# Keywords in Subversive Film/Media Aesthetics

# Keywords in Subversive Film/Media Aesthetics

Robert Stam
With Richard Porton
and Leo Goldsmith

**WILEY** Blackwell

This edition first published 2015
© 2015 John Wiley & Sons, Inc.

*Registered Office*
John Wiley & Sons, Ltd, The Atrium, Southern Gate, Chichester, West Sussex, PO19 8SQ, UK

*Editorial Offices*
350 Main Street, Malden, MA 02148-5020, USA
9600 Garsington Road, Oxford, OX4 2DQ, UK
The Atrium, Southern Gate, Chichester, West Sussex, PO19 8SQ, UK

For details of our global editorial offices, for customer services, and for information about
how to apply for permission to reuse the copyright material in this book please see our website at
www.wiley.com/wiley-blackwell.

*Library of Congress Cataloging-in-Publication Data*

Stam, Robert, 1941–
Keywords in subversive film/media aesthethics / Robert Stam with Richard Porton and Leo Goldsmith.
     pages   cm
   Includes bibliographical references and index.
ISBN 978-1-118-28892-4 (cloth : alk. paper) ISBN 978-1-118-28893-1 (paper)
1. Motion pictures–Aesthetics.   2. Motion pictures–Political aspects.
I. Porton, Richard.   II. Goldsmith, Leo.   III. Title.
PN1995.S83 2015
   791.4301–dc23

                                        2015015024

A catalogue record for this book is available from the British Library.

Cover image: © maximillion_studio/ iStockphoto

Set in 10/12.5pt Galliard by SPi Global, Pondicherry, India
Printed and bound in Malaysia by Vivar Printing Sdn Bhd

1   2015

# Contents

# Acknowledgments

*Keywords in Subversive Film/Media Aesthetics* is the work of three individuals. Robert Stam first formulated the proposal, devised the seven-chapter structure, chose and explained or formulated the majority of the concepts, invented new concepts (if concepts can be really called "new") and did the major part of the writing. Richard Porton and Leo Goldsmith contributed by writing specific sections (noted subsequently), as well as by reviewing the entire manuscript and making invaluable suggestions for concepts and examples. Richard Porton was responsible for the following materials: in Chapter One ("An Aesthetics of the Commons"), the passages on *Winstanley* in the section titled "The Aesthetic Commons"; the passage on *Leviathan* in the section titled "Revisionist Adaptation and the Literary Commons"; and the material on Mambety's *Hyenes* in the section titled "Cultural Indigenization." In Chapter Two ("The Upside-Down World of the Carnivalesque"), Porton wrote the material on Sasha Baron Cohen in the section titled "Contemporary Fools." In Chapter Three ("Political Modernism and its Discontents"), Porton wrote the material on "Apres Mai" in the section titled "Beyond Brecht," as well as the final paragraph of the section on titled "Political Cinema in the Age of the Posts." In Chapter Four ("The Transmogrification of the Negative"), Porton wrote most of the material in the section titled "Situationist Détournement," with the exception of the three final paragraphs devoted to the work of Emilio de Antonio. He also wrote the passages on Adam Curtis and on "archival foraging," the "aesthetics of failure," and on the work of Avi Mograbi in the section titled "Neo-Situationism and the Aesthetics of Failure." In Chapter Five ("Hybrid Variations on a Documentary Theme"), Porton wrote most of the section titled "The Strategic Advantages of Hybridization," with the exception of the materials on the work of Sergio Bianchi's *Mato Eles?*, authored by Stam. Porton also wrote the section titled "Performative Films." In the section titled

"The Essay Film and Mockumentaries," Porton wrote on "digressive aesthetics," "synecdochic strategies," and the "anti-hermeneutics of suspicion," along with the final paragraph in the chapter. The material on Chris Marker was co-authored with Robert Stam.

Apart from sprinkling the text with scintillating suggestions, Leo Goldsmith wrote the section on "The New Kino-Eye: Vision Machines" in Chapter Four, and also wrote most of the final chapter ("Aesthetic/Political Innovation in the Digital Era"), with the exception of only the material on Nollywood and the final section "In Guise of a Conclusion."

Richard Porton would like to acknowledge the modified appropriation of materials drawn from previously published essays. The discussion of *Sweetgrass* appropriates some passages from Porton's review of the film in the online edition of *Cineaste* (Vol. 35, 3, No. 10; http://www.cineaste.com/articles/webtakesemsweetgrassem). The discussion of Geyrhalter's *Our Daily Bread* adapts material from "*Our Daily Bread*" in *Cinema Scope* (Winter 2007, Issue 29, p. 56). The discussion of Marie Losier's *The Ballad of Genesis and Lady Jaye* incorporates some passages from Porton's "Documentary Cinema and Reality Hunger," published in *Cineaste* (Summer 2011, Vol. 36, Issue 3, p. 10). The discussion of Makavejev's *WR: Mysteries of the Organism* reworks some passages from Richard Porton's "*WR: Mysteries of the Organism*: Anarchist Realism and Critical Quandaries" in *Lola* (Issue 1: http://www.lolajournal.com/1/wr.html). Some of the passages on *Winstanley* and *Society of the Spectacle* appropriate material from Richard Porton's book, *Film and the Anarchist Imagination* (London and New York: Verso, 1999). Some of the discussion of Chris Marker's *Grin Without a Cat* relies on a review by Porton of the re-released version of the film, published in *Cinema Scope* (Spring 2002). Some of the discussion of *Hyenas* is partially derived from his "Mambety's *Hyenas*: Between Anti-Colonialism and the Critique of Modernity," which appeared in *Iris* (Spring 1995, Issue 18, pp. 95–103). The discussion of *Route 181* incorporates some passages from Porton's "Roads to Somewhere," published in *Cinema Scope* (Fall 2005; Issue 24, p. 12).

If not otherwise noted, Robert Stam wrote all of the remaining portions. While the vast majority of the material is completely new, the text revisits some issues raised in Stam's earlier texts, but now within a new lexicon format and with altered emphasis, developing similar ideas but using different filmic examples, or using similar examples but within different purposes. Chapter One, "An Aesthetics of the Commons," revisits some of the issues raised in a different way in *Unthinking Eurocentrism: Multiculturalism and the Media* (London: Routledge, 1994). The chapter on the carnivalesque revisits issues raised in *Subversive Pleasures: Bakhtin,*

*Cultural Criticism, and Film* (Baltimore: Johns Hopkins Press, 1989). The chapter on political modernism revisits issues raised in *Reflexivity in Film and Literature* (New York: Columbia University Press, 1992), and so forth. Some of the materials that constitute Chapter Four ("The Transmogrification of the Negative") formed part of a chapter titled "Palimpsestic Aesthetics: A Meditation on Hybridity and Garbage," in May Joseph and Jennifer Fink (eds.), *Performing Hybridity* (Minneapolis: University of Minnesota Press, 1999), but are here abbreviated, altered, supplemented, and reframed as part of a larger argument and with different films as illustrations.

During the long gestation of this book, much of the work by Robert Stam was first presented in the form of keynotes and visiting lectures. Stam would like to acknowledge the many institutions and individuals who invited him to address some of the topics discussed, and express appreciation for the comments and suggestions made by members of the audiences at such events, including: a 2011 lecture on "Politics and Aesthetics" at University of Massachusetts, Amherst; a 2011 (June 10–11) lecture on "Transmutations of Adaptation" at the Third International Conference on Film Adaptation, University of Bretagne, France; a 2011 (May 13) keynote on subversive aesthetics at Festival of Radical Film in Zaghreb, Croatia; a 2010 (June 1) keynote lecture on "Carandiru and the Discursive/Mediatic Spectrum" at the Recoveries of the Real conference in NYU Buenos Aires; a 2010 (May) "Theory and Practice of Adaptation" lecture at Federal University Niteroi (Brazil); a 2009 (April) lecture on "The Red Atlantic" at the Casa de Saber ("house of knowledge") in Rio de Janeiro; a 2009 (April) presentation of "The Red Atlantic: Tupi Theory and the Franco-Brazilian-Indigenous Dialogue" at the Shelby Cullom Davis Center, Princeton University; a 2008 (October 8–10) keynote at the Adapting America/America Adapted conference, Bogazici University, Istanbul; three 2008 (November 25, November 27, December 4) lectures in French at la Sorbonne Nouvelle (Paris III) concerning "Literature and Cinema"; a 2008 (December 5) lecture in French on "Critical Representations of First Contact" at L'Institut d'Amerique Latine in Paris; a 2008 (August 29) keynote "Globalization and Aesthetics from Below" in Puebla, Mexico; a 2008 (June 5) lecture on "The Aesthetics of Brazilian Documentary" at Monash University, Melbourne, Australia); a 2008 (May 12–15) keynote "Tupi or not Tupi a Tupi Theorist" at the Europe in Black and White conference, University of Lisbon; the "The Franco-Indigenous Dialogue" lecture at the Maison Francaise, NYU (April 22, 2008); the keynote "Conference on Political Cinema" at the Film Center, Oslo, Norway (October 13, 2007); the 2006 (November 23–27) invited lectures on "Brazilian Modernism" and "Politics and Aesthetics" at Nottingham University in Ningbo, China; three 2006 (October 14–17) invited lectures—"*Macunaima*," "Film Adaptation," and "Revolutionary Aesthetics"—at University of Alberta, Edmonton, Canada; a 2006 lecture in Portuguese on "*O Indio Brasileiro e a Cultura Popular*" at the Seminario Internacional de Cinema e Audio-Visual/Salvador/Bahia (Salvador: SEMCINE); a 2006 (October 16) lecture on "What Cultural Studies Can Learn from Tropicalia" at BRASA (Brazilian Studies Association), held at Vanderbilt University; a 2006 (November) lecture on "Tropicalia and Brazilian Cinema" at the Americas Society in New York City; a 2005 lecture (March 29) in Portuguese, "*Esteticas da Resistencia*," at the conference on "Cinema and Politics" at the Federal University in Salvador, Bahia; a 2005 lecture (March 9) on "Tropicalia and Postmodern Resistance," at the Conference on Latin American Cinema, University of Wisconsin, Milwaukee; a 2005 (February 4–5) lecture on "The Cultural Politics of Popular Music," "Art at the Margins," at the Center for Brazilian Studies, UCLA; a 2004 (December 2–5) lecture on "Multiculturalism within Brazilian Popular Music" at the Latin-American Institute, Berlin; a 2002 (March) lecture (in Spanish) on "*La Conquista en el Cinema de las Americas*" at ICAIC, Havana, Cuba; and a 2001 (July) lecture (in Spanish) on "*Esteticas de la Resistencia*" in Lima, Peru, at the Hemipsheric Institute for Performance and Politics.

   Robert Stam expresses gratitude as well for invitations to conduct seminars related to the issues of the book at: the University of Sao Paulo, Brazil (June 2014); the School of Communications, Federal University of Rio de Janeiro (2010); the Federal University of Cuiaba, Brazil (2010); the Institute for Postcolonial and Transcultural studies, Bremen University, Germany (June–July 2009); and the School of Criticism & Theory, Cornell University, 30th Summer Session (2006).

   Robert Stam would like to thank the following colleagues for facilitating the presentation of his work on politics and aesthetics: Sabine Broeck at the University of Bremen, Germany; Phillippe DuBois and Jacques Aumont at the Sorbonne Nouvelle (Paris III) and L'Institut d'Amerique Latine in Paris; Manuela Ribeiro Sanchez and the "Europe in Black & White" conference at the Centro de Estudos Comparatistas at the University of Lisbon, Portugal; the Alliance Francaise in New York City; Instituto Universitario De Pesquisas in Rio Janeiro, Brazil; Diana Accaria, the "Seminar on Postcolonial Theory," and the departments of English, history, and comparative literature at the University of Puerto Rico at Rio Piedras; Vermonja Alston at York University, Toronto; Diana Taylor and NYU's Hemispheric Institute of Performance and Politics, and the

Encuentros in Monterrey, Mexico, and Lima, Peru; Edward Said, Joseph Massad and Gil Anidjar and the Comparative Cultures University Seminar, Columbia University; and the "Area Studies in the Era of Globalization" seminar at the Social Science Research Council, New York.

Robert Stam would like to thank his superb assistants Jennifer Kelly, Belem Destefani, and Benjamin Han. He would also like to thank the following people for their stimulating comments on earlier drafts or sections, notably: Amalia Cordova, Chris Dunn, Patrick Erouart, Faye Ginsburg, Ismail Xavier, Manthia Diawara, Diana Taylor, Marcelo Fiorini, Randal Johnson, Randy Martin, Ella Shohat, and Robert Young. Steve Duncombe offered a close reading of an early version of the manuscript. Stam would like especially to thank his beloved editor Jayne Fargnoli for her extremely close attention and excellent advice, including in the form of "tough love" demands for more clarity and less elaboration. Finally, he thanks some of those friends who have immensely enriched his sense both of politics and aesthetics: Awam Amkpa, Manthia Diawara, Alessandra Raengo, Ismail Xavier, Joao Luiz Vieira, Chris Dunn, Patrick Erouart, Marcelo Fiorini, and, of course, Ella Shohat.

# Introduction

*Keywords in Subversive Film/Media Aesthetics* offers a conversational journey through the overlapping terrains of politically engaged art and artistically engaged politics, a journey with many watering holes and rest stops and off-ramps where travelers can take stock, catch their breath, and plot their own course through the contents. The book's somewhat unusual hybrid format combines a book-length essay on politics and aesthetics with an embedded lexicon of definitions, explications, and illustrations of almost a thousand concepts bearing on radical aesthetic strategies in film and the media. It foregrounds aesthetic interventions that generate an intellectual surprise or shock of social recognition by shifting the parameters of commonsense by interrogating regimes of power and privilege. These strategies offer an intellectual jolt, what Deleuze calls an intellectual "shock" or "vibration," in synaptic thrills that challenge the reigning order and thus catalyze a sense of social possibility.

This book combines various kinds of concepts and terms: (1) terms already well consecrated in relation to cinema (Brechtian *distantiation*, situationist *détournement*); (2) less-known film-related terms that deserve wider circulation (*cinematrix*, *surrealismo*); (3) terms drawn from other arts, disciplines, and movements (*audiotopia*, *anthropophagy*), and, finally, (4) a substantial portion of coinages and neologisms such as our own *candomblé feminism* and *potlatch strategy*. (To facilitate understanding, the initial entry concerning a given concept or strategy will appear in **bold**, with all subsequent mentions in *italics*.)

The volume aims to provide a theoretical toolkit for strategies germane to the analysis and even the practice of radical art. The book can be

*Keywords in Subversive Film/Media Aesthetics*, First Edition. Robert Stam with Richard Porton and Leo Goldsmith.
© 2015 John Wiley & Sons, Inc. Published 2015 by John Wiley & Sons, Inc.

approached in at least five ways: (1) read straight through as a narrative essay advancing a larger argument; (2) read selectively by chapter, each of which is devoted to a specific stream of radical aesthetics; (3) read in a more focused way using the subheadings as signposts for specific themes; (4) dipped into as a lexicon of concepts, with the index of terms as a guide; or (5) sampled for more in-depth analyses of films such as *Dr. Strangelove or: How I Stopped Worrying and Learned to Love the Bomb* (1964), *Les stances à Sophie* (1971), *Even the Rain* (2010), *Offside* (2006), *Shortbus* (2006), *Nostalgia for the Light* (*"Nostalgia de la Luz,"* 2010), *The Act of Killing* (2012), and so forth. Readers are encouraged to swan in and out of the text, to graze from concept to concept, to make their own intellectual leaps and pirouettes.

The volume will adhere to a few fundamental principles. First, the approach will be *pan-artistic*, that is, it will draw on all the arts, on the assumption that cinema has been endlessly enriched by its dialogue with the other arts. Second, the approach will be *pan-mediatic*, with examples taken from the widest possible spectrum of audio, visual, and digital arts and media: fiction film, documentary, television, music video, filmed performance, cable TV satire, sketch comedy, Internet parodies, and social network activism. Defying essentialist definitions, cinema's famed "specificity" consists precisely in its being *non*-specific and hospitable to the most alien and heterogeneous materials. The word "film" here serves as a synecdoche for the whole spectrum, what Jung Bong Choi calls the **"cinematrix,"** a term which locates cinema within broader industrial, geopolitical, and socioeconomic matrices whereby the production, distribution, and reception of texts produces social-artistic meaning.[1] The *cinematrix* has less to do with cinematic specificity than with interfaces and connectivities moving across various arts, media, and nations.

Rather than privilege feature films as the ontological quintessence of the "real film," *Keywords* regards all audio-visual moving-image materials as legitimate platforms for subversive art. The book expands the definition and range of "radical political film" in a digital age where the feature fiction film has become a "bit" in a larger mediatic stream. "Political film" today might mean not a feature fiction or a documentary but rather a music video such as "Somos todos Ilegales," a Colbert performance at the White House, a quickie YouTube protest spot, a web-based interactive site such as Eyal Sivan's Montage Interdit, or an open-access user-generated database such as Actipedia. And, now that virtually everything ends up being filmed, almost any text can be reconfigured and remediated to become a political film. The Internet brings tremendous advantages for both creation and dissemination. While 20 years ago most of the kinds of films mentioned in this book could have been seen only at art cinemas or film festivals, or in cinema studies courses, many are now available at the click of a mouse.

In a globalized age, meanwhile, the identity of the enemy is no longer quite so clear. Given the disenchantment with political movements based on the capture of state power, the word "revolution" has lost some of its charismatic power. While on one level contemporary struggles are against visible, or at least visualizable, abuses—wars of aggression, police brutality, sexual harassment, and so forth, on another level they are against the algorithmic features of an economic system. The enemy today is less likely to be a concrete, identifiable figure such as a factory boss, à la *They Don't Wear Black Tie* (1981) or *Tout va bien* (1972), or a colonial army, as in *The Battle of Algiers* (1966). The enemy now takes a more diffuse, abstract, and quasi-ungraspable form, encapsulated by words such as "privatization," "neo-liberalism," or "financial capitalism." With the digital revolution, meanwhile, it is difficult to see beyond the infinite riches offered to the Internet's consumers, in order to discern the underlying power hierarchies, the ownership structures, that possess and profit from the platforms and channels that constitute its infrastructure.

Third, *Keywords in Subversive Film/Media Aesthetics* takes on board the history of theorization of the relation between aesthetics and politics developed by a wide array of writers. Against the longer backdrop of the theories of canonical figures such as Plato, Aristotle, Kant, and Hegel, we will invoke some familiar names such as Bertolt Brecht, Fredric Jameson, Jean-Louis Comolli, Herbert Marcuse, Teresa de Lauretis, David James, Gilles Deleuze, Félix Guattari, Jacques Rancière, Judith Butler, Ismail Xavier, Henri Lefebvre, Nicole Brenez, Édouard Glissant, and David Graeber. But, rather than offer potted summaries of their thought, the book mobilizes (and sometimes amplifies or criticizes) their concepts in conjunction with our own concepts, using filmic examples as trampolines for our conceptualizations of emancipatory artistic possibilities.

Fourth, this book eschews the tyranny of the present by showing that the "new" often remediates the old. Although not a work of history per se, the book integrates historical understanding in its overall structure, in its individual chapters, and in the elaboration of specific concepts. It traces carnivalesque "social inversions" back to Greek Dionysianism, for example, and Kubrick's satire in *Dr. Strangelove or: How I Stopped Worrying and Learned to Love the Bomb* (1964) to Juvenal and Jonathan Swift via early 1960s "sick comics" such as Tom Lehrer. Fifth, the book deprovincializes the discussion in disciplinary terms by drawing on philosophy, literary theory, political theory, performance theory, and other relevant disciplines. Sixth, it deprovincializes debate in cultural-geographical terms through a *polycentric* approach which envisions an egalitarian restructuring of intercultural relations within and beyond the nation-state.[2] Within a polycentric vision, the world of cinema has many dynamic fields of power, energy, and struggle, with many possible vantage points. Therefore *Keywords* draws on theories and strategies not only from Europe and the United States but also from Latin America, Africa, Asia, the Middle East, and the indigenous world. Rather than starting from the center and venturing out into the periphery, we begin in the first chapter from what Faye Ginsburg calls the **periphery's periphery**, that is, the films of putatively "primitive" aboriginal people.[3]

In its option for the polycentric and the marginalized, *Keywords* distances itself from **Eurocentrism**, that is, the view that enshrines the hierarchical stratifications inherited from Western colonial domination, assumed to be inevitable and even "progressive."[4] *Eurocentrism* does not refer to Europe in its literal sense as a continent or a geopolitical unit but rather to an intellectual orientation rooted in colonial power, an interlocking network of buried premises, embedded narratives, and submerged tropes, that perceives Europe (and the neo-Europes around the world) as universally normative. Eurocentrism could equally well be called "coloniality" (Anibal Quijano), "European planetary consciousness" (Mary Louise Pratt), "the colonial mindset," "Euro-hegemonism," "Western hegemony," or the "occidental worldview."[5] Cherokee author Thomas King calls it the "unexamined confidence in Western civilization."[6] For the **coloniality/modernity project** of Arturo Escobar, Enrique Dussel, and Walter Mignolo, coloniality forms the inseparable dark side of modernity, just as postcoloniality forms the dark side of postmodernity.[7]

A key aspect of this **deprovincialization** is the embrace of emerging social actors and subjects of discourse who are creating cinema for the first time. Classically the objects rather than the subjects of representation, these groups, traditionally the *sans part*—"having no part," in Rancière's sense —are now taking part. Stated differently, they exemplify the artistic practices that Deleuze and Guattari call "minor," referring to literature written in a minoritized language (e.g., the Jewish literature of Prague) which bears a historically fraught relation to a dominant language. Minor writers live in a language which has an oblique or eccentric relation to the dominant, major language, which they reinvent from within. Minor practices are necessarily political in that each individual story "takes on a collective value" and is inseparable from a "collective enunciation."[8] **Minor cinema**, in this sense, is not only cinema made by minoritized people, but also cinema made in "minor" genres or formats, in a minor, dissonant, key, or that engages minor, disreputable, emotions, with an often combative relation to the dominant film discourse and language.[9] David James speaks of "avant-garde minor cinema" to refer to a "rainbow coalition of demotic cinemas: experimental, poetic, underground, ethnic, amateur, counter, non-commodity, working-class, critical, artists."[10]

At once a work of aesthetic theory, film history/analysis, and political critique, *Keywords in Subversive Film/Media Aesthetics* aims to provide a comprehensive overview of contemporary radical film/media aesthetics. Shamelessly eclectic, omnivorous, even anthropophagic, *Keywords* transfers Godard's dictum about film—that one should "put whatever one likes in a film"—to a book on radical aesthetics. To paraphrase a well-known Chinese aesthetic theorist, it "lets a thousand aesthetic flowers bloom," running the gamut from the experimental avant-garde to the left populist mainstream, moving from Maya Deren to Michael Moore, from Chris Marker to Patricio Guzmán. Throughout, the book foregrounds isolatable strategies rather than the nuances of authorship and the sinuous folds of narrative. The entries are not entitled "Godard" but rather "*distanciation*," not "progressive films about social rebellions" but rather "festive revolutionary practices," not "positive images of women" but "Medusan optics." The book is less interested in auteurs and canons than in fields of mediatic energy and the creation of new constituencies open to radical thought and praxis.

Within our rather ecumenical view, **radical politics** promotes an egalitarian, democratic, and non-authoritarian society that seeks the common good and heightens the sense of human and social possibility, as opposed to a reactionary politics that normalizes power hierarchies based on the mutually impacting relations of political economy, class, gender, race, empire, religion, sexuality, nation, or any other axis of social stratification. Although some analysts claim that changing class compositions and the digital revolution have rendered the old left–right polarity obsolete, a fundamental division remains. As long as the capitalist system and the racialized division of international labor generates and amplifies social inequality, a strong divide will separate those who defend that system as normal and acceptable from those who seek to reverse it or at least try to combat its abuses. A coherent left defends worker and civil rights and social entitlements gained through centuries of struggle, now threatened by neo-liberal privatization, and sees education, health, lodging, water, public transport, and childcare as public goods, all part of the *commons* that should be available to all. Our non-finalizing egalitarian synthesis draws on anarchism, Marxism, feminism, ecologism, left populism, critical race theory, border theory, queer theory, radical indigeneity, and many other currents, broadly favoring equality over hierarchy, freedom over authoritarianism, public over private, and the *commons* over *enclosure*.

In a refurbished version of the *laissez-faire* philosophy of Adam Smith, Thatcherite neo-liberalism sees the autonomous self-seeking individual as the foundational unit of the social world. Such a view delegitimizes all radical social transformation, proclaiming that "there is no alternative," while doing everything in its power to make that claim a reality by eliminating actual alternatives. Indeed, the right's virulent rejection of all things common and public (public schools, public radio, public television) goes hand in hand with a rejection of utopian alternatives. Radical art, by contrast, communicates a sense that another world is possible. If there are no alternatives, subversive art asks: Why do we keep imagining them? Responding to those who say there is "no outside to capitalism," David Graeber argues that the *commons* are always already "inside" capitalism. As evidenced by the constant outbreaks of protests and rebellions in Tunis, Cairo, Madrid, Madison, Istanbul, Tehran, and São Paulo, global capitalism has in some ways never seemed so discredited and vulnerable. At the same time, the hegemony of neo-liberal policies and the stranglehold power of banks show that capitalism remains dominant. At the same time, capitalism seems to be at the height of its arrogance and at the end of its rope. Yet, for Graeber, revolutionary thought

> can never really go away, because the notion of a redemptive future remains the only way we can make sense of the present: we can only understand the value of what surrounds us from the perspective of an imaginary country whose own contours we can never understand, even when we are standing in it.[11]

Despite the well-known Oscar Wilde quip from "The Soul of Man under Socialism"—"a map of the world that does not include **Utopia** is not worth glancing at"—commentators from various political perspectives often use the word "utopia" pejoratively. For orthodox leftists, utopianism is a frequent subject of derision because blueprints of future societies are viewed as fanciful and superfluous compared to political economy and the critical dissection of capitalist reality. (Marx derided the writings of his utopian socialist forebears—for example, Henri de Saint-Simon and Charles Fourier—as reactionary idealism.) Yet, other leftists such as Tom Moylan point to **critical utopias** which offer glimpses of alternative social arrangements. Although the anti-authoritarian left finds it difficult to point to actually existing societies that embody its tenets, anarchists and radical socialists tend to focus on **emancipatory moments**—the Paris Commune of 1871, the "Spanish Revolution" within the Spanish Civil War of 1936–1939, and May 1968—which provide brief glimpses of anti-hierarchical pathways to a more equitable political and social order. Catalytic historical interludes are prescient for the anti-authoritarian left because thy suggest the contours of what Ernst Bloch termed **concrete utopia**, a vision of the future that does not derive from cloud-cuckoo-land but is rooted in tangible historical struggles. (Bloch's utopian vision was highly appealing to New Leftists and liberation theologians during the late sixties and seventies.)

What Max Blechman labels "revolutionary romanticism"—an emphasis on the liberatory dimension of aesthetics[12] that can be traced from Schlegel and Novalis though Guy Debord—might be considered the aesthetic corollary of concrete utopia. Films that illustrate the principles of revolutionary self-organization often tackle the implications of key emancipatory moments in the history of workers' movements. The sequence, for example, in Peter Watkins's *La Commune (Paris 1871)* (2000), devoted to the events of March 28, 1871, the day the Commune was proclaimed following elections of a record number of workers to the municipal council, demonstrates how a liberatory aesthetic sheds light on the historical process of self-emancipation. As Antoine de Baecque observes, Watkins's method of **history reportage**, a modus operandi in which actors coordinated the writing of the script and were in ongoing dialogue with their colleagues concerning the film's polemical thrust, ruptured the "traditional relationship between 'filmer' and 'filmed' and redefined 'performance' as a form of political and active participation in the film, which in turn explicitly incorporated the personal experience of every member of the cast."[13] Consequently, there's a convergence between Watkins's egalitarian production process and the Communards' assertion, when interviewed by the slyly anachronistic Commune TV, that "proletarians will finally claim their rights and the fruits of their labor" and "the workers will be bosses."

A similar dynamic informs a key scene in Ken Loach's *Land and Freedom* (1995), a film that, in some respects, functions as a fictional cinematic equivalent of George Orwell's *Homage to Catalonia*. Like Orwell's journalistic account, Loach's vest-pocket epic is a tribute to the independent socialists and anarchists who battled Stalinist orthodoxy during the Spanish Civil War. The film's most effective scene, a 12 minute debate on the prospect of collectivizing a Spanish village during the height of the civil war, is also a prototypical example of emancipatory praxis—or, in Adornian terms, a negation of "the false totality" of bourgeois society. The scene crystallizes the grassroots, participatory direct-action ethos of the Spanish collectives, experiments in self-management that can be sharply contrasted with the Soviet Union's disastrous effort to impose collectivization on an unwilling peasantry.

The Paris Commune and the Spanish Civil War were epochal events accompanied by carnage on a massive scale. Hakim Bey posits the **temporary autonomous zone (TAZ)** as an alternative to

> violence and martyrdom. The TAZ is like an uprising which does not engage directly with the State, a guerilla operation which liberates an area (of land, of time, of imagination) and then dissolves itself to re-form elsewhere/ elsewhen *before* the State can crush it.[14]

The Cecilia commune, examined in Jean-Louis Comolli's *La Cecilia* (1975) is a case in point. The Cecilia of the title refers both to a woman— the young heroine of Giovanni Rossi's 1878 utopian romance, *A Socialist Commune*—and to the actual commune founded by Rossi and nine adherents in 1890. The idealized female figure and the parcel of land that becomes La Cecilia are not unrelated. The Italians' naïve belief that they can establish a liberated zone in Brazil is a symptom of perhaps unwitting ethnocentrism—an outgrowth of the unstated conviction that the colony is located in an ahistorical void. The commune eventually collapsed for a number of reasons: internecine squabbles, Rossi's hubris, and the supremely ironic fact that the land that made Cecilia possible had been bequeathed to Rossi by Dom Pedro II, the emperor of Brazil who was eventually overthrown by a republican coup.

"**Prefigurative politics**," a term coined by Wini Breines to characterize the desire of social movements within the New Left to imagine future forms of political and social organization, refashions the injunction of the IWW (Industrial Workers of the World). Radical science fiction is one genre that embodies what could be termed **prefigurative art**, an "art which would evoke the imagination of and a 'longing for' a better world."[15] Lizzie Borden's *Born in Flames* (1983) recast debates within **anarcha-feminism** in the form of a science fiction film that traversed the boundaries of dystopia and utopia and engaged in an imaginative variant of speculative politics. Borden's film is notable for postulating a society of the future where an American social democratic government implements a wages-for-housework program as a utopian means to a "radical transformation of society," as a ploy meant to defuse the direct action advocated by the radical feminist "Women's Army." Since the election of even a nominally social democratic government in the United States was as unlikely a prospect during the Reagan era, during which the film was made, as it is in the twenty-first century, Borden's insistence on demanding the impossible harnesses an optimism close to Bloch's concept of the **not yet**: "that which does not yet exist, which is in quest of itself in the core of things, and which is awaiting its genesis in the trend latency of the process."[16]

Radical art can play an indispensable role in challenging conservative discourses in general and neo-liberal doxa in particular. Art can loosen what Blake called the "mind-forg'd manacles" that restrain free inquiry. Nor do radical ideas always depend on conscious political options: intermittent flashes of radical energies can emanate even from politically problematic films and directors. (A Fanonian anticolonial current ripples down through even such a compromised vehicle as Quentin Tarantino's *Django Unchained* [2012].) Although most of the media-makers referenced here are on the left, our focus here is less on the artists' conscious political stance than on the social drift and artistic use-value of their strategies. Nor does *Keywords* endorse specific strategies as eternally progressive. The political valence of any given strategy is conjunctural, without guarantees. The *cinéma vérité* direct-address techniques that once seemed so revolutionary have by now become facile guarantors of "authenticity" in infomercials and reality shows. Once transgressive reflexive strategies are now easily neutered or co-opted and potentially available to any political tendency. Almost every strategy, even *détournement*, comes in a top-down and a bottom-up versions. Huge tech corporations, as Astra Taylor points out, encourage their users to imagine themselves as rebel remixers, repurposing bits of information even as the companies jealously exploit their own intellectual property and "snap up patents at breakneck speed."[17] Despite its transgressive aura, "its methods of appropriation are perfectly aligned with the profit-making logic of digital capitalism."[18]

Any discussion of subversive film aesthetics inevitably draws on the long history of **aesthetics**, a word derived from the Greek *aisthesis* in the sense of perception or sensation. Jacques Rancière calls *aesthetics* "the name for the category designating the sensible fabric and intelligible form of what we call 'Art'."[19] While Plato, despite the sensuousness of his writing, entertained a double prejudice against the senses, first, as a lure from the truth of the ideal and, second, as linked to the passion-driven demos, Aristotle granted art cognitive value as a sensuous way of knowing. In the West, *aesthetics* emerged as an autonomous discipline in the eighteenth century as the study of artistic beauty and of related issues of the sublime and the pleasurable. Kant drew on Baumgarten's idea of aesthetics as coextensive with perception to argue in *Critique of Judgment* (1790) for a view of aesthetic judgment as ideally disinterested, contemplative, and potentially universal. "Everyone must allow," Kant wrote, "that a judgment on the beautiful which is tinged with the slightest interest, is very partial and not a pure judgment of taste."[20] Aesthetic objects thus become autotelic instances of purposive purposelessness, detached in Kantian thought from any practical utility or from communal purpose, in a form of what Noel Carroll calls **radical autonomism**, or the view that "art is a strictly autonomous practice."[21] A methodological *via negativa* defined the aesthetic, like the divine, by what it is not—art was that which is *not* practical, *not* cognitive, *not* interested, *not* affiliated.

In the autonomist conception, art becomes cleansed of all base materiality and social connection in the name of transcendence. Through a kind of aesthetic "rapture," the artistic elect shed their mortal coils to ascend to a heaven of formal appreciation. Ben Highmore laments this transcendent view of art: "how does a form of inquiry that was once aimed at the entire creaturely world end up as a specialized discourse about fine art?"[22] Jacques Derrida, in *The Truth in Painting* (1987), critiques Kant's separating of intrinsic aesthetic beauty from the extrinsic non-aesthetic context; the frame, for Derrida, also forms part of the painting, and text and context always interpenetrate.[23] The art that interests us here, in contrast to Kantian proposals, is defiantly practical, material, worldly, interested, affiliated, constitutively impure. At the same time, Kantian "disinterestedness" can be recuperated for emancipatory aesthetics when reconfigured as a performative act enjoyed for its own sake, outside of instrumentalist productivism and the profit motive. But in this case art is seen not as an individual monadic experience but rather as a shared festival-like realm of freedom that imagines a life beyond labor as the alpha and omega of existence.

Although the aesthetics of the media are **specific**, they are not **autonomous**. The arts and media obviously have their specific material traits—literature is a single-track verbal medium, cinema a multi-track medium, and so forth—yet they are at the same time also embedded in a broader social ecology, in the entire history of the arts, in the history of the media, and in the jagged entanglements of history. To the classical conundrums of aesthetics, we would add other questions, premised on art's intrinsic sociality. How are notions of the beautiful shaped by history, ambient social values, and what Bourdieu calls **cultural capital**, the cumulative social advantages derived from not strictly economic means, such as education, physical appearance, good manners, and style of speech?[24] Has aesthetics itself been compromised by its association with the idolatrization of whiteness typical of the Baumgarten wing of the Enlightenment? Should art model a better, utopian world, or fashion dystopian demonstrations that we do *not* live in the best of all possible worlds? Or should art dialectically counterpose the utopian and the dystopian? Is art, as Oscar Wilde quipped, delightfully useless, with no purpose beyond its own onanistic self-pleasuring, or is it useful (*utile*) as well as sweet (*dulce*)?

In terms of film, radical aesthetics asks media-specific questions. What is the relationship between film technique and social intentionality? Do specific ideologies have clear aesthetic correlatives? Is a zoom shot in an ethnographic film necessarily predatory and voyeuristic? Does fascism lurk behind the militarized choreography of bodies in Busby Berkeley musicals, as Susan Sontag suggested? The focus in this book, in any case, is on the mutually stimulating encounter of artistic audacity and social invention as generative of new concepts, affects, and possibilities. While constantly concerned with form, *Keywords* rejects formalism—the exclusive valorization of artistic form over social content—which Edward Said compared to "describing the highway without the landscape."[25] At the same time, we will call attention to the historicity of form, the way that form itself expresses, relays, and impacts historical process. Thus one can distinguish between a decorative shallow formalism and the deep formalism of a historical poetics that sees form itself as situated, marked by the traces of the historical moment.

Rather than an out-of-body experience, art is thoroughly corporeal and intensely affective. Rancière posits three non-exclusive regimes of perception, affection, and thought, which he calls regimes of art: (1) the **ethical regime**, for example, the education of the citizenry as in classical Greek theater; (2) the **representative regime**, for example, modern realism as the mimetic adequation between the real and the copy; and (3) the **aesthetic regime of value**, which recognizes the specificity of art as reshaping material and symbolic space in order to undo hierarchical orders of representation in favor of a community of equals. Here Rancière echoes Schiller's linking of the aesthetic to equality: "Everything in the aesthetic State, even the subservient tool, is a free citizen having equal rights with the noblest."[26] All three regimes participate in what Rancière calls the *partage du sensible*, or "distribution of the sensible" (in the sense of that which is apprehended through the senses) by performing a spatiotemporal *découpage* that shapes what is allowed to be seen and heard and said: "Politics revolves around what is seen and what can be said about it, around who has the ability to see and the talent to speak, around the properties of space and the possibilities of time."[27] Beyond art per se, Rancière's phrase evokes the sensible fabric of experience, including institutions, practices, and affective modes. Film literalizes the concept of the distribution of the sensible in the sense that every filmic idea is embedded in a multi-sensorial web of image, sound, noise, and music.

The word "*partage*" in French conveys a social aporia by suggesting two apparently opposite meanings: the sharing and making perceptible of the common, but also the dividing up and even the *enclosure* of the common. It evokes the foundational mechanisms which generate exclusion and inclusion, the sharing, but also the rationing, of potentially common power and resources, both in a material sense (food, water, health) and in an artistic sense (in theatrical terms, the casting or the distribution, equal or unequal, of roles), and in the mediatic sense of the distribution of the sensorium via the different cinematic tracks. The tension between the two meanings—sharing and (unequal) dividing up—virtually defines the conflictual field of both the political and the artistic. For Rancière, radical politics emerges when those "who do not count" challenge the distribution of the commons. Reversing the longstanding association of aesthetics with elitism, Rancière sees it as suspending the hierarchical oppressions imposed on bodies by the unjust distribution of the sensible. Meg McLagen and Yates McKee, in the same vein, speak of **sensible politics** with reference to medial strategies where art and activism intersect to create sites of contestation.[28] This approach helps us move beyond mimetic representation to social affect, that is, the ways films relay and change the ways people experience what might be called the political economy of emotion, the parceling out of pleasure and pain, hope and despair, whether through hierarchical oppression or egalitarian conviviality.

Lurking in the interstices of our discussion are the politics of form itself. Form almost always embodies a politics, even if one cannot easily assign an unequivocal political valence to any given technique. Form has political expressivity in that it shapes affect and impacts its audience by communicating the imaginative sensation of social possibility. This purely formal aspect of the politics of art is perhaps most evident in the generally non-representational art of music. For example, jazz, purely as form, is more likely to awaken the mind, touch the emotions, and kineticize the body than "easy-listening" shopping mall music which shapes a social affect of passive compliance. For African-American artists, form and content have always been inseparable. Roland Rahssan Kirk's instrumental music, according to George Lipsitz, "called attention to his role as a black musician in a society controlled by whites."[29] Jimi Hendrix's distorted guitar version of "The Star-Spangled Banner" rendered the national anthem as a dissonant wail about war and oppression. Without being essentialist—virtually any genre or form can be deployed for or against established hierarchies—artistic forms do implicitly enact stances toward established codes. The formal provocations of some avant-garde films, for example, indirectly question regnant norms through a Rimbaud-style "*dérèglement*" of all the senses. Indeed, spectators accustomed to more conventional films can be more discombobulated by the stylistic aggressions of avant-garde films such as *Sleep* (1963), *Wavelength* (1967), or *The Act of Seeing with One's Own Eyes* (1971), than by explicitly revolutionary messages.

At its best, radical art shakes the ideological foundations by questioning the taken-for-granted of social life, transforming the unthinkable into the incontrovertible. Deleuze describes the revelatory power of the arts as follows: "painting makes visible forces that are invisible; music renders audible the inaudible; and philosophy renders thinkable the unthinkable."[30] As a synthetic art, moreover, film does all of those things *at the same time.* Film has the capacity to convey what freedom feels like, what equality looks like, and what democracy sounds like. Rather than a harmless superstructural *divertissement*, art is rather a consequential social practice, a crucial arena of struggle alongside the political and the economic. Proceeding from a broad understanding of the political, *Keywords* embraces strategies that challenge not only capitalism and state power but also the various modalities of social stratification—whether based on class, race, nation, gender, sexuality, or religion—all seen within what Kimberlé Crenshaw calls **intersectionality**, that is, the ways in which the various axes of stratification are interconnected and mutually impacting. Nicolas Bourriaud speaks of **relational aesthetics**, that is, an "aesthetic theory" which judges artworks "on the basis of the inter-human relations which they represent, produce, or prompt," fostering art that takes as its point of departure not the individual character and the individual author but rather the whole of human relations and their social context.[31] *Keywords* applauds all strategies that prod audiences to think and act more critically, openly, generously, equally, and effectively. At various moments, *Keywords* argues for radical humor as a crucial resource for a left often portrayed as a kill-joy. To paraphrase Breton, "the left must be fun, or it will not be," but with the addendum: "if it is *only* fun, it also will not be." At the same time, we question the artistic/mediatic hierarchies that construct, for example, the sacred word as infallibly deep and the image as idolatrous lure, or tragedy as noble and comedy as vulgar, or cinema as artistic and TV as a wasteland.

While not reducible to politics, all films nevertheless have a political dimension. For filmmaker Rui Guerra, "all films are political, *especially* those films that claim *not* to be."[32] Immediately inscribed in the *polis*, art models forms of sociability and attitudes toward relations of power, not only through character and plot but also through attitudes to the structures of discursive authority as mediated by formal parameters. The creation of artistic and narrative forms, as Fredric Jameson has tirelessly suggested in his work, is a political-ideological act that functions by inventing imaginary or formal solutions to apparently irreconcilable social contradictions. Filmic *mise-en-scène* and editing, in this sense, constitute ways of conceptualizing social relations. Thus one can ask of any film whether it pushes society toward a more egalitarian condition or normalizes inequality as natural and God-given. Which social voices and discourses resonate in film and which remain muffled or unheard? What social becomings are accelerated or blocked?

Although art does not in itself make revolutions or overturn global capitalism, it can nevertheless change consciousness and generate change. To paraphrase Gramsci: pessimism of the hardware, optimism of the software. Against the drift of high literary, iconophobic, and body-phobic prejudices against cinema, we take cinema very seriously—and comically, since comedy is also serious—as a form of thinking. One of Deleuze's signal contributions has been to show that cinema, similar to philosophy, generates concepts. Cinema makes concepts sensible, feelable, and able to impact on the sentient body. In the wake of film theory's "philosophical turn," Daniel Frampton speaks of **filmosophy**, or **filmind**, and **film-thinking** as the "projection, screenings, showing of thoughts ..."[33] For Alain Badiou, cinema transforms philosophy by transforming our understandings about what constitutes an idea.[34] The undeniable palpability of cinema, in this sense, challenges a Platonism that regards the senses as an enemy of thought.

*Keywords* addresses cinema/media as generating *political*/aesthetic concepts in a fused multi-sensorial whole. The book does not locate left politics only in films about politics or in choice morsels of dialogue that score points for "our side." Subversive cinema is less a genre than a field of energy that potentially pervades all genres. The metaphorics of writing also relay a political-aesthetic attitude. Many of the terms and coinages in *Keywords* deploy rhetorical figures of contradiction such as the **oxymoron**, that is, locutions which fuse opposite affects (e.g., the title of *Hiroshima Mon Amour* [1959]); or **xeugma**, the paratactic "yoking" of two apparently opposed concepts (e.g., Melville's "cannibals and colleges"); **antinomy** (a term used in Kantian logic and epistemology to explain the tension between what is rationally true and what is empirically experienced (time is infinite and time has a beginning; human beings are free and they are determined); and *discordia concors*, or the "harmonious discord" typical of metaphysical poets like John Donne. An oxymoronic aesthetic can mingle attraction and repulsion, pleasure and pain, harmony and dissonance. All these rhetorical figures emphasize the contradictory and the *dissensual* even while they cut through rigid polarities to reveal subterranean affinities or linked analogies connecting disparate poles. At the same time, terms like *dialogism, counterpoint, rhizome, molecular, becoming, polyglossia, pluristylism, heteroglossia,* and *polyperspectivalism* manifest a systematic option for the plural, the relational, and the transformational.

Aesthetic theory inherits antecedent questions concerning **artistic realism**. Originally linked to an oppositional attitude toward romantic and neo-classical models in fiction and painting, *realism* has provided one of the key source theories and practices of radical aesthetics. Underlying the realist impulse was an implicit teleology of social democratization favoring the artistic emergence of "more extensive and socially inferior human groups to the position of subject matter for problematic-existential representation."[35] Literary critics contrast this deep, democratizing realism with a shallow, reductionistic, and veristic **naturalism**, realized most famously in the Zola novels that modeled their human representations on the biological sciences. Brazilian critic **Ivana Bentes speaks of neo-naturalism** to characterize films such as *City of God* (2002) that give expression to auto-destructive impulses while capturing the "degradation, mutilation, usury, squalor, annihilation, as well as fleeting moments of hallucinatory delight in the exercise of killing."[36]

Bakhtin and Medvedev, in the late 1920s, offered a major corrective to antecedent conceptualizations by proposing what might be called a **discursive realism**, a kind of second-degree realism where the role of the artistic text is not to represent real-life "existents" in a verisimilar manner but rather to stage the competitions of languages and discourses.[37] For Bakhtin, human consciousness and artistic practice do not come into contact with the real directly but rather through the medium of the surrounding discursive-ideological world. The audio-visual media, in this sense, not only register the sounds and images of the world; they also chrontopically stage, through images, dialogue, and movement, the languages and discourses that refract and interpret the world. Within a double refractionism, art does not reflect or even refract the real; rather, it refracts a refraction of the stuff of life, offering a mediated version of an already textualized, discursivized, and ideologized socio-ideological sphere.

In relation to cinema, "realism" has been a constant, whether posited as an ideal or as an object of opprobrium. For Roland Barthes, realism is less than a sum of signifieds than a product of **reality effects**, that is, the artistic orchestration of apparently inessential details as guarantors of factual authenticity. Alessandra Raengo amends Barthes to speak of **reality a/effects** to refer to the affective dimension of realism, for example, to the black body as a paradigmatic visual sign (that wears its ontological status on its sleeve) as both product and trigger of an effect and affect of reality.[38]

With Deleuze, we move away from representation as a mimetic adequation between sign and referent to the concept of the film experience as the sensate feel of time and the mobile slidings of Bergsonian *durée* or lived duration. Finally, Alexander Kluge discerns a dialectic of complementary *attitudes* within realism, one that seeks exactitude in the representation of real experiences and another that points to the gaps between the real and what is hoped for, with both attitudes being equally part of the real.

Realism has often played a progressive role in art by relaying historically repressed perspectives of dominated populations, or more generally in conveying a sense that something is rotten in the state of capitalist society. The aesthetic referenced by György Lukács's phrase "critical realism" has generated an unending stream of progressive films that have seared social realities and subaltern struggles onto the general brain—the union struggle in films such as *Matewan* (1987), black and Latino struggles in *Lone Star* (1996), the struggle against racism in *Do the Right Thing* (1989), and so forth. Ken Loach's films, for example, combine a socialist ideology with a subtle dramatic-realist style to support past and present causes: the Irish War of Independence in *The Wind that Shakes the Barley* (2006), Republican resistance in the Spanish Civil War in *Land and Freedom* (1995), Latino union struggles in *Bread and Roses* (2000), labor rights in *Riffraff* (1936), and so forth.

At times, paradoxically, trans-realist art can touch the real in subversive ways. Larissa Sansour, for example, cunningly appropriates science fiction and slick CGI effects in her 2013 short *Nation Estate,* which depicts Palestine as a gigantic high-rise large enough to contain the entire Palestinian population. A pregnant woman (Sansour), after undergoing a retinal scan and fingerpint, enters a glossy lobby, graced with a giant Palestinian flag, where a poster reads: Nation Estate: Living the High Life." She enters an elevator where each floor represents a city in Palestine, with each stop offering simulacral vistas of the city in question. A keycard in the form of a Palestinian flag gives her access to an elegant flat where she waters a tree growing out of the floor, while the push of a button calls up an image of Jerusalem. Disrespecting the checkpoints of genre, Sansour draws on science fiction, real estate commercials, and corporate advertising to posit a utopian/dystopian solution in the form of a verticalized nation-state. As that state becomes less and less imaginable "on the ground," the artistic imagination posits a surreal solution for a surreal situation, thus becoming a form, paradoxically, of realism. The film's punning title hints both at the necessity of a Palestinian state and its apparent impossibility in a situation where it can only be realized in fantasy. Sansoor's trans-realist fantasy poking bitter fun at Palestine's shrinking territory was deigned too real, and more specifically "too pro-Palestinian," by the corporate sponsors of the Lacoste-Elysee Competition, who demanded that she "voluntarily" withdraw the piece, which she refused to do. The gesture of censorship ultimately backfired in that it provoked worldwide protests and a decision by the Swiss venue to break off relations with Lacoste, while Sansoor's new notoriety served to spread the word about her work.

Although realism can expose social mythologies and open up new social horizons, it can also foreclose radical possibilities. Borrowing the art world term "capitalist realism" (a play on "socialist realism") to refer to commodity-based art, Michael Schudson used the term in his 1984 book *Advertising, the Uneasy Persuasion* to describe the practices of advertising. Mark Fisher, meanwhile, speaks of capitalist realism in a more global way as a kind of invisible mental barrier to progressive change in the wake of universal commodification, where "competitivity" and the "privatization of stress" become central to capitalist hegemony.[39] *Capitalist realism* pervades everyday discourse, reflected in such expressions as "the bottom line is …" and "the reality is …," phrases which imply a rejection of any structural change in the name of the unforgiving reality principle. While claiming to be hard-nosed and pragmatic, capitalist realism is based on the ultimate fantasy—that crises are temporary, that the stock market will always go up, that nature is inexhaustible, that there will always be more oceans to pollute or, failing that, planets to colonize, and that capitalism, like the banks, is too big to fail.

Although realism is not the focus in *Keywords*, some of the most exciting contemporary work in film adopts an overall realist frame. Beatriz Jaguaribe speaks of "new registers of aesthetic realism" manifested globally in a revitalized political documentaries, in New Iranian Cinema, in the Dogma group, in the films of Mike Leigh, John Sayles, Michael Winterbottom, and Steve McQueen.[40] Many of these films mix actors with non-actors drawn from the milieu being depicted. After a longstanding avoidance of work as a subject fit for cinema, scores of films have treated the everyday challenges of work and labor. While eschewing any obvious political rhetoric, the films of the Dardennes brothers demonstrate a commitment, in Martin O'Shaughnessy's apt summary, "to characters who lack symbolic resources to make sense of their situations [and who] have to free themselves of any pre-elaborated discourse of value" and without recourse to more enlightened "third parties."[41] *La Promesse* (1996), for example, constitutes a kind of European *Huck Finn*, one haunted by the history of Belgian colonialism in Africa, where the adolescent son has to decide to go to hell by opposing the law of the racist father in favor of the ethical demands of the African widow.

The melding of fiction and documentary can generate non-fiction films every bit as suspenseful as the best fiction films. The blow-by-blow account of Edward Snowden's radical whistle-blowing in *Citizen Four* constitutes a startling **docu-thriller**. The Jose Padilha documentary *Bus 174* (2002), meanwhile, **sequesters suspense** by turning the real-life hijacking of a Brazilian bus by a homeless street person named Sandro into a **sociological mystery**. But, even more remarkably, the film hijacks Hitchcock in that its narrative structure strongly resembles that of certain memory-based Hitchcock films that proceed via a double and contradictory temporal movement—found in the tracing of the origins of Gregory Peck's amnesia in *Spellbound* (1945), or of Marnie's kleptomania in *Marnie* (1964)—in that the story simultaneously moves forward in terms of the unfolding events in the sequestered bus and backward toward the origins of a trauma.

The films of Jean-Marc Moutout explore these dilemmas as experienced from within the corporate world. The symptomatically titled *Violence des échanges en milieu tempéré* (2003), for example, shows the soft-spoken sadism of corporate downsizing, where a young employee, through a kind of hardening of the moral arteries, gradually aligns himself with management by firing those whom he knows very well do not deserve to be fired. Independent **Neo-neo-realist** films (A. O. Scott) such as *Slacker* (1991), *Reality Bites* (1994), and *Fight Club* (1999) in the United States, as Sherry B. Ortner points out, revolve around the harsh effects of Reaganite policies and "the unhappy nature of white-collar work under neoliberal capitalism."[42] While foregrounding cultural critique, or obliquely political indictments of the economic system, these films do not present idealized characters as models of activism or advance proposals for structural change; rather, they foreground the harshness of an era of downward mobility and in this sense could be called "we do not live in the best of all possible worlds" films.

Many radical documentaries—*The Corporation, The Shock Doctrine, Capitalism: A Love Story, Profit and Nothing Else, The Globalization Tapes, Master of the Universe, War by Other Means, Capitalism is the Crisis, Lifting the Veil,* and *Inside Job*—offer frontal critiques of the globalized capitalist order, often reaching large audiences. *The Corporation* (2004) is structured around a literalization of the neo-liberal metaphor of "corporate personhood." If corporations are people, the film argues, those "people" are psychopaths; they knowingly cause harm, show callous disregard for others, and are incapable of empathy and of sustaining human relationships. Joshua Oppenheimer's *The Globalization Tapes* contrasts the harsh realities lived by Indonesian workers and the euphoric nostrums of neo-liberal globalization. *Lifting the Veil* (2011) deploys Internet and original footage to create the first feature-length documentary on the Occupy Wall Street movement.

The We the Economy project, meanwhile, offers 20 short films about the economy by celebrated directors, all available free across cable, mobile, and video-on-demand (VOD) services. The purpose is to cut through the mystifying jargon of mainstream economics using any audio-visual means necessary—including the pop didacticism of animation, collage, puppets—to clarify the issues at stake. While Cable News abandons "the economy" as a term in favor of a pro-corporate "Business News" or individualistic "Your Money" rubric—the telespectator is addressed not as "citizen" but as "consumer" or "investor": "We the economy" stresses the collective dimension of economic relationalities, whether by highlighting the wealth abyss separating the 1% from the 99%, or by linking the tin embedded in our mobile phones to the brutal exploitation that makes mobile phones possible. While uneven and sometimes reformist in political terms, the more radical episodes deploy innovative strategies to cut through the murk of terms like "credit default swaps," "deleveraging," and "quantitative easing." The series suggests that language matters: calling corporations "downsizers" and "job exporters" rather than "job creators" carries a very different affective charge.

One James Schamus episode explores the essential weirdness of money by showing that, although it is often assumed to be the ultimate ontological real—"you can bank on it"—money is actually little more than a figment of our collective imagination. Those temple-like banks, furthermore, do not keep our money—they are legally obliged through the fractional reserve monetary system to have only 3% of their holdings actually "in" the bank—but rather loan it out at exorbitant rates. Furthermore, in a scam that staggers the imagination, the government prints money and gives it at virtually no interest to the banks, which then loan it, with interest, back to the government. The Adam McKay episode, meanwhile, follows three lollipop-loving cartoon alpacas (voiced by Amy Poehler, Maya Rudolph, and Sarah Silverman) whose adventures after graduation from "sweetness school" reveal diverse dimensions of class prejudice and income inequality. Two allegorical lemonade stands in the Ramin Bahrani episode illustrate the often sleazy ties between big business and government regulators.

One challenge for contemporary radical films, then, is to flesh out the abstractions of political economy, to trace contemporary immiseration back to the human decisions of the representatives of financial capital. A 1924 Vertov *Kino-Glas* film, all in reverse motion, traced the itinerary of bread from bakery to mill to storehouse to rye. In this sense, one could imagine a contemporary equivalent, a kind of financial *Memento* (2000 thriller movie by Christopher Nolan), which would move backward from the present in order to reveal the cruel mechanisms of political economy, by moving backward, for example, from scenes of starvation in contemporary Africa to the initial approval of an IMF austerity program, or from the current desperation of a barely working single mother to a Congressional decision to cut food-stamp subsidies. The contemporary equivalent of the stolen bicycle as tragic trigger mechanism in *The Bicycle Thief* (1948) might today be rendered as the student's initial acceptance of a "free" credit card or a student loan. Some activist films on the subject of debt—for example, *Maxed Out: Hard Times, Easy Credit, and the Era of Predatory Lenders* (2006) and *Profit & Nothing But! Or Impolite Thoughts on the Class Struggle* (2001) anticipate the kind of insights found in the book *Creditocracy and the Case for Debt Refusal* (2014), where Andrew Ross brilliantly brings together the many threads of contemporary social oppression, all linked to situations in which indebtedness becomes the precondition for material improvements in the quality of life and even for the requirements of a bare life existence.[43] Ross reveals the vast web that connects apparently disparate phenomena such as colonialism and Third World debt, slavery and reparations, public debt and austerity policies, student debt and political corruption, colonial resource extraction and contemporary debt bondage, climate debt and the ecological crisis. Profit accumulation through the exploitation of debt is the figure in the carpet that threads together major forms of oppression in the neo-liberal age. The contemporary dialectic is no longer between master and slave, or even between capital and labor, but rather between creditor and debtor. Excoriating the asymmetric moralism of Wall Street—that is, shameless exploitation combined with moralistic guilt-tripping for those who do not pay their credit card debts on time (even though banks prefer that we *not* pay on time)—Ross calls for a massive refusal of all illegitimate "odious debt" rooted in colonialism, neo-colonialism, and neo-liberal austerity policies. Making a killing off vital commons goods like education, health care, and urban infrastructure, for Ross, is a venal symptom of the neo-liberal transfer of fiscal responsibility from the state to defenseless individuals and disempowered constituencies.

Other activist documentaries have exposed the pathologies of neo-liberalism while promoting activist resistance. With films such as *The War on Iraq* (2004), *Walmart: The High Cost of Low Price* (2005), and *Iraq for Sale: The War Profiteers* (2006), Robert Greenwald and his Brave New

Films have been at the center of activist filmmaking that combines media-savvy political jeremiads with innovative ways of funding, producing, and distributing films through a mix of small budgets, short shooting schedules, grassroots house parties, online DVD sales, and the use of an array of new media outlets. *The Koch Brothers Exposed*, in its 2012 and 2014 versions, uses the two oil barons as one node in what Brecht called "the causal network of events," in this case a kind of toxic dump of right-wing libertarianism, ecological devastation, political corruption, Citizens United, anti-union politics, anti-black racism, voter suppression, and right-wing anti-government ideology.

In a Maussian **potlatch strategy**—in a very partial comparison to the gift-giving feasts practiced by the indigenous peoples of the Pacific Northwest—the various Occupy movements around the world have made a cornucopia of radical free films available on the Internet, including such the seven-part *Wall Street Occupation, Free the Network, Occupy the Imagination, 10 Arrests in 87 Minutes, Real Estate 4 Ransom, Occupied Cascadia*, along with the many films of the Zeitgeist movement. The idea of free films cuts against the very idea that films have to make money in a world where the corporate media report not on films but only on the box-office competition. In symbolic terms, potlatch replaces social Darwinist winners and losers with a social economy of gregariously competitive gift-giving. Indeed, the practice was banned in Canada and the United States because it was seen as unproductive, wasteful, and contrary to the central goal of capitalism—growth and accumulation. The apparently gratuitous giving of gifts, as elaborated in the writing of Marcel Mauss and Georges Bataille, also triggers reciprocal obligations to give, receive, and give back, a concept which completely contradicts the morality underlying classical economics, which insists on rational choice and the calculation of selfish interest. The gift of a film, in this sense, might trigger a response gift, for example, in the form not of financial recompense but rather of other films and energized activism.

At times, it is the cable TV comics who best manage to demystify the reigning economic doxa, who reveal through satire that some of the eternal truths of today are actually recent neo-liberal inventions. The right-wing persona of Stephen Colbert, for example, embodies what Bakhtin called **deep parody** that is, a form of parodic discourse that goes beyond a shallow mockery of manners, to create a profound ideological critique of right-wing thinking in general. Colbert's style and discourse parody conservative ideology not only through voice and body language (modeled on the macho blustering of cable gasbag Bill O'Reilly) but also by satirizing right-wing doxa through *ad absurdum* exaggeration. Colbert voices in laughable terms the right-wing economic nostrums—predatory social Darwinism, blind market fundamentalism, and heartless trickle-down economics. He has repeatedly lampooned not only the Super PACS with his own innocuously named "Making a Better Tomorrow, Tomorrow" Super PAC but also the pernicious trope of corporate personhood, which is being used to foster the complete corruption of political life in the United States. If corporations are persons, Colbert has argued, they should have the lifespan of persons and the children of CEOs ought to be able to marry them. One Colbert video takes Mitt Romney's "corporations are people" claim at its word through a mock political commercial which argues that, since Romney, as the head of Bain Capital, had snuffed out a number of other corporations, he was therefore a killer of people and should be renamed Mitt the Ripper.

John Oliver's HBO Show *Last Week Tonight* provides striking examples of what constitutes a "political film" in the twenty-first century. The episodes have all the standard attributes of a film—performance, moving images, editing, illustrative audio-visual materials, music tracks, and so forth. Combining hilarity with passionate denunciation, the episodes mix stand-up comedy, agit prop, satire, and direct-to-audience exhortation. One episode, entitled simply "Prison," excoriated the American prison-industrial complex system as cruel, racist, profit-oriented, and quite literally criminal. The episode ended with Muppets singing an educational song, whose Ogden Nash-style lyrics went:

> It's a fact that needs to be spoken
> America's prisons are broken
> It's hard truth that prisons are needed for civilization
> But mandatory minimums for heroin and crack
> Are stacked against Hispanics and blacks
> Our prison population is bigger than Slovenia
> We put people in jail instead of treating schizophrenia
> Prison conditions are a national disgrace
> With violence, maggots, and rape.

The sketch ended with a PBS-style nod of thanks to the sponsors: "The broken prison system is brought to you by—'decades of neglect, a lack of political courage, and a generous donation by the GEO group'."

Another episode treated the high-stakes issue of the Federal Communications Commission's (FCC) plan to end net neutrality by offering a special and profitable fast lane for corporations: corporations would fly the Internet first-class while the rest of us squirm in coach or economy, or not even get on the plane at all. After hailing the Internet (aka, "the electronic cat database") for everything it makes possible—doing one's taxes, applying for jobs, or "buying a bottle of coyote urine"—Oliver warned spectators of the threat to net neutrality and its premise of equality for all users. Although the Internet is not broken, he told his audience, the FCC wants to "fix it." Oliver compared Comcast's behavior toward Netflix to a mob shakedown enabled by the cozy relationship between cable corporations and Washington, and Obama's appointment of a cable lobbyist as FCC chair to "hiring a dingo as a babysitter" (a cartoon visual showed a dingo watching over a tiny tot). Noting the use of obscure legal niceties and lobbying to introduce and pass horrid legislation, Oliver revealed one of the trade secrets of corporate dominance—wrapping anti-popular policy in soporific and obfuscating legalese: "if you want to do something truly evil, hide it in something boring." Apple, he claimed, could include all of *Mein Kampf* in the iTunes user agreement, and everyone would mechanically click "agree" to its tenets.

The comic ended with a mock-melodramatic appeal to his audience, reminiscent of the "I'm-mad-as-hell-and-I'm-not-going-to-take-this-anymore!" chants from *Network* (1976)—in which he exhorted his audience to answer the FCC's invitation for "public comment" by inundating them with protest emails. Reminding the "Internauts" that they had been commenting passionately about utter trivia for years, Oliver urged the trolls to "get out there, and for once in your lives, focus your indiscriminate rage in a useful direction. Seize your moment, my lovely trolls … and fly my pretties, fly …!" The video subsequently went viral, crashing the FCC website, and stopping the momentum of a disastrous policy in the making. Addressing an urgent political issue, equal access to the collective intellectual legacy made available by the digital commons, the episode mobilized strategies drawn from the *artistic commons*, such as strategic hyperbole and mordant irony, to achieve its effects. Rather than follow the old model of films that require months or years of pre-production, fundraising, production, and post-production, the segment was generated in almost no time at all and its impact was virtually immediate. Of course, the aesthetician might object by asking "but, is it a lasting piece of art that will stand the test of time?" And the answer is that, first, of course it is indeed art both in its status and in its procedures and, while its topicality might mean that the episode itself might not stand such a test, the satiric strategies themselves are perennial and will perdure.

Rather than focus on auteurs, *Keywords in Subversive Film/Media Aesthetics* focuses on strategies and tactics forming distinguishable sources of alternative aesthetics. Each chapter highlights a different theoretical/ filmic current within the broader sea of alternative aesthetics. Chapter 1,

"An Aesthetics of the Commons," explores the multiple resonances of the commons, ranging from the literal sense of the communal ownership of land to the metaphorical sense of the transtextual commons of the artistic legacy in general. The chapter thus addresses two apparently antipodal forms of a commons aesthetic, one from the world of indigenous people as new social actors producing cinema from a native perspective, in relation to such concepts as **tribal auteurism**, "the high-tech Indian," and archaic modernism, and ab-originality, and the other having to do with the world's collective legacy of knowledge as conveyed, for example, through transtextual dialogism, revisionist adaptation, and postcolonial adaptation.

Chapter 2, "The Upside Down World of the Carnivalesque," explores another perennial stream within radical aesthetics, to wit, the subversive strategies and critical utopias linked to the popular festivities called up by Bakhtin's "carnivalesque" and by Lefebvre's "festival." Here we discuss festive-revolutionary practices as reflective of the culture of laughter, *parodia sacra*, social inversion, the woman on top, polymorphous celebrations, ideological parody, corporate impersonation, and offside cinema as part of an ongoing subversive lineage.

Chapter 3, "Political Modernism and Its Discontents," both elucidates and critiques a long dominant current on the left, what David Rodowick calls "political modernism," especially as incarnated in Brechtian theory and its practical extensions in the form of reflexive realism, alienation effects, and counter-cinema. After explicating this rich heritage, the chapter moves to the feminist, critical race, and postcolonial attempts to go beyond that heritage, while examining such concepts as visceral spectatorship and the affective-corporeal turn.

Chapter 4, "The Transmogrification of the Negative," explores a particularly vibrant current that breaks the link between aesthetics and beauty, a trend that transfigures the low, the despised, and the trashy into the social sublime. This current moves historically from modernist collage to Brazilian anthropophagy on to the situationists and their latter-day culture-jamming progeny. Here we explore such concepts as the undercommons, the aesthetic of mistakes, anthropophagic modernism, the aesthetics of garbage, eco-feminist subversion, *détournement*, culture jamming, and media jujitsu.

Chapter 5, "Hybrid Variations on a Documentary Theme," explores another major source of aesthetic renewal: the cross-pollination or reciprocal chameleonism that has energized and transformed both documentary and fiction, as evoked in terms such as "mockumentaries," "hybrid authorship," and "intermediality." The chapter addresses an especially striking feature of recent documentary—the democratization of authorship through the emergence of new social subjects of discourse.

Chapter 6, "Hollywood Aristotelianism, the Fractured Chronotope, and the Musicalization of Cinema," moves from a critique of the orthodox Hollywood chronotope to an exploration of a cornucopia of transrealist strategies such as Menippean satire, magic realism, the aesthetics of anachronism, shamanic cinema, trance Brechtianism, audiotopias, and contrapuntal history.

Chapter 7, "Aesthetic/Political Innovation in the Digital Era," extends the book's concepts into the era of the new social media by highlighting such concepts as hydra-media, the interface effect, rhizomatic production, FutARism, and virtual heterotopias.

The overall argument of *Keywords in Subversive Film/Media Aesthetics* is not stated explicitly but worked out slowly over the course of the book. Diverse leitmotifs are woven into the various chapters, creating a kind of musical echo effect whereby the same themes emerge in different contexts. The seed idea of the aesthetics of the commons sprouts throughout the various chapters. The concept of the indigenous land commons in the first chapter is echoed in the discussion of the digital commons in the latter portions of the chapter. The early feminism of *Les stances à Sophie* (1971) in the second chapter (carnival), similarly, rhymes with later forms of feminism in the third chapter (Brecht), and so forth. Throughout, the book stresses the dialectics of critique and celebration, protest and utopia, all seen as complementary and mutually constitutive concepts. Critique without celebration is disheartening and ultimately disempowering, while celebration without critique is facile and disingenuous. Undergirding the book is the idea of critical utopia, that is, utopia not as blueprint or prediction but as a past- or future-based critique of the present. Alexander Kluge speaks of "the utopia of film" as the search for a "quality about which one vaguely knows that it existed at some point in the past" conjoined with the idea that "there could be something other than this insufficient present of the moment."[44] "The encounter with the truth of art," for Herbert Marcuse, occurs "in the estranging language and images which make perceptible, visible, and audible that which is no longer, or not yet perceived, said and heard in everyday life."[45]

At once a quietly passionate manifesto and an opinionated lexicon, *Keywords* names and illustrates strategies of very diverse provenance, all of which foster radical conceptualizations of film and politics. This archive includes strategies rooted in the longstanding legacy of artistic forms and chronotopes such as the carnivalesque (the world upside down, the grotesque body); strategies deriving from the historical avant-gardes (collage, found objects); strategies emerging from cable comedy (fake news, ideological impersonation) and from the new social media (hactivism). What all these strategies have in common is their exuberantly recombinative capacity, their joyous mash-ups of possibilities, their simultaneous recognition and renewal of antecedent texts and practices. Whatever does not come from the tradition, as Buñuel put it in a boutade, "is plagiarism." Underlying this book is a transpersonal notion of creativity that goes beyond an auteurism rooted in the mystique of the romantic author as secret legislator of mankind, to embrace a common creativity rooted in the shared intergenerational transtext that we will be calling the aesthetic commons.

## Notes

1   Jung Bong Choi, "Of Transnational-Korean Cinematrix," in *Transnational Cinemas* 3(1): 3–18.
2   For an in-depth discussion of polycentrism, see Ella Shohat and Robert Stam, *Unthinking Eurocentrism: Multiculturalism and the Media* (London: Routledge, 1994).
3   Faye Ginsburg, "Peripheral Visions: Black Screens and Cultural Citizenship," in Dina Jordanova, David Martin-Jones, and Belén Vidal (eds), *Cinema at the Periphery* (Detroit: Wayne State University Press, 2010), p. 84.
4   On Eurocentrism, see Ella Shohat and Robert Stam, *Unthinking Eurocentrism*, and Robert Stam and Ella Shohat, *Race in Translation: Culture Wars around the Postcolonial Atlantic* (New York: New York University Press, 2012).
5   See Anibal Quijano, "Coloniality of Power, Eurocentrism and Latin America," *Nepantla* No. 3 (Durham: Duke University Press, 2000), and Mary Louise Pratt, *Imperial Eyes: Travel Writing and Transculturation* (New York: Routledge, 1992).
6   Thomas King, *The Inconvenient Indian* (Minneapolis: University of Minnesota Press, 2012), p. 265.
7   See, e.g., Walter Mignolo, *The Darker Side of Western Modernity: Global Futures, Decolonial Options* (Durham, NC: Duke University Press, 2011).
8   Gilles Deleuze and Félix Guattari, *Kafka: Towards a Minor Literature*, trans. Dana Polan (Minneapolis: University of Minnesota Press, 1986; originally published as *Kafka: Pour une litterature mineure*, 1975), pp. 16–17.
9   To our knowledge, David Rodowick was the first scholar to extend the idea of minor literature to minor cinema: see D. N. Rodowick, *Gilles Deleuze's Time Machine* (Durham, NC: Duke University Press, 1997).
10  David E. James, *The Most Typical Avant-Garde: History and Geography of Minor Cinemas in Los Angeles* (Berkeley: University of California Press, 2005), p. 13.

11 David Graeber, *Revolutions in Reverse: Essays on Politics, Violence, Art, and Imagination* (New York: Autonomedia, 2011), p. 9.

12 Max Blechman, "The Revolutionary Dream of Early German Romanticism," in Max Blechman (ed.), *Revolutionary Romanticism* (San Francisco: City Light Books, 1999), p. 30.

13 Antoine de Baecque, *Camera Historica: The Century in Cinema*, trans. Ninon Vinsonneau and Jonathan Magidoff (New York: Columbia University Press, 2012), p. 199.

14 Hakim Bey, T.A.Z.: *The Temporary Autonomous Zone, Ontological Anarchy, Poetic Terrorism* (New York: Autonomedia, 1991), p. 101.

15 Bernard Lazare, quoted by Jesse Cohn in "What is Anarchist Literary Theory?" *Anarchist Studies*, 15(2) (2007): 125.

16 Quoted in Martin Jay, *Marxism and Totality* (Berkeley: University of California Press, 1984), p. 183.

17 See Astra Taylor, *The People's Platform* (New York: Henry Holt, 2014), p. 154.

18 Taylor, *People's Platform*, p. 155.

19 Jacques Rancière, *Aisthesis: Scenes from the Aesthetic Regime of Art* (London: Verso, 2013), p. ix.

20 Immanuel Kant, *The Critique of Judgment*, trans. James Creed Meredith (Oxford: Clarendon, 1982), pp. 42–43.

21 Noel Carroll, *Beyond Aesthetics: Philosophical Essays* (Cambridge: Cambridge University Press, 2001), p. 295.

22 Ben Highmore, "Bitter Aftertaste: Affect, Food, and Social Aesthetics," in Melissa Gregg and Gregory Seigworth (eds), *The Affect Theory Reader* (Durham, NC: Duke University Press, 2010), pp. 321–322.

23 Jacques Derrida, *The Truth in Painting* (Chicago: University of Chicago Press, 1987).

24 Pierre Bourdieu, "The Forms of Capital," in J. Richardson (ed.), *Handbook of Theory and Research for the Sociology of Education* (New York: Greenwood, 1986), pp. 241–258.

25 See Edward Said, *Culture and Imperialism* (New York: Knopf, 1993).

26 Friedrich Schiller, *On the Aesthetic Education of Man* (Mineola, NY: Dover, 2004).

27 The idea of the *partage du sensible* forms a part of many of Rancière's books, but see especially *Le Partage du sensible: esthetique et politique* (Paris: Fabrique, 2000), published in English as *The Politics of Aesthetics: The Distribution of the Sensible* (New York: Continuum, 2004), p. xi.

28 Meg McLagan and Yates McKee, *Sensible Politics: The Visual Culture of Nongovernmental Activism* (New York: Zone Books, 2013).

29 George Lipsitz, *Time Passages: Collective Memory and American Popular Culture* (Minneapolis: University of Minnesota Press, 2001), p. 3.

30 Deleuze makes these statements in his series of 1988–1989 interviews on DVD with Claire Parnet, *L'Abécédaire de Gilles Deleuze* (Editions Montparnasse, 2004).

31  Nicolas Bourriaud, *Relational Aesthetics* (Paris: Presses du Reel, 1998), pp. 112–113.
32  Interview with Robert Stam.
33  Daniel Frampton, *Filmosophy* (London: Wallflower, 2006), p. 5.
34  Alain Badiou, *Cinema* (Paris: Nova, 2010), p. 323.
35  Erich Auerbach, *Mimesis: The Representation of Reality in Western Literature* (Princeton: Princeton University Press, 1953), p. 491.
36  Ivana Bentes, "Global Periphery: Aesthetic and Cultural Margins in Brazilian Audiovisual Forms," in Jens Andermann and Álvaro Fernández Bravo (eds), *New Argentine and Brazilian New Cinema: Reality Effects* (New York: Palgrave Macmillan, 2013), p. 114.
37  P. N. Medvedev and M. M. Bakhtin, *The Formal Method in Literary Scholarship: A Critical Introduction to Sociological Poetics*, trans. Albert J. Wehrle, rev. edn (Cambridge, MA: Harvard University Press, 1985).
38  See Alessandra Raengo, *On the Sleeve of the Visual: Race as Face Value* (Hanover, NH: Dartmouth University Press, 2013).
39  See Mark Fisher, *Capitalist Realism: Is There No Alternative?* (UK: Zero Books, 2009).
40  Beatriz Jaguaribe, *O choque do real* (Rio de Janeiro: Rocco, 2007).
41  Martin O'Shaughnessy, *The New Face of Political Cinema: Commitment in French Film since 1995* (New York: Berghahn, 2007), p. 109.
42  See Sherry B. Ortner, *Not Hollywood: Independent Film at the Twilight of the American Dream* (Durham, NC: Duke University Press, 2013).
43  Andrew Ross, *Creditocracy and the Case for Debt Refusal* (New York: Or Books, 2013).
44  Alexander Kluge, "Die Utopie Film" (1964), quoted in Christopher Pavsek, *The Utopia of Film: Cinema and Its Futures in Godard, Kluge, and Tahimik* (New York: Columbia University Press, 2013), p. 1.
45  Herbert Marcuse, *The Aesthetic Dimension: Toward a Critique of Marxist Aesthetics* (Boston: Beacon, 1977), p. 72.

# 1

# An Aesthetics of the Commons

Most studies of subversive aesthetics take political modernism as their point of departure. But *political modernism* is hardly the only path to radical aesthetics. Modernism was too often premised on a stagist *mythos* whereby the new simply replaces the old, whereas in fact the old and the archaic can be mobilized in favor of the new and the radical (Gomez-Pena speaks of the "junkies of futurity").[1] The modernist "cult of the new"—what Alexander Kluge called in a film title "The Assault of the Present on the Rest of Time"—offers diminishing returns in an era when mass media have annexed co-optable features of the avant-garde while evacuating any semblance of political radicalism. Within what might be called **corporate avant-gardism**, intertextual parody and reflexivity have become mass media staples, as common and bland as white bread.[2] The transtemporal editing techniques deployed by contemporary TV commercials—which resemble those that first transfixed the spectators of *Last Year at Marienbad* (1961)—are now used by corporate TV commercials to promote a gravity-free world of consumerist pseudo-freedom. Entertainment capitalism's **accelerationist aesthetics** favors excess and transgression as motors of capital expansion.[3] The ads of transnational corporations, in this sense, offer a transrealist aesthetic of globally integrated cityscapes, a world without center or borders, conjured up in a hyperkinetic proliferation of deterritorialized simulacra; however, all their wildly dispersive centrifugal energies are ultimately disciplined by the centripetal force of the corporate brand.

*Keywords in Subversive Film/Media Aesthetics*, First Edition. Robert Stam with Richard Porton and Leo Goldsmith.
© 2015 John Wiley & Sons, Inc. Published 2015 by John Wiley & Sons, Inc.

## The Aesthetic Commons

The "brand new" often ages badly; it inevitably becomes old, which is why few genres date more rapidly than "futurist films." Our goal here is not to rescue the avant-garde but rather to shift attention to a more venerable arsenal of stratagems. Alternative aesthetics rooted in millennial traditions such as *Menippean satire* and *carnivalesque inversion*, we will argue, bear perennial relevance; they remain always already available for renewal. Rather than search for "new stories," "new techniques," and "new apps," artists/theorists can make old stories new by reimagining them through alternative artistic traditions with ancient roots.

This vast planetary archive of ideas and strategies forms a kind of **aesthetic commons**. At once archly traditional and hyper-contemporary, the metaphor of the "*commons*" has appealingly multiple resonances, evoking everything from ancient patterns of communal land ownership— the poet Shelley's "equal participation in the commonage of nature"—to the contemporary digital commons of the "copy left" movements. For Jacques Rancière, "politics is the sphere of activity of a *common* that can only ever be contentious."[4] The notion of commonly held land forms a social norm shared by societal formations ranging from the thirteenth-century England of the "Great Charter of the Forest" to the longstanding communal social systems of countless indigenous peoples. The "**commons**" evokes a cornucopia of socio-political ideals—Tom Payne's "Common Sense," Marx's "primitive communism," the "Boston Commons," the "Common Wealth," the "common people," the Paris Commune, the "Creative Commons," and the indigenous "common pot." The *commons* counters the fetishizing of exclusive proprietary rights that fuels the corporate drive to privatize everything from Amazonian biodiversity to the lyrics of the "Happy Birthday to You" song. Vesting property in the community, the *commons* evokes "communism," but without its Stalinist baggage, and "socialism," without the bloodless social-democratism that so easily turns it into capitalism-with-a-human-face.

While it might seem utopian to speak of *the commons* in an age of relentless privatization, the vaguely remembered plenitude and the future possibilities of the commons trope provides a thread that links many social struggles.[5] In a political age where US conservatives keep moving the ideological goalpost to the right by redefining a mild liberalism—seen in many countries as a form of *laissez-faire* conservatism—as if it were socialist radicalism, the idea of the *commons* moves the goalpost to the left by calling for a deep restructuring to restore the common good. Rather than propose a mere tax on oil corporations, it questions the very idea of anyone such as the Koch Brothers actually "owning" a public good such as oil and exploiting it for profit to the detriment of the populace and the planet. Such utopian ideas are usually dismissed as naïve, but the point is not the immediate realizability of the proposal but rather the directionality of the critique. Currently proliferating in the writing of figures as diverse as Naomi Klein, Slavoj Žižek, Vandana Shiva, Elinor Ostrom, David Graeber, Jacques Rancière, Peter Linebaugh, Michael Hardt, and Antonio Negri, "*the commons*" haunts privatizing neoliberalism with the specter of communalizing egalitarianism. The term evokes resistance to "**enclosure**" in all its forms, from its early proto-capitalist form of fencing in shared European land, to its colonialist form of appropriating indigenous land, on to its contemporary global capitalist form of the "**second enclosure**"— that is, the marshaling of juridical "patent" and "intellectual property" to assert the corporate ownership of ideas. In the wake of the fall of communism and the crisis of capitalism, the "*commons*" calls up the planetary struggle to reclaim the "common wealth." Many recent protest movements have taken place, revealingly, amidst the leafy vestiges of the traditional commons, in the form of public squares and parks.

The popularity of the *commons* trope was triggered, perhaps, by the disenchantment with nation-state-based forms of socialism and communism, by the crisis in productivist forms of Marxism, by the growing visibility of indigenous-led resistance, and above all by the rapidly worsening climate change, which is generating a widespread consciousness of capitalism as a menace to the planet. Naomi Klein speaks of **Blockadia** as a "roving transnational conflict zone" of resistance to the extractive projects of corporations.[6] From a leftist perspective, meanwhile, David Harvey has delineated the conjunctural complexities of the "*commons*." Some provisional *enclosures*, he points out, might be necessary to *protect* the commons in a broader sense.[7] Elinor Ostrom has shown that the commons which actually last are not completely "open" or "free," but rather "stinted" with restrictions.[8] The challenge is to avoid fetishizing private property, and yet preserve creators' rights to make a living while also protecting privacy as an inalienable right against the panoptical surveillance of corporations or of NSA. Small-scale indigenous societies, paradoxically, might want to "enclose" their collective "privacy," their biodiversity, their herbal remedies, and spiritual secrets to safeguard them from new-age Indian wannabes and predatory pharmaceutical companies. Free-software enthusiasts sometimes forget that, in many communities, certain kinds of knowledge are restricted to tribal insiders, or to men, or to women, or to the initiated. In this sense, the libertarian metaphor/fantasy of absolutely free circulation can operate in tandem with overly romantic (often exploitative) attitudes toward indigenous forms of knowledge circulation. In Australia, Aboriginal activists protested the virtual appropriation of a major sacred site (Uluru, in English: "Ayers Rock") in the virtual world of *Second Life* in 2003.[9] Édouard Glissant speaks of the right to **opacity**, that is, the right of first peoples or other besieged groups not only to represent themselves but also to refuse representation in the name of a communal form of *opacity*.[10]

Contemporary *enclosure* forms a direct threat not only to indigenous people—threatened with the loss of their land, streams, biodiversity, and even knowledge—but also to the ecological sustenance of the entire planet. At the same time, *enclosure* sabotages artistic and political creativity by fencing in the *commons* of artistic ideas and human creativity. A number of films have portrayed the **historical commons** within Europe. Nominally based on David Caute's 1961 novel *Comrade Jacob*, Kevin Brownlow and Andrew Mollo's film *Winstanley* (1975) chronicles the eponymous hero's (Gerrard Winstanley) efforts to maintain a communal experiment in Surrey during the 1640s—the determination to dig up and collectively manure this piece of land exemplifies a rage against the royal enclosure that robbed the English poor of their land. Early on in the film, strategically placed quotations from Gerrard Winstanley's *The New Law of Righteousness*, thunderously exhorting that the "earth shall be made a common treasury for all," accompany austere shots of the Surrey countryside. Winstanley's appeal to an anarchistic ideal of freedom, celebrating "the man who will turn things upside down," segues to a shot of the mansion inhabited by Winstanley's main antagonist, the wealthy Parson Platt, the implacable enemy of the Digger commune.

# From Columbus to Indigenous Media

The struggle over the commons links perennial global conflicts that go at least as far back as the conquest of the Americas and the creation of the Red Atlantic. "Contact between the two disconnected halves of the world five centuries ago," as Paul Chaat Smith puts it, was "the profoundest event in human history... [one that] created the world we live in today...."[11] In this sense, people everywhere live under the shadow of Columbus and 1492. Iciar Bollain's feature film *Even the Rain* (2010; "*También la lluvia*" in Spanish) links the colonial theft of indigenous land with the contemporary threat to the literal aquatic commons tied to the basic human/animal need for water to survive. Bringing the sixteenth-century debates about Columbus and the Conquista into the present, the film follows Spanish filmmakers in Bolivia shooting a critical film about Columbus that aims to underscore Spanish exploitation and indigenous rebellion. Columbus' exploitation of the Tainos is juxtaposed with the exploitation of the Quechua people by multinational corporations. While the conquistadores lusted after gold, the multinationals crave for water; what has changed is only the material to be extracted. The film connects the two historical moments through a local man named Daniel, who plays the role of the Taino rebel leader in the film-within-the-film, but whose role in "real life" is that of an activist leading demonstrations against the corporations that would privatize "even the rain." (The rebel is named "Hatuey" in homage to the Taino *cacique* who led the fight against Spanish colonialism in Hispianola.) Set in the period of the "Water Wars," the film points not only to the general commodification typical of neoliberal globalization where commodification extends even to hitherto public goods such as water, but also to the successful struggle against commodification by groups such as the "Coordinating Committee for Water and Life."[12]

*Even the Rain* portrays a tripartite exploitation: the conquistadores' lust for gold, the multinationals' thirst for raw materials, and, to a lesser degree, the filmmakers' need for extras and cheap labor. While classical Marxism is anticapitalist yet ultimately productivist, the Andean movements portrayed in *Even the Rain* are often more radically anticapitalist in their assertion that "mother earth" should not be commodified. This culturally instilled refusal was the idée-force that helped energize the Bolivian movement and enabled it to defeat powerful transnational corporations. The Andean movements are just one example of the **radical indigeneity** expressed in the burgeoning movements among indigenous peoples, variously called "first peoples" or "fourth world," that is, those still-residing descend-ants—estimates range from 250 to 600 million people—of the original inhabitants of lands subsequently taken over by or circumscribed by European conquest. Indigenous peoples, who have a link to communal ownership of land and who share a history of dispossession by Western colonialism, tend to be minoritized within the various nation-states whose hegemony they suffer, including within the "Third World." Just as English and Irish peasants revolted against the enclosure of communal lands in the early days of capitalist industrialization, so indigenous peoples today are in the forefront of the struggle against the extractive aggressions of transnational corporations.

It is in this context that it becomes imperative to speak of the burgeoning phenomenon of "**indigenous media**," that is, the use of contemporary technologies (camcorders, VCRs, digital camera, the Internet) to fore-ground the stories, values, and perspectives of indigenous peoples. (Maori filmmaker Barry Barclay coined the term **"Fourth Cinema"** to refer to the indigenous film movement in his 1990 book *Our Own Image*.) Indigenous cinema is innovative less in aesthetic terms than in terms of being produced by new social actors or subjects of discourse. Within "indigenous media," the producers are themselves the receivers, along with neighboring communities and, at times, distant cultural institutions or festivals such as the Native film festivals held in many parts of the world. Although indigenous film has come to form a significant branch of what is variously called "world cinema" or "transnational cinema," **first people's cinema**, as programmer Jesse Wente (Ojibwe) notes, fits awkwardly into the usual paradigms. As Wente explains on the inaugural website of the 2012 "First Peoples' Cinema: 1500 Nations, One Tradition," *First People's Cinema* defies the dominant categories and modes of interpretation. "To see these films," he writes, "is not only to discover a heretofore neglected wing of film history, but to reconsider what film itself is and can be."

*Indigenous media* comprise an empowering vehicle for communities struggling against geographical displacement, ecological deterioration, and cultural annihilation. The three most active centers of indigenous media production are Native North American (Inuit, Yup'ik, Cree, Dineh), Indians of the Amazon Basin (Nambiquara, Waiapi, Hunikui, Ikpeng), and indigenous Australian and Maori "auteurs" such as Rachel Perkins, Taika Waititi, the late Barry Barclay, and Merata Mita. The films of this transnational movement incorporate what Faye Ginsburg calls **offscreen regimes of value** that counter the neoliberal commodification of culture by recognizing indigenously made films as rooted in social relationships, with potential impact on local communities.[13] For Michelle H. Raheja, **"transnational indigenous media"** radicalizes Audrey Lorde's dictum that 'the masters' tools will never dismantle the master's house' by insisting that the very foundations of the master's house are indigenous and should be *reterritorialized* or repatriated.[14] In a very different context, Deleuze writes of the re-appearance of the **missing people**: "The moment the master, or the colonizer, proclaims 'There have never been people here'," Deleuze writes, "the *missing people* are a becoming, they invent themselves, in shanty-towns or in camps, or in ghettoes, in new conditions of struggle to which a necessarily political art must contribute."[15] Although Deleuze describes a process of *"becoming Indian,"* it is, in some cases, not a matter of "non-Indians becoming Indian" but rather of "Indians themselves becoming Indian." In the Amazon, for example, many people formerly described as "mestizos," or "peasants," have "come out" as self-identifying "Indians." In tandem with activism, indigenous film and video production forms an integral part of this movement.

*Indigenous media* has long had to confront the dumb intellectual inertia of Eurocentric trap concepts such as "authenticity," "tradition/modernity," and "real Indians." The default setting of Hollywood films, even in those that portray Indians positively, mandated that they be seen as obstacles to the forward momentum of progress. Indigenous media is subjected to all sorts of double-binds: it cannot be too modern, too avant-garde, or too technically polished, in which case it is "not really Indian." It must be traditional to be authentic, but if it is *too* traditional, it is judged opaque and inaccessible. An **allochronic politics** (Johannes Fabian) relegates native peoples to historically condemned time, rendering them as "vanished," or "extinct," as road-kill splattered on the freeway of progress. But genocides rarely achieve their fantasy of total annihilation. Even the supposedly extinguished Pequot in Massachusetts now have their digitally equipped museums, while the descendants of the "extinct" Tainos appear on websites participating in festivals and family gatherings.[16] Indigenous media, in this respect, proclaims: "We're here, we're now, get used to it!"

A related prejudice mandates that indigenous peoples remain pristine and undefiled by "Western" technology. But indigenous peoples have been entangled with technology for millennia. The true history of indigenous people, as Paul Chaat Smith points out, is one of "constant change, technological innovation, and intense curiosity about the world. How else do you explain our instantaneous adaptation to horses, rifles, flour, and knives?"[17] Philip J. Deloria, similarly, speaks of "**Indian Modernity**" to delineate the fraught situation of Native American actors performing "Indianness" within the Hollywood system.[18] At the same time, "*indigenous media*" should not be seen as a magical panacea either for the concrete challenges faced by indigenous peoples or as a salvage operation for an anthropological discipline eager to shed its colonial roots. Indigenous media projects can foster factional divisions, and can be appropriated by international media as facile symbols of the ironies of the postmodern age.[19]

Indigenous media-makers confront what Ginsburg calls a "**Faustian dilemma**": on the one hand, they use new technologies for cultural self-assertion; on the other, they spread a technology that might ultimately foster their own disintegration.[20] At its best, however, indigenous media transcends the standard conventions of commercial or even so-called independent cinema by producing work literally "grounded" in their own territorial commons. The view that warns indigenous peoples to flee the media to avoid Western contamination, in this sense, denies them the indispensable tools of self-defense in the digital age. Undeterred by Promethean/Heideggerean pessimism, the children of recently contacted groups—allochronically designated "stone age tribes"—now use Facebook and post YouTube videos to introduce themselves to multiple publics. In the aboriginal film *Ringtone* (2014), the members of an aboriginal community in Northern Australia explain the complex cultural motivations for their choice of cellular ringtones, which mingle ancestral clan songs with hip-hop music, suggesting what one of the film's directors calls the **"generative power of the ancestral."**[21] In South America, Mapuche and Aymara activists use the Internet, Facebook, and YouTube to disseminate hip-hop protest songs, while in North America, Native Americans hold "cyber-pow-wows."[22] Meanwhile, the Internet connects both continents Bilingual Purépecha speakers in Chicago are now in contact via the Internet with Aymaras in Bolivia, Yanomami in Venezuela, and Guarani in Paraguay.[23]

Contemporary indigenous youth in North America have also felt drawn to rap and reggae as forms of cultural protest. The rap music video "Indigenous Holocaust," by native (Anishinabe) hip-hop artist Wahwahay Benais, and directed by Missy Whiteman (Arapaho/Kickapoo), revisits the oppressive history of Indian boarding schools where native children were separated from their parents and shorn of their hair, their language, and their culture. The opening "de-vanishes" the Native American by having the ghostlike artist emerge from the haze into clarity. The artist's literal coming-into-focus metaphorizes the crystallization of the image of a formerly marginalized cultural identity. Accompanied by archival photos of deeply sad young Indian faces, victims of the ordeal of colonial schooling, the refrain of Benais' rap goes as follows: "They took his son from his home/Yeah, they pulled 'em apart/They took her daughter from her home/They were forced to depart ... Another native fell victim to the holocaust." As Benais raps direct to camera, first against a forest background and then against a starry nighttime sky, the lyrics tell us of "priests stealing children" and "girls raped," of "women sterilized," where the Bible served to "teach 'em and bleach em" and where native mouths were washed with soap if they dared speak in their native tongue. Musically modeling a symbolic red/black/white coalition, the video conjoins a largely black performance style—hip-hop—with "red" percussive chants, together with a largely white musical genre (country) in the form of video samples from the Dixie Chicks:

> Forgive, sounds good
> Forget, I'm not sure I could
> They say time heals everything
> But I'm still waiting...

The cited lyrics, from the 2006 song *Not Ready to Make Nice* —the Dixie Chicks' response to right-wing demonization for having criticized George Bush—on one level offer an homage to fellow musicians combating the same enemy, but they also constitute a native appropriation of country music for the collective purposes of indigenous peoples, who are also "still waiting" for justice and sovereignty. "Indigenous Holocaust" gives audio–visual–musical form to what Lakota scholar Maria Yellow Horse Brave Heart calls **"historically unresolved grief and trauma"**—the "cumulative emotional wounding ... across generations, emanating from massive group trauma."[24]

Hollywood films have loomed large for Native Americans because, as Paul Chatt Smith puts it, "they have defined our self-image" by telling the "entire planet how we live, look, scream, and kill."[25] Within this picture, native actors have played an ambiguous role. Through a kind of ethnic misrecognition, Will Rogers, a Cherokee, became one of the highest-paid actors in Hollywood, yet was not recognized as Indian, while Iron Eyes Cody, who claimed to be Cherokee but was really Sicilian, became famous playing Indians. A critique of Hollywood stereotypes animates the scene in Chris Eyre's *Smoke Signals* (1998) where Victor instructs Thomas on how to "look Indian" by being solemn, silent, and stoic, similar to "a movie Indian" who looks as if he just walked off the set of *Dances with Wolves*. When Thomas objects that his ethnic group only caught salmon, Victor suggests adopting a more powerful animal as the tribal symbol, reminding him that the title was "*Dances with Wolves*" and not "*Dances with Salmon*"! When a white racist allegorically "occupies" their seats on the bus, they respond with a satirical John Trudeau song about John Wayne.

Many Native American films perform **perspectival reversal** by examining colonial conquest from an indigenous point of view. Creek/Seminole filmmaker Bob Hick's *Return of the Country* (1994) also recalls the cultural massacre performed by religious boarding schools. The film opens with a pseudo extract from a parodically colonialist film—*The Magnificent Savages*—but then the film reverses this oppressive situation through a dream–fantasy of reversal; this time, it is Euro-American culture and Christianity that are outlawed (a white child is ordered to destroy his Bible), and the courts, the congress, and the presidency are all in native hands. The "rez" is now reserved for whites.

## First Peoples, First Features

Many indigenous films reanimate connectivities with the land, traditions, and languages by translating ancient genres of storytelling, drawn from indigenous cultural commons, into the idiom of a modern medium. The story of Chris Eyre's *Skinwalkers* (2002) is constructed around Navajo legends about the *Yea-Naa-gloo-shee*, powerful spirit-beings that take shape-shifting animal form. In the same director's *A Thief of Time* (2004), a mysterious Anasazi spirit-woman protects a native archaeological site. Shirley Cheechoo's *Bearwalker* (2000), the first fiction feature to be directed by an aboriginal Canadian, begins by initiating the spectator into native lore about the powerfully mischievous "darkside" spirit called "bearwalker." A voice-over adds a note of cultural counterpoint: "Christians calls it the devil. My people call it bearwalker." The Maori film *Whale Rider* (2003), similarly, was based on an ancient genealogical myth of origins about a culture hero, Kahutia Te Rangi, who was saved by a whale that transported him to Whangara in New Zealand, where he was renamed *Paikea* in honor of the creature who saved him. For those supposed within the Hegelian tradition to be "peoples without history," these films show that history can also take the oral form of stories, myths, and songs, resulting in a **transgenerational audiovisual archive**. In Vincent Carelli's *The Spirit of TV* (1990), a member of the Waiapi tribe reflects on the transgenerational benefits of the video image: "I didn't have images of my relatives; now … young people will be able to see the old ones." Within **tribal auteurism**, such filmmakers see themselves as primarily accountable to family and clan rather than to producers or sponsors. In this spirit, videos such as Dean Barclaw's *Warrior Chiefs in a New Age* (1991) and Victor Masayesva's *Itam Hakim, Hopiit* ("We, Someone, the Hopi People," 1982) give a prominent voice to elders. As Leslie Marmon Silko explains, Masayesva's films show the undiminished "power of communal consciousness, perfected over thousands of years …."[26]

Some indigenous productions have reached large audiences through **televisual indigeneity**. The seven-part, indigenous-directed series *First Australians* in 2008 offered an alternative to settler colonial history, from pre-contact to the present. In the same year, the five-part "American Experience" PBS Series "We Shall Remain," featuring Native American directors such as Chris Eyre (Cheyenne/Arappaho) and Dustin Craig (Apache), explored key moments in Native American history. The hugely successful *Raven Tales*, from the Canadian Aboriginal People's Television Network (APTN), meanwhile, offered a series of half-hour computer-animation-based TV programs targeted at school-age children—portrayed in the series itself as savvy wired kids—in order to disseminate native cultural traditions and legends in an entertaining way. The episodes relate the adventures of the trickster god Raven, who found the first humans hiding in a clamshell and brought light to the world. (Raven might be seen as fighting enclosure in that he tricks a mean old chief who *hoards* the light.) The Mayan people of Mexico, meanwhile, have produced a 21-episode *telenovela*, entitled *Baktun* (2013), performed in Mayan by the residents of Tihosuco, Mexico. The title refers to a megacycle of the Mayan Long Count Calendar that was widely misinterpreted in the media as predicting the "end of the world," when in fact *Baktun* refers only to the end of one cycle and the beginning of another.

At this point, indigenous filmmakers have made scores of feature films, many of them successful, for example, the Native American *Smoke Signals*, the Inuit-produced *Atanarjuat: The Fast Runner* (2001), and the aboriginal *Bran Nue Dae* (2009).[27] *Atanarjuat: The Fast Runner*, directed by Zacharias Kunuk, is set in the ancient past, retelling an Inuit legend about love and revenge, passed down through centuries of oral tradition, whose origins predate European conquest. Thanks to digital cameras, the spectator is initiated into the daily rhythms of pre-contact Inuit life. A key movement in the film—Atanarjuat's desperate naked sprint across the gleaming Arctic ice—involves spirit-guidance and a magical leap. Yet, the film does not glorify a "natural" pre-modern people unsullied by technology; the closing credits show the indigenous cast and crew outfitted with headphones and cameras. We are far from the constructed naïveté of the putatively low-tech Indian of *Nanook of the North* (1922), where Flaherty had his Inuit protagonist bite into the gramophone record, even though Nanook (aka Allakarialak) was well-versed in technology. Paul Chaat Smith credits *Atanarjuat: The Fast Runner* with turning "Igloolikians into movie stars," and elevating an isolated Indian town "to the first rank of international cinema."[28]

Rachel Perkins' **aboriginal musical** *Bran Nue Dae* (2009), similarly, defied the myth of aboriginal themes and actors as "box-office poison" by achieving immense artistic and commercial success. The film invests a *Grease* (1982)-style high school musical with the critical energies of Spike Lee's *School Daze* (1988), treating the theme of aboriginal dispossession in an upbeat style marked by black-inflected (and country) musicality. That almost all the performers—except Geoffrey Rush as a cartoonishly villainous priest—are aboriginal invests the musical genre with fresh meaning. The male protagonist (Willie) responds to the priest's racist remarks with music: "There's nothing I would rather be/than be an aborigine/ and watch you take my land away."

As liminal figures both inside and outside the borders of the imagined nation, the "Indian" has been endlessly romanticized, allegorized, nation-alized, and instrumentalized, with little consideration of an indigenous point of view. Despite their cruelly reduced demographic presence,

"Indians" have played a primordial role in how the colonial settler-states of the Americas imagine themselves. Thus, indigenous media in Brazil, for example, must be seen against the longer historical backdrop of the venerable archive of Indian stereotypes, often superficially "positive" yet still paternalistic, exemplified by such figures as the *romantic Indian* of silent cinema (*Iracema*); the *harem-fantasy Indian* (*I Married a Xavante*, 1955); the *soft-core Indian* of the pornochanchadas (*A India*, 1980); the *ecological Indian* (*Taina*, 2000); and the infantile "Let's Play Indian" of the Xuxa children shows.

One of the most prolific of the *indigenous media* movements is *Video nas Aldeias* ("Video in the Villages") in Brazil, which since 1986 has been affirming indigenous cultural identity and supporting indigenous struggles by protecting territorial and cultural patrimonies. Video in the Villages has trained scores of native filmmakers and generated almost a hundred films representing some 37 indigenous peoples of the Amazon, such as the Kayapo, the Xavante, the Ashaninka, the Ikpeng, the Guarani, the Waiapi, and the Kuikuro. Video in the Villages projects such as *Xina Bena* ("New Era," 2006), *Prinop: My First Contact* (2007), and *De Volta a Terra Boa* ("Back to the Good Land," 2008) **repurpose the archive** by using non-native footage to their own ends. In *Prinop: My First Contact*, Ikpeng villagers, in conjunction with the screening of a film by the Villas-Boas Brothers about their encounter with the Ikpeng in the early 1960s, re-enact their first experience of whites arriving in planes. In *Ja me Transformei em Imagem* ("I've Already Become an Image," 2008), Huni Kui tribal leaders reenact their version of first contact, and community members watch and comment on footage screened in their own village. Mingling the declarations of the elders, photographs, archival footage, and first-person narration, the Huni Kui relate their own history as a series of traumatic ruptures, from the communal "time of the *malocas*" (thatched-roof longhouses) when they lived in peace, followed by the disruptive "time of first contact," followed by the time of massacres when the whites tried to "clear" the land, followed by "the time of captivity," condemned to being a semi-enslaved workforce engaged in rubber extraction. Western "progress," for the Huni Kui, has meant dispossession, solitude, exploitation, debt peonage, and the loss of collective festivity. The only relatively happy note comes with the final period of the "time of rights," characterized by the struggle to reclaim land, natural resources, and traditional means of survival. The future lies in the recovery of the past.

Many indigenous films present "**bottom-up**" **history** conveyed through popular memory, legitimizing oral history by "inscribing" it on the screen. George Burdeau's *Pueblo Peoples: First Contact* (1990), for example, offers the Zuni (Pueblo) peoples' version of the arrival of the conquistadores in what is now the US Southwest. The film has a Zuni elder renarrate the initial encounter between the conquistadores and the Zuni, giving pride of place to Zuni narratives within a communal atmosphere of domesticated storytelling. Seen from a Zuni perspective, the invaders become abstracted, depersonalized Goya-esque figures of menace and looming catastrophe. As Steven Leuthold points out, Burdeau forges a graphic connection between the Zuni people and the land through dissolves from an elder's wrinkled face to light reflected in water, or dissolves from still photos of ancient structures to similarly formed landscapes.[29]

Mexican indigenous filmmaker Dante Cerano Bautista (Purépecha), meanwhile, incorporates the literal **agricultural commons** into his experimental short video *Xanini*. Inspired by his grandfather's warning that the corn would take revenge if it were not taken care of, the film offers a **vegetative gaze**, in that the story is told from the point of view of wild corn. In Amalia Cordova's account, the film opens with a point of view relaying the perspective of a mestizo bureaucrat surveying the cornfield. A shift of perspective then unfolds the same scene from the corn's point of view. Speaking Purépecha, the corn stalks warn each other of danger and expel the bureaucrat. In the end, the corn ponders the haunting question—when will the native people who have migrated to El Norte return?"[30] For Michelle Raheja, such works constitute **"virtual reservations,"** or imaginative sites of physical and imaginary *reterritorialization*, where indigenous people can develop indigenous epistemologies and contest and reconfigure media representations.[31]

*Indigenous critique* is usually less concerned with inclusion within the settler colonial nation-state than with sovereignty apart from it or alongside it. Nor is Western "freedom" necessarily attractive. For indigenous consensus societies, the West was not the teacher of freedom: rather, it deprived those societies of a freedom they already enjoyed and were fighting to keep. Rather than a tokenistic "inclusion," on the one hand, or a passive **"bare life"** (Agamben) of merely physiological survival exposed to the lethal power of the modern state, indigenous peoples seek what Anishinaabe writer Gerald Vizenor calls **"survivance,"** a word that fuses survival and resistance, a trickster-style outwitting of domination through a reciprocal use of nature that enables indigenous peoples to survive while changing. Alanis Obomsawin (Abenaki), the *doyenne* of First Nations filmmaking, provided a filmic celebration of *survivance* in her inspirational film *Kanehsatake: 270 Years of Resistance*. For Aileen Moreton-Robinson, such films forge an **embodied sovereignty**, which is at once "ontological (our being) and epistemological (our way of knowing), and ... grounded within complex relations derived from the intersubstantiation of ancestral beings, humans and land ... [in contrast with] Western constructions of sovereignty ... predicated on the social contract model, the idea of a unified supreme authority, territorial integrity, and individual rights."[32] Indeed, many indigenous critics propose a multi-leveled idea of sovereignty, variously termed "**intellectual sovereignty**" (Robert Warrior, Osage), "**visual sovereignty**" (Jolene Rickard, Tuscarora), or a "**cinema of sovereignty**" (Randolph Lewis), defined as "the ability for a group of people to depict themselves with their own ambitions at heart."[33]

## The Storytelling Commons

In Michael Hardt and Antonio Negri's expansive view, the "common is not only the earth we share but also the languages we create, the social practices we establish, [and] the modes of sociality that define our relationships..."[34] To expand on Hardt and Negri, the *common* is also the collective inheritance of artistic and narrative practices bequeathed to humanity. There is a link, we would argue, between reinventing the *common* in a political sense and reinventing artistic theory and practice in an aesthetic sense. Just as it is often said that human beings use only a tiny portion of their brain power, so mediatic storytellers have used only a tiny proportion of the world's stories, and only a tiny proportion of cinema's potential as a medium to tell those stories. Speaking of his film *Jom* (1982), Ababacar Samb-Makharam envisions storytelling as "an endless source where painters, writers, historians, filmmakers, archivist, and musicians can come and feed their imaginations."[35] Just as the indigenous natural world harbors much of the planet's biodiversity, so the indigenous cultural world could be said to harbor much of the world's of **bio-narratological diversity**.

Some of the most innovative literature in Latin America has drawn on the **storytelling commons** of indigenous myths and legends. Miguel Angel Asturias' Nobel Prize–winning novel *Hombres de Maiz* (1949) draws on the *Popol Vuh* (the Mayan encyclopedia of theogony, cosmogony, and astrology that Asturias himself had translated). Leslie Marmon Silko's *Almanac of the Dead* (1991) revolves around an attempt to retrieve a Mayan almanac hidden from the Spanish by a native guardian. Mário de Andrade's 1928 novel *Macunaíma*, and the 1968 film adaptation, in this sense, form an example of **archaic modernism**, in that both novel and film innovate artistically by drawing on the *bio-narrational* energies of the dense forest of Amazonian myth. To create his novel, de Andrade drew on the primordial magma of Amazonian cosmos of myth and legend, seen as an indispensable source of the world's narrative oxygen. The astounding *freedom of invention* of *Macunaíma* derives on the one hand from *artistic modernism* and on the other from the animistic matrix of Amazonian myths, creating a mytho-poetic universe where characters metamorphose into animals and heroes turn into constellations after death. De Andrade's principal source was the **indigenous corpus** of legends as collected by the German anthropologist Theodor Koch-Grunberg in the headwaters of the Orinoco between 1911 and 1913 and published in his two-volume *Vom Roraima zum Orinoco* (1917).[36] In a creolized anthology of folklore, de Andrade scrambles together oaths, nursery rhymes, and proverbs. Macunaíma himself is a cultural bricolage, a "hero" without psychological depth or biographical density; his "backstory" is not familiar or generational but rather ancestral and millennial.

Anticipating Foucault's notion of a "pervasive anonymity of discourse," Bakhtin argues that "autographed literature" forms merely a drop in an ocean of anonymous folk literature. De Andrade, in this sense, "interbreeds" tales from one **legendary commons** (e.g., Amerindian) with tales from another *legendary commons* (e.g., African or European) within an exuberant artistic miscegenation. Folktales become part of a productive combinatory by which the collective language of the tribe is transformed into literary *parole*.[37] De Andrade himself, within this communal transtextual spirit, repeatedly claimed that his revolutionary novel had invented nothing new; that he had merely woven indigenous and African tales into a tapestry informed by the tradition of Apuleius, Rabelais, and Lazarillo de Tormes. A teeming rainforest of invention, *Macunaíma* offers an Amazonian proliferation of narrative life forms. Characters literally turn into stars, as they do in indigenous legends, becoming allegorical constellations to be deciphered by the amazed "readers" contemplating them from planet earth.

Just as human social life is embedded in a common ecology, so artistic life is embedded in the shared ecologies of the *aesthetic commons*. In his discussion of Shakespeare as the heir of cumulative artistic bounty, Bakhtin speaks of **"embeddedness."** The "semantic treasures Shakespeare embedded in his works," Bakhtin writes, "were created and collected through the centuries and even millennia: they lay hidden in the language and … in the diverse genres and forms of speech communication … shaped through millennia."[38] The "global village" of the media, similarly, is "embedded" in the larger history of the *aesthetic commons*. The notion of *embeddedness* goes far beyond the literary–historical philological tradition of tracing "influences" to embrace a more diffuse dissemination of ideas energized by the deeper currents of global culture. Film aesthetics, to borrow Bakhtin's words about literature, also forms "an inseparable part of culture [that] cannot be understood outside the total context of the entire culture of a given epoch."[39] Just as individuals cannot be understood purely as autonomous individuals but only as wrapped in an environing sociality, so art cannot be understood apart from its surrounding social ecology.

Oxymoronic formulations such as **"revolutionary nostalgia"**—Walter Benjamin's idea that the past can be mobilized as a vital resource for renewing the present—and Negri's **"futur anterieur,"** or Bennet and Blundell's **"strategic traditionalism"** as referring to indigenous media,[40] all convey the paradoxical temporality of using the old to construct the new. In the artistic equivalent of a backward tracking shot combined with a forward zoom, some of the most innovative artistic works have also been the most stubbornly traditional. The surrealists' **absurd enumerations**— heterotopic lists of incommensurable items—go back to the tongue-in-cheek erudition of the Menipeia and Rabelais; the taboo-shattering avant-garde draws on the taproot of carnivalesque inversion, and so forth. Some of Pasolini's films, similarly, practice **atavistic modernism**, whereby the ancient world, with its rich lode of myth and ritual from the Bible and Sophocles and *A Thousand and One Nights*, is used to revivify alienated modernity.[41] Pasolini modeled his visual style, meanwhile, on the frescoes of Masaccio and Giotti.

As we move from hieroglyph to the quill pen to the smartphone, the stratagems persist but morph through technological remediation. There are few "new techniques" that cannot be traced, at least conceptually, to some earlier precedent. Our concern here, then, is with a paradoxical **archaic innovation**, the creation of the new on the foundations of the old. Just as the European avant-garde became "advanced" by drawing on the "archaic" and "primitive," so non-European artists have drawn on the most traditional elements of their cultures, elements less "premodern" (a term that embeds modernity as telos) than **"paramodern,"** that is, the tradition of the new existing alongside the modern, not in subordination to it but rather participating in a different temporal logic. Implicitly defying the "progressive" stagist view of art, Laura Marks, in *Enfoldment and Infinity: An Islamic Genealogy of New Media Art* (2010), notes the uncanny similarities between the hypnotic experience of a twenty-first-century experimental artwork (Ulf Langheinrich's *Hemisphere*) and that of the dome of a fourteenth-century mosque in Yazd, Iran, both of which feature shimmering firmaments of astronomical geometric complexity.[42] Marks draws on Deleuze's Leibnizian concept of **the fold**— *le pli* in French, a word that, for Deleuze, is redolent of the creases of fabric, the origins of existence, the intersections of time, the layering of thought, and the folding or doubling of one writer's thought " 'into' the thought of another."[43]

The temporalities of art, in this sense, are necessarily enfolded and temporally mixed. The distinction of archaic/modern, for example, is often not pertinent, in that both modernist and para-modern aesthetics challenge the protocols of mimetic realism as the verisimilar imitation of phenomenal appearance. In their attempts to forge a liberatory language, alternative film traditions make artistic use of *paramodern* materials such as popular religion and ritual magic—phenomena that exist outside of the tradition/minority binarism. It is thus less a question of juxtaposing the archaic and the modern than of deploying the archaic in order, paradoxically, to innovate, within a **dissonant temporality** that combines a past imaginary *communitas*—the memory of the commons—with an equally imaginary future utopia. A more adequate formulation would thus speak of a planetary **palimpsestic time** to refer to the scrambled temporalities operative everywhere, where the premodern, the modern, the postmodern, and the paramodern, along with the colonial, neocolonial, and postcolonial, coexist globally, although the "dominant" might vary from region to region.

*Artistic modernism* was usually defined in contradistinction to realism as an outmoded norm in representation. However, outside of the West, realism had rarely been the dominant aesthetic. Thus, non-Western cultures became the catalysts for the supercession, within Europe, of a culture-bound verism. Modernism as a reaction against realism, therefore, can be seen as a rather provincial, site-specific rebellion. In India, the *rasa* **aesthetic** (Sanskrit for "flavor" or "taste" or "savor"), which is more than 2,000 years old, was articulated in the *Natyashastra*. Usually attributed to the sage Bharata, the *Natyashastra* is often compared in its historical positionality to Aristotle's *Poetics*, in that it provided a foundational matrix for a theory of performance arts, and generated an endless series of revisions and commentaries. Unlike *Poetics*, *Natyashastra* was based not on *mimesis* (representation) or *mythos* (story) or character (*ethos*), but on the subtle "culinary" orchestration of feelings and tastes. At once mystical and practical, the *Natyashastra* combines spirituality— each rasa has a presiding deity—with very practical recommendations about stagecraft, makeup, costume, music, and dance. Rather than discuss dramatic structure, the treatise elaborates eight (later nine) *rasas* such as love, pity, anger, heroism, terror, comedy, and so forth. For many scholars, the *rasa* aesthetic not only shaped the forms of classical Indian music and dance but also the modalities of Indian cinema. Indeed, Indian director Shyam Benegal has recently spoken of a **pan-Asian *rasa* aesthetic** that he himself had been practicing unawares, one shared by the popular entertainment cinemas of much of Asia.[44] (Richard Schechner, meanwhile, has developed a theory of **Rasesthetics** in relation to contemporary performance theory.)[45]

We find a strikingly **literal reanimation** of Hindu classicism in the 2008 Internet feature *Sita Sings the Blues*. Written, directed, produced, and animated by American artist Nina Paley with the help of a computer in her Chicago apartment, the film might be called a **digital blockbuster**, an epic film created not with millions of dollars and a cast of thousands but only with 2D computer graphics and flash animation. *Sita Sings the Blues* counterpoints a feminist version of the *Ramayana* story, about the relationship between Prince Rama and the endlessly patient and devoted Sita, and the story of the artist's breakup with her husband, in such a way as to link Sita and the author as two women tormented by the slings and arrows of male insensitivity. The two stories are then interwoven with a third "series"—the 1920s jazzistic scorned-love crooning of Annette Hanshaw—"sung" (in the Bollywood "playback" manner) by a simulacral Sita, visually presented, thanks to vector graphic animation, as a reincarnation of Betty Boop.

This already layered and multi-temporal construction is then interspersed with amicably impromptu voice-over commentaries by three Indian friends, incarnated on screen as silhouetted shadow puppets who debate the validity of different versions of the story. Episodes with dialogue are enacted through painted figures of the characters in profile in a manner resembling the eighteenth-century tradition of *Rajput* brush painting, a tradition historically associated with illuminated manuscripts telling epic stories such as the *Ramayana*. The syncretic dialogue shifts temporal and stylistic registers by mixing the noble epic stylistic register with vulgar colloquialisms such as "Your ass is grass." The deliberate lack of composition-in-depth reminds us of the modernity of the traditional, in that modernist painting too eschewed the Renaissance perspective in favor of flatness and de Cirico-style contradictory perspectives.

Downplaying "originality," Paley alluded to the *artistic commons* by stressing that she had pilfered ideas "that have been around for thousands of years." But just as germane as the film's relation to the literary commons is its quite literal relation to the **digital commons**. As an artist–activist, Paley made the film available on the Internet under the free distribution model so it could be copied, shown, and broadcast legally and for free. The credit to the producer of the film reads "You" and the financier is "Your Money." Thus, the film forms the meeting ground of the *artistic commons* and the **creative commons**—the non-profit organization devoted to expanding the range of creative works available for others to build upon legally and to share. At the same time, the film triggered another form of *enclosure*—the **religious enclosure** claimed by Hindu fundamentalist critics demanding what Kevin Dodd called "sole hermeneutic custody" of the sacred text.[46]

## Revisionist Adaptation and the Literary Commons

We spoke earlier of the *embeddedness* of art within the deep geological strata of artistic creation. The semiotic study of widely shared narrative structures and cultural topoi called **narratology** can, in this sense, be regarded as a somewhat impersonal and scientistic unpacking of the archeological layers of artistic embeddedness and the **narrative commons**. Henry Fielding referenced the **literary commons** in *Tom Jones* (1749) when he compared the work of the ancient writers to "a rich Common, where every Person who hath the smallest tenement in Parnassus hath a free right to fatten his muse."[47] Building on Bakhtin's "**dialogism**"—or the philosophical–linguistic–literary concept of the necessary relation between any utterance and other utterances—and Kristeva's "**intertextuality**," Gerard Genette, in *Palimpsestes* (1982), proposes the umbrella term "**transtextuality**" to refer to everything that "puts one text in relation, whether manifest or secret, with other texts." Genette posits five types of *transtextuality*: (1) "**intertextuality**," or the "effective co-presence of two texts" in the form of quotation, plagiarism, and allusion; (2) "**paratextuality**," or the relation between the text proper and its "paratext" (postfaces, epigraphs, dedications, illustrations), in short, all the accessory messages surrounding the text; (3) "**metatextuality**," or the critical relation between one text and another; (4) "**architextuality**," or the generic taxonomies suggested or refused by titles or subtitles; and (5) "**hypertextuality**," or the relation between one text, which Genette calls "hypertext," to an anterior text or "**hypotext**," which the former transforms, modifies, elaborates, or extends.[48]

We find *hypertextuality* in the winding twists and transtextual turns that leads from Greek oral-epic recitation to Homer's *Odyssey* (eighth century BC) to Virgil's *The Aeneid* (29–19 BC) to Joyce's *Ulysses* (1918–1920) to Godard's *Contempt* (1963), on to the Coen Brothers' *O Brother Where Art Thou?* (2000) and Guy Maddin's *The Keyhole* (2011), which compresses Odysseus's journeys across the wine-red sea into the narrow confines of a single domicile. Much of the history of the arts has been caught up in this ongoing whirl of texts generating other texts in an endless process of recycling, transformation, and transmutation, with no clear point of origin. In the broadest sense, **transtextual dialogism** refers to the infinite and open-ended possibilities generated by the entire matrix of communicative utterances within which the artistic text is situated, and reach the text not only through recognizable influences, but also through a subtle process of what Derrida calls **dissemination** or the process of semantic slippage by which signs enter new contexts to become signifying terms within a spiraling proliferation of allusive transformations. To paraphrase an anonymous *boutade* about postmodernism, *dissemination* means, in a textually transmitted disease, that any text that has slept with another text has slept with all the other texts that that other texts have slept with. Jay David Bolter and Richard Grusin, meanwhile, propose **"remediation"** as part of their argument that the so-called "new digital media" actually gain their cultural significance by absorbing and refashioning earlier media and artistic practices. Before one spoke of **intermedia**, writes Alain Badiou, cinema was itself its own intermedia.[49] Here, we are not far from McLuhan's **rear view mirror theory**—that the content purveyed by each new medium is drawn from antecedent media. For Bolter and Grusin, *remediation* brings into the media age the Foucauldian view of **genealogy** as a matter not of origins but of affiliations and resonances.[50]

We find a non-Eurocentric version of transtextual theory in Brazilian **modernist anthropophagy**, which proposes the cannibalistic devouring of the European historical avant-garde corpus as a way of absorbing its power without being dominated by it, just as the Tupinamba Indians devoured the bodies of European warriors to appropriate their strength. Brazilian modernist Oswald de Andrade's 1928 *Anthropophagic Manifesto* posed the challenge to Brazilian artists: "Tupi or not Tupi: that is the question," that is, whether Brazilian artists should be proud Tupi "Indians" or be servile mimic-men parroting metropolitan culture. (The North American 1950s version of this Indianist metaphor pitted literary "redskins" against "palefaces.") This cannibalistic twist on the most famous phrase from *Hamlet* was reenacted in 2009 in a 6-hour version of the Shakespearean play by Brazilian *dramaturg* Jose

Celso Martinez Correa. The play, available in its filmed version in a box set of DVDs, begins with all the performers, and the audience, singing a musical version of the "Tupi or not Tupi slogan." Further amplifying the hybridities already present in the play itself, the performance turns the play into an **anthropophagic musical** by interspersing original musical numbers related to the themes and characters: "Ophelia's *Fado*," "Polonius Blues," "Guildenstern's Ballad," "Canticle of the Furies," and so forth. Tupinizing Shakespeare, the lyrics celebrate the rebel Indian, the one who does not drop his bow and arrows when the conqueror arrives.

Shakespeare's plays have inspired a rich vein of *revisionist adaptations.* In *Une Tempête* (1969), Aime Cesaire turned Shakespeare's *Tempest* into a **Fanonian manifesto** merely by tweaking the text for anticolonialist purposes. Caliban became the revolutionary "Caliban X" (as in Malcolm X), Ariel becomes the mulatto Uncle Tom intellectual, and Prospero the colonialist patriarch. Indeed, Shakespeare has often been "multiculturalized," whether through non-traditional casting (the Julie Tyamor version of *The Tempest*) or through indigenous rewriting, as when Cherokee writer William Sanders, in his "The Undiscovered," has Shakespeare shipwrecked off Virginia and ultimately adopted by the Cherokee who rename him "Spearshaker" and who teach him the Cherokee language and stage a revisionist version of *Hamlet* as a comedy.[51] *Te Tangata Whai Rawa o Weniti* ( "*The Maori Merchant of Venice*," 2002), the first feature film spoken in the Maori language, meanwhile, is, according to its director (Don Selwyn), an attempt to "colonize Shakespeare." In Houston Wood's account, the film calls attention "to the parallels between how the Jews and the Maori have been treated by white Christians."[52] In this sense, the film correlates the twinned oppressions of Europe's internal and external others, through what we have elsewhere called, riffing on Raymond Williams, "**analogical structures of feeling**."[53]

Many filmic adaptations draw on the taproot of the **literary commons**. Adaptation in this sense can be seen as a form of **textual poaching**, a metaphor redolent of the agricultural commons, described by Michel de Certeau in *The Practice of Everyday Life* (1984) as comparable to nomads poaching their way across fields, and borrowed by Henry Jenkins to apply to the subcultural appropriation of mass culture. As a form of cross-artistic file-sharing, film adaptations "stretch" their verbal source-texts to fit a multi-track medium that draws on all the arts integral to the cinematic medium, resulting in the **amplification of intertexts**. An insistence on strict fidelity in adaptation, in this sense, can constitute a form of hermeneutic "*enclosure*" that asserts ownership on the meaning of a text, as opposed to a view open to transtextual remodelings of a source text. Bakhtin speaks of the "**surprising homecomings of the text**" as it is reinterpreted over "great time." Film adaptations, in this sense, are almost necessarily "unfaithful," not only because of the change from a single-track verbal medium into a multi-track medium, but also because of the passage of time or change of context. Alessandra Raengo speaks of a **biocultural dimension of adaptation** as a way to reconceptualize the relation between literary source and derivative text as a never-completely-realized assimilation. Filmmaker Claire Denis compares the relation between her films and their literary sources—for instance, between her *Beau Travail* (1999) and Melville's *Billy Budd, Sailor* (1924)—to **grafts**, analogous to a heart transplant, a negotiation between two immune systems.[54]

**Revisionist adaptation**, or the critical adaptation of canonical texts, in this sense, draws on the *literary commons*, available to be borrowed, stolen, transformed, and re-invoiced for the aesthetic and social needs of the present. Some film adaptations perform the **radicalization** of their source texts, thus recapitulating on another level a process already commonplace within literature itself, where many well-known novels have been rewritten from the perspective of secondary or even imaginary characters. Miguel de Cervantes' *Don Quixote* (1605) has thus been re-envisioned from a female perspective (Kathy Acker's *Don Quixote: A Novel* [1994]), and Margaret Mitchell's *Gone with the Wind* (1936) from the perspective of the enslaved (Alice Randall's *The Wind Done Gone* [2001]). Herman Melville's *Moby-Dick; or, The Whale* (1851; henceforth referred to as "*Moby-Dick*"), meanwhile, has been recast from the point of view of the wife of the monomaniacal captain (Sena Naslund's *Ahab's Wife: Or, The Star-gazer* [2005]). One could easily imagine other revisionist adaptations of *Moby Dick*, from the point of view of Queequeeg, for example—how did that homoerotic love-fest in that Nantucket inn look to him?—or from the point of view of the whale.

Although not an adaptation of *Moby Dick* from the whale's point of view, Lucien Castaing-Taylor's and Vérena Paravel's documentary *Leviathan* (2012) does follow in the literal wake of a whaling ship not unlike Melville's *Pequod*. By registering the sometimes sordid processes of industrial fishing off the coast of New England, the film offers the perspective, if not of the whale, then at least of the whaling ship. Inspired by the *Book of Job* and Hobbes' *Leviathan or The Matter, Forme and Power of a Common Wealth Ecclesiasticall and Civil* (1651; henceforth referred to as "*Leviathan*") as much as by *Moby Dick*, the film imbues what is purportedly a documentary on the fishing industry with a rich, allusive texture that reflexively incorporates a number of other genres and approaches to filmmaking. With the aid of 11 digital cameras handed back and forth between the filmmakers and the fishermen, the film details life at sea in a non-naturalistic style that evokes abstract expressionism and the films of Stan Brakhage. On another level, the piscatorial carnage resembles a horror film, where the blood from a day's catch mingles with ominous shots of gulls reminiscent of Hitchcock's *The Birds* (1963). While this modernist documentary offers a plunge into Hobbes' "state of nature," it is, for the most part, **anti-anthropomorphic** and **anti-anthropocentric**; although the result of labor is at the film's epicenter, human beings only play a marginal role in *Leviathan*'s universe of discourse.

In the colonial and postcolonial eras, literature and film have often practiced the critical rewriting of canonical European texts. Jean Rhys's *The Wide Sargasso Sea* (1966), for example, retells Charlotte Bronte's *Jane Eyre* (1847) as the story of Bertha Mason, Mr. Rochester's first wife (and the by-now celebrated "madwoman in the attic" of feminist criticism), leading us to reassess the racialized presentation of Bertha as a "Creole savage." Filmic adaptations obviously exist on a continuum with these other "rewritings." We find **transtextual subversion** when a recombinant text challenges the socially retrograde premises of preexisting hypotexts or genres, or calls attention to their repressed subversive features. Given the almost three centuries separating Daniel Defoe's *Robinson Crusoe* (1719)from its latter-day film adaptations, it is hardly surprising that the Defoe novel has been repeatedly subjected to revisionist critique. For politically conscious directors, colonialist and misogynistic novels such as *Robinson Crusoe* trigger a kind of **obligatory infidelity**, or reading "against the grain." We see this revisionist process already within the literary field (Michel Tournier's *Vendredi, ou les limbes du Pacifique* [1967], J. M. Coetzee's *Foe* [1986]) as well as in poems (Derek Walcott's *Castaway* [1965]). The conventional schoolmaster's view of Crusoe that makes him the embodiment of practical courage, ingenuity, and perseverance completely "edits out" *Robinson Crusoe*'s status as perhaps *the* paradigmatic capitalist and colonialist novel. The narrative not only recapitulates the history of colonialism and slavery, but also stages a Crusoe–Friday relationship marked by linguistic, religious, and economic subordination. Crusoe imposes on Friday his language (English) and his religion (Christianity), while relegating Friday to what amounts to slave labor, an enslavement euphemized and prettified so as to resemble a cheerful collaboration.

The filmic adaptations of the novel, going back to the first *Crusoe* in 1902 up to *Castaway* (2000) and the reality show "Survivor," have at times "written back" against empire. Jack Gold's *Man Friday* (1976), for example, takes a very irreverent stance toward the Defoe source novel.

Made at the height of the international "counter-cultural" movement, in the 1970s, after the formal demise of colonialism, *Man Friday* can be seen as a **"proto-postcolonial film,"** that is, a text that touched on post-colonial themes before the advent of postcolonial theory per se. Within this adversarial optic, Defoe's colonial romance mutates into a counter-cultural anticolonialist allegory. While *Man Friday* endorses a communal narrative, it also literally engages the issue of *the commons,* albeit in a some-what superficial manner. First, by having the village chief authorize Friday to tell his story, the film designates Friday's story as a **collective narrative**, a communal tale belonging to the entire tribe. Second, specific sequences revolve around rival conceptions of property. When Friday "borrows" Crusoe's hat, Crusoe tries to explain the laws of ownership, but Friday fails to understand why any one would be so deranged as to believe in individual property. (Here, the film unfortunately reverts to a "positive" stereotype about indigenous peoples, imagined as enjoying a golden age innocent of "mine and thine," when in fact it is usually *land* that indigenous people hold in common, not personal objects such as clothing.)

What is most promising in this film, which is problematic in many ways, is its groping toward what Bakhtin called the "counterpointing of chrono-topes" and what Edward Said calls **"contrapuntal readings"**—that is, the mutual haunting, within the larger arc of colonial domination, of one set of times, spaces, histories, and perspectives by another set of times, spaces, histories, and perspectives. Friday becomes a lucid, broken-English Montaigne, the native exegete of cultural relativism. In this sense, the film links narratological procedures to ideological issues through a recurring shuttle between Crusoe's perspective and Friday's, or, to be more precise, between (1) a patently satiric version of Crusoe's perspective, and (2) a generally sympathetic version of the perspective of Friday and his community, seen as a kind of (anti) Greek chorus commenting on the action. Patrick Keiller's' *Robinson* trilogy (*London* [1994], *Robinson in Space* [1997], and *Robinson in Ruins* [2010]), finally, follow the odysseys of an eponymous protagonist—really Keiller himself, with a subtle nod to Defoe's famous castaway—crisscrossing the English landscape on a kind of Baudelairean jaunt and pausing to contemplate the relics and ruins of globalization, (post-)industrialization, and nuclear armament found along the way.

Other *revisionist adaptations* practice **epidermal subversion** by casting actors of color in roles usually assumed to be white—a practice going at least as far back as Orson Welles' all-black "Voodoo Macbeth" in 1936—thus triggering subtle changes in representation and reception. Most adaptations of Emily Bronte's *Wuthering Heights,* for example, portray Heathcliff as a stormily Byronic (implicitly white) rebel personified by actors such as Laurence Olivier and Ralph Feines, ignoring the novel's cues that Heathcliff was a person of color. Heathcliff is described as a dark-skinned gypsy found wandering the streets of Liverpool, a key port in the slave trade frequented by runaways of many races. By casting two actors of Afro-Caribbean ancestry as Heathcliff, the Andrea Arnold version brings to the surface the submerged ethnicity of the novel, subtly transforming its affect and drift. The illicitly transcendent passion uniting Catherine and Heathcliff becomes as much about overstepping boundaries of race as well as of class. The Arnold version privileges Heathcliff's subaltern perspective through a constantly moving subjective camera accompanying his agitated zigzag across the moors, accompanied by the close-in anxious sounds of his breathing. A Fanonian reading might see this new Heathcliff as casting a colonial-style "look of envy" on the relatively comfortable lily-white world. In a return of the historical repressed, the whippings, the insults, and Heathcliff's reduction to the status of a virtual slave come to evoke colonial slavery and thus take on a broader **Black Atlantic** civilizational meaning.[55]

## Cultural Indigenization

Many African films practice **revisionist Africanization** by indigenizing prestigious European source texts. Djibril Diop Mambety's *Hyènes* (*"Hyenas,"* 1992) radically "recasts" a modernist touchstone by offering an ingenious Senegalese adaptation of Friedrich Dürrenmatt's classic absurdist play, *The Visit* (1956). As with the play, the film too revolves around a wealthy old woman's vindictive return to the village where, years earlier, she had been "seduced and abandoned." The desolate town of Colobane, with its rapacious petite bourgeoisie, forms a microcosm of the contradictions of Senegalese society in the era of the eroding of revolutionary hopes and of traditional solidarities.

Linguère Ramatou, the film's vengeful elderly woman, agitates Colobane's populace to the point of frenzy by promising a future of untold wealth. "Ramatou is coming back ... richer than the World Bank!" The local politicians and clergy view Ramatou's largesse with her "sovereign funds" as the only possible solution to the never-ending cycle of poverty and exploitation. The film's **transnational allegory** creates an analogy between individual resentment and debt-collecting with neocolonial dependency and the suffering imposed on African countries by "structural adjustment," and the IMF's attempt to control the internal polices of debtor nations by coercing them to increase exports and curtail social spending, thereby ensuring social misery. In the final analysis, however,

Mambety's thematic tapestry is geared more toward narrative polyphony than toward moralistic oppositions; as in all complex parables, the interpretive work of decipherment is left to the audience.

In his comprehensive survey of African oral literature, Isidore Okpewho shows how writers such as Ousmane Sembene and Wole Soyinka subvert traditional **trickster narratives** for the purpose of radical social critique. In works such as *The Road* (1965) and *Kongi's Harvest* (1965), traditional solidarity with victims is transformed into barbed attacks on entrenched power. *Hyènes*'s parodic, tragicomic stance is less prescriptive and programmatic than Sembene or Soyinka's fictional jeremiads. With a skillful deployment of what Bakhtin termed "**double-voiced discourse**"— that is, a discourse that introduces into a pre-existing discourse a semantic intention directly opposed to the first voice— *Hyènes* expertly frames motifs from both the oral tradition and from more earnest, hopeful African films. *Hyènes* also arguably exhibits "**double consciousness**"—W. E. B. Du Bois' term to evoke a dual existence as American person and as oppressed black minority, two conflictual ideals within the same corporeal consciousness. While Du Bois was describing African-Americans' anguished oscillation between black identity and American selfhood, filmmakers such as Mambety must delicately balance African identity with a modernist legacy that influenced an earlier generation of African intellectuals, most notably the founders of the journal *Présence Africaine* (founded in 1956 in Paris).

In a formulation rich in implication for filmic adaptations, Bakhtin suggested that "every age **reaccentuates** in its own way the works of [the] past."[56] Often based on novels written decades or even centuries earlier, the *reaccentuations* of revisionist adaptations provide **ideological barometers** that register the shifts in the social/discursive atmosphere. Women filmmakers, for example, have reenvisioned Victorian heroines through a feminist grid. In the initial sequence of Jane Campion's adaptation of Henry James' *Portrait of a Lady* (1996), contemporary young Australian women speak rapturously of first love; their embrace of romantic clichés becomes linked to the fate of Isabel Archer—the film's nineteenth-century heroine, a woman ultimately trapped by her capitulation to insidious assumptions concerning romantic love. Many adaptations are invested in "filming back" against a source text or genre by giving voice to characters or subject positions silenced in the original. Thus, *Brokeback Mountain* (2005) "**queers**" the Western genre, much as *Thelma & Louise* (1991) feminizes the road movie.

Every cross-cultural adaptation of a novel, by the same token, filters its source-text through a national or regional culture. Ketan Mehta's *Maya*

*Memsaab* (1993)—an Indian rewriting of Gustave Flaubert's *Madame Bovary* (1856)—offers an example of **cultural indigenization**, whereby the French culture of the source novel is mediated through by the adapting Indian culture.[57] The double-edged effect is both to universalize and "provincialize Europe" (Chakravarty). Transposed names indigenize Flaubert's story; "Maya," for example, shares the same phonemes as "Emma" but brings a philosophical note since "maya" is Sanskrit for "illusion." Within the indigenizing process, Mehta systematically substitutes things Indian for *la chose francaise*. He replaces Flaubert's Rouen with the picturesque resort town Shimla, exploiting the town's association with the British Raj and with adulterous playboys and mistresses. Rouen cathedral is replaced by "Scandal Point," while Flaubert's indefatigable tour guide is replaced by a hustler pushing drugs and cheap hotel rooms. The religious associations of the Rouen Cathedral's Last Judgement tableau, as Flaubert's ironic commentary on a sordid affair, give way to a merely secular sleaziness in the film. In Flaubert, Leon and Emma's lovemaking takes place in a horse-drawn carriage, but in the Mehta version the carriage becomes a train, with shades drawn down as in Flaubert, while sexual congress is evoked through a cinematic *clin d'oeil* to the climactic train entering the tunnel of Hitchcock's *North by Northwest* (1959).

While relatively realist within Bollywood norms, *Maya Memsaab* also features the extravagant musical production numbers typical of Bombay cinema. Through a generic division of labor, the non-musical episodes represent life in a fairly verisimilar manner, while the songs represent life as dreamed and fantasized. While the plot resembles life, as Ratnapriya Das puts it, the songs represent dreams.[58] Along with Govind Nihalani, Mrinal Sen, and Shyam Benegal, Mehta belongs to the **"third way" Indian cinema**, a style that negotiates between apparently antagonistic traditions. Mehta strives for a **"middle cinema" aesthetic** located between the fantastic, colorful, dance-dominated, and very popular Bollywood cinema, on the one hand, and the austere, low-budget, independent, and programmatically realist "new Indian Cinema" on the other. Mehta's foiling of genres and style forms an apt correlative to Flaubert's artistic procedures, to wit, his orchestration of multiple styles, perspectives, and centers of consciousness. By pitting the exalted, romantic, metaphoric, and grandly literary style against the flat, banal, metonymic style, all translated and filtered through specifically cinematic techniques and genres, the Mehta version forges the equivalent of Flaubert's stylistic counterpoint between mimetic realism and bookish fantasy.

*Maya Memsaab* can be seen, on one level, as a **postcolonial adaptation**, a genre subdividable, according to Sandra Ponzanesi, into four sub-groups: (1) **adaptations of colonial novels** (e.g., *A Passage to India* [1924] or *Out of Africa* [1937]) that are not necessarily postcolonial in spirit; (2) **postcolonialized classics** (the already cited *Mansfield Park* [1814]); (3) **art film adaptations of postcolonial texts** (*The English Patient* [1992]); (4) **doubly postcolonial films** (novels adapted by postcolonial filmmakers—such as Deepa Mehta's *Earth* [1998] or Shirin Neshat's *Women without Men* [2009]).[59] As an example of the second category, Patricia Rozema re-envisions Jane Austen's *Mansfield Park* through Edward Said's analysis of the novel in *Culture and Imperialism* (1993). The adaptation counterpoints middle-class England with the colonized Caribbean, using the Sir Bertram character to foreground the slavery backgrounded in the novel. The film's audacious reimagining of the novel through an anti-Orientalist grid outraged critics who found its emphasis on slavery "unfaithful" to the novel. The scene in which Fanny Price discovers Tom Bertram's pornographic sketchbook of brutal scenes from the Antigua plantation was seen as an anachronistic and politically correct rubbing of slavery in the noses of (the presumably white) fans of the novel. However, as Tim Watson points out, the novel can be productively seen within the context of two cross-historical debates, those about slavery at the time of the novel's production, and those about reparations at the time of the film's release. The adaptation simply "unsilences" the critique of slavery elided in the novel, where Fanny's question about slave trade remains unanswered.[60]

In *Bride and Prejudice* (2004), meanwhile, Gurinder Chadha not only contemporizes the original but also casts a **postcolonial-feminist** look at another canonical Austen novel, blending, as Ponzanesi puts it, "success-ful commercial strategies with mildly subversive narratives."[61] The film hybridizes two popular traditions through a **masala** (spicy mix) of Bollywood and latter-day musicals such as *Grease*. While hardly as inventive as *Maya Memsaab*, *Bride and Prejudice* practices **cross-cultural analogies** by suggesting certain subterranean affinities between Austen's England and Chadha's India: the similar sexual modesty; the strategic role of dance balls in charting the trajectories of romance; and the comparable role of wealth in marriage, whether in the form of Western marriages for financial convenience or in the form of Indian arranged marriages. The intra-national class differences that mark the Austen novel transmute into the transnational cultural differences of the Chadha adaptation, so that the romance between the American Darcy and the Indian Lalita come to homologize the geo-political romance of India and the United States in the period of the film. In a perhaps unduly reciprocal portrayal, both American and Indian have to abandon some of their prejudices.

A number of revisionist adaptations perform **actualization/relocalization as critique**, whereby a change in period and setting generates revelatory differences between the source text and the film. In the wake of *West Side Story* (1961), which sets *Romeo and Juliet* in a stylized Manhattan "slum," Lúcia Murat's *Maré, Nossa História de Amor* (2007) resets *Romeo and Juliet* in the actual Rio de Janeiro slum named in the title. Abdellatif Kechiche's *L'Esquive* (English title *Games of Love and Chance*, 2003), meanwhile, stages a modern-day adaptation of an eighteenth-century play, Marivaux's *Les Jeu de l'Amour et du Hasard* ("The Game of Love and Chance," 1730), as a springboard for exposing the social fractures of contemporary French society. In a reflexive move, Kechiche does not adapt the play, but rather stages the process of adaptation of the play in a surprising contemporary location—a present-day high school in the marginalized *banlieux* of Paris, literally "suburbs," but, more accurately, low-income housing projects inhabited by immigrants and their children. The French expression "*Marivaudage*" suggests highly articulate flirtation and identity disguises against the backdrop of class relations between noble rich and servant poor, where the rich pretend to be poor and the poor pretend to be rich. For the film's high-school drama teacher, the point of the play is that the rich should fall in love with the rich and the poor with the poor, without any pointless cross-class masquerade. The restaging of Marivaux' dialogue by *banlieu* adolescents dramatically transforms the meaning and affect of the play, however. Since the students are *all* relatively poor, the class contrasts central to the play become less pertinent, while other issues, such as religion, nationality, color, ethnicity, and police harassment, come to the fore.

In *L'Esquive*, the **symptomatic time-gap** in centuries between the source play and adaptation transmutes into an ethnic-cultural gap—the all-white French of the play have become the multi-racial children of a postcolonial France transformed by the historical karma of massive immigration from the former colonies. The contrast now is between the class structures relayed by the play, where noble and servant share a common world, but one structured by clear social hierarchies, and those of the film, where the most salient differences reflect the divide between the wealthy French center and the impoverished *banlieu*, or what some have punningly called "the place of the banned." The playful romantic banter of the eighteenth-century comedy gives way to the pungent street argot of the adolescents, an immensely creative rush of obscenities, *verlan*, gangster French, Black American English, Arabic, and Wolof. Within a thoroughly creolized contemporary French, the film foregrounds what Glissant, in *Poetics of Relation* (1990), calls the "internal multiplicity of languages."[62]

## The Archival Commons and the Ab-original Musical

We have spoken in this section of artistic strategies that engage the *aesthetic commons*, the long-standing archive of genres, techniques, and texts perpetually available for recombinant creativity. It is in this perspective that we turn to two very different, literally antipodal, examples of appropriation of the *artistic commons*, the first by a European auteur addressing an imagined community of cinephiles, the second by an aboriginal Australian woman director signifying on two classical Hollywood film genres for the transformative purposes of her own community.

We find a cinephiliac embodiment of the *aesthetic commons* in Godard's monumental **metafilm** *Histoire(s) du Cinema*, his collage-essay film about the history of cinema and about history *tout court*. For Godard, cinema, in all its forms, is the medium where the history of the twentieth century is rendered palpable and made flesh. This historicity is not restricted to the most obvious site of the so-called "historical film"— often little more than a collection of formulaic signs about how history itself is envisioned at a specific moment—but rather in the entire range of audiovisual productions. For Godard, all films bear the marks of history. In this sense, the film clips form archival–geological time capsules, exempla of a time and a place and its technologies of expression and representation.

A decade in the making, *Histoire(s) du Cinema*, constitutes an **archival epic** that works over the materials contained in Godard's video archive of some 3,000 cassettes embracing all genres: fiction films, documentaries, archival materials, and TV shows. The film hyperbolizes many recurring features of Godard's work—the orchestration of citations, the hybridization of media, the recombinant absorption of the other arts, and the endless permutations of *intellectual montage*. All have in common the idea of archival *remediation*. The quotes are *transartistic*—literary, philosophical, cinematic, theatrical, and musical. Christopher Pavsek compares the result to a "junk-heap of cultural history ... available for ... utopian collective recycling."[63] Godard displays the creative sparks that occur when a film juxtaposes, or rather fuses, in an undecidable *polysemy*, the image of a Monet painting with a text about the Holocaust and underscored by the music of a Schoenberg. Dipping into the ocean of antecedent creativity, cinema becomes the infinite combinatory of the pre-existing that we have called the *artistic commons.*

At the same time, the excerpts are never simply quoted; all are transformed through voice-over narration, reframing, superimposition, and the insertion of new sounds or snippets of music. Godard creates an **anachronistic transtextuality** by weaving and overlaying snippets and moments and sounds from different time periods, genres, and countries. The fascination, with Godard's film, is not only with the cited films *qua* films, but with the possibilities of crossbreeding they open up. *Histoires,* moreover, not only raids the *artistic commons* but also explicitly engages questions of intellectual property. As a long-time advocate of cinematic pilfering, Godard has often said that one should put "whatever one likes in a film"—whether an Aznavour song, an Eluard poem, or a shot from *Joan of Arc.* In this same vein, Godard has long proposed, and realized, Walter Benjamin's ambition of a **text entirely composed of quotations** through films without newly written dialogue but with only orchestrations of transtextual fragments. Through a kind of **cine-electro-shock**, Godard explodes, fragments, disperses, and recontexualizes the texts that go into his audio-visual collage.

Such a practice was not designed to please the corporate advocates of intellectual property rights, and when Godard first screened sections of *Histoires(s) du Cinema* in 1988 at Cannes, the assembled journalists obsessed over how he had obtained the rights. Godard argued "fair use" and "educational purposes" while also making all the citations very brief. Although one of the founders of **auteurism**—a romantic individualist theory that sees a film as belonging to the director whose unique personality it expresses—Godard has nonetheless given public support to the idea of the *artistic commons.* The "socialism" of his *Film Socialism,* he has said, lies precisely in its undermining of the idea of intellectual property, beginning with that of artworks. At the same time, Godard's films proliferate in cinematic "footnotes"; he does not borrow without acknowledgement. Significantly, Godard concludes *Film Socialism* with a shot of the well-known FBI copyright warning, joined with a quotation from Pascal: "If the law is unjust, justice proceeds past the law." Godard offered a different critique of private property in his earlier film *Weekend,* through a citation of Engels's essay "The Origin of the Family, Private Property and the State," where Engels, drawing on Lewis Henry Morgan's work in *Ancient Society,* praised the profoundly democratic organization of the Iroquois League. For Marx and Engels, the Iroquois meshed a communal economic system with a democratic political organization, thus offering a model of economic equality achieved without state domination, in a society devoid of nobles, kings, governors, soldiers, and police, and where all, including women, were free and equal.

In the context of indigenous media, meanwhile, aboriginal Australian activist–anthropologist Marcia Langton speaks of **Ab-originality** as "a field of intersubjectivity … remade over and over again in a process of dialogue, of imagination, of representation and interpretation."[64] Indigenous films often constitute an *"ab-original"* form of *archaic innovation*, in the sense that they are concerned with the generation of what Ginsburg calls **future imaginaries** based partly, paradoxically, on the recuperation of a past linked to a sense of **intergenerational responsibility**.[65] A key issue separating colonizing modernity from indigenous cultural values had to do precisely with the issue of property. A particularly powerful critique of Western notions of "enclosed" land as private property marks aboriginal Australian filmmaker Rachel Perkins' 1-hour fiction, *One Night the Moon* (2001). If Godard is preoccupied with the *intellectual commons*, Perkins' **aboriginal musical** is concerned with the **literal commons** in the form of land, an issue very much in the news in the wake of the 1992 Mabo Decision that overturned the Australian founding doctrine of *terra nullius*. The film is based on actual events that transpired in Australia in 1932 and more specifically around the aboriginal tracker Riley, whose scouting skills in the service of the Australian police won him a King's Medal. Perkins' musical drama revolves around a young white child who follows the moon and goes missing in the Outback. The father, out of racist arrogance and an exacerbated sense of private property, refuses the proffered help of a savvy Aboriginal tracker. Ultimately, the father's scorn for alternative forms of knowledge (**subaltern gnosis**) leads to the death of his own child, since the tracker, given his intimate familiarity with the land, could have saved the daughter's life.

But what is most striking in aesthetic terms is the film's revisionist orchestration of two genres—the Western and the musical—to make a point about the commons in an almost literal sense. From the perspective of colonized people of color, both genres might well be seen as suspect examples of what Maori filmmaker/theorist Barry Barclay calls the "**invaders' cinema**" typical of colonial settler-states. A submerged settler-state ethos/ethnos haunts both genres. The Hollywood Western consecrated the dispossession of native peoples by narrativizing Manifest Destiny, while the Hollywood musical choreographed this narrativization, as when the lyrics of the theme song of *Oklahoma!*—a state ripped out of traditionally native territory, bearing an indigenous name—tell us that "We [whites] know we belong to the land/and the land we belong to is grand." The hybrid Western musical *Calamity Jane*, where natives are called "painted varmits," has white settlers singing the glories of the Black Hills—the sacred lands of the Sioux—as belonging to whites. Ironically, this lyrical act of appropriation borrows from Indian conceptions of "belonging to the land."

In both the United States and Australia, settlers butted up against indigenous peoples as part of what Glissant calls **"straight-arrow" conquest**. In both countries, nation-states destroyed long-standing systems of communally held land in favor of Dawes Act-style deeds of private ownership. There is nothing that divides the Western worldview from the indigenous worldview as much as the conception of the land as what Thomas King calls the "defining element of Aboriginal culture," which "contains the languages, the stories, and the histories of a people [and] provides water, air, shelter, and food."[66] As a revisionist amalgam of musical and Western, *One Night the Moon* tells the story of an Australian *contact-zone* through indigenous eyes. The film hybridizes the Western with the musical, furthermore, by showcasing the country-and-Western music popular not only in the American Southwest but also in the Australian interior. This technique reaches its paroxysm in an open-air production number alternately sung by the white settler and the aboriginal tracker. In a form of **musical-socio-ideological antiphony**, the lyrics counterpose two views of the land, As the two men stride off in opposite directions, the settler's refrain is "This land is mine," owing to his having "signed a deed on the dotted line," which is answered by the tracker's refrain: "This land is *me*... this land owns me," culminating in a claim of indigenous knowledge and of settler alienation: "You only fear what you don't understand."

Voiced in the most direct monosyllabic terms, the production number stages a discursive duel in the sun, an ideological standoff over competing views of the land. The tracker gives voice to what Chadwick Allen calls **native indigeneity**, or the aboriginal collective view of the land as sacred and communally owned, while the white farmer voices **settler indigeneity**, or the Western view of newly cultivated land as alienable private property.[67] The question evoked in the lyrics goes far beyond an individual piece of farmland; it was at the very heart of Western colonialism and the Lockean doctrine of *terra nullius*, which decreed that the land did not rightfully belong to the indigenous people unless they had fenced it off and practiced sedentary agriculture. To merit ownership, those who had lived on and cared for the land for millennia had to mix it with their labor in order to make it productive of commodities. What is ultimately a philosophical/political/epistemic confrontation here takes the form of a well-choreographed musical number staged as part of a Western-style genre and set against the backdrop of the very land where sovereignty is in dispute.

Franny Armstrong's drama–documentary–animation–essay film *The Age of Stupid* (2009), finally, links the digital commons to the planetary commons in its discussion of climate change. The film was highly innovative in its funding, production, and distribution, just as it was innovative its style and its mix of genres and formats. A kind of **cyber-blockbuster**, the film's methods were the polar opposite of the Hollywood version. Working in collaboration with NGOs and organizations such as Greenpeace, Move-On, and the performance group Yes-Men, the film-makers encouraged public involvement through an interactive website. In order to have full independence, the film was financed independently through the crowdfunding model and pioneered a new distribution system called Indie Screenings, a web-based form of film distribution, whereby anyone, anywhere could screen the film publicly and keep whatever profits ensued. Rather than procure profit, the filmmakers multiplied screenings. Linked by satellite to scores of cinemas around the United Kingdom (and later around the United States and elsewhere), the premiere received the Guinness World Record for being the largest film premiere in history, for an estimated total of a million spectators, a feat rarely achieved by a leftist documentary.

In aesthetic-narrative terms, the film borrows a very old literary frame-device—**shipwreck narration**—where a sole survivor of a disaster, *à la* Ishmael in *Moby-Dick*, remains to tell the story, with the difference that the shipwreck, in this case, is not of a single ship but of spaceship earth. The narrator, played by Pete Postlethwaite, lives in a 2005 post-apocalyptic world, where he presses on the icons and rubrics of his computer screen in a high-tech tower called The Global Archive. The Archive gives him access to the **intellectual-mediatic commons** in the form of a vast repository of everything that has been written or filmed, which he probes for clues as to how the planet earth and its people somehow managed to commit collective suicide. In this sense, the narrator is the keeper of the flame of memory, a planetary *griot* or custodian of the surviving store of art and knowledge.

After an evocation of the beginnings of the universe—conveyed in minimalist fashion through the slow-motion stirring of milk in a glass—the opening animation reveals a planet devastated by climate change—Las Vegas swallowed up by the desert, Sydney in flames, the Alps transformed into a snowless desert, and the Taj Mahal consumed by vultures in a war-devastated India. Also innovative in narrative terms, the film transposes the interwoven stories of the "network narratives" (Bordwell) of a film such as Soderberg's *Traffic* (2000) into a documentary format. As a futuristic restrospective Cassandra, the narrator marshals evidence for an indictment of the short-sighted passivity that allowed the apocalypse. A polyphony of voices intermingles individual tableaux of characters from seven countries: an Alpine climber in despair of the disappearing snow, a Nigerian woman afflicted by the polluted water generated by corporate-owned oil, a wind-farm developer fighting corporate lobbyists, and a literal life saver in the wake of Hurricane Katrina.

Despite its gloomy subject, *The Age of Stupid* manages to be both entertaining and reflective by mingling the star power of Postlethwaite, the music of Mobe, combined with witty graphics, video clips, lively animation, pleasurable bike-riding protests, and interviews with leading figures of the anti-globalization movement. In an ethic/aesthetic of global connectivity, the film politicizes the network narrative to reveal Brecht's *"causal network of events,"* and specifically the emerging central political issue—the connection between private ownership, the dominance of fossil fuels, and the devastation of our common planet.

Coming full circle, we can link the commons as conceived by indigenous **Red Atlantic** cultures to the theory and praxis of the commons within the West itself (going back to the "Charter of the Forest" section of the Magna Carta), all part of a multi-pronged struggle against various forms of "enclosure." While asymmetrical, the two enclosures— the colonial enclosure of the indigenous world, and the capitalist enclosure of the commons in the West—are metaphorically and metonymically linked. Henry George's cry that "we must make land common property" in *Progress and Poverty* (1979) echoed the cries of the Native American leader Tecumseh, who argued in 1810 that the only way "to check and stop this evil [of landgrabs]—is for all the Redmen to unite in claiming a common and equal right in the land [which] belongs to all for the use of each."[68] The expulsion from their land of millions in the Global South recalls the enclosures of the commons elsewhere. In *La Revolucion India* (1969), Bolivian indigenous writer Fausto Reinaga lauded an "immortal pre-American socialism" as a "luminous concrete reality" that existed thousands of years before Marx, Engels, and Lenin had been born."[69] In a spirit of revolutionary nostalgia, Reinaga argued that the future of humanity must be communal as with "our ancient indigenous communities."[70]

Unlike the peasantry for Marx, first peoples *are* now capable of representing themselves. In the Granada TV documentary *Kayapo: Out of the Forest* (1989), the Kayapo and other native Amazonian peoples stage a mass ritual performance to protest the planned construction of a hydroelectric dam that would flood their communities. The Kayapo chief Raoni appears with the rock star Sting in what turned out to be a successful attempt to capture international media attention and cancel the World Bank loan that would have financed the project. Two decades later, native activists are opposing yet another attempt to dam the Xingu River—the Belo Monte Dam—shrewdly taking advantage of the world-wide success of *Avatar* to enlist James Cameron into their cause and describing themselves as the Na'vi of the Amazon. In the Amazon, "First Contact" is still occurring, but this time the "Indians" come armed not with bows and arrows but rather with books, computers, digital cameras, websites, blogs, and listserves; the *indigenous commons* meets the *digital commons.*

## Notes

1   Guillermo Gomez-Pena, *Conversations across Borders* (London: Seagull, 2011), p. 120.

2   Decades ago, avant-gardist Kenneth Anger complained that every advertising agency in New York had pilfered from *Scorpio Rising* (1963); such are the wages of co-optation.

3   See Steven Shaviro, "Accelerationist Aesthetics: Necessary Inefficiency in Times of Real Subsumption," *E-flux* (2013) <http://www.e-flux.com/journal/accelerationist-aesthetics-necessary-inefficiency-in-times-of-real-subsumption>.

4   Cited in Ibid., p. 350.

5   Fredric Jameson, *Marxism and Form: Twentieth Century Dialectical Theories of Literature* (Princeton: Princeton University Press, 1974), p. 82.

6   Naomi Klein, *This Changes Everything: Capitalism vs. the Climate* (New York: Simon and Schuster, 2014), p. 294.

7   See David Harvey, "The Future of the Commons," in *Radical History Review*, Issue 109 (Winter 2011): 101–107.

8   See Astra Taylor, op. cit., p. 173.

9   See Faye Ginsburg, "Indigenous Counterpublics," in Meg McLagen and Yates McKee (eds.), *Sensible Politics: The Visual Culture of Nongovernmental Activism* (New York: Zone Books, 2012), p. 563.

10  See Édouard Glissant, *Poetics of Relation* (Ann Arbor: University of Michigan Press, 1987), 189.

11  Paul Chaat Smith, *Everything You Know about the Indian is Wrong* (Minneapolis: University of Minnesota Press, 2009), p. 71.

12  By way of background, in 1998, a conservative Bolivian government, in conjunction with corporations such as Bechtel and Suez, and with the support of the World Bank, had privatized water in Cochabamba. After water prices sky-rocketed and service was eliminated for those who could not afford water, mas-sive demonstrations in April 2000 forced Bechtel out of the country and ushered

in socialist and indigenous president Evo Morales, who argued that water must be free. On April 22, 2010, the tenth anniversary of victory in the Water Wars, the government issued the "People's Agreement on Climate Change and the Rights of Mother Earth."

13   From a talk by Faye Ginsburg, "Screening Disabilities: Visual Fields, Public Culture, and the Atypical Mind in the 21st Century," May 16, 2011, at Porter College, University of California, Santa Cruz.

14   See Michelle Raheja, *Reservation Reelism: Redfacing, Visual Sovereignty, and Representations of Native Americans in Film* (Lincoln: University of Nebraska Press, 2010), p. 18.

15   Gilles Deleuze, *Cinema 2: The Time Image* (Minneapolis: University of Minnesota Press, 1989), p. 217.

16   See Maximillian C. Forte, "Amerindian@Caribbean: Internet Indigeneity," in Kyra Landzelius (ed.), *Native on the Net: Indigenous and Diasporic Peoples in the Virtual Age* (London: Routledge, 2006), pp. 132–151.

17   Paul Chaat Smith, op. cit., p. 4.

18   See Philip Deloria, *Indians in Unexpected Places* (Lawrence: University of Nebraska Press, 2004), p. 68.

19   For a critical view of indigenous film projects, see James C. Faris, "Anthropological Transparency: Film, Representation and Politics," in Peter Ian Crawford and David Turton (eds.), *Film as Ethnography* (Manchester: Manchester University Press, 1992). For a critique of the Faris critique, see Terry Turner, "Defiant Images: The Kayapo Appropriation of Video," in *Anthropology Today*, 8(6) (December 1992): 5–16.

20   Faye Ginsburg, "Indigenous Media: Faustian Contract or Global Village," *Cultural Anthropology*, 6(1) (February 1991): 92–112.

21   See Jennifer Deger. "The Jolt of the New: Making Video Art in Arnhem Land," *Culture, Theory, and Critique*, 54(3) (November 2013): 355–371.

22   Indeed, Dan Umstead, the founder of the Oneida Indian web site proudly joked that they founded the site even before the White House homepage was up. See Landzelius (ed.), *Native on the Net*, p. 292.

23   Gomez-Pena, *Conversations across Borders*, p. 81.

24   Quoted in Amy Lonetree, *Decolonizing Museums: Representing Native America in National and Tribal Museums* (Chapel Hill: University of North Carolina Press, 2012), p. 5.

25   See Paul Chaat Smith, op. cit., p. 37.

26   Leslie Marmon Silko, "Videomakers and Basketmakers," *Aperture* 119 (Summer 1990): 73.

27   See Faye Ginsburg's piece on the film, "Beyond Broadcast: Launching NITV on Isuma TV," at: <http://mediacommons.futureofthebook.org/imr/2009/05/03/beyond-broadcast-launching-nitv-isuma-tv>

28   See Paul Chaat Smith, op. cit.

29   See Steven Leuthold, *Indigenous Aesthetics: Native Art, Media, Identity* (Austin: University of Texas Press, 1998), pp. 110–112.

30   See Amalia Cordova's PhD-in-progress dissertation (NYU) on indigenous media, provisionally entitled "Nomadic/Sporadic: The Pathways of Circulation of Latin American Indigenous Media."

31   See Michelle Raheja, op. cit., p. 238.

32   Moreton-Robinson (ed.), *Sovereign Subjects: Indigenous Sovereignty Matters* (Crows Nest: Allen ad Unwin, 2007), p. 2.

33   Randolph Lewis, *Alanis Obomsawin: The Vision of a Native Filmmaker* (Lincoln: University of Nebraska Press, 2003), p. 175.

34   See Michael Hardt and Antonio Negri, *Commonwealth* (Cambridge, Harvard: 2009), p. 350.

35   Cited in Mark Cousins, *The Story of Film* (London: Pavilion, 2011), p. 429.

36   See Theodor Koch-Grunberg, *Vom Roroima Zum Orinoco: Ergebnisse einer Reise in Nord Brasilien und Venezuela in den Jahren 1911–1913.* Vol. II, *Mythen und Legenden der Taulipang und Arekuna Indianer* (Stuttgart: Strocker & Schroder, 1924).

37   Haroldo de Campos, *Morfologia de Macunaíma* (São Paulo: Perspectiva, 1973).

38   M. M. Bakhtin, "Response to a Question from the *Novy Mir* editorial staff," in M. M. Bakhtin et al. (eds.), *Speech Genres and Other Late Essays* (Austin: University of Texas Press, 1986), p. 5.

39   Ibid., p. 2.

40   See Bennett, T. and Blundell, V. "First Peoples: Cultures, Policies, Politics," *Cultural Studies*, 9 (1995): 1–24.

41   As a proto-transnationalist, Pasolini's embrace of disparate traditions is somewhat stymied by his tendency to reduce the cultural traditions of Africa and the Middle East to idealist constructs and thereby paper over their complexity.

42   Marks, op. cit., p. 1.

43   See Gilles Deleuze, *Le pli—Leibniz et le baroque* (Paris: Editions de Minuit, 1988).

44   Benegal made his remarks about pan-Asian *rasa* aesthetics in a public interview at the "Subversive Film Festival" in Zaghreb (May 2011) and in conversations with Robert Stam. He remarked that he had not published anything on the subject.

45   See Richard Schechner, "Rasaesthetics," *The Drama Review* 45(3) (Fall 2001).

46   See Kevin Dodd, "Film Review: *Sita Sings the Blues*," *Journal of Religion & Film*, 13 (2) (October 2009).

47   Quoted in Lewis Hyde, *Common as Air: Revolution, Art, and Ownership* (New York: Farrar, Strauss, and Giroux, 2010), p. 46.

48   Gerard Genette, *Palimpsestes: La Litterature au Second Degree* (Paris: Seuil, 1982).

49   Alain Badiou, op, cit., p. 346.

50   See Jay David Bolter and Richard Grusin, *Remediation: Understanding New Media* (Cambridge: MIT Press, 1999).

51   See Jodi A. Byrd, op. cit., p. 42.

52 Houston Wood, Native Features*: Indigenous Films from Around the World* (New York: Continuum, 2008), p. 169.

53 The idea of analogical structures of feeling is explored in Shohat/Stam, *Unthinking Eurocentrism* (London: Routledge, 1994).

54 See J-P Renouard and Lise Wajeman, "The Weight of the Here and Now: Conversation with Claire Denis," in *Journal of European Studies*, 34 (2004): 1–2.

55 The Kate Bush music video of *Wuthering Heights*, meanwhile, performs transgenerational female identification, proclaiming Bush's trans-generational solidarity with the Catherine character.

56 Mikhail Bakhtin, *The Dialogic Imagination: Four Essays* (Austin: University of Texas at Austin, 1982), p. 421.

57 Robert Stam treats this film in *Literature through Film* in less detail. This version, unlike the video without subtitles on which the earlier discussion was based, is based on access to the DVD of the film.

58 Unpublished paper written for Robert Stam's "Film and Novel" course.

59 Sandra Ponzanesi and Marguerite Waller (eds.), *Postcolonial Cinema Studies* (London: Routledge, 2011).

60 See Tim Watson, "Improvements and Reparations at Mansfield Park," in Robert Stam and Alessandra Rengo (eds.), *Literature and Film* (Oxford: Blackwell, 2005).

61 Sandra Ponzanesi, "Postcolonial Adaptations: Gained and Lost in Translation," in Sandra Ponzanesi and Marguerite Waller (eds.), *Postcolonial Cinema Studies* (London, Routledge, 2011).

62 Édouard Glissant, *Poetics of Relation* (Ann Arbor: University of Michigan Press, 1997), p. 119.

63 Christopher Pavsek, *The Utopia of Film: Cinema and its Futures in Godard, Kluge and Tahimk* (New York: Columbia, 2013), p. 47.

64 Corinn Columpar, *Unsettling Sights: The Fourth World on Film* (Carbondale: Southern Illinois Press, 2010), p. xiv. Marcia Langton, "Aboriginal Art and Film: The Politics of Representation," *Rouge* (2005).

65 See Faye Ginsburg, "Australia's Indigenous New Wave: Future Imaginaries in Recent Aboriginal Feature Film," Adrian Gerbrands Lecture (May 29, 2012).

66 See Thomas King, op. cit., p. 218.

67 See Chadwick Allen, *Blood Narrative: Indigenous Identity in American Indian and Maori Literary and Activist Texts* (Durham: Duke University Press, 2002).

68 Quoted in Peter Linebaugh, *The Magna Carta Manifesto: Liberties and Commons for All* (Berkeley: University of California Press, 2008), p. 246.

69 Fausto Reinaga, *La Revolucion India* (La Paz: Hilda Reinaga, 1970), pp. 15–16.

70 Ibid.

# 2

# The Upside-Down World of the Carnivalesque

This chapter focuses on another "archaic" source of alternative aesthetics, to wit "**carnival**," a rowdy tradition whose history runs (to speak only of Europe) from Greek Dionysian festivals and Roman Saturnalia, through the medieval "carnivalesque" of Rabelasian grotesqueries and later baroque theater, to Jarry, Surrealism, and on to the counter-cultural mischief of recent decades. Over five centuries in the Americas, these European traditions of salutary misbehavior meshed with the recombinant traces of the sacred-musical festivities of West Africa, generating the world of what Joe Roach called "**circum-Atlantic performance**"—that is, the mingled indigenous, African, and European performative currents found all around a *Black Atlantic* impacted by the slave trade and the diasporization of Africans. More than merely an archaic "survival," carnival is a dynamically evolving contemporary practice. The most well known carnivals are those held in Rio de Janeiro and Trinidad, but there also are mini-carnivals in the Global North, such as the Notting Hill Carnival in London, Caribana in Toronto, and the Labor Day Parade in New York—all now mediated through the morphing forms of the mass media.

## The People's Second Life

Nearly all cultures have carnival-like traditions that point to an alternative cosmovision of the common people. The Holi festival in Kishan Garhi in India features myriad sorts of **social inversions**—untouchables mocking Brahmins, women ridiculing men, and so forth. A Dutch traveler to eighteenth-century Africa (Guinea) described a carnival-like

*Keywords in Subversive Film/Media Aesthetics*, First Edition. Robert Stam with Richard Porton and Leo Goldsmith.
© 2015 John Wiley & Sons, Inc. Published 2015 by John Wiley & Sons, Inc.

"feast of eight days, accompanied with all manner of singing, skipping, dancing, mirth, and jollity: in which time a perfect lampooning liberty is allowed, and scandal so highly exalted, that they may freely sing of all the faults, villanies, and frauds of their superiors ... without punishment."[1] Among the Hopi, ritual clowns puckishly upend conventional social decorum. The Saturnalia of ancient Rome and the Feast of Krishna in India have translated popular insurgency through images of millenarian reversals. In Japan, meanwhile, Imamura's film *Eijanaika* (1981) portrays a carnival-style revolt through an 1866 historical episode in Japan just prior to the turbulent events that led to the Meiji Restoration, when swirling, gyrating crowds of revelers would chant *"Eijanaika!"* ("Why not!") while charging into the streets, ultimately invading the palace. But perhaps the closest counterpart to Bakhtin's affectionate analysis of Medieval and Renaissance carnival is Pasolini's "Trilogy of Life," based on three thoroughly carnivalized classics—*The Decameron* (1971), *Canterbury Tales* (1972), and *The Arabian Nights* (1974)—which depict a festive life prior to capitalism and the Industrial Revolution, a life characterized by utopian jouissance, the celebration of the bodily lower stratum, and free and familiar contact.

As theorized by Bakhtin, carnival embraces an **anti-canonical aesthetic** that rejects formal harmony and unity in favor of the asymmetrical, the heterogeneous, and the miscegenated. Carnival's **"grotesque realism"** hyperbolizes a body in constant transformation, turning conventional aesthetics on its head in order to locate a new kind of convulsive, rebellious beauty, one that reveals the grotesquerie of the noble and the latent beauty of the "vulgar." Carnival's **oxymoronic aesthetic** impregnates everything with its opposite, within an alternative logic of permanent contradiction and nonexclusive polarities that transgresses the monologic true-or-false thinking typical of a certain kind of positivist rationalism. Carnival promotes what Bakhtin calls **gay relativity**, or the ludic suspension of the imperious rules of logic in the name of freedom of thought. Carnival is **utopian** in the sense of Marcuse's claim that art in general is utopian, in that it "opens a dimension inaccessible to other experience, a dimension in which human beings, nature, and other things no longer stand under the law of the established reality principle."[2]

Bakhtin's notion of the *carnivalesque* opens up a rich repertoire of concepts and strategies for analyzing and even creating art. Carnival evokes a deep social unconscious and collective desire for gregarious pleasure among equals. Artists often practice carnivalesque strategies, and audiences enjoy them, without necessarily knowing their historical genealogy or conceptual basis. Carnival gives expression to **"the people's second life,"** a sacred/profane time-out for imaginative play and alternative cosmovisions. Undoing the false equation of wisdom with gravitas, Bakhtin saw carnival's **culture of laughter** as penetratingly deep, and Rabelais as most profound when he was laughing the most heartily. Perhaps picking up on the Schillerian idea that people are the most human when they play, Simon Critchley, echoing Bakhtin, links laughter to gregarious community, as "a convulsive movement ... contagious and solidaristic [with] an ethical function insofar as the simple sharing of a joke recalls to us what is shared in our life-world practices ... as a minimal form of *sensus communis.*"[3] The court echoing with derisive female laughter, provoked by the sexist declarations of the prosecutor, in Marleen Gooris' film *A Question of Silence* (1982), calls up an anticipatory utopia imbued with laughter's unifying force, its subversive refusal of ready-made definitions, its choral intimation of nascent collective "becomings."

The usual argument against the political use of laughter in art is a kind of **mimetic fallacy**—the "rule" which mandates that style should match subject—for example, a painful subject must be treated in a "pained" manner," with what Tom Waugh calls **"indexical sobriety."**[4] The mimetic prejudice against humor sometimes takes the form of rhetorical questions: "how can the artist laugh, when so many people have suffered..." But a contrary view would say that any theme can be susceptible to humorous or satiric treatment. The key question is, who is the *butt* of the joke—the powerful or the powerless? (The *purimspiel*, for example, makes fun of Haman, not of Esther; it mocks the tyrant, not the Jews.) The culture of laughter is linked even to the trope of **laughing at death**, a levity made possible by the knowledge that, while individuals die, the people as a collectivity continue. Laughing at death, in this sense, is not an act of cynicism but of faith. Rabelais' **grotesque realism** evokes the ongoing trans-individual voice of the people and **"the grotesque body of the people"** as encapsulated in the ambivalent figure of the **pregnant hag**, near death, giving bloody birth to fresh new life—while simultaneously evoking the timeless processes of artistic renovation.

Carnival is the people's self-pleasuring, a party the people offers to itself, a little miracle, as in love, of a sharing of social fantasies. But carnival is not only a living social practice but also a general, perennial fund of popular forms and festive rituals summed up in the term **"carnivalesque,"** or the transposition into art of the spirit of popular festivities. For Bakhtin, the *carnivalesque* promotes **participatory spectacle**, a "pageant without footlights," erasing the boundaries between spectator and performer. As a kind of dress rehearsal for revolution, carnival suspends hierarchical distinctions, barriers, and prohibitions. It installs a qualitatively different kind of communication based on **"free and familiar contact"** or transparent non-hierarchical communication within a community of equals. Barbara Ehrenreich calls carnival an acknowledgement of the "miracle of our simultaneous existence."[5] As a danced version of Habermas' rather academic **"ideal speech situation,"** carnival fosters convivial relations between people, including with strangers, in an atmosphere free of paranoia and competition. In vertical terms, carnival turns **the world upside-down**—or, from another perspective, "right side up." The carnivalesque spirit thus sees social and political life as a perpetual **"crowning and uncrowning"** where the inevitability of change becomes a source of what Ernst Bloch called "the principle of hope."[6]

Carnival also has a philosophical side. As with cinema, it **generates concepts**, to paraphrase Deleuze, in blocks of music, polyrhythm, movement, and performance. Carnival translates concepts of social emancipation into collectively created gestures and improvised movements. In Bakhtin's marvelously inclusive and egalitarian formulation, carnival entails the suspension of all "hierarchical structure and ... everything resulting from socio-hierarchical inequality or any other form of inequality among people."[7] Many of the symbolic power reversals that proliferate in contemporary films can be traced back to the comic festivals analyzed by Bakhtin. **Carnival** often featured corpulent Lords of Misrule who decreed seasons of obligatory revelry and indecorous behavior. Bakhtin's conceptual categories illuminate a rich archive of transtextual and transartistic tropes. The **banquet imagery** of feasts and symposia, for example, traces its long-term origins to celebrations of harvests and survival. The phenomenon of **transvestitism** foregrounded by Bakhtin, similarly, has been an endless source of comedy, from Aristophanes to *Tootsie*, *La Cage aux Folles*, *Mrs. Doubtfire*, and *White Chicks*, up to more radical forms of drag and gender-bending.

The *carnivalesque* is at once spiritual and material; it transfers all that is spiritual, ideal, and abstract, to the material sphere of earth and the body. Rather than reduce life to the material, however, carnival invests the material with profound significance. If carnival turns the world upside down, it also exalts the social bottom by celebrating the *bodily lower stratum*. By focusing on the shared physiological processes of bodily life—copulation, birth, eating, drinking, defecation—the *carnivalesque* aesthetic offers a temporary suspension of hierarchy and prohibition. **Sacred excrement**, as a literal expression of the *bodily lower stratum*, forms part of the fecund imagery of the *grotesque*. The festive slinging of cow dung ("*le jeu de la merde*"), typical of old-time European carnivals, was later sublimated into more refined aggressions such as throwing tomatoes, talcum, and water balloons, metamorphosing into the tossed custard pies of slapstick comedy. As with animal dung in certain African artistic traditions, urine carries great dignity within the carnivalesque aesthetic. Rabelais' Gargantua urinates on the multitude, just as Mário de Andrade's child Macunaíma "pisses hot on his old mother, frightening the mosquitoes" and is shat on by vultures and geese. Within an excremental vision, feces and urine enjoy auratic prestige.

## Sacred Parody

Perhaps the most direct link between Bakhtin's analysis of Medieval carnival and cinema takes the form of scenes that make irreverent use of Biblical topoi to deride theological propriety and ecclesiastical institutions. Many subversive films deploy what might be called **strategic blasphemy**. The Medieval **parodia sacra**, or sacred parodies, that is, all the popular festivities that played irreverently with Biblical texts and ecclesiastical institutions, took very diverse forms, such as the **festa stultorum** (feasts of fools) and the **risus paschalis** (Easter Laughter), a genre favored by the lower clergy, presided over by infantile "boy bishops" and "lords of misrule." The final multiple crucifixion scene in *The Life of Brian* literalizes "Easter Laughter" by having Brian/Christ invite his fellow crucifixees to try and look at "the bright side of death." The **"coena cipriani,"** or Cyprian Suppers, meanwhile, revolved around Christ's Last Supper with his 12 disciples. The Last Supper easily lends itself to parodic desacralization because its various elements can easily be transferred to a material level. Kidnapped by a subversive intention, the Eucharist bread and the wine can become fuel for themes of gluttony, drunkenness, and orgiastic excess. At the same time, revised versions of the Last Supper can stage issues of power: in a social transubstantiation, the Christ figure can be replaced by a blasphemous stand-in. In a liturgical *coup d'etat*, Judas can occupy the place of Christ, and the 12 disciples can be replaced with incongruous surrogates. Such gestures are not necessarily anti-Christian, since some millenarian versions of Christianity see Jesus himself as a stigmatized outcast who sleeps in a manger and rides into Bethlehem on a donkey, subversively preaching his own version of the "world upside-down" theme—that the meek shall inherit the earth and that the last shall be first.[8]

Endlessly memorialized in canonical art, the Last Supper has been parodied in a wide variety of media. The echoes of *parodia sacra* resound within the walls of the orgiastic cloister that is Bunuel's oeuvre, the constant site of black masses, monkish pranks, and theological burlesques. Bunuel offered a locus classicus of the *coena cipriani* genre in his *Viridiana*, where a literal "beggars' banquet" in an aristocratic residence turns into an orgiastic replay of the Last Supper, all against the musical backdrop of the Hallelujah chorus from Handel's *Messiah*. The beggars gathered around Don Jaime's table arrange themselves in the configuration familiar from the Da Vinci painting, as a prostitute lifts her skirt to take an imaginary photo with her lower bodily "camera obscura." The scene enacts a class revenge in the guise of a banquet, as the "lower orders" mock the manners of their "betters." It is not for Bunuel a question of applauding the behavior of the beggars but rather of deploying the performative image of unruly behavior in order to enact the comic degradation of the social rules that privilege all that is classy, noble, and aristocratic.

The Last Supper has triggered an infinite chain of impious transtextual variations. Parodic versions of the Last Supper can be sighted in Pasoloni's *Mama Roma* (1962) and Robert Altman's *M\*A\*S\*H\** (1970), and, decades later, on *The Simpsons*, *The Sopranos*, and *The Colbert Report*.[9] Such parodies become truly subversive, however, only when they go beyond mere pastiche to trouble deeply entrenched religious/social/ racial/sexual hierarchies. The artist Alfred Hrdlicka, picking up on the homosociality of the world portrayed in some of the paintings, for example, turned the Last Supper into a homosexual orgy. Many *coena cipriani* create **multicultural Last Suppers**. Jamaican–American artist Renee Cox challenged racial and gender hierarchies in her five-panel photographic montage, entitled "Yo Mama's Last Supper," which depicted 12 black male apostles gathered around the naked black artist herself as Christ. Given that the apostles were people of what would now be called "Middle Eastern appearance," one wonders why a non-Aryan Jesus and disciples would provoke outrage. (A sketch by the Arab–American sketch comedy group "Axis of Evil" has the Three Wise Men get racially profiled on their way to Christ's manger.) In Kevin Smith's *Dogma*—another *parodia sacra* film—the Chris Rock character argues that Jesus was black and complains that "the mofo owes me 12 dollars."[10]

The Renee Cox piece provoked an apoplectic reaction on the part of right-wing New York mayor Rudy Giuliani, who called for a "decency panel" to snuff out such sacrilege. Yet, there is something faintly comic about such Quixotic efforts to stop the advance of a two-millennia stream of transtextual blasphemy, rather like putting a finger in a dike against an artistic tsunami. From another perspective, this kind of censorship could be seen as a form of spiritual **enclosure** striving to fence off the **religious commons** or the shared stock of religious topoi and tropes. Presumably, the mayor would have been even more shocked by Stephen Colbert's mockery of the idea of using religion to "cure the gay." A Catholic himself, Colbert offered his barbed support for a religious antidote to homosexuality: "Get down on your knees, drink a little wine, and take a symbol of the male body into your mouth!—what better way to cure the gay!"

Many of the *coena cipriani* films form **remediated parodia sacra**, directed not at the Last Supper per se but rather at its various artistic reiterations. One Colbert gambit placed the comic at Jesus' side pointing to the Lord as if to say "here's my new best friend." In *Monty Python at the Hollywood Bowl*, an obstreperous and obscenity-spewing Pope (John Clease) badgers a Cockney-accented Michelangelo for painting a Last Supper featuring three Christs (one fat, two skinny), 28 disciples, and a kangaroo. A George Carlin book features the author with forks raised, asking "*When Will Jesus Bring the Pork Chops?*" In his HBO show, Robin Williams has the apostles eat Chinese take-out and invents a new sibling for Jesus—"Jesse the brother of Christ"—seething with sibling-rival rage about his brother's celebrity status. Invited by the Virgin Mother for a trip to the beach, the "I-coulda-been-a-contender" brother shouts: "Sure, Ma. Jesus walks on the water and I come home with sand in my ass!"

Mel Brooks, for his part, **rejudaizes** the Last Supper in *The History of the World: Part One*, a historically plausible move since the Last Supper was originally a Jewish Passover meal (Pesach), graced by Passover *matzot*. In the Brooks version, Christ and his disciples dine in an ancient Roman inn strangely reminiscent of a Borscht Belt hotel. The supper here becomes the scene of vaudevillian repartee, as a humorlessly Waspish Savior, confusing a common curse with his own name, repeatedly takes the waiter's exclamation "Jesus!" as literally addressed to him. Shu Lea Cheang's *Color Schemes*, for its part, stages a multicultural Last Supper, again in the frontal tableau manner, with a Native American woman in Christ's position, surrounded by African-Americans, Asian-Americans, and Latinos. Here, the Last Supper becomes a school of etiquette for people of color undergoing their assimilationist ordeals of civility. The film spoofs melting-pot ideals through the metaphor of a "color wash," whereby the very non-Aryan "disciples" undergo four ethnic "wash cycles": soak, wash, rinse, and extract.

Tomas Guttierez Alea's film *The Last Supper* (1976), whose very title evokes the *coena cipriani*, lends fleshly historicity to the Last Supper topos. The film is based on actual events toward the end of the eighteenth century, at a time when plantation overlords were haunted by the specter of Haitian-style slave rebellions. Drawing on Fraginals' classic study *El Ingenio* ("The Sugar Mill," 1964), Alea adopted the true story of a count's historical decision to gather 12 of the slaves for a ritual exercise in humility whereby, in *imitatio Christi*, he would serve them dinner at his own table. When the count violates his promise of a day off for Good

Friday, the slaves angrily burn down the sugar factory. (By displacing events that transpired in 1789 to 1804, the year of Haitian Independence, Alea links them to the rebellions that generated the first Black Republic in the Americas.)

The events of the film transpire over the 5 days of Holy Week, the sacred counterpart to the profane social inversions of carnival; the Last shall be First, as the Bible says, but only for a few days. The Frenchified count is dressed in the *ancien régime* style, with crimson attire and cakey makeup. The *mise-en-scène* of the hour-long supper is modeled on the Da Vinci painting. As the count, in the Christ position, gathers the slaves around him, his visage bears a look of beatific self-satisfaction. In a filmic mimicry of Da Vinci's technique, Alea has soft candlelight "bless" the master's powdered wig. Fantasizing of himself as a new Christ surrounded by his disciples, whom he repeatedly compares to slaves, the master, in a Brechtian *gestus*, kisses the slaves' feet but immediately wipes his mouth in disgust.

The later arrival of the fugitive slave Sebastian, whipped to the point of collapse, leads to a quasi-**Hegelian master–slave encounter**. The scene addresses the perverse reciprocity of the politics of recognition under slavery—the master despises the slave, yet his wealth is the creation of the slave labor on which he depends. When the battered Sebastian returns to the master's table, the master forgives the "transgression" and, echoing Christ's question to the disciples, asks: "Who am I? Do you recognize me?" The slave responds by spitting in the master's face, as if to say, "Yes, I recognize that you have mastered me, but I do not recognize your mastery." Judas' hypocritical kiss is replaced by Sebastian's insurrectionary spittle. Were it not Holy Week, such a rebellion would have surely triggered punishment by death, but instead the count treats it as one more trial to be borne in a Christ-like manner. But later the count shifts from self-satisfied benevolence to sheer disciplinary force. Tearing the mask off the count's "charity," the film demystifies the figure of the "friendly master." Forced to work on Good Friday, the slaves rebel and seize the overseer. In response, the master has all the slaves decapitated, but Sebastian escapes to freedom. The master reveals himself to be just as brutal as the slave driver; his humility is fake. The film shows that virtually all of the whites—the priest, the overseer, the teacher, the sugar-maker—form indispensable cogs in an oppressive and very modern industrial system. The film concludes with a Foucauldian **disciplinary spectacle** on Easter Sunday morning, a Golgotha-like scene showing the heads of the slaves impaled on stakes; only the stake of the by-now-escaped Sebastian remains empty.

## Festive-Revolutionary Practices

Many of Bakhtin's chronotopes and topoi—carnival, banquet imagery, marketplace speech, free and familiar contact—are indissociable from the festive takeover of public space. These topoi help us rethink media aesthetics because they privilege the movement inherent in the word "cinema" and "movies"—that "move" people and hopefully get people to move together, to turn ideas into activist social "movements," to join a kinetic *communitas*. Bakhtin's conceptualization, which has deep affinities with Moylan's **"critical utopia"**[11] and with Lefebvre's **"festival,"** provides a touchstone for this particularly vibrant strand within subversive aesthetics. A 1966 situationist pamphlet famously asserted that "revolutions will be festivals or they will not be, for the life they herald will itself be created in festivity."[12] In "Toward a Permanent Cultural Revolution," Lefebvre summed up the goals of festive revolution: "The festival rediscovered and magnified by overcoming the conflict between everyday life and festivity ... such is the final cause of the revolutionary plan."[13]

Some films, such as Marcel Camus' *Black Orpheus* (1959), offer a tantalizing glimpse of the collective joy of carnival, but eschew the trope of social inversion in favor of primitivist celebration. Orson Welles' never-released documentary *It's All True* (1942), in contrast, emphasized multi-racial and cross-class gregariousness of carnival as well as the real-life activism of black and mestizo Brazilians taking to the streets to protest the urban "renewal" that devastated "Little Africa," a neighborhood nucleus both of carnival and of cultural resistance. Many decades later, Arnaldo Jabor's film *Tudo Bem* offers **carnival as social allegory** by injecting carnival-like energies into the between-four-walls theatrical space of a bourgeois apartment in Copacabana. When the well-off couple invites workers to come repair the apartment, they are gradually invaded by an anarchic assemblage of Brazil's marginalized masses—Carioca maids, construction workers, *favelados*, Northeastern peasants—who gradually take over the bourgeois space. Crowding all of Brazil's class and racial contradictions into a single apartment, the film stages a quite literal carnival surging from the maids' quarters into the living room. The subaltern characters reenact the samba pageant by singing a carnival samba dedicated to the "Black Admiral" (João Cândido Felisberto), who in 1910 led a mutiny against corporeal punishment in the Brazilian navy. The apartment becomes the site of festive irreverence, popular mysticism, and the vernacular memory of historical resistance. The *Senzala* (slave quarters), in Glauber Rocha's felicitous phrase, invades the *Casa Grande* (big house).[14]

A number of Brazilian films literally model their narratives and staging on Rio's carnival pageant. Carlos Diegues' *Xica da Silva* (1976) develops what might be called a carnivalesque **samba-pageant aesthetic** by having the titular Xica celebrate her manumission from slavery by leading a costumed carnival dance through the streets of eighteenth-century Minas Gerais. In fact, Diegues conceived *Xica da Silva* as a "**samba-enredo**" (samba-narrative), that is, as formally analogous to the collections of songs, dances, costumes, and lyrics that form part of the annual samba-school pageants. Indeed, *Xica da Silva* (1976) and Walter Lima Jr's *Chico Rei* (1982) were first presented as samba school pageants for Rio's carnival and only later transposed into feature films.

What especially interests us here is what Claudia Orenstein calls "**festive-revolutionary practices**" as a perennial source of radical art. In film after film, the festive takeover of the streets becomes a metaphor for retaking the commons for emancipatory purposes. Barbara Hammer's carnivalesque *Superdyke* offers a militant lesbian example of the trope, showing the exhilaration of coming out together into the public sphere. The film features feminist superwomen, sporting "Superdyke" tee-shirts and bearing cardboard shields emblazoned with the word "Amazons," rescuing women from various dangers while proudly occupying the streets with their gay parade. Marching in time in battalion formation, their helmets carry the inscription: "Out of the closet, into the streets." Thus, lesbian collective glee disrupts the **hetero-normative order**—a concept disseminated by Michael Warner and rooted in Gayle Rubin's notion of the "**sex/gender system**" and what Adrienne Rich calls "**compulsory heterosexuality**," that is, the social regime, aligning bio-logical sex, sexuality, and gender identity, that posits heterosexuality as the normal sexual orientation.[15]

The trope of dancing crowds taking over public space has deep appeal and profound social meaning. The well-known chant goes: "Whose streets? Our streets!," while one direct action group dubs itself "Reclaim the Streets." In a free-wheeling, soft-peddling version of the **situationist derive**—ambulatory drifting through socially varied neighborhoods— "critical mass" bike riders snake through the metropolis as what Stephen Duncombe calls "a living organism."[16] The demonstration that shut down the financial center of London in 1968 was dubbed "carnival against capitalism." Carnival-like activities figured in Seattle's "Festival of Resistance," while Occupy Wall Street protests often featured drum circles, which, as Mark Greif points out, have long been linked to Afro-diasporic culture (Congo Square Drum Circle), ultimately forming "partly imaginary, partly historic attempts to live out suppressed anticolonial traditions, of Native

American spirituality and survival, and the African diaspora in the Americas and Caribbean."[17] What Greif calls "leaderless, spontaneously coordinated polyrhythmic and pluralist drum circles" manifest emerging forms of conviviality. Carnivalizing protest, the drums trigger primal feelings of oceanic celebration and ecstatic feelings of union, not only between body and mind but also with other human beings. While democratic assembly depends on the spoken word, drumming depends on "a kinetic and continual, unbroken out loud bodily manifestation of the rhythm, an experience of others' moves within a generality of constant movement, sound, and rhythm" within a common space where authority does not overrule "life-giving expression."[18]

The politics of actually existing carnival and of carnivalesque artistic strategies are conjunctural; no strategy is *essentially* progressive or regressive. In Jamesonian terms, carnival is a master code in which competing discourses fight for hegemony. As what Bakhtin calls a "**situated utterance**," that is, a communicative event shaped by history and asymmetrical power, carnival's political valence depends on who is carnivalizing whom, in what historical conjuncture, in what style, and to what ultimate purpose. Historically, the repression of carnival has often gone hand in hand with the repression of African and indigenous cultures and a proselytizing animus against Afro-diasporic religious expression. In the *Black Atlantic*, the suppression of carnival has often taken on racial overtones, whereby the banning of drums, dancing, and Afro-diasporic religious practices was triggered by anxieties about the possibility of slave rebellions. The maintenance of slavery required the suppression of dance, trance, possession, and everything that smacked of communal joy or an alternative to slavery. (Nelson Perreira dos Santos' *Tenda dos Milagres* describes this process as it occurred in turn-of-the-century Brazil.)

Within carnival's *upside-down world*, implausible kings are enthroned in an atmosphere of contagious hilarity. The musical comedy short film *Rufus Jones for President* (1933), a kind of music video *avant la lettre*, offers a lively example of the trope. In this oddly prescient fantasy, Ethel Waters puts her young son Rufus—played by an 8-year-old Sammy Davis Jr.—to sleep with a comforting bedtime story, in which he becomes president of the United States. Thanks to a campaign energized by music and dance in the streets, Rufus wins the highest office in the land. While framed as a fantasy–lullaby to calm a child, the film provides a comic–musical outlet for dreams of black empowerment. Taking the dominant ideology at its word—the mother reminds the boy that "anyone can be president"—the short film instantiates that claim in mischievous form. The narrative embeds the carnivalesque trope of the boy king (**puer rex**)—just as it resonates historically with Afro-diasporic celebrations such as "Negro Election Day" and "Jubilee" in the United States and the "Congada" in Brazil.[19] (One of the long-term antecedents of Jubilee was the ancient practice of periodic debt cancellation, for example, in Sumer and Babylon, whereby slaves were freed, debts were annulled, and seized property was returned to its rightful owner.) Thus, long before the first filmic black presidents (played by actors such as James Earl Jones, Morgan Freeman, Chris Rock, and Dennis Haysbert), this 1933 short film turned what was then unthinkable—a black president in apartheid America—into the triumphant image of a dancing boy. The film represented an early stage in the painfully slow process by which black people came to occupy symbolic as well as literal positions of power—including through tropes of musical royalty (*Count* Basie, *Duke* Ellington, *King* Oliver)—the process that culminated in the election of Barack Obama.

## Unruly Women

The carnivalesque celebrates the **bodily lower stratum**—that is, everything that sex-fearing puritanism considers base: bodily fluids, sweat, urine, sperm, excrement—in sum, the fundaments of our common existence, still considered taboo and obscene. Miranda July's *Me and You and Everyone We Know* has 6-year old Robby offer a ludic ode to the *bodily lower stratum* in the form of a scatological exchange: "I want to poop back and forth. I'll poop into her butthole and then she'll poop it back into my butthole ... and we'll keep doing it back and forth with the same poop. Forever." The carnivalesque also favors **marketplace speech**, the frank and vulgar exchanges of the marketplace and the *agora* in Socrates' time, or the seven "dirty words" sacralized by George Carlin on American television. On a more profound level, Bakhtin's conceptual categories point to the transindividual sources of pleasure in art, pleasures that go beyond vicarious identification with individual success to more collective and open-hearted aspirations for shared conviviality.

Carnival's delicious grotesquerie privileges **the protuberances and orifices** of the body, its points of opening and extension, the body as it changes and transforms itself: eating, drinking, defecation, and other elimination (sweating, blowing of the nose, sneezing), as well as copulation, pregnancy, dismemberment, and swallowing up by another body—all these acts are performed on the confines of the body and the outer world. In all these events, the beginning and end of life are closely linked and interwoven.[20]

Bakhtin emphasizes the interplay between the body and the world, the points where the membrane between self and other becomes permeable. Singing the body electric in all its glorious obscenity, he extols the active, sweating, farting, secreting, lubricating, menstruating, orgasming body, always in relation to other bodies and other selves, in short, to something beyond itself.

The sexualized body defies classical aesthetic norms because it exists in a realm both below and beyond notions of the beautiful and the ugly. In reference to the unique mix of desire, awkwardness, and grotesquerie in Catherine Breillat films such as *Romance* and *Fat Girl*, Damon Young has coined a variation on the word "sublime"—"**subslime**"—to refer to the status of the nether regions of the female body in Breillat's works, at once the site of sublime ineffability—awesomely ominous like the ocean—and, paradoxically, also of the all-too-physical materiality, embodying the non-transcendability of material existence, or what Teresa de Lauretis has called the "corpse implicit or latent within the organism."[21] One is reminded of Bakhtin's three spasms—birth, orgasm, and death—and of Yeat's "god of love" who "pitched his tent/near the place of excrement."

Picking up on the old pornographic literary device of the **speaking vagina**—used most famously in *Vagina Monologues*—feminist artists have explored the comic–didactic inscription of the *bodily lower stratum*. In a performance piece entitled "Interior Scroll," filmmaker–performer Carolee Schneeman, after reading from *Cezanne, She Was a Great Painter*, spread her legs and pulled out a scroll of text from her vagina in order to critique patriarchal oppression. In the "Finger in the Dyke" production "Singing Vulva" (available on YouTube), a woman rapper, sporting a vulva costume, mocks the anxieties that fuel misogyny. Lauding the orifice as both "hairy" and "scary," she reminds us of the primordial truth that "we all come from this hole, and none other" In the cabaret spectacle "Vaudeville of the Vulva," meanwhile, the performance artist and sexual health activist Laura Doe, garbed in a nun's habit but playing British academic Virgina Regina, PhD, explores societal prejudices toward the female genitalia. Feminist corporeality meets the *parodia sacra* in a sisterly salute to the vulva as God's "greatest work of art," performed in the artist's "pink period." Since the secretions emitted in orgasm favor charity, she concludes, orgasm is "the Christian thing to do." Rosa von Praunheim's *Ein Virus Kennt Kein Morale*, meanwhile, offers a more earnest Lutheran version of the *parodia sacra*. The film's Brechtian refrain sums up the film's activist stance. To the tune of "He's Got the Whole World in His Hands," a transvestite chorus sings direct to the camera/audience: "You've got your own fate/in your hands." Fatalistic religiosity and the platitudes of demagogic politicians give way to activist politics.

Barbara Hammer films such as *Menses* (1974), *Superdyke* (1975), and *Dykatectics* exemplify these carnivalesque tendencies. *Menses* celebrates the *grotesque body* as literally open, secreting, and self-transforming. The film opens with the camera panning slowly and lovingly over the crotches of naked women in a North California field, as a superimposed animated egg floats from woman to woman, as the soundtrack repeats, mantra-like, "menses ... menses ... menses..." In a Sapphic *parodia sacra*, a woman in white proffers a communal wineglass whose red liquid overflows and trickles down her body. We are reminded of Bakhtin's exaltation of all of the body's "base" secretions—feces, sperm, urine, menstrual flow—in sum, all that are banned from respectable representation because of a Manichean notion of the body's fundamental uncleanliness. *Dykatectics* (1974), meanwhile, renders lovemaking as caress rather than thrust, while *Superdyke* emphasizes the collective pleasure of a "gay outing" of lesbians playfully but proudly asserting their identity in the public sphere, defying the patriarchal taboo against women making a "spectacle of themselves."

*Les Stances à Sophie* (1971), directed by Moshe Mizrahi but based on Christine Rochefort's 1963 feminist novel, features a vivid example of an **unruly woman** protagonist. Written and produced in the wake of the **gynocentric** (women-centered) **writing** of Simone de Beauvoir, Marguerite Duras, and Francoise Sagan, but prior to the **theoretical feminism** of Kristeva, Iragaray, and Cixous, the film was made just as the MLF (Movement for the Liberation of Women) was emerging from the teargas mists in the aftermath of May 1968, a period when radical women were becoming disillusioned with sexist male revolutionaries who expected women to prepare the coffee but not deliver the speeches. The *carnivalesque* title refers to a ribald song from the Rabelaisian tradition of obscene medical student limericks, lines of which form the epigraph to the text: "I met you one night in the street where you were vomiting tripe. Ah, if I had known you were only a whore." The stanza evokes the sexual double standard, whereby women are adjudged whores for exercising freedoms that men assume as their birthright.

Both the novel and the film are deeply feminist—in their critique of gender subordination, their display of female solidarity, and in the defiant agency of the main character/narrator. Significantly, the film foregrounds *female authorship* at a time when the *caméra-stylo*—Astruc's "camera-pen," to be used by directors to create films as personal as novels—was largely wielded by men making films from a masculinist and individualist point of view, or what Geneviève Sellier calls the "**first-person masculine singular**."[22] At one point, in a **writerly** *mise-en-abyme*, the three major women characters collectively pen a sexually libertarian feminist manifesto.

We witness the formation of what Sianne Ngai calls **compound subjects** or the "combining of dual or multiple subjects into a single force or agency."[23] The film instantiates, in this sense, a feminist *politeia*, what Wendy Brown calls "the singularly human practice of constituting a particular mode of collective life."[24]

Both novel and film explore the carnivalesque figure of the **woman-on-top** that defies patriarchal power through boisterous hilarity, a figure that anticipates the bawdy, crotch-grabbing, Roseanne-style figure celebrated by Kathleen Rowe in *The Unruly Woman*.[25] Perhaps a distant descendant of Lilith, the first wife of Adam in Jewish folklore, the aggressive woman-on-top represents the **succubus** or female demon with immense powers of liberatory sexual mischief. *Les Stances a Sophie* proliferates in feminist provocations. When her future husband Philippe criticizes her on their first encounter for kissing three different men during their visit to a commune, Celine mocks his patriarchal surveillance by claiming that she would have kissed more men if she had had the time. Instead of treating bourgeois marriage as "happy end," here both novel and film end with Celine's buoyant opting *out* of marriage: "I breathe. Finally. Alone." In illustration of Bakhtin's dictum that all political struggle passes through language, and in keeping with the tenets of what Andrew Ross calls **language feminism** *à* la Kristeva and Cixous—where "'the feminine' is yoked to an explicitly anti-sexist ... approach to language and subjectivity"— much of the conversation in the film revolves around the **gender-differentiated understandings** of "love," "freedom," and "happiness."[26]

Iris Marion Young has written about the differentiated ways in which men and women relate to the body and to physical space.[27] Mizrahi's *mise-en-scène*, in this sense, shapes a **gendered space of interlocution**, which reveals that men and women, even when sharing the same space, sometimes inhabit different affective–discursive worlds. Within a Renoir-like depth of field and multi-layered acoustic space, the film has the men converse in the foreground while the women, in the background, riff ironically on their masculinist and racist discourse, without the men even noticing that they are being mocked. When her husband's friend tries to seduce her, Celine invites *him* to strip, while informing him that she favors truly free love and not a competitive fuck behind her husband's back; humiliated, he retreats with his tail, as it were, between his legs. For the surrealism-inflected Celine, love is a creative disorder and utopian dream; for the men, it is ownership, conquest, and bottom-line realities.

*Les Stances à Sophie* could easily fit into the genre that Teresa de Lauretis dubbed **Oedipus-Interruptus films**, that is, films that perform *social inversion* by deconstructing the male-centered Freudian narrative of generational revolt against the paternal phallus and the nuclear family of Daddy, Mommy, and Me.[28] This interruption of the Oedipal scenario can take place through the witty unpacking of a musical comedy (Chantal Akerman's *The Golden Eighties*), or through the parodic invocation of oracular Lacanianism by a phallocratic professor (Yvonne Rainer's *The Man Who Envied Women*), or through the media-spoofing bicycle-riding militancy (Lizzie Borden's *Born in Flames*). Rather than merely sabotage voyeurism *à* la Godard, such films gleefully deconstruct/reconstruct conventional film language, canonical genres, and social hierarchies.

## Polymorphous Celebrations

As we shall see in Chapter 3, many on the left have been understandably wary of the abuse of sexuality in cinema. These critics were perhaps reacting not only to the commercialized cynicism of most porn, but also to the earlier over-valorization of sexuality by the avant-garde itself. This over-investment was visible in Amos Vogel's tumescent claim, in *Film as a Subversive Art*, that the filmic revelation of orgasm, which he calls "the only ecstatic experience left to man [sic]—a moment of total self-surrender by dissolution into the beloved and therefore into the world," would in effect overthrow "the final visual taboo."[29] While pertinent in an era when erotic imagery was repressed and forced underground, the present-day massive availability of orgasmic representations makes Vogel's faith in the subversive power of the making visible of the orgasm seem extraordinarily outdated and naïvely phallocentric.

If we were to reformulate the real taboo, however, as being not on orgasm or even sexuality per se but rather on open, free, and equal sexuality enjoyed by loving partners in an atmosphere of laughing and caring collectivity, without puritanical taboos or capitalist–productivist performance anxiety, and without any over-determining cash-nexus, Vogel's claim might perhaps be more persuasive. Such representations (and practices) might express a contagious playfulness that betokens, and helps fashion, a non-productivist transindividual pleasure bathed in mutual respect, where sexuality is inseparable from intimacy and community. Any number of films, in this sense, have treated sexuality creatively and honestly in many of its dimensions. One thinks of the yearnings of the separated couple in Vigo's *L'Atalante*; the carceral homo-eroticism of Genet's *Chant d'Amour*; the domestic–oceanic couplings of *Fuses*; the ludic bisexual romps of Broughton's *The Bed*; the self-mocking lesbian correctness of *Go Fish*; the carnivalesque mayhem of Zee Cockettes in *Tricia's Wedding*;

and the Reichian gambols of *WR: Mysteries of the Organism*. Such films suggest that is possible to present sexuality in all its multi-faceted richness of feeling and meaning, at once as naughty as sin and as innocent as the games of children; as inevitable as hunger and as necessary as food; as tragic as loss and as comic as a giggle; and as ethical as friendship and as spiritual as a whirling dervish.

Fleeing **erotophobia**, some feminists have full-throatedly embraced egalitarian forms of eros and the *bodily lower stratum*. Lauren Berlant warns against the erotophobic attitude that sees sex "as a threat to happiness, thinking of the appetites as a threat to sociality, when there is no sociality without them."[30] In this sense, such work resonates with Bakhtin, who, while hardly a feminist, does at least celebrate the self-differentiating body, the bowels, the belly, the gaping mouth, and the anus—corporeal zones where the male–female binary becomes non-pertinent. Carol Schneemann, who attributed her feminism to a reading of de Beauvoir's *The Second Sex*, celebrated her own couplings in *Fuses* (1967). Within an avant-garde aesthetic of frenetic superimpositions simultaneously evoking fireworks, surf, electricity, and the oceanic fusion of selves, Scheemann turned eroticized bodies, in her words, into "tactile sensation of flickers."[31] Orgasms explode constantly in the film, not as overriding telos but rather as part of a quotidian domesticity, where ejaculation and moistening become less performative goal than currents in a general flow. By painting, scratching, and dying the celluloid, Schneeman calls attention to the physicality both of film and of love, revealing both to be layered, tactile, multi-sensorial, and synaesthetic. Scheemann unabashedly places her own body center-frame, making a "gift of [her] body to other women."[32]

The proud display of her own nakedness, in Scheemann's words, was meant to break "the taboos against the vitality of the naked body in movement, to eroticize my guilt-ridden culture, and further to confound this culture's sexual rigidities—that the life of the body is more *variously* expressive than a sex-negative society can admit."[33] Schneemann's film, as Ruby Rich puts it, is "devastatingly erotic, transcending the surfaces of sex to communicate its true spirit, its meaning as an activity for herself, and … for women in general."[34] The film constitutes what David James calls "a new copulation between the filmic and the erotic … in which female sexuality is enacted as a practice of mutuality," all filmed from the perspective of the couple's cat Kitch, or what James punningly calls the "pussy's point of view."[35] In the film's "own eroticism, its autoeroticism, its skin is slipped upon the celluloid, displaced from the closure of mimetic identification and freed from the economy of its syntax, suddenly a tactile material, palpably aroused."[36] Decades later, pro-porn artists and scholars such as Susie Bright, Candid Royalle, Mireille-Miller-Young, Laura Kipnis, Lisa Duggan, Kate Ellis, Carol Vance, Constance Penley, Annie Sprinkle, and Nina Hartley continued to defend eros and the pulsating body against the puritanical hysteria of the Christian right and the Women against Pornography movement.[37]

Bakhtin's theory of laughter accords well with what Ruby Rich calls **"Medusan" feminist films**. Rich takes the term from Helene Cixous' "Laugh of the Medusa," where the French theorist celebrates the potential of feminist texts to "blow up the law, to break up 'the truth' with laughter."[38] Lizzie Borden's *Born in Flames*, Nelly Kaplan's *A Very Curious Girl*, and Ana Carolina's *Mar de Rosas* can all be seen as mischievous Medusan films that direct mocking laughter against what Luce Iragaray calls *"l'esprit de serieux"* of phallocentrism. *Tricia's Wedding*, performed by the gay transvestite group "Cockettes," meanwhile, portrays Richard Nixon as a closeted homophobic macho who makes a pass at a Mick Jagger look-alike. The perennial tropes of carnival—transvestitism, comic crownings, and uncrownings—are deployed in a campy attack on the sexual and political repression underlying Nixon's law-and-order discourse.

What Genevieve Yue calls **Medusan optics** take the Medusa myth, wherein Medusa, the gorgon whose terrible gaze turns anyone she sees into stone, as a lens or optic through which gender, vision, and the production of images can be viewed. *Medusan* optics, for Yue, conjure up the dangers and desires critical to the Medusa myth, tracing the power of the irresistible look, Medusa's violent beheading by Perseus, and the forbidden image of a woman who at once constitutes and stands apart from her own image. In this way, *Medusan optics* are invested with almost mystical power, from the *fascinum* of the evil eye as described by Jacques Lacan to the *curiositas* of spectacle discussed by Tom Gunning.[39] Yet, *Medusan optics* are not bound to cultural histories of the Medusa myth or, indeed, ancient Greek mythology, nor are they restricted to specific genres, forms, or production contexts. Because they offer a *mode* of viewing moving images, rather than a *type* of image, *Medusan optics* can be deployed to critically interrogate instances where the figures of women, and the violence done against them, are linked to the terrible and alluring power of the medium itself.[40]

John Cameron Mitchell's *Shortbus* (2006), for its part, stages what Linda Williams calls a **pornotopia**. The Shortbus Club becomes the site of **polymorphous perversity**—Freud's term, further elaborated by Wilhelm Reich, to refer to the human capacity to seek sexual gratification outside of socially normative sexual behaviors. Actual rather than simulated, the film's sexuality is what Linda Williams calls **"on/scene"** as opposed to "obscene" or off-stage. The film also instantiates Bakhtin's account of carnival as erasing the barrier between private and public. The film's infinite permutations of sexual connectivities, as Michael O'Rourke and Karin Selberg point out, constitute what Erin Manning, in the context of the shifting relations between sensation and thought in the body in movement in dance, calls **relationscapes**, in this case one "of tangled, rotating, and recombinative bodies...."[41]

Mitchell's Sodomite *Kama Sutra* is saturated with liquidity, as men perform self-fellatio, urinate in the bathtub, ejaculate on their own faces, and project their sperm, in a joke on action painting, on the drippings of Jackson Pollock-style paintings. "Queer-friendly but not queer-exclusive" (Williams), *Shortbus* has its orgiasts perform daisy-chain sex while singing the national anthem into a participant's anus, with everyone collapsing into giggles at the end. The digital "camera" emerges from the nose of the Statue of Liberty to fly through an animated brightly colored Manhattan to peek in, à la *Mondo Cane*, on a cast of characters in what Williams calls "in medias sex." As Damon Young points out, the film's utopia is somewhat compromised by an American exceptionalism that "aligns the spectator's view with the statue's look." The illuminist symbol of Enlightenment Republicanism orients the whole enterprise, as Sofia's long-deferred orgasm relights the torch of Lady Liberty, in a film that is haunted "from beginning to end" by images of Ground Zero and the War on Terror.[42] *Shortbus* also falls short of Bakhtin's popular carnival in the upscale character of the club, in the impeccably buff normative beauty of the performers, and in the focus on the performative telos of the "Big O" of orgasm.

## Stand-up Comedy and Nuclear Catastrophe

While the carnivalesque often expresses itself through playful parody, it can also take the more angry form of **satire**, classically defined as exaggeration to prove a point. In the eighteenth century, Jonathon Swift created satiric versions of a popular genre of his time, that is, the **"modest proposals"** or scientistic schemes for social progress. Swift's specific modest proposal was for the devouring of Irish children as a "rational" response to the Irish famine, as a way to kill two birds with one stone by (a) reducing the numbers of the Irish poor, and by (b) feeding the rich with the well-spiced buttocks of Irish street urchins. One episode of Michael Moore's *Awful Truth*, actually entitled "*modest proposals*" in direct homage to Swift, offered "private-sector solutions" for the public problem of homelessness in New York City. The episode proposed turning Manhattan Mini-Storage boxes—"safer and bigger than any New York City shelter"—into "homes" for the homeless, offering the "benefits" of cardboard protection, climate control, central Manhattan location, nearness to subways, and low price (US$3/month).

Satire deploys **strategic hyperbole** to skewer the powerful. And who exercised more raw power than the titans of nuclear war, those sovereigns who could potentially reduce the entire world to a condition of death, or at best *bare life*, Agamben's term for a minimal, merely biological existence? In 1964, at the very height of the Cold War, Stanley Kubrick's *Dr. Strangelove or: How I Stopped Worrying and Learned to Love the Bomb* (referenced as *Dr. Strangelove* from this point forth) adapted Peter George's suspense-thriller *Red Alert*, in which a psychotic general orders B-52s to attack the Soviet Union. On one level, an **apocalyptic tragedy** that ends not with just a few corpses as in a Shakespearean play, but rather with the entire world as a funeral pyre, *Dr. Strangelove* on another level qualifies as **Swiftian satire**, a tradition going back to Juvenal in the classical period and Swift in the modern period. Indeed, the film references Swift by having the exuberant bomber-pilot "King Kong" refer to "LaPuta" (Spanish for "whore"), the philosophers' island in *Gulliver's Travels*.

Although the novel treated its subject in a realistic mode, Kubrick decided that absurdist comedy was the only approach adequate to a superpowers arms race whose acronym was MAD (Mutually Assured Destruction) and which threatened to destroy the planet in the name of ideological differences that would later seem as petty and ridiculous as Medieval disputations about the sex of angels. At the time, the subject of nuclear warfare seemed somehow at once real and unreal, impossible and inevitable, leading to a general anaesthetization in the face of a horror that had become anodyne. Kubrick chose to break through that *blocage symbolique* by turning the realistic novel into a dark nightmare comedy. The film's technique of **radical simplification** made the Cold War understandable even to a child by portraying the generals as grossly cartoonish and infantile. Hearing of the other side's brand new "Doomsday Device," one general, similar to a child coveting a neighbor's toy, peevishly whines: "I want one too!" Peter Sellers' Dr. Strangelove character, meanwhile, exemplifies Bergson's theory of comedy as rooted in **automatism** or the reduction of the human to the mechanistic. Strangelove's reflexive Nazi salutes, accompanied by equally automatic "Sic Heils," somatize fascist ideology by inscribing it on the body, reflecting a fascist personality in corporeal–linguistic tics. The very name "Strangelove" came to form the archetype of the nuclear madman, an epithet attached to Cold Warriors such as Henry Kissinger at the time, and to Dick Cheney and the neo-cons later.

In a **psychoanalysis of militarism**, both the title—"*Dr. Strangelove*"— and the self-help-style subtitle—"*or: How I Stopped Worrying and Learned to Love the Bomb*"—articulate the psychosexual with the politico-military, so as to underline a neurotic psychosexual dimension of the Cold War itself. The perversion implied by "Strange Love" is immediately reinforced by the opening images of refueling jets imaged as gigantic birds enjoying sexual congress, all further underlined by the non-diegetic romanticism of an instrumental version of "Try a Little Tenderness." In this space-age twist on love and death, seen as geopolitical *liebestod*, the Cold War is depicted as a co-dependant bipolar relationship between super powers. The two heads of state on the "hotline" argue like two quarrelling love birds, and the generals deploy military language to speak of sex, with "countdown" for foreplay and "takeoff" for orgasm, much as the film's plot proceeds from military foreplay to the "climax" of nuclear explosion. Symbolically castrated in his wheelchair, Dr. Strangelove becomes "erect" with Hitlerian sexual fantasies. In their speculations about the post-nuclear world, the generals fantasize about post-apocalypse underground harems.

Within the satiric tradition, virtually all of the characters have improbably allegorical names redolent of sexual passion and aggression. The Russian premier is named "Kissoff," which, besides sounding Russian and rhyming with "piss off," also implies some sort of kissing competition. "Jack Ripper" references an infamous sexual psychopath, while "Buck Turgidson" is quadruply masculine in its simultaneous evocation of a male deer, a macho man, a blood-swollen male organ, and a male child. For the tumescent Turgidson, war is an aphrodisiac. The name of the US president—"Merken Muffly"—meanwhile, is redundantly feminine, since "Merken" designates a woman's pubic hairs and "Muff" is a colloquial term for the female genitalia.

*Dr. Strangelove* renews satire by dialoguing with a specific homegrown American form of the carnivalesque, an underground mode of sketch comedy variously known as "**sick humor**" or "**black humor**." In the American context, this very Jewish underground current ultimately goes back to carnival-like festivities such as Purim, where the costumed powerless laugh at the powerful, including within the community itself, now mediated through Greenwich Village and Borscht Belt sketch comedy. Incarnated by such figures as Lenny Bruce, Tom Lehrer, Shelley Berman, Stan Freeberg, Mel Brooks, Mike Nichols, and Elaine May, this tradition, especially in its early phase, probed such "touchy" topics as racism, anti-semitism, and nuclear war. In the tradition of carnival's *laughing at death*, the humorist Tom Lehrer performed satirical songs about nuclear destruction, sung in an insouciant sing-along manner.

Within a refurbished **Brechtian cabaret** style, the bitterness of Lehrer's lyrics trouble the hootenanny good cheer of the music. The refrain of one such song consisted of variations on "We'll all go together when we go/every Hottentot and every Eskimo." Another song, delivered in a country and Western hillbilly style, recounted the delights of watching Atomic mushroom clouds rising over Nevada test sites: "Mid the yuccas and the thistles, we'll watch the guided missiles, dropping bombs in the cool, desert air," all climaxing with an ecstatic "yahoo!" anticipatory of Slim Pickins' yelp as he rides the nuclear warhead like a bucking bronco.

In *Dr. Strangelove*, Kubrick borrows specific techniques as well as themes from "*sick comedy*." Many of the stand-up sketches, for example, those of Shelley Berman and Mike Nichols and Elaine May, involved single-voiced or double-voiced telephone conversations. At a time when military and communications technologies were becoming symbiotically interlinked, it is striking that *Dr. Strangelove* proliferates in scenes involving telephones, intercoms, public address systems, and other communication devices. Thus, the abortive communications taking place through diverse media become an uncannily apt metaphor in a story where the slightest *mis*communication could easily entail nuclear disaster.

Made at a time when the US power elite was mobilizing paranoia to buttress a political system dominated by what Eisenhower called the "military–industrial complex," *Dr. Strangelove* targets paranoia itself as satiric object. Rather than stoke panic, *Dr. Strangelove* transmutes fear and pain into artistic pleasure and social awareness. The film copes with existential fear through **apocalyptic hilarity**—the artistic exorcism of that very same fear, in a caustically comic version of the catharses of classical tragedy. Bakhtin's Carnival, we recall, took place against the backdrop of real plague and eschatological anxiety, forming a symbolic victory over cosmic terror and pious paranoia. *Dr. Strangelove*, in this sense, gives artistic shape to a shared nightmare, telling us that we are not alone in being afraid, or in thinking that our "leaders" are crazy. At the same time, the film conjures away existential panic by turning powerful villains into objects of derision. Almost two decades later, the documentary *The Atomic Café* filtered the satirical spirit of *Dr. Strangelove* through strategies of *media jujitsu* by using public service films to expose the inadvertently sick humor of government recommendations that young pupils simply "duck and cover" under their desks to avoid the effects of radiation.

## Contemporary Fools

Many present-day comedians have carried on the tradition of sick humor in what amounts to a renaissance of political satire. In "Forms of Times and the Chronotope," Bakhtin speaks of the "time-honored bluntness of fools" who create their own special **chronotope**. The fool's masks, for Bakhtin, "grant the right not to understand, the right to confuse, to tease, to hyperbolize life; the right to parody others while talking, the right to not be taken literally, not 'to be oneself'… and the right to rage at others with a primeval (almost cultic) rage…."[43] Bakhtin's words perfectly describe Steven Colbert as a pre-eminent example of **the contemporary fool**.

Closely related to the *fool* is the *faux* **naïf**, a figure going at least as far back as Cervantes' Don Quixote, who takes chivalric romances for gospel truth, and Voltaire's philosophical fable *Candide*, where the titular character takes literally Leibniz's notion that we live in "the best of all possible worlds." As a *faux naïf* blinded by his ideological *idees fixes*, Colbert pretends not to realize that the audience is laughing at *him*! Colbert's left-inclined audience—whom he allegorically addresses as "nation"— serves as an in-studio Greek chorus. They voice the tacit norms that regulate the performance, the truth that goes counter to Colbert's nonsensical pronouncements; their laughter plays the role of **episteme** (knowledge) against his **doxa** (opinion). Colbert's interactions with congressional figures, meanwhile, display the fool's capacity to confuse, to tease, "hyperbolize," and to "parody others while talking." Through quick-witted sophistry, Colbert "proves," for example, that Eleanor Holmes Norton, as an official representative of Washington, DC, is not from the United States, since Washington, DC is "not a state."

Colbert's skewering of President Bush at the April 2006 White House "Roast" cut even more deeply. The Roast, usually an **ersatz carnival**, an innocuous ritual of merely apparent social inversion, where comedians make fun of a president's mannerisms but not of his politics, became in this instance the scene of high-risk drama. As court jester in a warmongering time, Colbert spoke truth in the literal face of power, all in the guise of ironic praise for "my hero, George W. Bush." Colbert ridiculed Bush's penchant for strong assertions of belief by emptying his firmly held beliefs of all substance. In a kind of imbecile's credo presented with passionate intensity, Colbert dramatically declares: "I believe in America." But he follows that declaration with empty trivialities. "I believe [America] exists. My gut tells me that I live there… and I strongly believe it has 50 states." Then Colbert mocked the public relations construction of Bush as a courageous man who "takes a stand" by playing with the word "stand" itself: "I stand by this man. I stand by this man because he stands for things. Not only for things, he stands *on* things. Things like aircraft carriers and rubble and recently flooded city squares," all of which shows that America will respond to disaster with the "best photo-ops in the world." But Colbert reserved his most cutting barbs for the media by suggesting that they should be even *more* servile to power:

> Let's review the rules. Here's how it works: the president makes the decisions. He's the decider. The press secretary announces those decisions, and you people of the press type those decisions down… Just put 'em through a spell check and go home… Write that novel you've got kicking around in your head. You know, the one about the intrepid Washington reporter with the courage to stand up to the administration. You know—fiction!

It was all as if a digital camera had recorded a Shakespearean fool in the act of mocking both the self-deluded king and his obsequious courtiers. But while Elizabethan fools addressed only those present in the court, Colbert's **YouTube Fool**, initially ignored by the very media whose cowardice he had mocked, subsequently went viral to become one of YouTube's biggest hits, seen by millions of people, to the point that a website called "Thank You Stephen Colbert" logged tens of thousands of "thank you's." What was usually a hollow ritual became the site of edgy hilarity, a symbolic crowning and uncrowning of the powers that be, as Colbert cut through the heavy atmosphere of pious obeisance cultivated by the new monarchs.

The performances of Colbert build on the subversive protocols of earlier performers in the avant-garde tradition. A key figure, in this sense, is the avant-garde performance artist (and philosopher) Adrian Piper. While hardly comic in her approach, Piper too fashioned provocative personae who triggered socially revelatory responses. In what Piper's exegete John Bowles calls Piper's **"self-aware performance of stereotypes,"** Piper "sets the stage for her audience to expose their own insecurities."[44] Her basic strategy is summed up in the title of one of her series—**Catalysis** (1970–1973)—in that her **catalytic performance** of self-transformation into a "Third World man" or a "foul-smelling homeless young woman" is designed to catalyze socially symptomatic reactions to her partially permutated persona as a "gendered and ethnically stereotyped art commodity."[45] In these unframed performances, Piper became a trigger-mechanism for the prejudices of an art world where the gatekeepers were almost invariably white and male. In "The Mythic Being: I/You(Her)," Piper darkened her skin, donned sunglasses, and sported an Afro in order to incarnate white America's deepest fear—the African-American male. Piper describes her street performance: "I swagger, I stride, lope, lower my eyebrows, raise my shoulders, sit with my legs wide apart on the subway so as to accommodate my protruding genitalia."[46] The neurotically phantasmatic character of the panicked reaction to her persona was even more markedly irrational, given that Piper is herself not only a woman but also rather petite and even frail in appearance.

Decades after Piper's intervention, *The Couple in the Cage* (1993), by Coco Fusco and Guillhermo Gomez Pena, demonstrated the possibilities of **performance hoax as ideological Rorschack**. Made as part of the anti-quincentennial protests against Columbus, the film tells the story of a performance by the two authors, a satire of the tradition of colonial expositions, where the pair posed as "recently discovered natives" from an hitherto unknown Caribbean island. Dressed in *Gilligan's Island* skirts, the pseudo-aboriginal couple watched TV while speaking gibberish that mingled Spanglish, pseudo-native languages, and Japanese brand names. (A plaque affixed to the cage explained the allusion to colonial expositions.) In the end, the film is less about the performance itself than about the varied *reactions* to the performance. Some got the joke, whereas others took the spoof at face values; some liberals protested the caging of the natives, while some conservatives found proof of the savagery of people of color. The goal was to provoke the audience into an awareness of its own investment in such primitivist images. But as the artists themselves acknowledged, they underestimated the sheer inertia of the colonialist imaginary as the spectacle was often not understood in the sense they intended.[47]

The films and performances of Sasha Baron Cohen offer a more politically ambiguous variation on *catalytic performance*, most notably in his fictional characters such as the rapper Ali G, the Kazakh patriot Borat, and the flamboyant fashion reporter Bruno. Although the Ali G character resembles the Colbert persona, in that Cohen plays idiotic characters who interact with people unaware that they are being set up, in the case of the Borat and Bruno characters, the *faux naïf* provokes the truly naïve into simply funny or, in some instances, racist, sexist, and homophobic responses. Cohen's Borat character, featured in both HBO's *Da Ali G Show* and Larry Charles's *Borat: Cultural Learnings of America for Make Benefit Glorious Nation of Kazakhstan* (2006), uses scatological humor to score racism. Troels Degn Johansson labels Cohen's comic guerilla tactics, in which the comic as scam artist ambushes clueless celebrities or people in the street, "a perfect example of "**the performative tactics of failure**."[48] What this means in practice is that the Jewish Cohen performs a sort of ritual self-abnegation (perhaps close to Kristeva's status of the "**abject**") in the form of the persona of a racist anti-Semite. This persona, tied to the chameleon-like motivations of a media trickster who has his eye simultaneously on the box office and on his satirical targets, both endears and offends, since Cohen's satire hits its target with a centripetal force whose impact is difficult to calibrate in advance.

Some viewers have found Cohen's mockery of Kazakhs and Kazakhstan "anti-Islamic," and his play with anti-Jewish stereotypes "anti-Semitic." Cohen practices what might be called **buckshot critique**, that is, a social assault that bags legitimate satiric prey while also spraying completely innocent victims as collateral damage. The Borat ruse forces viewers to accept "politically incorrect" slapstick alongside more "progressive" pranks, with the two strands disconcertingly co-mingled in any single piece of Cohen *shtick*, a modus operandi both brilliant and perverse. One *Ali G. Show* skit—Borat as an aspiring country singer sharing his priceless ditty "Throw the Jew Down the Well" with a receptive audience—seems targeted at the patrons' obliviousness to casual anti-Semitism. Less straightforwardly, a scene from *Borat* that highlights the mock-journalist's effort to infiltrate an elite dinner of Southern WASPs is dizzyingly scattershot from an ideological perspective. Borat's delight in proudly presenting his feces to his hosts pays homage to the *bodily lower stratum*, while his bringing an African-American prostitute to the event scandalized his implicitly racist hosts but also struck some as a gratuitous nod to a racist and sexist stereotype.

Thumbing his nose at civility is both Cohen's cash cow and his opportunity to puncture selected pretensions, a stance that straddles conformism and sporadic subversiveness. What is perhaps most productive for subversive aesthetics is his device of deliberately provoking **socially symptomatic behavior**. The hysterical reaction of the wrestling fans to staged homosexual lovemaking in *Bruno*, for example, reveals homophobic panic in all its irrational horror. Wrestling offers the titanic struggle of two secret-sharers in love with one another. The anguished howls of execration provoked by the performative revelation of the secret code of wrestling also illustrates Rene Girard's analysis of the primordial role of the scapegoat, hated for its putative horrendousness, but loved for its socially unifying function.[49] Cohen's spoof reveals the great unsaid of wrestling—its encoding of male homosocial desire. Henry Jenkins calls WWF wrestling a form of **masculine melodrama**— a genre that had the function of provoking emotional release. Jenkins cites Norbert Elias and Eric Dunning's classic study *The Quest for Excitement: Sports and Leisure in the Civilizing Process* as evidence of sports as a social institution that produces and elicits affective excitement. As Jenkins puts it: "Melodrama allows for the shedding of tears, while sports solicit shouts, cheers, and boos."[50]

The hysterical reaction of the "patriots" to Borat's pro-Kazakhstan version of the American national anthem, similarly, exposes the irrational pathos undergirding chauvinistic nationalism. The real butt of the joke in *Borat* is less Kazakhstan than American racist super-patriotism. In this sense, Borat's singing at a rodeo of a pro- Kazakhstan anthem to the tune of the Star-Spangled Banner provokes the xenophobic audience into a righteous frenzy, acted out in a crude and libidinal form reminiscent of the bloodlust of lynch mobs and tar-and-feathering parties. Setting aside the complex ethical and even legal questions raised by such tactics, they have the salutary effect of showcasing the pathologies of prejudice in all their grotesqueries.[51]

## Pedagogic Humor and Provocation

Another major purveyor of carnivalesque vulgarity is Michael Moore. Despite his achievement of winning a vast audience for left documentaries, a certain left both loves and feels superior to Moore; he is often seen as "in excess," as "too much"—too slovenly, too working class, too unsubtle, and too fat (similar to the obese Rei Momos of Brazil's carnival). Although dismissed by some as "Jackass for Lefties," Moore's broad appeal to a mainstream audience partly derives from his unkempt, hamburger-eating, baseball-cap-wearing Americanness. As the shuffling, potbellied embodiment of the working-class, a distilled quintessence of Midwestern normalcy, he is the very antithesis of the right-wing bogeyman—the effete latte-sipping liberal. The standard complaints about Moore's "narcissism" really constitute a kind of *genre mistake*, where the critic judges an artistic text according to generically inappropriate categories. The presence of Moore's ungainly body in the frame is not a testament to vanity, but rather the index of a **self-staging author** (Cecilia Sayad) whose artfully fashioned persona (at least in some of his films) is that of the hapless everyperson seeking honest answers from the systematically mendacious.[52] This clueless Quixote imagines that he can persuade a Nazi/Aryan/Klan encampment to abandon racism if only a multi-racial cohort of balloon-wielding dancers will blow them kisses while singing "Stop in the Name of Love."

As an artist and persona, Michael Moore is multiple: part *faux naïf*, part portly lord of misrule, part agit-prop provocateur, part stand-up comic, part moralist, and part satirist. In his early films, Moore plays the role of an information-challenged bumpkin trying to get corporations to stop abusing the populace. Moore's ludic provocations are more than mere pranks, however. Apart from the fact that his pranks sometimes win concrete results, they also have a conceptual basis. Moore's **satiric vignettes** cut through the corporate idolatry that passes for political wisdom in the US media, capturing the malignancies of global capitalism and the dumb inertia of the comatose American political system. Moving beyond the usual defensive apologetics of the Democratic Party, Moore takes the offensive by turning everything upside down. His work offers one corrective to a failure of the reformist left to creatively shape narratives that clarify the oppressive nature of capitalism as a system. Satirists such as Moore rush into the vacuum left by mainstream liberals who shy away from challenging neoliberal dogma because they are themselves complicitous with it. He couples his critique with celebration through what Tom Moylan calls **critical utopias**—social utopias based not on scientific blueprints but rather as emerging out of the negativities and dissatisfactions of capitalist life—by delineating the contours of another possible world.[53] Moore carnivalizes right-wing power while also proposing a **counter-utopia** in the name of a collective dream. Going against the grain of a certain left-wing rationalism, Moore at times makes an unabashed appeal to emotion, not in the name of sentimentality and facile affect but rather in hopes of touching on socially generated emotions of outrage and sympathy, anger and love.

Just as Quixote embraced the romantic fictions of chivalric literature, Moore's *faux naïf* of *Roger and Me* pretends to take capitalism's self-advertising literally, really and truly believing that corporations are what the commercials say they are: warm and fuzzy, empathetic, virtually human social ensembles that "care about you." Within the feudal logic of "if the king only knew" (about nobility's outrageous abuse of the peasants), Moore's naïve persona, at least in early films such as *Roger and Me*, pretends to believe that the contemporary nobility known as CEOS will stop abuses against workers once they are informed about them. Moore plays the putative ignoramus who thinks that he really can convince General Motors CEO Roger Smith to help foreclosed former workers. He feigns surprise when corporate flacks refuse to let him film his exposés inside of corporate headquarters. Within the larger goal of **satiric didacticism**, the real point is not the naiveté of the persona, but rather the process of **disalienation** of the spectators themselves.

For Jacques Rancière, radical politics calls for a new **theatricality** that refuses the existing distribution of roles and of the goods of the commons, within a new dramaturgy where new social actors, performing on a redesigned public stage, recast their own role in order to have equal participation in the commons. In this sense, Moore's films can be seen as one intermittently successful attempt to forge an activist dramaturgy. Many episodes from Moore's *The Awful Truth* and *TV Nation* model a mischievous politics that he calls **slacktivism** or lazy activism. *Slacktivism* again revives the spirit of Melville's Bartleby, the scrivener who "prefers not to" collaborate with the boss's demands, but moves from passive resentment to active resistance. (One wonders whether a contemporary Bartleby, who after all worked on Wall Street, would have joined the Occupy Movement.)

Eschewing the sobriety of many left documentaries, Moore's festive **social entertainments** combine raw and righteous anger at corporate or congressional malfeasance with the unbridled joy of choreographed group performance. One sketch features a merry band of pranksters called the "gay freedom riders"—a queer reincarnation of Ken Kesey's "Merry Pranksters"—stalking the homophobic pastor Fred W. Phelps. A pink "sodomobile" carrying a bevy of orgiasts zigzags across the Midwest with the express purpose of violating all the laws of the various states where homosexuality is illegal. As the bus bucks back and forth thanks to ardent sexual rocking and rolling, its side poster reads "Sodom is for lovers" and "Buggery on Board." Moore's vehicle "cruises" through the Midwest, in an automotive embodiment of what Jose Munoz calls a **cruising utopia**.[54] Moore literally mobilizes an activist citizenry in ways that invoke historical currents of solidarity, in that the very name of the troupe as "gay freedom riders" projects the gay liberation movement as a logical extension of the black liberation movement.[55]

Subversive cinema often plays with various modalities of the **counterfactual**. While the **dystopian counterfactual** hyperbolizes the pathologies of the cynical ethos promoted by global capitalism, the **utopian counterfactual** prods us to imagine more generous alternative social arrangements. Both the utopian and the dystopian can serve subversive purposes. A portrayal of the New York subway as the site of Darwinist slaughter in the name of greed evokes one possible outcome of contemporary urban trends, while portrayal as a singing, dancing *communitas* suggests a carnival of gregarious equality. The activist performances of the Yes Men—the activist team and its network of supporters created by Jacques Servin and Igor Vamos (real names?)—in this sense, practice subversive permutations of the counterfactual. If corporations are people, then artists certainly have the right to impersonate them. The "Yes Men" have perfected this practice through what Amer Day calls **identity nabbings**, that is, they actually impersonate, if not corporations, at least their human avatars by becoming fictitious spokesmen for the World Trade Organization (WTO), McDonalds, and the Dow Chemical Company.[56] Carrying subversion to dizzying and legally hazardous heights, the Yes Men create fake corporate websites in order to get themselves invited to appear in the media as CEOs. In their **anti-corporate purimspiels**, they mock the oppressive contemporary Hamans, "infiltrating" what Rancière calls "the networks of domination."[57]

Success in the contemporary corporate world, as Richard Sennett has pointed out, has less to do with performance on the job than with performance of the self; executives practice a kind of "deep acting."[58] By re-appropriating the dress-codes, manners, and discourses of corporate "suits," the Yes Men deploy a non-canonical form of method acting in the service of the **dramatization of corporate villainy**. Two films, *The Yes Men* and *The Yes Men Fix the World*, showcase Mike Bonanno and Andy Bichlbaum (invented names) as imposter delegates who go into the very belly of the corporate beast to make outrageous (and even murderous) "modest proposals" at business conferences and WTO meetings— proposals that, similar to Swift's, are sometimes taken at face value. No matter how repellant—Big Macs made out of recycled human feces, or foul-smelling candles purportedly made from decaying human flesh (actually animal flesh)—no idea strikes the business people as out-of-bounds, as long as a profit is to be made. For a WTO convention, the pair presents a futuristic gold "management leisure suit" meant to solve two challenges for transnational corporations—(1) keeping track of workers in faraway places; and (2) increasing leisure time for the overworked executive class. The suit opens to reveal a giant golden phallus—a kind of **corporate-penile ambulatory panopticon**—whose tip bears the "Employer's Visualization Appendage" thanks to which the CEO can monitor Global South workers (shown through archival footage) even while jogging or hiking in the Alps. The reaction of the attendees is not shock but polite applause and a mechanical "thank you" for "the very interesting talk," which leaves the Yes Men wondering if "there is anything that the corporate world cannot get away with."

In a **Swiftian spoof** of Ayn Randian survivalism, the Yes Men also modeled an inflatable "Survivaball," a self-contained personal living system for the post-apocalyptic businessman trying to survive global warming. Many in the corporate audience were intrigued, rather than horrified, at the idea. The group's "vivoleum project," meanwhile, promised to keep fuel flowing by transforming the corpses of the victims of oil-based calamities into crude oil. In their most notorious prank, the corporate mimic Jacques Servin appeared on BBC News as "Finisterra" (etymologically, "end of the world")—invited as an official representative of Union Carbide—and announced that the corporation, notorious for its artful dodging of all legal responsibility, had decided to fully compensate, to the tune of billions of dollars, the victims of the poisonous explosion at the (formerly Dow Chemical-owned) gas plant in Bhopal, India. The explosion killed over 2,000 people and left hundreds of thousands in danger of blindness and kidney failure. The "news" of massive compensation sparked a dramatic downturn in the value of Union Carbide Stock and reminded the world of a man-made catastrophe that the corporation had hoped everyone would forget. Eventually accused of lying, the Yes Men, in a nod to Platonic idealism, protested that they had given a completely accurate representation of what the corporation "*should* have done." Addressing dystopian abuses through utopian declarations, the Yes Men simply declare their utopias as established fact, such as when they published and distributed perfect simulacral copies of *The New York Times*, announcing all the (counterfactual) news "fit to print": the end of the Iraq War, George Bush's prosecution for treason, and the establishment of National Health Care.

## Tropes of Social Inversion

A number of carnivalesque films turn the social world upside down through **historical inversion**. Don Featherstone's *Babakiueria*, for example, upends Euro-Australian discourses, policies, and media representations of Aborigines in Australia. Framed as Aboriginal TV reportage, *Babakiueria* has an indigenous woman reporter initiate the spectator into the "strange culture" of whites. Mingling anthropological and social-welfare discourses of "typicality," she introduces us to a "typical white family," residing in a "typical white house," in a "typical white ghetto," practicing "typical white rituals," and exhibiting a typically white "predilection for violence" (evidenced by clips of soccer brawls). Seen through an Aboriginal grid, Euro-Australian customs are estranged, as colonial practices formerly applied to Aborigines (the denial of self-representation, forced adoptions, and relocation programs) are now applied to whites under the guidance of the "Ministry of White Affairs." Euro-Australian representations of Aborigines boomerang against their perpetrators.

Through a similar kind of jujitsu, black artists such as Spike Lee and Marlon Riggs have deployed stereotypes, and even minstrelsy, to black advantage. Racial stereotypes were, of course, central to the traditional minstrel shows, where (usually white) men blacked up their faces and wore fright wigs while performing a caricatural version of blackness. In the United States, the practice has often provoked protest. Spike Lee's *Bamboozled* (2000) inflates stereotypes to comically grotesque proportions, so that the audience has to confront them directly. Satirically exposing the process of production of the stereotype, the film jujitsus blackface, as it were, into a denunciation of exploitation and internalized colonialism in the entertainment industry, In Alessandra Raengo's words, *Bamboozled* "deploys blackface as a hermeneutics of the surface and a way to facialize the commodity form."[59] The racist memorabilia that crowd the film constitute **second-degree stereotypes**, where the referent is not the human subject but rather the stereotype itself in reified form.

Shifting our attention to Brazil, we find both carnivalization and *social inversion* in the Gilberto Gil music video of "Mao de Limpeza" ("Hand of Cleanliness"). As a cultural figure—at once pop star, intellectual, activist, and former minister of culture—Gil has enjoyed a special relation to Brazilian carnival, in that he frequently participates in and has written songs about Bahia's carnival Afro-blocos such as the "Sons of Gandhi," named in homage to the Indian anticolonialist pacifist. Carnival, for Gil, constitutes an "assured accomplishment of Brazilian blacks" and "a maximum point of the aesthetic agglutination of the forces of celebration."[60] In the video of "Hand of Cleanliness," Gil resignifies what would usually be seen as the irredeemably racist performance mode of blackface through **subversive deployment of the stereotype**. As performed by Gilberto Gil and Chico Buarque de Holanda in a music video, the lyrics of Gil's song "Hand of Cleanliness" satirically upend a racist Brazilian proverb to the effect that black people always screw up: "They say that when blacks don't make a mess at the entrance/They make it at the exit." But Gil's lyrics contradict and "interrupt" this piece of racial doxa: "Imagine! The slave mother spent her life/Cleaning up the mess that whites made!" Even after slavery was abolished, Gil points out, blacks continued cleaning clothes and scrubbing floors: "How the blacks worked and suffered!" The lyrics then go beyond labor and suffering to invert the trope of dirtiness classically wielded by racists against blacks:

> Black is the hand of cleanliness
> Of life consumed at the side of the stove
> Black is the hand that puts food on the table
> And cleans with soap and water
> Black is the hand of immaculate purity

The song concludes with a complete inversion of the trope of Black dirtiness:

> What a damned lie! Look at the dirty white guy!

"Hand of Cleanliness" exemplifies what W. T. Lhamon Jr. calls "**optic black**," the strategy that "acknowledges and works through stereotypic effects, usually turning them *inside out*."[61] Stated differently, Gil's song provokes a Brechtian *alienation-effect* (*verfremdungseffekt*); it makes strange the doxa of racist commonsense, asking us to imagine how anyone could ever have associated blackness with dirtiness! The visuals further complexify the meaning of the lyrics. The phenotypically white singer Chico Buarque appears in blackface and is dressed in black, while Gilberto Gil appears in whiteface and is dressed in white. "Hand of Cleanliness" reconfigures the usually white-dominant representational practice by counterpointing black-face with whiteface. Historically, blackface was unilateral—there was no whiteface—and white spectators often took the representation as "authentic." But here the choice of performance mode comes not from racist white media entrepreneurs, but from the black artist himself. In a sly Brazilian rewrite of the costumed inversions of Genet's *Les Noirs*, the song overturns the equation of blackness with dirtiness; blackness now connotes immaculate purity, while whiteness connotes the dirtiness of the *branco sujao* (dirty white guy). While the *mise-en-scène* underlines an apparently black/white schema, the performance itself implies the transcendence of that schema. As they dance together, the two singers are obviously friends playing at a kind of carnival—in fact, they can barely restrain their laughter—and having a splendid time. The racism of the proverb does not mean that whites and blacks cannot be friends or fight together against racism.

## Offside Cinema

Sport is often a trigger for carnival-like activities and what one sociologist of sport calls "Saturnalia-like occasions for the uninhibited expression of emotions which are tightly controlled in our ordinary lives."[62] Although the case of "monkey taunts" against black players, rooted in centuries of colonial simianization of black people, reveals sports' potentially dystopian side, sports spectatorship can display a more positive side as well. Ever since the 1979 Islamic Revolution in Iran, women have been forbidden from watching "the beautiful game" of soccer in Teheran's Azadi (Freedom) Stadium. For sheer love of the game, Tehran's female fans have corseted their bosoms, hidden their long flowing locks, and masqueraded as men in order to root for their favorite teams and players. In November 1997, Iran's victory against Australia enabled it to advance to the World Cup for the first time since the Islamic Revolution. After the victory, the streets of Tehran became the site of carnivalesque revelry as women threw off the *hijab* and partied in mixed company. When the team returned to Iran, thousands of women went to the Azadi Stadium to join in the celebration. Refused admission, they chanted: "Aren't we part of the nation? We want to celebrate too!"

Jafar Panahi's 2006 film *Offside* transgresses literal and imaginary lines, and in this sense constitutes an example of **offside cinema**, by analogy to the "offside" rules in soccer. The context of production of the film matched the situation portrayed in the film, in that Panahi, similar to the women in the film, also had to do an "end run" around the authorities. One of the most censored of Iranian directors, Panahi used **strategic mendacity** to get the film made, creating a decoy director and a fake synopsis to get past a maze of censorial entities. In a hybrid mix, Panahi used non-professionals as actors in a fictional story filmed during an actual soccer match (with Bahrain in 2005). Partially inspired by his own daughter's request to attend a soccer game, the film accompanies women as they try to sneak into the stadium. Some are caught and placed in an open-air cell on the edges of the stadium, where they can hear the roars of the crowd but not see the game. (There is not a single shot of the playing field in the entire film.) The film sutures us into the women's viewpoint, not only by subjectivizing them through point-of-view shots, but also by leaving the spectators maddeningly unable to see the game. In this sense, the film forces all spectators to suffer from the restrictions on the women. Thus, the laws penalizing the women characters also penalize us as spectators by frustrating our sports scopophilia.

In an **inversion of stereotypes** about the gendered hierarchies of cultural capital, these unruly women know more about soccer than the guards. One rather butch woman sports an army uniform, in implied protest against sexual segregation in the armed forces. The female dialecticians repeatedly demolish their male guardians' arguments in defense of gender segregation. When the guard explains that women are barred from the matches to protect them from vulgar masculine speech, one woman retorts, "We hear all those things at home, we won't listen!" When a guard asks one of the women to cover her eyes to shield herself from the graffiti, she promises, "I won't look." In an aporia of masculinist chivalry, men see themselves as moral lepers, as so filthy-minded that women have to be protected not only *by* men but also *from* men. As the women consistently outwit the men, sexual segregation is revealed as logically—and logistically—indefensible and even unenforceable. The prerogatives of Bakhtin's *bodily lower stratum* actually enable one of the women to evade the guards. Alleging urinary emergency, she insists on being accompanied to the male restroom, while hiding her identity as a woman behind a poster of the face of a soccer star. Once in the men's room, she tricks her guard and slips into the crowd. The literally **leaky body** comes to metaphorize the porosity of social barriers in general. After the victory, the women, in a violation of patriarchal gender etiquette, join in the open-air celebrations in the streets. As a provisional, ephemeral, laughing *communitas*, they actively participate in the carnivalesque takeover of the public sphere.

The meanings of the title—*Offside*—come to ripple outward from the literal denotation of transgressing an invisible yet consequential virtual soccer line to evoking the symbolic transgression of other lines—both visible and invisible, between law and desire, between etiquette and its disruption, between inside and outside, between men and women, and between documentary and fiction. Challenging one invisible line—for example, in relation to gender—subtly impacts all the other lines. Social change along one axis of social stratification such as gender can thus lead to challenges along other axes, such as ethnicity or religion, challenging the various codes that underwrite social hierarchy. A revolution in one site can spread to another, which is why the authorities, aware, in their own upside-down way, of what Kimberlé Crenshaw calls "*intersectionality*," take challenges on any specific axis as a threat on all axes.

Once the film was made, the regime sabotaged its Oscar chances by postponing its Iran release, since Oscar nominee films have to be released first in the home country. In December 2010, the Iranian regime accused Panahi of shooting without permission, of supporting the Green Revolution, and of making propaganda against the system. The director was banned from making films, from traveling abroad, and from giving interviews. Panahi's defiant answer to the ban was a film entitled *This is not a Film* (2011), in the great tradition of **architextual negation**, as exemplified by Diderot ("Ceci n'est pas un conte") and Magritte ("This is not a pipe"). Distributed in France by Kanibal Films, this no-budget celluloid-less digital home movie was technically not a film but rather a self-labeled "effort."

As in *Offside*, Panahi again blurred the borders between inside and outside by sending a home movie to the Cannes Film Festival, famously smuggling the film out of Iran on a USB drive hidden in a cake—reflexive film meets *Rear Window* meets home movie meets *Waiting for Godot*! Confined to his own home, Panahi turned his own house arrest into a microcosmic inside-four-walls **national allegory**. At home, Panahi shows himself surfing the Internet as he turns his own home into a *cinemateque*, exhibiting segments from his own films such as *Crimson Gold* and *The Circle*. Panahi's co-director Moyjaba Mirtahmash reads the film script that Panahi had been forbidden to shoot, a *mise-en-abyme* story about a girl locked up in her home by her parents. Carrying the idea of "art thrives on constraints" to a kind of paroxysm, Panahi offers an object lesson in **iPhone cinema** as a way of thwarting repression and taunting the censors. Ironically, the 4-day shoot coincided with the fireworks marking the Iranian festival *Chaharshambe Suri* that precedes *Nouruz* (Persian New Year). Panahi records the announcement on the news that Ahmedinejad has banned the fireworks and bonfires that usually form part of the festival. Thus, Panahi himself has been declared "offsides" by the regime. In political terms, he had advanced beyond the line, just as the masquerading women were "too forward," as used to be said of women who were just a little too free.

## Notes

1   Barbara Ehrenreich, *Dancing in the Streets: A History of Collective Joy* (New York: Holt, 2009), p. 89.
2   Herbert Marcuse, *The Aesthetic Dimension: Toward a Critique of Marxist Aesthetics* (Boston: Beacon, 1977), p. 72.
3   See Simon Critchley's essay "Comedy and Finitude: Displacing the Tragic-Heroic Paradigm in Philosophy and Psychoanalysis," in *Constellations*, 6(1) (March 1999).
4   Tom Waugh, "Notes on Greyzone," in Brenda Longfellow, Scott MacKenzier, and Thomas Waugh, *The Perils of Pedagogy: The Works of John Greyson* (Montreal: McGill-Queen's University Press, 2013), p. 31.
5   Barbara Ehrenreich, op. cit., p. 261.
6   Ernst Bloch, *The Principle of Hope*, 3 vols (Oxford: Blackwell, 1986).
7   See M. M. Bakhtin, *Problems of Dostoevsky's Poetics*, trans. Caryl Emerson (Minneapolis: University of Minnesota, 1984), pp. 122–123.
8   Thanks to Steve Duncombe for reminding me of this tradition within Christianity.
9   Dan Savage has compiled a list of such parodies: see "Forum: Gays Mocking the Last Supper," at *Prince.org*, available at: <http://prince.org/msg/105/246670?&pg=13>
10  In their *faux* denunciations of a non-existing "war on Christmas," Fox News anchors have insisted that "Jesus was a white man," exemplifying what Ella Shohat has called the pictorial "de-Semitization" of Christ, refashioned as an Aryan, similar to the blue-eyed Robert Powell in Zefferelli's *Jesus of Nazareth*, thus "deemed more appropriate [to represent] a supreme being within a white normative ethos." See Ella Shohat, "Sacred Word, Profane

Image," in Robert Stam and Alessandra Raengo (eds.), *A Companion to Literature and Film* (Oxford: Blackwell, 2008), p. 37.

11    See Tom Moylan's *Demand the Impossible: Science Fiction and the Utopian Imagination* (New York: Methuen, 1986).

12    Lenora Champagne, *French Theatre Experiment Since 1968* (Ann Arbor, University of Michigan Press, 1984), p. 6.

13    Claudia Orenstein, *Festive Revolutions: The Politics of Popular Theater and the San Francisco Mime Troupe* (Jackson: University of Mississippi, 1999), p. 29.

14    Glauber Rocha, *Revolucao do Cinema Novo* (Rio: Embrafilme, 1981).

15    Adrienne Rich, "Reflections on Compulsory Heterosexuality," *Journal of Women's History*, 16 (2004).

16    Stephen Duncombe, *Dream: Re-Imagining Progressive Politics in an Age of Fantasy* (New York: The New Press, 2007), p. 137.

17    Mark Greif, "Drum Circle History and Conflict," *Occupy # 2* (November 19, 2011).

18    Ibid.

19    On these black-led entertainments in antebellum America, see David R. Roediger, *The Wages of Whiteness: Race and the Making of the American Working Class* (London: Verso, 1991).

20    M. M. Bakhtin, *Rabelais and His World* (Cambridge: MIT Press, 1968), p. 317.

21    Damon R. Young discusses "subslime" in his as-yet unpublished dissertation, entitled *Making Sex Public: Cinema and the Liberal Social Body* (PhD dissertation, University of Carolina, Berkeley, 2013). With permission of the author.

22    Geneviève Sellier, *Masculine Singular: French New Wave Cinema* (Durham: Duke University Press, 2008).

23    Sianne Ngai, *Ugly Feelings* (Harvard University Press, 2007), p. 137.

24    Wendy Brown, *States of Injury: Power and Freedom in Late Modernity* (Princeton: Princeton University Press, 1995), p. 38.

25    Kathleen Rowe, *The Unruly Woman: Gender and the Genres of Laughter* (Austin: University of Texas, 1995).

26    As summarized by Ngai, op. cit., p. 310.

27    See Iris Marion Young, *Throwing Like a Girl and Other Essays in Feminist Philosophy and Social Theory* (Bloomington: Indian University Press, 1990), pp. 141–159.

28    See Teresa de Lauretis, *Technologies of Gender: Essays on Theory, Film, and Fiction* (Bloomington: Indiana University Press, 1987).

29    Amos Vogel, *Film as Subversive Art* (New York: D.A.P./C.T. Editions, 2005).

30    March 22, 2013 interview with Lauren Berlant (<http://www.xtra.ca/public/Toronto/Lauren Berlants queer otpimism-13`73.aspx>).

31    Robin Blaetz (ed.), *Women's Experimental Cinema: Critical Frameworks* (Duke University Press Books, 2000), p. 110.

32    Ibid., p. 107.

33    Ibid., p. 108.

34   B. Ruby Rich, *Chick Flicks: Theories and Memories of the Feminist Film Movement* (Durham: Duke University Press Books, 1998), p. 27.

35   David James, op. cit., p. 317.

36   Ibid., p. 320.

37   For an anthology of this work, see Tristan Taormino, Celine Parrenas Shimizu, Constance Penley, and Mireille Miller-Young, *The Feminist Porn Book: the Politics of Producing Pleasure* (New York: The Feminist Press, 2013).

38   See Robert Stam, *Subversive Pleasures: Bakhtin, Cultural Criticism, and Film* (Baltimore: Johns Hopkins, 1989), p. 120.

39   Lacan writes: "The evil eye is the *fascinum*, it is that which has the effect of arresting movement and, literally, of killing life"—*The Four Fundamental Concepts of Psychoanalysis: The Seminar of Jacques Lacan, Book* IX, trans. Alan Sheridan (New York and London: Norton, 1988), p. 118 (emphasis original). Gunning cites Augustine's use of the term *curiositas,* or "the lust of the eyes," which, "in contrast to visual *voluptas* (pleasure) … avoids the beautiful and goes after its exact opposite 'simply because of the lust to find out and to know'"—"An Aesthetic of Astonishment: Early Film and the (In)Credulous Spectator" (1989), in Leo Braudy and Marshall Cohen (eds.), *Film Theory and Criticism*, 6th edition (New York: Oxford University Press, 2004), pp. 862–876, citation on p. 871).

40   See Genevieve Yue, "Medusan Optics: Film, Feminism, and the Forbidden Image" (PhD dissertation, University of Southern California, 2012).

41   Michael O'Rourke and Karin Sellberg, "John Cameron Mitchell's Relationscapes," in *medias res*, January 31, 2011.

42   From Damon R. Young's as-yet-unpublished chapter "Through the Window from *Psycho* to *Shortbus*: Cinema and the Liberal Sexual Subject," part of his dissertation, entitled "Making Sex Public: Cinema and the Liberal Social Body" (PhD dissertation, University of Carolina, Berkeley, 2013). Cited with permission from the author.

43   Stam, *Subversive Pleasures,* p. 113.

44   See John P. Bowles, *Adrian Piper: Race, Gender, and Embodiment* (Durham: Duke University Press, 2011), p. 11.

45   Ibid., p. 35.

46   Piper: "Notes on *The Mythic Being*," quoted in John P. Bowles, op. cit., p. 7.

47   For a Native American critique of the Fusco-Gomez performance, see Jodi A. Byrd's brilliant *The Transit of Empire: Indigenous Critiques of Colonialism* (Minneapolis: University of Minnesota Press, 2011).

48   See Troels Degn Johanssen, "Notes on Failure: Mistakes, Errors, and Failure in the Performative Tactics of Art and Product Design," Presentation, International Association of Societies of Design Research, The Hong Kong Polytechnic University, November 15, 2007. Available at: <http://www.sd.polyu.edu.hk/iasdr/proceeding/papers/>

49   Rene Girard, *La Violence et le Sacré* (Paris: Grasset, 1972). English translation: *Violence and the Sacred*, trans. Patrick Gregory (Baltimore: Johns Hopkins University Press, 1977).

50   Henry Jenkins, *The Wow Climax: Tracing the Emotional Impact of Popular Culture* (New York: New York University Press, 2007), p. 80.

51   John Greyson calls attention to the homoeroticism of another sport—hockey—in a hockey/dance routine in his film *The Making of Monsters* (1991) and through a slow-motion hockey pileup that literally throws the players into each other's arms.

52   See Cecilia Sayad, *Performing Authorship: Self-Inscription, Corporality, and the Cinema* (London: I. B. Tauris, 2013).

53   See Tom Moylan, *Demand the Impossible: Science Fiction and the Utopian Imagination* (London: Methuen, 1986).

54   See Jose Esteban Munoz, *Cruising Utopia: the Then and There of Queer Futurity* (New York: New York University Press, 2009).

55   For a discussion of the limitations and complications of the black/queer analogy, see David Eng, *The Feeling of Kinship: Queer Liberalism and the Racialization of Intimacy* (Durham: Duke University Press, 2010).

56   See Amber Day, *Satire and Dissent: Interventions in Contemporary Political Debates* (Bloomington: Indiana University Press, 2011), p. 7.

57   See Jacques Rancière, *Le Spectateur Emancipe* (Paris: La Fabrique, 2008), p. 81.

58   See Richard Sennett, *The Corrosion of Character: The Personal Consequences of Work in the New Capitalism* (New York: W.W. Norton, 1998), p. 112.

59   See Alessandra Raengo, *On the Sleeve: Race as Face Value* (Hanover: Dartmouth, 2013). On *Bamboozled*, see also Harry J. Elam, Jr., "Spike Lee's Bamboozled," in Harry J. Elam, Jr. and Jackson Kennell (eds.), *Black Cultural Traffic Crossroads in Global Performance and Popular Culture* (Ann Arbor: The University of Michigan Press, 2005); and Ed Guerrero, "*Bamboozled:* In the Mirror of Abjection," in Mia Mask (ed.), *Black Contemporary American Cinema: Race, Gender and Sexuality at the Movies* (New York: Routledge, 2012).

60   See Cassia Lopes, *Gilberto Gil: A Poetica e a Politica do Corpo* (São Paulo: Perspectiva, 2012), p. 25.

61   W. T. Lhamon Jr., *Raising Cain: Protecting the Emotional Life of Boys* (Cambridge: Harvard University Press, 1998), p. 113.

62   Allen Guttmann, cited in Ehrenreich, *Dancing in the Streets*, p. 225.

# 3

# Political Modernism and Its Discontents

An ongoing aesthetic debate bears on whether cinema should be narrative or anti-narrative, realist or anti-realist. The debate is concerned, in short, with cinema's relation to **modernism**. Here, we can distinguish between **modernity** as an epoch—covering the half millennium since Columbus' voyages and encompassing colonialism, transatlantic slavery, the Enlightenment, industrial capitalism, and imperialism—and **artistic modernism**, as the ensemble in the arts (both inside and outside of Europe) that emerged in the late nineteenth century, flourished in the first decades of the twentieth century, and became institutionalized as high modernism after World War II.

The project of "*political modernism*" was rooted in the utopia of a transformative liaison between the aesthetic and the political avant-gardes, one that would mobilize artistic energies in conjunction with the transformation of social and political life.[1] The filmic possibilities of such a liaison were most vividly and dramatically glimpsed, perhaps, in Eisenstein's unrealized project of an adaptation of Karl Marx's *Das Capital*, conceived to show spectators how to "think dialectically" in a film whose style would be inspired by Joyce's *Ulysses*. (*Kluge's News from Ideological Antiquity: Marx, Eisenstein, Capital* [2008] was partially inspired by the Eisenstein project.) Peter Burger, in *Theory of the Avant-Garde*, refined the discussion of modernism by distinguishing between two trends: a **radical avant-garde** embodied in Surrealism and Dada, which attacked the bourgeois canons and institutions of art, and an **apolitical high modernism** that merely institutionalized the formal innovations of movements such as Cubism and Abstractionism, seen as an ideal set of traits such as abstraction, fragmentation, and the reflexive foregrounding of the materials and processes of art.[2]

*Keywords in Subversive Film/Media Aesthetics*, First Edition. Robert Stam with Richard Porton and Leo Goldsmith.
© 2015 John Wiley & Sons, Inc. Published 2015 by John Wiley & Sons, Inc.

## The Two Avant-Gardes

According to Nicole Brenez, the term "avant-garde" was first used in a fourth-century Hindu treatise to refer to the elephants that lumbered ahead of the soldiers in war. In this sense, the metaphor evokes an advance group courageously (or blindly) exposing itself to risk.[3] Later, this risk-taking became associated with the French Revolution and a 1794 publication entitled *Avant-Garde*. Although the *avant-garde* has often been seen as the artistic wing of revolution, the relations between the two have in fact been constantly shifting. *Artistic Modernism* proved compatible with a wide spectrum of political positions ranging from Marxism (Brecht) to anarchism (Vigo) to anticolonial Marxism (Oswald de Andrade) to conservatism (T. S. Eliot) and even to fascism (Marinetti, Pound). Even close collaborators could move in opposite directions; the Bunuel of *Chien Andalou* went left, while his co-director Salvador Dali (aka *Avida Dolars*) flirted with fascism. The two avant-gardes have thus at times run on parallel tracks, at times converged, and at times sharply diverged.

In terms of the temporalities of the two movements, some, such as David Graeber, have argued that moments of revolutionary effervescence "always seem to be followed by an outpouring of social, artistic, and intellectual creativity," resulting in the creation of "new horizons of possibility" and "a radical restructuring of the social imagination."[4] At the same time, Graeber sees the two currents as operating in symbiotic interfecundation, with "a persistent tendency to overlap with revolutionary circles," in spaces where "people can experiment with radically different, less alienated forms of life" in relatively free territories for experimentation with new forms of work, exchange, production, and leisure.[5] In cinema, the two *avant-gardes* achieved a tentative symbiosis during certain privileged historical moments, for example, in the experimental 1920s films and theories of Eisenstein and Vertov in the post-revolutionary Soviet Union.[6] Against the backdrop of a remarkable flowering of experimentation in theater, painting, literature, cinema, and theory, these filmmaker–theorists combined radical ideas with the practical challenge of constructing a socialist film industry. Despite the diversity of their theories and styles, all of these artists privileged **montage** as the basis for a **socialist cine-poetics**.

Although Eisenstein's theories evolved over time, *montage* formed a constant both in his writing and in his films. In the early stages, Eisenstein favored a variety-show style **"montage of attractions"**—sketch-like blocks of sensational turns—while in later stages he moved toward a layered, **dialectical montage** aesthetic. In "Methods of Montage," Eisenstein developed a full-scale typology of increasingly complex forms of montage, such as **metric, rhythmic,** tonal, overtonal, and intellectual—each generating specific spectatorial effects. Eisenstein was also the theorist of contrapuntal sound, a concept developed in a 1928 manifesto signed by himself, Pudovkin, and Alexandrov, where the three directors, on the eve of the sound revolution, warned against the temptation of a literal synchronous use of sound, favoring instead a metaphoric counterpoint between sound and image.

In incendiary essays and manifestos, Dziga Vertov made even more radical proposals. To excoriate cinema's dominant forms, Vertov drew on a wide range of derisive tropes, including magic ("the cinema of enchantment"), drugs ("electric opium"), and religion (the "high-priests of cinema"). As an alternative, he called for the "sensory exploration of the world" through kino glas or "cinema eye," in "unplayed films" that caught life in all its raw veracity with a view to prodding the working class to better comprehend the mechanisms of social life. For Vertov, montage pervaded all the stages of filmmaking, from initial conceptualization through filming to editing and postproduction. His concept of intervals—the artistic deployment of movement and proportional relation between frames—injected musical theory into film editing. Vertov mobilized the brave new world of mechanical velocity in the service of socialism; the literal and figurative "electricity" of cinema vibrated with the Soviet slogans of "tractorization" and "electrification of the countryside." Demonstrating the power of cinema to generate social concepts, Vertov would use graphic matches between various wheels—of trains, sewing machines, and the turning wheels of cameras and projectors—as a way of evoking a continuum of the productive labor of progressive modernity. (Vertov's theories later impacted the radical film aesthetics of groups as varied as the Workers Film and Photo League in the United States, *cinema verité* [the French translation of Vertov's *Kino Pravda*] in 1960s France, and the "Dziga Vertov group" in the 1970s.)

Decades later, the *two avant-gardes* converged again in the various New Waves (Jean-Luc Godard and Chris Marker in France; Tomas Guttierez Alea and Santiago Alvarez in Cuba; Fernando Solanas and Octavio Gettino in Argentina; Glauber Rocha and Leon Hirzman in Brazil; Kluge and Fassbinder in Germany; and Mrinal Sen and Ritwik Ghatak in India). These filmmakers built on the achievements of the Russian theorists/filmmakers but also went beyond them. Godard spoke of a "struggle on two fronts" and opted for Vertov over Eisenstein by founding the "Dziga Vertov Group" with Jean-Pierre Gorin. Glauber Rocha, meanwhile, proposed the reinvention of Latin American film language through an unlikely amalgam of the neo-realism of Zavattini and the transrealism of Eisenstein. In *Dialectics of the Spectator*, filmmaker/theorist Tomas Guttierez Alea proposed a viewer's dialectic—a synthesis of Eisensteinian "pathos" and

Brechtian "distance," with both filtered through Latin American cultural politics. Citing Brecht, Alea rejected the emotion/reason dichotomy, seeing emotion as stimulating reason, and reason as purifying emotion.

## The Brechtian Legacy

From the 1930s through the 1970s, the theory and practice of German dramatist Bertolt Brecht formed a crucial link between the formal and the political avant-gardes. Leftist film theory and practice drew especially on Brecht's Marxist-inflected critique of the dramatic realist model operative both in traditional theater and in the classical realist film. The Brechtian critique influenced not only countless filmmakers (among them Welles, Losey, Resnais, Duras, Straub-Huillet, Makavejev, Tanner, Oshima, Sen, and Ghatak), but also countless film theorists (Jean-Louis Comolli, Peter Wollen, Colin MacCabe, Julia Lesage). Here, we will first outline Brechtian aesthetic concepts and strategies, and then note some of the attempts to both incorporate and transcend Brecht andpolitical modernism.

In *Brecht on Theater*, Brecht theorized his general goals for the theater while proposing techniques for their realization, many subsequently extrapolated to the sister-art of film.[7] Repelled by the exploitation of pathos both in bourgeois drama and in Nazi spectacle, Brecht rejected the totalizing aesthetic of the Wagnerian *Gesamtkunstwerk*, that is, the total work of art that enlisted all the theatrical "tracks" (lighting, staging, acting, music) in the service of a single, spectacular totality of overwhelming emotion. The redundant Hollywoodean style, whereby all of the filmic tracks work toward the same visceral/emotive effect—attractive stars = pro-filmic kissing = romantic backlighting = Chopinesque music = romance-effect—could be called "Wagnerian" in this totalizing sense.

Key to Brecht's aesthetic was the nurturing of the **critical spectator** as opposed to the narcoleptic "zombies" engendered by the lachrymose sentimentality of bourgeois theater, on the one hand, and the irrational enthusiasms of Nazi spectacle on the other. Art for Brecht was a **call to praxis** that prodded the spectator not to merely contemplate the world but rather to criticize and change it. For Brecht, this meant **changing production relations**—that is, altering **the industrial apparati** that mediate and distribute art. Here, Brecht partially aligned himself with Frankfurt School theories of the **"culture industries"**—that is, the factory-like and profit-oriented approach to cultural production within capitalist society—while never endorsing Adorno's call for an austerely difficult high-modernist art.

Brechtian dramaturgical theory was consciously anti-Aristotelian. Instead of the concatenation of Fate, identification, and catharsis typical of Aristotelian tragedy, Brecht favored a democratic theater of ordinary people making their own history. Brecht rejected what Christian Metz, drawing on Melanie Klein, would later call **"good object cinema,"** that is, the industrial cinematic system that fabricates its own consumers by habituating them to certain standardized satisfactions.[8] Rather than merely produce predictable gratifications so as to ensure the circulation of art as commodity, Brecht's goal was not to **be popular** in the box office sense, but rather to **become popular**—that is, to generate new emancipatory forms of entertainment that would also generate a new audience and new political constituencies. The goal was to change the frame through transformative forms of pleasure, shaping a desire for change rather than merely satisfying the old desires for glamour and happy endings.

While literary critic Georgy Lukacs took the novels of Balzac and Stendhal as his model for **social realism**, Brecht favored what might be called **reflexive realism**—a theater realist in its social portraiture but modernist-reflexive in its forms. Haunted by the Nazis' fondness for overweening spectacles that exploited blind, elemental emotions, Brecht called for a fragmented dramaturgy that fostered critical distance through the systematic demystification of dominant discourses and social relations. For Brecht, realism did not consist in a faithful mimicry of phenomenal appearances, but rather in the critical exposure of the **causal network of events**, that is, the fundamental social mechanisms, the algorithms, as it were, of social power, all presented within a self-aware anti-illusionist style.

A key Marxist-inflected concept that animated Brechtian theater was the idea of **contradiction**, at once social, characterological, and aesthetic. In an isomorphism of form and content, the thematic social contradictions between the working class and the bourgeoisie would intersect with the formal contradictions between sound and image, music and mood. Contradiction also took place within characters themselves; the psyche became the arena of oppose voices, discourses, and ideologies. In this sense, Brecht's idea of contradiction can be usefully enriched through the Bakthinian concept of **heteroglossia** (etymologically "many-languagedness") or the interanimation of competing social languages and discourses generated not only by class hierarchies as in Brecht but also by sexual, racial, economic, cultural and generational differences. The languages of *heteroglossia* furnish a rich aesthetic resource, for they may be juxtaposed to one another, contradict one another, and be dialogically interfaced. The Brechtian aesthetic of tension can also be enriched by

Jacques Ranciere's concept of **dissensus** as the force that disrupts entrenched hierarchies in a struggle, at once artistic and political, over the redistribution of the sensible. *Dissensus* strives to fashion new "improper" social subjectivities partially by reinvisioning the field of artistic perception based on the assumption of radical human equality. Both art and politics, for Ranciere, form theatrical spaces where social (and thespian) actors perform the *mise-en-scène* of equality, designing what Ranciere calls "a new landscape of the visible, the sayable, and the doable."[9]

Rejecting overt didacticism, Brecht favored **immanent meaning**, that is, an approach whereby the play's significance had to be worked out by the active spectator, obliged to adjudicate the contradictory voices and discourses. The audience was to become a kind of jury mulling over the play's contradictory evidence. Related to *immanent meaning* was Brecht's assumption that radical theater, in times of bourgeois hegemony, should **divide the audience**. Rather than fabricate a mythical social unity through a façade of populist togetherness, Brecht preferred to polarize the audience by confronting it with its own contradictions.

Along with his general goals, Brecht also proposed specific techniques for achieving them. Easily transposable to cinema, these techniques, include: first, **fragmented mythos**, that is, instead of an organic and linear narrative, a "theater of interruptions" based on a cabaret-style dramaturgy that juxtaposes scenes rather than develop a fluid movement of causality. Whereas tragedy and melodrama move inexorably toward the catharsis that purges the tensions constructed by the narrative, in Brecht's **epic theater** the narrative line exhibits its own kinks and knots to avoid the "swindle" of illusionistic staging that fosters the impression that theatrical events are not pre-arranged but simply "happen."

Second, Brecht defended an **anti-hero/anti-star aesthetic**. Brecht preferred to make ordinary people the protagonists, rather than the extras, of history/story. ("Happy is the Land," went the famous Brecht aphorism, "that has no need of Heroes.") Rejecting the exaltation of charismatic heroes both through their positive character traits and through theatrical technique, Brecht discerned a homology between the social *mise-en-scène* of hierarchical social systems and the dramaturgy that privileges heroes through lighting, *mise-en-scène*, performance, and the orchestration of the gaze. (Riefenstahl's *Triumph of the Will*, for example, constructs Hitler as the godlike avatar arriving from the sky, the figure toward whom everyone's earthly gaze is turned.) This anti-heroic approach eschewed any **aesthetic fascism** that would decree that "good" characters be beautiful and well-coiffed, "bad" characters be physically unattractive, and the unbeautiful and improper be mocked or stigmatized.

Third, Brecht defended **de-psychologization**, that is, an approach less concerned with the nuances of individual consciousness and affective memory *à la* Stanislavski than in collective, intersubjective, socially molded patterns of behavior. Feminist theorists, in Brecht's wake, spoke of a trans-individual **situational identification**. Yvonne Rainer, following Brecht, questioned the political effectiveness of films that relied on emotional identification with characters when all that was needed were "situations"— the terminology itself evokes the work of Jean-Paul Sartre and Simone de Beauvoir—in which female spectators could imagine themselves, "within a structure of distantiation which ensures room for critical analysis."[10] While not strictly feminist, Godard's *Une Femme Mariee* offers *situational identification* through its treatment of a typical case of Parisian adultery, rendered as an abstract and equilateral triangle of husband/wife/love treated as interchangeable units granted equal screen time and engaging in exactly the same rituals—where the point is no longer suspense about the outcome of an erotic competition, but rather the exemplary social geometry of the triangular situation in general.

Fourth, Brecht favored **gestus**—that is, the stylized acting out of power hierarchies between human beings in a given period and society, conveyed through ritualized postures and body language, with the purpose of illuminating unequal social relationships. In one of his HBO standup specials, Chris Rock brilliantly embodied the racial *gestus* of the Jim Crow South by enacting the servile body language and "yes massa" speech of an Uncle Tom-era Negro, who, the minute "Mister Charlie" is out of sight and hearing, explodes into proud boasts, angry threats, and anti-honky invective. Rock thus anatomized the socially generated performance repertoires mandated for blacks in the Apartheid South.

Fifth, Brecht used **direct address** to destroy fourth-wall illusionism and undercut the gravitational pull of the spectacle. Hardly a novelty, *direct address* formed part of an *artistic commons* that included the *magister ludis* of ancient theater, the "lords of misrule" of Medieval carnival, the "dear reader" commentaries of eighteenth-century novels, and the in-your-face antics of vaudeville and stand-up comedy. In these **breakouts**, performers drop their mask and address the audience not as characters but as performers. While in the theater the device entailed *direct address* by characters to the audience, in cinema it entailed *direct address* by intermediary figures or by characters to the camera (and indirectly to the audience), such as when Godard has Jean-Paul Belmondo address the spectator directly, both by look and by words, in the first few minutes of *Breathless* (1960). Against the convention that actors should never look at the camera/audience and thus disturb spectators in their comfortable position as protected voyeurs, direct address was calculated to make the spectator conscious of theater as theater (or film as film) and to see themselves as active interlocutors with the performance.

A foundational concept for Brechtian-style *political modernism* is "**reflexivity**," along with its myriad satellite terms such as "**self-referentiality**," "**metafiction**," and "**antiillusionism**." Borrowed from philosophy and psychology, the term first referred to the mind's capacity to be both subject and object to itself within the cognitive process. *Reflexivity* informs some of the most celebrated dicta of philosophy, such as Socrates' grammatically and philosophically reflexive "know thyself" and Descartes' *cogito ergo sum*, where the skeptical observation of consciousness, consciousness watching itself "consciousing," becomes the key to epistemology. In the wake of Kant's call for reflexive philosophical judgment, social scientist/philosopher Pierre Bourdieu called for "reflexive sociology," while anthropologists such as Talal Asad and George Marcus called for "reflexive anthropology." The term "**artistic reflexivity**" extends reflexivity in the root psychological/philosophical sense to apply to the metaphorical capacity for self-reflection of a medium or language or text to reveal the principles of its own construction. *Artistic reflexivity* comes in many forms: authorial self-consciousness, meta-theoretical reflection, the display of the apparatus, the *mise-en-abyme* of narrative, the relativization of perspective, and the mutual alienation of genre.[11] Reflexivity subverts the assumption that art can be a transparent medium of communication, a window on the world. Dropping the pretense of "slice-of-life" naturalism, the approach becomes **presentational** rather than **representational**.

Here, we will briefly mention just two filmic examples of cinematic reflexivity, both of which treat the filmmaking milieu. Julie Dash's *Illusions* (1982) filters reflexive realism *à la* Brecht through a black feminist consciousness. Set in a Hollywood studio in the segregated 1940s, the film calls attention to *the apparatus*, while also dissecting Hollywood's pathologies of race. A study in the "disappearing" of black talent and labor, the film features two kinds of "**submerged ethnicity**" in the form of two black characters: Mignon Dupree (Lonette McKee), invisible as an African-American studio executive passing as white, and Esther Jeeter (Rosanne Katon), the invisible singer hired to dub the singing parts for white film star Leila Grant. Jeeter performs the vocals for a screen role denied her by Hollywood's institutional racism. While black sounds are enjoyed, black images remain taboo, as black talent is sublimated into a haloed. But while *Singin' in the Rain* exposes the *intra*ethnic appropriation whereby silent movie queen Lina Lamont (Jean Hagen), thanks to dubbing, appropriates the silky voice of Kathy Selden (Debbie Reynolds), *Illusions* reveals the *inter*racial dimension of this same procedure within the broader context of the white appropriation of black talent by separating out what had been artificially fused into white dominant. By reconnecting the black voice with the black image, the film makes the black presence "visible" and therefore "audible," while revealing the double erasure and Hollywood's often hidden indebtedness to black performance. (In a further twist on the demystifying of the titular "illusions," the credits reveal that the voice of the singer does not belong to the actress playing Esther Jeeter, but to Ella Fitzgerald.)

As its title suggests, John Waters' *Cecil B. Demented* offers a more out-rageously farcical version of the reflexive mode. The film revolves around a student film "cell" that is violently opposed to the studio system, to expensive blockbusters, the star system, and formulaic plots. The cell members conspire to kidnap Hollywood star Honey Whitlock (Melanie Griffith) to call attention to their cause. Chanting the praises of "Underground" and "guerrilla" cinema, each member of the cell is tat-tooed with the name of one of cinema's great rebels such as Kenneth Anger, Rainer Fassbinder, and Andy Warhol. The kidnapped star, rather similar to Patty Hearst, finally embraces the cause of her captors, in the underground equivalent of a happy ending.

Although designed to deconstruct the axioms of Western capitalist societies, Brechtian techniques are also extrapolable for other political systems, and have sometimes been used to criticize communist societies as well. Wajda's *Man of Marble*, for example, practices **anti-Stalinist reflexivity**. Here, the film-about-filmmaking format—in this case, a filmmaker's plan to demystify the official propaganda that fabricates the image of the worker–hero—becomes a springboard for a critique, at once social and cinematic, of a bureaucratic communist regime. Another anti-Stalinist film from what was once called the "socialist bloc," Dusan Makavejev's *WR: Mysteries of the Organism* (1971), an ingeniously constructed amalgam of fiction and documentary, for its part, points the way to unraveling the intertwined obstacles to political and aesthetic vanguardism. Taking as its point of depar-ture the turbulent career of Wilhelm Reich, the movie offers an eviscerating critique of Stalinism while slyly subverting one of the most venerable strains of cinematic avant-gardism—Soviet montage. If Eisenstein used cinema as a tool for galvanizing the masses and leading them toward a single goal, Makavejev's variant of montage is less programmatic and more playful.

Preferring to term his modus operandi **"collage"** instead of montage, Makavejev's anarchist thrust is conveyed through an accretion of paradoxes. Stale assumptions concerning the consumerist West and the benighted East are imploded through a series of incongruous transitions and juxtapositions. Eminently suitable for **critical foraging**, *WR: Mysteries of the Organism*'s narrative offers a number of multi-layered paradoxes.

Milena, a Yugoslav feminist activist and sexual revolutionary whose exhortations that Reichian theory should be wedded to orgasmic practice receive a jaundiced reception from her male colleagues, is the driving libidinal force of the latter half of the film. Yet, when pontificating about "free love," she comes off as a party hack spouting liberatory slogans—for example, "Our road to the future must be life-positive ... socialism must not exclude human pleasure from its program." Her authoritarian paeans to sexual freedom pigeonhole her as a peculiarly repressed apostle of emancipatory desires. Milena's sexual politics are also compromised by her infatuation with a visiting Russian ice-skater, the facetiously named "Vladimir Ilyich" (as in "Vladimir Ilyich Lenin"). From a **social-allegory** perspective, Milena's oscillation between reformist zeal thinly disguised as a Yugoslav-style "revolution within a revolution" and a man who embodies Soviet rigidity mirrors the contradictions of Tito's own rupture with Stalinism.

Although reflexivity per se has no intrinsic political valence, **Brechtian reflexivity** deploys artistic self-consciousness for political ends by **fore-grounding the apparatus**, in this case the **cinematic apparatus**, defined as the totality of interdependent operations that make up the cinema-viewing situation, including: (1) the technical base of film equipment including camera, lights, film, and projector; (2) the conditions of film projection; (3) the projected film; and (4) the mental machinery of spectatorship that constitutes the viewer as a subject of desire. Godard's films at one point or another have explored virtually every nook and cranny of the *apparatus*, whether by displaying the camera (*Le Mépris*, 1963; *Passion*, 1982), foregrounding the conditions of projection (*Masculin Féminin*, 1966), or reflecting on the mental machinery of spectatorship (*Les Carabiniers*, 1963; *Histoire(s) du cinéma*, 1998). Godard's short contribution to the omnibus anti-war film *Loin du Vietnam* (1967) largely consisted of shots of Godard's own camera, overlaid with his voice-over musings on the apparatus and on the modalities of his mediated solidarity with the Vietnamese people.

Some films practice **financial reflexivity** by highlighting the economic dimension of filmmaking, as when Godard opens *Tout Va Bien* (1972) with the signing of the checks allotted for the production. *A Margem da Imagem* ("On the Margins of the Image," 2003), Evaldo Mocarzel's film about the exploitation of images of the homeless of São Paulo, similarly includes a scene where the director explains the financial arrangements to the film's impoverished participants. In his contribution to the collective film *Far from Vietnam* (1967), Godard, similarly, offers **self-critique as artistic resource**. Given his social distance from both French workers and Vietnamese revolutions, Godard concludes that his support for Vietnam must consist in combating Hollywood and Mosfilm by creating "one, two, many Vietnams" within the cinematic field. Jean-Luc Godard, J. P. Gorin, and Anne-Marie Miéville's *Ici et ailleurs* (1974), similarly, attempts to bridge the gap between disparate political and national perspectives—French and Palestinian—by employing video technology to unite an associative chain of images in one shot. The technological sleight of hand reinforces the affinities between the French working-class and the Palestinians, in a procedure that parallels the "creative activity" that Bakhtin calls "**exotopy**," as a process that alternates between two stages in every creative act—the first stage of empathy or identification (the novelist or filmmaker puts himself or herself in the place of his or her character), and the reverse movement of a return to critical distance.[12] In a doubly reflexive movement, the filmmakers empathize with " the oppressed" while also conceding the limitations of their **mediated solidarity** (Walter Benjamin) and their own subjectivity.

Sixth, Brecht also fostered critical distance toward the spectacle through denaturalizing strategies such as **tableau effects**—a kind of social freeze-frame generating stylized group portraits of human ensembles frozen into socially revelatory postures, a technique easily transposable to cinema through literal freeze-frames. The very unnaturalness of these voguing-like scenes sought to make power arrangements visible through a process of **denaturalization**. And while *tableau* drew on the pictorial arts, another denaturalizing strategy—**literarization** or the proliferation of text—drew on the verbal arts.

Seventh, Brecht favored **distantiated acting** as opposed to empathetic or identificatory acting. Techniques such as having actors speak in the past tense or in the third person, or announce their own stage directions, were designed to help actors see their roles socially and historically rather than psychologically, engendering critical distance between actor and role, and between character and spectator. Godard films, in this sense, create distantiation by having actors speak directly about their own acting ( *Une femme mariée*, 1964), or by having actors speak in "unnatural" ways, whether through a striking *lack* of affect (the Ubuesque monotone of the bumpkins in *Les Carabiniers*), or, conversely, through an **excess** of affect and rhetoric.

Eighth, Brecht recommended that actors envision **acting as quotation**, a technique increasingly deployed by Godard in films whose dialogue consist largely in quotations from his favorite authors, with no scripted dialogue at all.

Ninth, Brecht favored **the radical separation of elements**, that is, a structured architectonics that set scene against scene, character against discourse, music against feeling, and film track against track. In an intersectional struggle for supremacy between words, music, and staging, the various tracks would mutually relativize or even discredit one another rather than reinforce one another in a totalizing fashion. This process could consist in a metaphorically vertical separation, for example, through paradigmatic contrasts between tracks (sweet music against bitter image), or in metonymically horizontal separations, as with the syntagmatic separating off of neighboring segments or sketches within the discursive chain, sliced up into "chapters," "facts," "tableaux," etc.

Finally—tenth—Brecht also practiced what we would now call **multimedia** or **intermedia** through the mutual alienation of "sister arts" such as film, photography, and music, a proleptic version of what media theorists such as Andre Gaudreault would later call **intermediality**, or the convergent intercourse of the various arts and media within a single artistic utterance or across the wider spectrum of media.

Closely related to the fashioning of an active spectator was Brecht's **opposition to voyeurism** and the "fourth-wall convention" that would have spectators imagine themselves as peeping into a private world to which they were magically granted access. Filmmakers such as Godard and Farocki undermine voyeurism through a kind of **erotic sabotage** that calls attention to spectatorial voyeurism while refusing to placate it. Godard's *Sauve qui peut (la vie)* (*Every Man for Himself*, 1980) stages the sexual fantasies of a CEO—a technocrat's wet dream; the Taylorization of sexual production—programmed by the science of management. In this example of **porn reflexivity**, Godard has the boss, rather similar to a filmmaker, assign precise movement and positions to the "actors" (his assistant, secretary, and a prostitute). As with the assembly-line workers in Chaplin's *Modern Times*, the orgiasts are reduced to well-defined jerks, twists, and quivers. Within this highly anti-erotic presentation, there are no writhing bodies but only the empty multiplication of sexual signifiers in a kind of caricatural formula of an orgy—an orgy rendered as sign.

In *Contempt* (1963), Godard has the pro-filmic camera eye, which in conventional cinema surreptitiously marries itself to the gaze of the spectator, focus on the spectators themselves, in an apparitical equivalent of *direct address*. The Playmate-like images of Brigitte Bardot in *Contempt* are echoed in Harun Farocki's *An Image* (1983), which deconstructs the image-production of an actual Playmate. Shot at the *Playboy* studio in Munich, the film impassively registers the entire process of construction of the kind of images sold and masturbated over by millions, now emptied of their eroticizing power through a disenchanting focus on the technical fabrication of the images and the cold professionalism of the technicians. Their request for a "saucy look" throws cold water on any spectatorial delusion that such performative flirtation is really sincere or somehow directed at them. Similar to performance artist Annie Sprinkle's parodic image of herself as a Playmate suffering the slings and arrows of excruciatingly tight bras and awkward poses, the film's stress on the model's physical discomfort undermines erotic fantasy and projection. (In other projects, such as the video *I Thought I Saw the Prisoners*, Farocki anatomizes another kind of voyeurism, that of the panoptical surveillance deployed not only by a high-security California prison but also by a supermarket.)

Brechtian strategies are not the exclusive province of European "art films." A number of directors who spent time in Hollywood—Orson Welles, Fritz Lang, Joseph Losey, Haskell Wexler—were also influenced by Brecht. We find a latter-day Brechtian film in the 1981 musical *Pennies from Heaven*, based on a BBC TV drama by Dennis Potter and directed by Herbert Ross. The film injects the artificial naturalism of the musical comedy with Brechtian irony, turning the pleasures of the musical against escapism, while still remaining pleasurable. Set during the Great Depression, the film centers on an incorrigibly optimistic Chicago sheet-music salesman Arthur Parker (Steve Martin), whose business and marriage are failing. In the depths of economic despair, Parker dreams of living in the enchanted world of the musical comedy, where money falls from the sky and women are ambulatory dreams. The film illustrates the thesis of Andrew Berman's book on Great Depression-era "backstage musicals" (*We're in the Money*), where the films form allegories about "getting the (economic) show on the road," so that wealth, as the title song suggests, might once again rain down on the unemployed.[13]

The narrative form of *Pennies from Heaven* follows the guidelines laid out by Brecht in his schema contrasting **dramatic-versus-epic theater**. In his schema, Brecht proposed a series of contrasts that allied **epic theater** with **narrative** (not with dramatic theater's **plot**); with **decisions** (not with drama's **sensations**); with **montage** (not **growth**); with human beings as **process** (not as **fixed point**); and with **reason** (not **feeling**). Rather than organic plots where one scene leads logically into the next *à la* dramatic theater, **epic theater** works through the juxtaposition of autonomous scenes. Brecht detested the fake naturalism that has the actors pretend not to notice that they have left the register of plain speech to enter that of song. The songs in *Pennies from Heaven* therefore highlight their own artifice through cutaway sets, and the inter-cutting of staged scenes with anthological production numbers featuring Fred Astaire. The musical numbers are clearly marked as illusory solutions to real economic problems. Steve Martin's boyishly awestruck acting becomes a *gestus* that renders visible the naiveté of those who believe in Horatio Alger-style success fantasies. The title song is performed by a stuttering accordion-playing tramp who, after wolfing down two meals in a Hopperesque diner, metamorphoses into a balletically graceful dancer and charismatic crooner. The rainstorm becomes a shower of golden coins, but the background photos depicting the Great Depression's casualties contradict the hopefulness expressed in the song, undermining the Technicolor fantasies of Hollywood musicals.

## Beyond Brecht

In many countries, the 1970s were the site of passionate debates about politics and aesthetics. The Olivier Assayas 2012 film *Apres Mai* ("Something in the Air") stages some of these debates as they took place in France. Set in the early 1970s, when the memory of the 1968 events still burned brightly, this semiautobiographical film chronicles the political and erotic coming-of-age of budding painter Gilles (Clement Metayer). During a meeting of leftist militants in Italy, a screening of a leftist film generates the kind of aesthetic quarrels typical of the era. Why, one radical spectator asks, should revolutionary films be made in a bourgeois style, when "revolutionary films call for revolutionary syntax?" A member of the film collective then argues for a "proletarian syntax understandable by workers." The exchange mirrors many of the debates of the time, which pitted Lukacsian realism against Brechtian/ Adornonian modernism, populist Costa-Gavras against deconstructive Godard, and popular "accessibility" against avant-garde hermeticism.[14] These debates generated extremely rich formulations about the politics of film aesthetics. In an influential 1969 *Cahiers* editorial, Jean-Louis Comolli and Jean Narboni provided a schema that posited an ideological spectrum of films ranging from those completely complicitous with prevailing aesthetic and political norms, through to mildly critical reformist films, to those that made a frontal assault on the reigning political and artistic institutions. In their "**category-e,**" the authors pointed to the sly subversion of films that seemed to be under the sway of the dominant ideology but where perverse disjunctions in the *mise-en-scène* exposed the strains and fissures of the official ideology through formal **gaps and fissures** that offered an escape from the dominant ideology. Raymond Williams later argued that no hegemony goes uncontested, and distinguished between **residual, emergent,** and **dominant** cultural forces. (Re-elaborating Williams, the cultural studies of the 1980s further displaced critical agency from the text itself to the spectator, as in Stuart Hall's later analysis of **dominant, negotiated,** and **resistant readings** of the mass media.[15])

In the 1970s, some theorists turned Brechtian concepts into a rather austerely rigorous reflexive schema. *Cahiers* in its Marxist phase, and *Cinetique* developed very rigorous (and often contradictory) standards whereby few films passed the ideological test. Peter Wollen's formulations of "**counter-cinema**" can serve as a summary of the key principles of the trend. Wollen's schema mapped the contrasts between mainstream cinema and counter-cinema in the form of seven binary features: (1) **narrative intransitivity** versus narrative transitivity (i.e., the systematic disruption of the flow of the narrative); (2) **estrangement versus identification** (through Brechtian techniques of acting, sound–image disjunction, direct address, etc.); (3) **foregrounding versus transparency** (systematic drawing of attention to the process of construction of meaning); (4) **multiple versus single diegesis**; (5) **aperture versus closure** (rather than a unifying authorial vision, an opening out into an intertextual field); (6) **unpleasure versus pleasure** (the filmic experience conceived as a kind of collaborative production/consumption); and (7) **reality versus fiction** (the exposure of the mystifications involved in filmic fictions). Wollen subsequently distanced himself from distance, as it were, by pointing out that the complete refusal of mainstream pleasures was a dead end: "Desire, and its representation in fantasy," Wollen wrote in the early 1980s, "far from being necessary enemies of revolutionary politics ... are necessary conditions."[16]

Claire Johnston, meanwhile, offered a feminist version of the schema in her essay "**Women's Cinema as Counter-Cinema**," which attempted to fuse Althusserian Marxism, Metzian semiotics, and Lacanian psychoanalysis with a feminist project. Since the 'truth of oppression cannot be captured on celluloid with an 'innocent' camera," feminist cinema had to refuse conventional kinds of identification by creating new meanings that would "[disrupt] the fabric of male bourgeois cinema."[17] Laura Mulvey, meanwhile, called for and practiced a **feminist avant-garde cinema** as a "counterpoint" to the Hollywood film.[18] The critical current based in this feminist trend would subsequently valorize films such as Chantal Akerman's *Jeanne Dielman, 23 quai du Commerce, 1080 Bruxelles* (1975); Mulvey and Wollen's *Riddle of the Sphinx* (1977); and Sally Potter's *Thriller* (1979).

In its more rigid versions, counter-cinema schemas, while suggestive, in some ways simply reversed old dyads instead of transcending them. To signify on Roberto Schwarz's phrase "**national by subtraction**"—that is, a critical term denoting the essentialist view that sees the nation as a pure, essential core to be unearthed through the removal of all "foreign" elements—those one might call the **hyper-Brechtians** practiced a revolutionary **aesthetics by subtraction**. The goal became the successive stripping away of all the layers of dominant cinema's taken-for-granted pleasures—the infantile malady of a childlike absorption in stories, the identificatory bonds of affection with characters, the fetishistic joys of scopophilia—leaving intact only the filmic apparatus itself reflecting on its own procedures. (The only honest film, Godard famously claimed, would consist in a camera filming itself in a mirror.) The logical telos of this iconoclasm was a *personne-a-ma-gauche* aesthetic brinkmanship. A Dziga-Vertov Collective document asked if "at certain moments in history, the most important thing might be to *not* make films."[19] In David James words, the endpoint was the total "repudiation of the illusionist narrative codes of the commercial feature [as] only the first step in a *via negativa* of unprecedented severity." Film ended up consuming itself; "even as it discredited all previous film production, it supplied the grounds for its own discrediting."[20]

In some ways, *hyper-Brechtianism* departed from Brecht's own axioms. While Brecht endorsed popular forms of culture such as sport and the circus, the *hyper-reflexive* theories offered only a morbid carnival of negations of the dominant cinema. While Brecht relished stories and fables—arguably a hard-wired feature of the human mind—mythophobic latter-day Brechtians saw narrative as a kind of original sin. Some theories were built on the self-defeating idea of completely destroying spectatorial pleasure. Peter Gidal (1975) spoke of "**structural-materialist**" **films** that would represent nothing beyond their own fabrication. In a male-feminist vow of representational chastity, he also, at one point, promised never to show a woman's body in his films, a vow instantly mocked by many feminist critics as a pointless masculinist gesture. A theory based simply on negations of the conventional pleasures of cinema because of the alienated uses to which they have been put, moreover, risks a dead-end **cine-anhedonia**—the incapacity for experiencing (filmic) pleasure. Apart from ignoring the socialized delights of the *carnivalesque* and *festive revolutionary* traditions discussed earlier, such a view forgets that, to be effective, films—and social movements—must offer their quantum of pleasure and desire, something to discover or see or imagine, a glimpse of what, as Nina Simone put it in a song, "it feels like to be free." Brechtian *distantiation*, after all, only works if there is an emotion or a desire to *be* distanced. The view that simply bemoans audience delight in spectacle betrays a puritanical distaste for pleasure itself.[21]

The deconstructionist **critique-of-ideology** approach performed a service by unmasking the ideology at work within cinematic forms themselves and denouncing the potential for exploitation in identification with streamlined plots, glamorous stars, and idealized characters. Totally deconstructive films, as Metz has pointed out already in the 1970s, require a libidinal transfer whereby the traditional satisfactions of entertainment are replaced by the pleasures of intellectual mastery, or what psychoanalytically inclined theorists called the "sadism of knowledge."[22] The infantile pleasure in the toy is exchanged for the even more infantile pleasure of breaking the toy, when the goal might better be to use the toy for new purposes, or even better, to invent a new toy and invent new, disalienated forms of pleasure. As we shall see in the chapter on the *fractured chronotope*, films can play with and multiply fictions through *narrative proliferation* rather than eliminate them; tell stories, but also question them; and articulate the play of desire and the pleasure principle as well as the real-world obstacles to their concretization.

While 1970s film theory promoted formal *reflexivity* as a political panacea, in the postmodern and post-postmodern era, such strategies began to be seen as having exhausted their charisma. The reflexive "**baring of the device**"—that is, revealing the mechanisms of art—has become virtually ubiquitous, featured on everything from CNN "behind-the-scenes" reports to the visible cameras of reality shows. How can reflexivity maintain a critical edge in an age where directors expose their own techniques through DVD commentaries and when every middle-class adolescent can make films with smartphones? An apolitical reflexivity has become the "new normal" in the mass media, no longer producing shock or social knowledge but only a blasé sense of *déjà vu* on the part of the media-saturated spectator. At times, the demand for *reflexivity* became a form of narcissistic superiority rooted in *cultural capital*: "My literate sophistication allows me to see clearly and reflexively what you—poor fool—are incapable of seeing!" Bruno Latour has therefore called for **infra-reflexivity** as a critical check on the arrogance of those who wield reflexivity as an elitist weapon.[23]

While effective in its time, the Brechtian legacy, and especially what might be called **hyper-Brechtianism**, can be retrospectively seen as occasionally haunted by a number of pitfalls, some having to do with the blind spots of certain orthodox forms of Marxism, notably: (1) **economism**, whereby the economic base (infrastructure) simply determines the superstructure of ideology and culture; (2) **scientism**, a blind faith in the progressive metanarrative of science, easily aligned, in the 1970s, with Althusser's "scientific Marxism"; (3) **rationalism**, an exorbitant belief in enlightened reason and an extreme suspicion toward the kinds of empathic identification stereotypically associated with the feminine and the non-Western; (4) **objectivism**, or a rationalistic objectivity placed under suspicion by Adorno and Horkheimer (*The Dialectics of Enlightenment*), by Fanon (for whom "objectivity always works against the native"), and by feminist "standpoint theory"; (5) **class reductionism**, the elevation of a single axis of social domination (class) over other axes such as race, gender, sexuality, and nation; and (6) **pedagogic authoritarianism**, linked to a vanguardist or nation-statist stance which suggests that the vanguard party, as with Ranciere's "ignorant schoolmaster," knows what is best for the people.

Just as some *hyper-Brechtians* were gravitating toward puritanical austerity and arid theoreticism, radical performance artists were moving in the opposite direction, toward irreverence. In the theatre, directors such as Heiner Muller opened up the latent possibilities of Brecht's **Lehrstücke** (learning plays) in plays such as *Mauser* (1975) and *The Mission* (1982). Augusto Boal's democratizing **"forum theater,"** meanwhile, strove to reduce the gap between actor and audience through the concept of the **"spect-actor,"** where members of the audience, regardless of their race, gender, or class, can literally become the actors by getting up on stage to actively intervene in the drama. While Boal spoke of a **Theater of the Oppressed**—a dramaturgical correlative to educator Paulo Freire's *Pedagogy of the Oppressed*—fellow Brazilian avant-garde theater director and filmmaker Ze Celso, whose blog is called **"Anthropophagic Macumba,"** spoke of a **Theater of Discovery** that combined Brecht with Brazilian carnivalesque anthropophagy. (Ze Celso was literally post-Brechtian, in that he had begun by staging Brecht plays in the early 1960s.) With Ze Celso's Oficina group, the theatrical experience becomes an orgiastic (and sometimes lysergic) festivity aimed at social rebellion and experimentation, where dancing crowds, mingling actors and spectators, spill out into the neighboring streets.

Along the symbolic borders of the United States and Mexico, we find not only the feminist **border theory** of Gloria Anzaldúa and Cherríe Moraga—an analytical literal and metaphorical grid used by feminist, Chicana/o studies, and queer scholars to explore all kinds of literal and metaphorical borders—but also the vibrant performance art films of Guillermo Gomez Pena (sometimes with Coco Fusco). The Latino performance trio *Culture Clash*, whose work made its way not only into theaters but also into TV sitcoms, PBS shows, and short films such as Lourdes Portillo's *Columbus on Trial*, in this sense provides a model of **post-Brechtian performance**. Moving out from their roots in Salvadorean Circuses, Chaplin and Cantinflas, Teatro Campesino, Bay Area Radical Theatre (the Mime Troupe), and the stand-up comedy of Lenny Bruce and Richard Pryor, *Culture Clash* came to occupy a terrain similar to that occupied by such figures as Tony Kushner (*Angels in America*), Anna Deveare Smith (*Fires in the Mirror*), and George C. Wolfe

(*The Colored Museum*), all of whom, in their different ways, combined filmed performance with political radicalism, documentary veracity, trans-realist audacity, and, importantly edgy humor.

The films of John Greyson, meanwhile, invoke Brechtian precepts while "queering" them through a campy **aesthetic of excess**. Two of Greyson's key strategies, for Cindy Patton, are **queering**, or the exposure of the buried erotic and homoerotic layers of the dominant society, and **buggery**, or the violent defamilization that estranges the societal normal as monstrous.[24] While classical Marxism had traditionally privileged class and anti-capitalist struggles, Greyson goes beyond Brecht by endlessly engaging the intersectionalities of race, class, sexuality, and empire in such films and videos as *The Jungle Boy* (an anti-Orientalist dissection of *The Jungle Book* as a homoerotic imperialist film) and *Kipling Meets the Cowboys*, which links British imperialism in India to American racism toward the "other Indians"—that is, Native Americans.

Greyson's *The Making of "Monsters"* actually stages the 1938 Brecht–Lukacs debates about realism in quasi-farcical form by making Brecht, reincarnated as a talkative (and gay) catfish, the director of the made-for-TV "Monsters" film-within-the-film, while making Lukacs the producer (jokingly confounded with the other George Lucas, known for his "socialist realist classic *American Graffiti*" and the "blockbuster indictment of multinational capitalism," *Star Wars*). The debate in the film revolves around the correct cinematic treatment for the theme of gaybashing, whether to opt for a bathetic approach, which the film's "Brecht" rejects, or for a meta-cinematic deconstructive approach, which "Lukacs" rejects. You are just "trying to get the audience to cry," the voice-of-catfish-narrator sneers, and "your clichéd cross-cutting achieves the opposite of what you want!"

Throughout, Greyson respects the Brechtian injunctions of *distantiated acting*, stylized staging, and the *separation of the elements*, along with reflexive *mise-en-abyme*, here achieved through the film's self-presentation as a film-about-the making-of-a-documentary-about-the-making-of-a-docudrama about gay bashing. The film further references Brecht by featuring "Lotte Lenya" (the actress–singer from the Berliner Ensemble, the theater group founded by Brecht) as a black lesbian singing "Gay Bash Back." At the same time, the film "*queers Brecht*" by excavating the suppressed homoeroticism that generates homophobia. In an inversion of an inversion that reveals the normality of monstrosity, those who were conventionally seen as monsters—gay "deviants"—trade places with the real monsters—the homophobic killers presenting the appearance of "normal," well-behaved, middle-class boys.

## The Affective-Corporeal Turn

In its more theoreticist versions, *hyper-Brechtianism* at times seemed less concerned with combating dominant cinema than with destroying the "lure" of the image itself. A certain **neo-Platonic iconophobia** was reflected in the theoretical return in the 1970s to the "Allegory of the Cave," now interpreted to evoke benighted spectators spellbound in the ideological darkness of the movie theater. Speaking more broadly, hyper-rational approaches sometimes showed a distaste for the unseemly "embodiedness" of film; the "seen" was regarded as "obscene." For the literati, film was inconveniently corporeal in its incarnated, fleshly, enacted characters; its real locales and palpable props; its carnality and visceral shocks to the nervous system; its sounds that can damage eardrums; and its images that can provoke desire.

The film experience cannot be reduced to the celluloid object in a metal container, or to the film moving through the projector, or to bits and pixels of streamed digital information. Films take place in the spectator's mind and body; they come alive only when sparked into life by the sensorial apprehension of the spectator. Hyper-rationalist approaches forget that that we go to films and to artistic events not only to learn but also to feel, indeed to learn about new ways of feeling, in situations where emotion can be *integral* to cognition, a partner rather than an enemy of knowledge. The **affective-corporeal turn** in recent theory has paid renewed attention to bodily knowledge and embodied spectatorship, in ways that are implicitly critical of a rationalist modernism. The shift from critical dissection of the gaze to reflections on the body, on performance, and on masquerade—developed in distinct ways by scholars such as Vivian Sobchack, Richard Dyer, Thomas Elsaesser, Laura Marks, Steven Shaviro, Jennifer Barker, Margaret Morse, Alessandra Raengo, Corinn Columpar, and Sophie Mayer (and countless others) inside of film studies, and Judith Butler, Elizabeth Grosz, Lauren Berlant, Jonathon Crary, Inderpal Grewal, Caren Kaplan, Eve Sedgewick, and Brian Massumi (and count-less others) outside of it—has opened the way for a more complex view of the role of the body in spectatorship. Linda Williams, in *Hardcore* (1989), began to redeem the **body genres** (notably melodrama, horror, and porn) from critical contempt, genres that provoked visceral sensations in the spectator similar to those portrayed or enacted in the films.[25] For Williams, films arouse us in different ways, and sexual arousal can also be a legitimate aim of art.[26] The supercilious scorn for "low" body genres is ultimately indissociable from contempt for the *bodily lower stratum*, linked to phobias about the body and about not maintaining rational distance from a film, as if the King Kong of the libido were about to break its chains and invade the space of the spectator.

In order to "make sense," films engage with the senses. For Vivian Sobshack, we see and comprehend films "with our entire bodily being, informed by the full history and carnal knowledge of our acculturated sensorium.[27] For Steven Shaviro, "the flesh is intrinsic to the cinematic apparatus, at once its subject, its substance, and its limit."[28] For Deleuze, films can open up "**conceptual-affective flows**" between bodies, understood not as bounded units but as a nexus of multiplicities. Brian Massumi distinguishes between **emotion**, as naming specific codified feelings such as fear and love, and **affect**, as referring to less localizable "intensities." For Masumi, "affect holds a key to rethinking postmodern power after ideology."[29] Bringing to the fore precisely those issues sidelined by apparatus theory—such as "emotion, sensation, corporeality, and pleasure"—Corinne Columpar and Sophie Mayer speak of the **"politics of the palpable."**[30] The theoretical rediscovery of the spectatorial body took many forms: the critique of **ocularcentrism** by Martin Jay in *Downcast Eyes: The Denigration of Vision in Twentieth-Century French Thought*; the renewed attention to sound, on the part of scholars such as Rick Altmann and Claudia Gorbman, against the view which saw film as an exclusively "visual medium" that is "seen" by "spectators" rather than heard by "auditors"; the seminal phenomenological work of Vivian Sobchack; and the Deleuzian explorations in Laura Marks' *The Skin of the Film: Intercultural Cinema, Embodiment, and the Senses*, with its stress on **"haptic visuality"** or film-seeing as related to the sense of touch. Reflecting this affective turn, Thomas Elsaesser and Malte Hagener subtitled their *Film Theory* book "*An Introduction through the Senses*,"[31] while a popular online journal bears the name *Senses of Cinema*. Ranciere's concept of the *partage du sensible*, or the conflictual division/ distribution/ redistribution/sharing of the *common* sensory world, also forms part of this *affective-corporeal* turn.[32]

Not entirely new, the affective turn was latent in classical film theory. Eisenstein's "intellectual montage," Deleuze reminds us, was accompanied by "sensory thought" and "emotional intelligence."[33] In any case, this body of work has made an enormous contribution by illuminating the interaction of cinema with our sensate bodies. Steven Shaviro, in his Deleuzian defense of the corporeal in *The Cinematic Body*, speaks of film spectatorship as a "visceral" experience. In her influential *The Address of the Eye*, and later in *Carnal Thoughts*, Vivian Sobchack criticized the theoretical slighting of the spectators' lived body and cinema's sensual address to our "corporeal-material being."[34] In language that itself mingles the conceptual with the corporeal, Sobchack speaks of "tactile foresight" and the **"carnal foundations of cinematic intelligibility."** The concept of the **cinesthetic subject**, for Sobchack, mingles synaesthesia (the intermodal stimulation of the senses) and what she calls **coanaesthesia** (the pre-logical unity of the sensorium and the perception of one's body as the sum of its somatic perceptions).[35]

As part of this *affective turn,* a number of queer-feminist writers have usefully foregrounded the politics of human emotion. Lauren Berlant's concept of **cruel optimism** analyses the contemporary crisis of neoliberalism due to the fading of fantasies of upward mobility in Western liberal societies. For Berlant, this historical disillusionment is felt affectively before it is understood through discourse or ideology. *Cruel optimism* constitutes a feminist updating of the old Hegelian–Marxist concept of **false consciousness**, that is, the process by which capitalist structures and ideologies obscure the true power relations between the owners of the means of production and those who merely endure it, between those who make money, and those whose money makes money. The concept of *cruel optimism* psychoanalyzes this process by stressing the ways that subjects invest in and are attached to the toxic normalcy of institutions and relationships and social systems that actually undermine any possibility of social happiness.[36]

At its best, this extremely rich vein of research and analysis proposes a kind of *corporeal* materialism rather than (or at times in tandem with) a Marxist *historical* materialism. Many writers in this vein (e.g., Laura Marks, Hamid Naficy, Linda Williams, David Martin-Jones) made indispensable connections between the body and radical politics in relation to a particular corpus of films—intercultural, minoritarian, exilic, and so forth. Others, such as the cognitivists, remain relentlessly apolitical. The question is how we might distinguish in political terms between the corporeal-affectivity of different films and genres, for example, between a violent blockbuster and that of a film that challenges the *partage du sensible* in an egalitarian direction. At its best, the affective turn provides an illuminating analytical framework for understanding the different ways subjects live the social sensorium and what might be called the political economy of pleasure and pain, hope and despair. The potential weakness in some versions of the *corporeal-affective turn* is a fetishization of the individual body—what Bakhtin in his critique of the Formalists saw as the empty sensations of the individual consumer of art—rather than the sensations that pass *between* and *among* individuals as part of a **transindividual subjectivity**.[37]

In her book *The Documentary: Politics, Emotion, Culture,* Belinda Smail contests the downplaying of the role of emotion in analyses of documentaries.[38] Some documentaries manage to touch the depths of what might be called the **social body**. Patricio Guzmán's *La Memoria Obstinada* ("Obstinate Memory," 1997), in this sense, demonstrates the power of cinema to catalyze historical emotion through **visceral–cognitive spectatorship**, provoking a strong reaction that is at once personal and public, physical and mental. *Memoria* embeds traces of Guzmán's epic documentary *The Battle of Chile* (1973–1976)—a film that registered the historical process by which Salvador Allende came to power until he was removed by a US-supported *coup d'etat* on September 11, 1973. *The Battle of Chile* plunges us into the vortex of events through agile in-your-face cinematography, giving us a very physical sense of the kinetic joys and dangers of street demonstrations and even of the risk of death—for example, in a heart-stopping sequence where an Argentinean cameraman films his own death during an attempted military *coup*. Indeed, many of the activists shown in *The Battle of Chile*, including Guzmán's own cameraman Jorge Muller, were subsequently murdered by the *junta*. Guzmán went into exile, and the film was smuggled out of Chile and edited abroad with the help of Chris Marker. Celebrated internationally upon its release in 1976, the film, anathema to the dictatorship, remained unseen in Chile itself.

As the political situation opened up in the mid-1990s, Guzmán returned to his homeland to show the film to selected audiences. *La Memoria Obstinada* offers Guzmán's account of showing *The Battle of Chile* to students who grew up under the *junta*. Shaped by a repressive environment that rendered taboo any positive memory of the Allende period, some of the students recite the official line that Allende had created a chaotic situation, that the *coup* was necessary, and so forth. One unforgettable sequence records the reactions of a group of theater students to the film. As they watch the finale of *The Battle of Chile*, the students, their bodies slumped, look thunderstruck. What follows is a volcanic eruption of long-buried emotion, a **mediatic exorcism**, a demonstration of film's power to move and even transform people in ways that inescapably involve the body. One young woman begins the post-film discussion by speaking, voice breaking but persistent, of her pride in the bravery of the Chilean people. Another stuttering young man recalls that, for him, as a child, September 11 represented nothing more than the infantile pleasure of a "day off from school"; he breaks down as he expresses horror at the events portrayed and reflects on his own blithe unawareness at the time. Another man, of indigenous appearance, weeps uncontrollably in a paroxysm of grief and pain. It is, paradoxically, the complete breakdown of speech that testifies to the powerful emotions triggered by the film. Inarticulateness becomes a form of eloquence. Unlike the media's cynical tactic of "getting the victim to cry" after a disaster, here the images and sounds catalyze a **return of the historical repressed**, an explosion of buried emotion triggered by the sheer, irrefutable facticity of the audiovisual evidence, evoking events of which the young people were perhaps vaguely aware but which had long been covered over by a mendacious official discourse.

*La Memoria Obstinada* communicates, in short, the fraught **historicity of spectatorship**. Its emotional reception reminds us of something often forgotten in the age of instant transmission, smartphones, and omnipresent screens, that is, the prosthetic identificatory power of cinema, something that the earliest spectators were aware of when they spoke of cinema as a "magic carpet" flying them away to faraway places. One could argue, of course, that the young peoples' reaction will be ephemeral, that of a touching Hollywood drama easily forgotten the next morning. The difference is that, with *La Memoria Obstinada*, it is a question not of fictional characters but rather of Chile's own story, present but dimly remembered by young spectators who had never been allowed any substantive sense either of the vibrant audacity of the activism of that period, or of the horrific brutality of the *coup*.

We find an analogous example of *visceral–cognitive spectatorship* provoked by film-watching in Margaretha von Trotta's *Marianne and Julianne*, where two German high school students, after seeing a film about the Shoah, immediately throw up in the school bathroom, in a direct corporeal response to a horrible revelation about events linked to the history of their country. The collectively produced activist film *Winter Soldier* (1971), meanwhile, provides another example of the power of irrefutable, stomach-turning facticity. As what might be called a **film brut** (raw film) about brutality, the film registers, with minimal authorial intervention, the testimony of American "Veterans Against the [Vietnam] War," who relay, with a mixture of anger, shame, disgust, and confessional release, the unspeakable brutalities that they had witnessed, and, sometimes, themselves committed. As they are visibly flooded by feelings of inchoate rage and pain, they are moving in their very incapacity to speak. At times, the breakdown of speech condenses **transgenerational emotions** of epic proportions, as when a Native American veteran breaks down with the horrible realization that he had become in Vietnam, in a colonial chiasmus, the kind of racist soldier that had massacred his own ancestors, In sum, such films convey a vivid sense of film's awesome capacity to resuscitate buried pasts as lived through the body.

The film-related events staged by such organizations as "Future Cinema," "Punchdrunk," and "Secret Cinema," meanwhile, provoke and stimulate the body in a different way, by bringing the fiction film into the three-dimensional world through *participatory spectatorship*. Building both on avant-garde theater's penchant for involving and even assaulting the spectator, as well as on interactive games and theme parks, these participatory projects offer **immersive reception** through cultural experiences where a temporary location—announced, rave-like, at the last moment—is transformed into a constructed world inspired by the screening of a specific film such as *The Battle of Algiers* (1966). In an inversion of the colonial expositions that displayed the triumphs of imperialism, "Secret Cinema" (April–May 2011) turned the tunnels under London's Waterloo Station into a *tableau vivant* of 1950s French-dominated Algeria. Before the screening, alongside the recreated *souks* and squares of "Algiers," actors impersonating French officers, in character and speaking in French, dragged audience members to the gendarmerie to interrogate them about their links to "terrorism." Spectators could peek in at torture scenes glimpsed through prison bars. The "Secret Cinema" presentation conveyed what might be called the **visceral politics of imperialism** as a form of **biopower**, or the state or imperial regulation of their subjects through the subjugation of bodies and the control of populations. Although set in the 1950s, the event triggered powerful allegorical resonances in the age of the "War on Terror" and Abu-Ghraib.

More recently, analysts speak of a post-classical **immersive cinema** whereby the spectator is plunged less into a linear narrative than a roller-coaster-like succession of sensations. The question is: *immersion* to what end? While disaster blockbusters try to trigger useless sensations of panic, a film such as *12 Years a Slave* (2013) communicates with tremendous skill the realities of slavery. Spielberg's *Amistad* (1997), meanwhile, although politically problematic in many ways, does create a visceral effect in the scene in which live black bodies are thrown overboard from the slave ship, providing a dramatically literal "*immersive effect*" on those spectators for whom the phrase "the Middle Passage" might have been merely an unfelt historical abstraction. Spielberg references a kind of *visceral spectatorship* in his comments about what he sees as the wave of the future—screenless, enveloping, game-like immersive entertainments where the "player" (not the spectator) dwells inside an interactive simulacral entertainment. Thanks to Oculus Rift, a strap-on virtual headset, "players" might soon be able to participate directly in the disciplinary spectacle of the guillotine through a simulator: "Twist your neck and you see crowds of spectators; look down and you see the basket waiting for your head."[39] While Spielberg has in mind commercial entertainments, one imagines the possibilities of using such media not for "entertainment" but for a **virtual pedagogy** that would offer the simulacral yet visceral experience of a lynching, or of enslavement, or of police harassment, from the victims' point of view, or, for that matter, of a revolution from the participants' point-of-view.

Thanks to new media technologies, meanwhile, documentaries have achieved unprecedented levels of veracity and immersive effects. Jehane

Noujaim's *The Square* (2013), for example, plunges us into the vortex of the events of the Arab Spring through a vivid blow-by-blow account of the unfolding events in Tahrir Square. As with *Battle of Chile* four decades earlier, the film registers the day-to-day challenges facing a mass movement, not at a safe distance but rather close up and *sur-le-vif*, where the excitement in the streets bleeds into the film and into the movie theatres. The film combines the account of the unfolding events with a more focused portrayal of a gallery of activist "characters" representing a cross-section of the demonstrators – actor Khalid Abdalla, an Egyptian-British upper-class son of a dissident and star of *The Kite Runner,* now a vigorous media spokesman for the activists in the Square; Ahmed Hassan, a big-hearted and tireless natural leader formed by the Cairo streets, a more articulate Egyptian Ali-la-Pointe; Magdy Ashour, an open-minded Islamist and a victim of Mubarak regime torture, torn between his allegiance to the Muslim Brotherhood and the more secular democratic ideals of his new-found friends from the Square, along with two minor artist-characters, Aida El Kashef, a filmmaker, and Ramy Essam, a singer-songwriter who became the troubadour of the revolution in the tradition of Bob Dylan and Victor Jara.

Like *Battle of Chile*, *The Square* sympathizes broadly with the left but lets the representatives of all tendencies, including rightists and Islamists, speak their mind. And like *Battle of Chile*, *The Square* conveys the passionate engagements of a moment when masses of people suddenly glimpse their national desire. Incorporating footage shot by activists on the ground, the film shows a short-lived utopian moment where gender, class, and religious divides begin to break down. Culled from 1600 hours of footage, the film was made under the *"risk of the real,"* (Comolli) interrupted by arrests, physical injuries, interrogations, and confiscated cameras. We are painfully aware that the filmmakers are dodging live bullets, tossed tear-gas canisters, and onrushing military vehicles. *The Square* gives a visceral and kinetic sense of events, not shying away from images of torture, beatings, and government thugs running their trucks over demonstrators. Just as *Battle of Chile* showed an Argentinian cameraman filming his own death, *The Square* shows us a policeman dragging a murdered body across the street and dumping it in the garbage, footage later picked up by international networks. Rather than interviews, voice-over, and talking heads, we witness activists in dialogue with one another, improvising responses to events as they occur. *The Square* is a *Battle of Chile* or a *Battle of Algiers* for the YouTube generation, a low-budget film made with camera-phones and Canon 5D camera. Charting the collision of utopian hopes and dystopian power structure, the film follows a trajectory from mass euphoria to exasperation, from activism to coups d'etat, but also insists, with a lucid if chastened optimism, that even after defeats, *la lucha continua*. Although the movement was not ultimately successful, *The Square* gives a sense of what revolution might feel like.

Culled from 1,600 hours of footage, the film was made under the "*risk of the real*," (Comolli) interrupted by arrests, physical injuries, interrogations, and confiscated cameras. We are painfully aware that the filmmakers are dodging live bullets, tossed teargas canisters, and onrushing military vehicles. *The Square* gives a visceral and kinetic sense of events, not shying away from images of torture, beatings, and government thugs running their trucks over demonstrators. Just as *The Battle of Chile* showed an Argentinean cameraman filming his own death, *The Square* shows us a policeman dragging a murdered body across the street and dumping it in the garbage, footage later picked up by international networks. Rather than interviews, voice-over, and talking heads, we witness activists in dialogue with one another, improvising responses to events as they occur. *The Square* is *The Battle of Chile* or *The Battle of Algiers* for the YouTube generation, a low-budget film made with camera phones and a Canon 5D camera. Charting the collision of utopian hopes and dystopian power structure, the film, similar to *The Battle of Chile*, follows a trajectory from mass euphoria to exasperation, from activism to *coups d'etat*, but also insists, with a lucid if chastened optimism, that, even after defeats, *la lucha continua*.

## The Rediscovery of Pleasure

*Hyper-Brechtianism* sometimes betrayed Brecht by falling prey to a certain **puritanism**—defined by George Bernard Shaw as the "terrible fear that someone, somewhere, is having a good time." Despite Brecht's own love of fun, humor, and entertainment, the hyper-Brechtians valorized a quasi-Lutheran "working" as opposed to the "playing" and "enjoying" spectator, an ideal redolent of the Weberian Protestant work ethic and premised on the very un-Brechtian idea that playing cannot generate knowledge. And while the *historical avant-gardes* had often experimented with sexual avant-gardism—albeit in a masculinist way—this concern had little appeal for the hyper-Brechtians. While right to be wary of sexualized exploitation, to reject all sexualized representation would be rather similar to banning banquet scenes since eating might lead to food poisoning.

Feminists were critical of the masculinist bias not only of Brecht but also of an avant-garde seen as hostile to "feminine" values stereotypically linked to empathetic identification, passive consumerism, and an irrational love for soap operas.[40] The choice of "identification" as conceptual villain betrayed a hostility to what would normally be seen as a virtue—the capacity to empathize with others. Revolutions, after all, work both through **identification** with a trans-individual collective project and through **disidentification** with the hegemonic ideology. For Ranciere, *disidentification* evokes a critique of the idea of one's "natural place" in society, while the same term, for Jose Munoz, evokes the creative strategies deployed by racial and sexual minorities in order to negotiate majority culture by transforming mainstream works for their own cultural purposes The stigmatization of emotion was premised on the false dicthomy of reason and emotion dichotomy, when, in fact, reason, as Brecht well understood, can be emotional, even passionate, without ceasing to be reasonable, just as rationalism can be hysterical, a mask of objectivity hiding deeply irrational forms of pathos. Education, meanwhile, can be what Nietzsche called a *frohliche wissenschaft* or—as Godard put it in the title of his treatise on audiovisual pedagogy—a *gai savoir*.

In 1992, Ruby Rich celebrated cinematic pleasure by joyfully heralding the advent of the **new queer cinema** that she described as "irreverent, energetic, alternatively minimalist and excessive [and] ... full of pleasure."[41] The movement included such films as Todd Haynes' *Poison* (1991), Tom Kalin's *Swoon* (1992), Marlon Riggs' *Tongues Untied* (1989), and Gregg Araki's *The Living End* (1992). For Jackie Stacey, films such as Sheila McLuaghlin's *She Must Be Seeing Things* (1987) went beyond humanist "positive images" to draw on queer performance to "explore cinematic pleasures beyond the heterosexual gaze and to play with the meanings of taboo issues, such as the fluid boundary between lesbian and heterosexual desire, the pleasures of voyeurism, and the tensions of interracial romance."[42] Summarizing Gayle Kimball's conclusions in "Women's Culture: The Women's' Renaissance of the Seventies," Richard Dyer spoke of **lesbian cultural-feminist cinema** as having the following features: (1) the deployment of images of female power, including in the form of goddesses and female figures from Biblical and Greek mythologies; (2) the reclaiming of Amazons and witches from patriarchal denigration; (3) an emphasis on the personal and autobiographical as exempla of a more general, collective female existence; and (4) the celebration of the self-transforming female body and, specifically, female experiences such as childbirth and menstruation.[43]

Many feminist directors turned away from the frosty impersonality of *counter-cinema* to propose a feminist **counter-cinema of the personal**. For Alison Hoffman, Miranda July's defiantly quirky films seek to create the sense of a "community of feeling" based on shared vulnerability, beckoning us toward what Peggy Phelan calls "possibilities in thought and in practice ... still to be created, still to be lived...."[44] While Godard moved toward the short-circuiting of eroticism, Peggy Ahwesh, in *The Color of Love*, went in a more pro-sexual direction in a found-footage film made out of decomposing, jerky Super-8 porn footage, where the physical defects evoke not only the precarious material support of the film itself but also the fragile, trembling nature both of sexuality and sexual representation.

The feminist challenging of the comparmentalizateion of public and private, personal and political, had concrete implications for filmic practice. Yvonne Rainer, in *Film About a Woman Who...* (1974), wove together life and art, the public and the private, the historiographical and the autobiographical. This concern with the personal recalls Maya Deren's metaphor, drawn from a *minor* musical genre, of a **chamber aesthetic**— an echo, perhaps, of Virginia Woolf's "room of one's own"—as a way to surpass the gendered division between public and private. As articulated in Deren's "Statement of Principles," **chamber films** were attuned to "different values than one expects of symphonic orchestrations [and, by analogy, to] values quite different from those of feature films."[45]

Other feminist filmmakers recuperated the notoriously sentimental epistolary genre to develop the **epistolary film**, or what Ruby Rich calls **correspondence films**, whereby filmmakers such as Yvonne Rainer, Chantal Akerman, and Mona Hatoom, taking advantage of the polyperspectival structure of the epistolary form, deployed letters to convey female interlocution and reciprocal *écriture féminine*.[46] Yvonne Rainer practices a different kind of **perspectival narration** in her doc-fiction hybrid *Privilege* (1990), a film that mixes *cinema verité*-style interviews with a self-reflexive film-within-the-film (a documentary on menopause by the director's African-American alter ego "Yvonne Washington"). The film counterpoints diverse perspectives related to intersectional variables of gender, race, class, and age, toward the announced topic of the film—privilege—specifically that of bohemian artists who form part of another kind of "vanguard," of gentrification. More generally, Rainer creates a **cinema of self-questioning** in terms of the privileges of the white-middle-class lesbian filmmaker herself, for whom the story is not paramount but merely "an empty frame on which to hang images and thoughts...."[47]

Michelle Citron, meanwhile, practices **feminist intersubjectivity** in *Daughter's Rite* by interweaving home movies and documentary interviews to create a synthetic feminine subject and a polyperspectival approach to questions of mother–daughter relations. While Scott MacDonald speaks of the **home movie aesthetic** of filmmakers such as Marie Menken,[48] others spoke of **herstory** as what had been occluded by **his-story**. Catherine Russell described Su Friedrich's films, meanwhile, as **auto-ethnographies** where the director understands "her personal history to be implicated in larger social formations and historical processes."[49] Sadie Benning's early Pixel-vision films such as *Me and Ruby Fruit, Jollies* (1989), and *If Every Girl Had a Diary* (1990), resemble diary entries in their playful, confessional style, and document the joys and anxieties of the young filmmaker coming out into her lesbian identity. Many of the feminist films constitute what Bakhtin calls **hidden polemics**, that is, texts that engage in a metatextual dialogue with some (usually unnamed) antecedent text. Marjorie Keller's *Misconception* (1977), for example, forms what Anne Friedburg calls a "loving critique" of the masculinist approach to childbirth in Stan Brakhage's 1959 *Window Water Baby Moving*.[50]

## The Legacy of the V-Effect

Is Brechtianism dead in the postmodern age? Alexander Kluge's mixed mode opus *News from Ideological Antiquity* implies as much by having two actors from the Berliner Ensemble (the theater group founded by Brecht) read passages from Marx, which, it turns out, they do not actually understand at all. Confusing idealism in its colloquial sense as opposed to the philosophical sense, they ask, "Why does Marx say we shouldn't be idealist?"; and, "Isn't it good to be idealist?" In a larger sense, Kluge can be seen as offering historically informed and imaginative transmutations of the basic themes of Brechtian theory. Brecht's *"art as praxis"* becomes Kluge's view of art as conducive to the construction of an **oppositional public sphere**; Brecht's (and Benjamin's) idea of "changing the apparatus" becomes Kluge's ideas of **counter-production** and **counter-commodities**. Brecht's call for a "democratic opera" becomes Kluge's "opera as a power plant of emotion." Brecht's **active spectator** becomes the **spectator–collaborator**. The fractured mythos of Brecht's epic theater becomes the splintering of the narrative continuum in Kluge's *The Patriot* (1979). And if Brecht tried to right the balance in favor of rational distance, Kluge, in the wake of hyper-Brechtianism, restores the balance again in the title of his film *The Power of Emotion*.[51]

Brecht's estranging operations remain highly pertinent at a time when the Western left has found it difficult to break through the dominant commonsense and make its project appealing to the majority. One of Brecht's most politically generative concepts, in this sense, was the *verfremdungseffekt* (aka V-Effect), variously translated as distantiation, estrangement, or **alienation-effect**—that is, deconditioning devices by which conventional societal arrangements are relativized and cast in a critical light. The translation of V-effect as "distantiation" is problematic because it is sometimes read as "distance" and "indifference" when the real goal is for the spectator to see through the veils of sentimentality that obscure social vision. As a politicization of the Russian Formalist concept of **ostrenanie** or "making strange," *verfremdungseffekt* aimed at **denaturalization**, at freeing socially conditioned phenomena and understandings from the stamp of familiarity so as to reveal them as unnatural, even shocking. Since the dominant ideology normalizes an oppressive social order, *alienation-effects* are one way to break through the passivity-inducing formulae that blind us to the inequalities that structure our everyday life but whose mechanisms remain largely invisible. Brechtian *alienation-effects* were designed to provoke the spectator to reconceive and hopefully change hegemonic modes of social understanding. An excellent example of turning the unthinkable into the obvious through an *alienation-effect*, in this sense, is the slogan "We are the 99%." In one fell swoop, what had been seen as a beleaguered leftist minority deployed the power of a concept to turn itself into a potentially overwhelming majority, consisting of all those not forming part of the exclusive club of the "owners" of the United States."

Within Brecht's theory, *alienation-effects* were closely tied to Marxist analyses of "**alienation**," the process by which human beings lose control of their labor power and institutions along with their critical consciousness about their real conditions of existence. The goal of *alienation-effects* was to reveal through shock-effects the ultimate strangeness and mutability of taken-for-granted social arrangements. Part of the point of *alienation-effects* is to connect the dots of social oppression by demonstrating the links between phenomena that are usually thought of in compartmentalized ways. For example, during the same post-financial crisis period where absolutely no one from Wall Street was being arrested for massive financial crimes, thousands of New Yorkers were being arrested and subsequently imprisoned for petty drug-related crimes such as having a joint in one's possession. An episode of *The Daily Show* (August 13, 2013) used an *alienation-effect* that connected these two social realities, dramatizing the left-wing axiom that the real social problem in the United States is not the "crime in the streets" but "the crime in the suites." The episode spoofed Mayor Bloomberg's defense of his "Stop and Frisk" policy, which mainly targets blacks and Latinos. *The Daily Show* had its black "correspondent" Jessica Williams surprise liberal guest host John Oliver with her ringing endorsement of "stop and frisk." Picking up on Bloomberg's comment that "the police go where the crime is," Williams reported direct from a "high-crime area"—Wall Street—as a place where profiling was absolutely necessary. Those most likely to commit corporate crime, she pointed out, usually fit a certain profile—well-dressed, affluent, and "fond of using sunscreen." So if "you're a white, upper-East Side billionaire with ties to the financial community, like Michael Bloomberg," she warned, "you just have to expect to be roughed up once in a while."

In a left-populist vein, Michael Moore's oeuvre provides a treasure trove of **neo-Brechtian alienation-effects**, now filtered through American popular entertainment and standup comedy. First under the title "TV Nation," and later "The Awful Truth, " Moore became what Doug Kellner calls "one of the most high-profile critics of corporate capitalism, US military policy, the Bush–Cheney administration, the US health industry, and the manifold injustices of US society."[52] One Michael Moore TV episode, a parody of the show "Cops," where police routinely brutalize "illegal aliens" and black drug dealers, performed a social reversal similar to the Jon Stewart bit, by having the cops abuse CEOs instead of lower-grade criminals. The basic drift of Moore's work has been to mock America's criminal corporatocracy and its profit-driven corporate media, but in a style that "picks up on the playful and ironic side of postmodern/Gen X culture and uses humor, jokes, irony, and stunts to break up the sobriety of the classic documentary."[53] In his earlier work, Moore feigned naiveté in order to effect the "disalienation" or **deniasement** (French "*denaiving*") of American spectators who mechanically reiterate their blind exceptionalist faith in "the greatest country in the world." *Sicko* (2007), for example, "de-naives" the Americans who ritualistically praise the pathogenic American health system as "the best health care system in the world." Doing what cautious liberal commentators rarely do, Moore **models alternatives** by calling attention to other countries where health care is treated simply as a universal right. Through the mutual illumination of social systems, we learn that, in Britain, cashiers *dispense* rather than receive cash, that Cubans (and even GITMO prisoners) enjoy better health care than the average American, and that insurance companies, far from "caring about you," as the ads proclaim, spend inordinate energy in order *not* to help customers, by weeding out the unhealthy (i.e., unprofitable) customers.

Some of the topoi of Moore's films make a cumulative point through repetition. One leitmotif is that of the breezily overconfident Moore trying to penetrate the inner sanctums of corporate capitalism. In a familiar routine, Moore is first received by the authorities with icy politesse, followed by veiled threats, and finally by physical force, almost invariably accompanied by the assertion of a legal/philosophical principle: "You are on private property." What becomes clear through this quasi-ritualistic repetition is that it is **corporate enclosure** and the reign of private property that prevent the solving of the most obvious problems. Moore tears the mask off corporate propaganda, forcing the corporations to reveal their true face behind the public-relations makeup. His **comical *lehrstuckes*** have a Bergsonian, mechanical quality, since we always know how they will end—just as we always know that Don Quixote will get beat up—the suspense only concerns how long the beating will be postponed. But the inevitable progression from genteel hostility to threats of expulsion and the assertion of private property rights is in itself a lesson about a system that values property over life and health. The measure of Moore's success, then, lies less in the real-world effects of his intervention than in the pedagogic power of the example.

Everyday life in the capitalist society is anxiogenic, leaving the average person haunted by myriad insecurities about jobs, debt, foreclosures, bankruptcy, and health care, and a general lack of access to what should be common. Moore's films are perhaps best understood in an American political situation where right-wing populists constantly exploit what Sianne Ngai calls **ugly feelings**—unconfessable emotions of irritation, envy, and *ressentiment*.[54] Not only does Moore directly address the right-wing exploitation of frustration—for example, in the *South Park*-style animation pinpointing the role of the phobic fear of black men in American politics—but he himself also mobilizes anger for more progressive social purposes. By cutting through the right's exploitation of racialized fear and misdirected anger as politically combustible, without which it cannot hope to win elections, Moore transforms "base" emotions into the gold of political consciousness.

## Political Cinema in the Age of the Posts

The partial eclipse of political modernism and the avant-garde must also be seen in the light of **postmodernism** and its proclamation of the end of utopian metanarratives of science and revolution, which led to a questioning of the premises of political modernism and a more decentered remapping of political and cultural possibilities. In what is by now a standard narrative, a discourse of "revolution" slowly gave way to an idiom of "resistance," indicative of a shifting vision of the emancipatory project redefined as "posts"—post-Marxist, post-Brechtian, post-structuralist, post-modernist, post-feminist, and post-colonialist. Substantive nouns such as "revolution" and "liberation" transmute into a largely adjectival opposition: "counter-hegemonic," "subversive," "adversarial," and "insurgent." Instead of a macro-narrative of revolution, the focus shifts to Foucauldian micropolitics and a decentered Deleuzian multiplicity of localized struggles.

The era of the posts also witnesses the rise to prominence of intellectuals affiliated with the Global South such as Edward Said, Gloria Anzaldúa, Nestor Garcia Canclini, Arjun Appadurai, Anibal Quijano, Enrique Dussel, Vandana Shiva, and Achille Mbembe (and countless others). The transdisciplinary field of **postcolonial theory**, in this sense, explores issues of the colonial archive and hybrid postcolonial identity in work inflected by the poststructuralist theory of Derrida, Lacan, and Foucault. With postcolonial theory, the Manichean opposition of colonizer and colonized, oppressor and oppressed, and First World/Third World gives way to a more nuanced yet still power-laden spectrum of subtle differentiations, in a new global regime where First World and Third World (now redubbed the "Global South") are seen as inextricably commingled. Notions of ontologically referential identity made way for identity seen as an endlessly recombinant play of constructed differences. Once-rigid boundaries are presented as more porous; imagery of barbed-wire frontiers between the French and Algerian quarters in *The Battle of Algiers* (1966) have given way to the more subtle barriers between *banlieu* and city center of *La Haine*. Instead of binary oppositions, we find mutual shaping and indigenization within a Bakhtinian "in-between."

Perhaps no filmmaker encapsulates this moment of the converging "posts," with its erosion of essentialist binaries through the ramifying "politics of difference," better than Isaac Julien. If Fanon embodied the theory and practice of Third World nationalism, Julien embodies the theory and practice of postcolonial postnationalism in the metropole. Just as Fanon mixed genres and discourses in his writing, Julien in *Black Skin White Masks* (1996) mixes cinematic genres in his film, mingling archival footage; interviews with Fanon's family members, fellow psychiatrists (Azoulay), and scholars (Francoise Verges, Stuart Hall); quoted fiction films; and staged scenes featuring soliloquies by the actor (Colin Salmon) playing "Fanon." At the same time, the film instantiates the skeptical spirit of the posts by offering a fairly "cool" take on Fanon's incendiary prose, conveying both political identification with Fanon and generational distance from him, while effecting a carefully calibrated departure from Third-Worldist rhetoric.

The Julien film picks up on a striking feature of Fanon's work—its constant preoccupation with the clash of gazes, or what might be called, paraphrasing Jane Gaines, (**colonial**) **looking relations**.[55] In *Wretched of the Earth*, Fanon casts colonialism itself as a painful crossing of looks, where the black man has to meet the white man's eyes, where the colonizer trains on the colonized a look of prejudice, surveillance, desire, and appropriation, while the native looks on the settler town with lust, envy, and rage. The colonialist's greatest crime, meanwhile, was to make the colonized look at themselves through colonizing eyes. In the wake of Sartre, de Beauvoir, and Fanon's theorizations of *le regard*, Julien's film constitutes a theorized orchestration of racialized and sexualized looks, captured and analyzed in all their permutations: Fanon's direct look at the camera/spectator; de Gaulle's archival paternal look at Algeria as he parades through Maghrebian streets; the uncomprehending look of French soldiers on Algerian women and their misreading of the hermeneutics of the veil; and the sympathetic look of the woman observer (cited from *The Battle of Algiers*) who cries empathetically as she witnesses torture. The most disturbed look is Fanon's look at two men kissing; the gaze is returned when one of the men looks back at Fanon, after which Fanon looks away as if unable to sustain a homosexual gaze. In an instance of **queer postcoloniality**, the look is disrupted, named, disturbed, and critiqued, giving a sense of homoerotic panic, a frightened form of **dis**identification.

Since the 1990s, the situation of the left has both dramatically improved and disastrously worsened. Despite victories by the Latin American left and by indigenous peoples in the Americas, the left has been battered by the disappearance of actually existing socialism, the ebbing of Third-Worldist anticolonial revolution, the decline and cooptation of unions, and the spreading reign of finance capital. Socialism, meanwhile, has become little more than a third-way capitalism, as became obvious when the French Socialist Party contemplated nominating a former head of the IMF (and a sexual predator to boot) as its presidential candidate! For philosopher/economist Yann Moulier-Boutang, a third age of capitalism is typified by **cognitive capitalism** as a new iteration of capitalism where work becomes co-extensive with life itself, a successor to the **mercantile capitalism** of the eighteenth century and the **industrial capitalism** of the nineteenth and twentieth centuries.[56] Global capitalism, meanwhile, practices what David Harvey calls **accumulation by dispossession**, or the brutal transformation of non-capitalist sectors into capitalist sectors.[57] Global capitalism has devoured more and more of the earth's resources while sucking the air out of the democratic process in Western liberal democracies. While colonial capitalism classically cannibalized the Global South, postcolonial capitalism is now cannibalizing the wealth of the Global North itself by appropriating public goods such as pensions and education.

Capitalism and authoritarianism have never been so strong and, at the same time, so vulnerable to bursting financial bubbles, post-partisan protests, and "Twitter revolutions." To those who recite the Thatcherite mantra that "there is no alternative," Graeber points to aspects of social life that have not succumbed to privatization and the cash nexus. In a very different language, Deleuze and Guattari suggest that the schizophrenic logic of capitalism calls forth its own resistant "anti-production." At this point in the history of art and politics, it is necessary to question the potentially elitist, authoritarian, and Eurocentric aspects of political modernism and the avant-garde itself. Political avant-gardism assumes that the oppressed, due to a knowledge-deficit, need pedagogical guidance. Middle-class intellectuals are the possessors of the **episteme** or rational knowledge, while the people are the victims of the **doxa**, or fallacious ordinary opinion.

Just as one can assume, *à la* Jacques Ranciere, a basic **equality of intelligence** within a society, so one can assume the equality of intelligence between cultures and societies. In his influential article "The Twilight of

Vanguardism," David Graeber poses the provocative question: "... if the role of revolutionary intellectuals is not to form an elite that can arrive at the correct strategic analyses and then lead the masses to follow them, what precisely is it?" Although Graeber does not offer a definitive "solution" to this quandary, he does invoke a gallery of nineteenth-century artists with anarchist sympathies to suggest that, rather than being a political vanguard leading the way to a future society, radical artists almost invariably saw themselves as exploring new and less alienated modes of life. Graeber, whose anthropological study of indigenous peoples inflects his argument, suggests a way out of the cul-de-sac of vanguardism by proposing a "form of **auto-ethnography**, combined, perhaps, with a certain utopian extrapolation; a matter of teasing out the tacit logic or principles underlying certain forms of radical practice in communities, and then, not only offering the analysis back to these communities, but using them to formulate new visions."

## Notes

1    For a thoroughgoing analysis of political modernism, see D. N. Rodowick, *The Crisis of Political Modernism: Criticism and Ideology in Contemporary Film Theory* (Berkeley: University of California Press, 1994).
2    See Peter Burger, *Theory of the Avant-Garde* (Minneapolis: University of Minnesota Press, 1984).
3    Nicole Brenez, *Cinémas d'avant-garde* (Paris: Cahiers Du Cinéma, 2007).
4    David Graeber *Revolutions in Reverse: Essays in Politics, Violence, Art, and Imagination* (New York: Autonomedia, 2011), pp. 60–61.
5    Ibid., p. 98.
6    On the "two avant-gardes," see Peter Wollen, "The Two Avant-Gardes," in Peter Wollen, *Readings and Writings: Semiotic Counter Strategies* (London: Verso, 1982).
7    See *Brecht on Theatre: The Development of an Aesthetic*, trans. John Willet (New York: Hill & Wang, 1957).
8    See Christian Metz, *The Imaginary Signifier: Psychoanalysis and the Cinema* (Bloomington: Indiana University Press, 1981).
9    On dissensus, see Jacques Ranciere, *Dissensus: On Politics and Aesthetics* (London: Continuum, 2010). On landscapes of the visible, see Ranciere, *Le Spectateur Emancipe*, p. 84.
10    David E. James, *Allegories of Cinema: American Film in the Sixties* (Princeton: Princeton University Press, 1989), p. 324.
11    This reflexivity need not be literal. The films of Michael Snow and Hollis Frampton, for Annette Michelson, promote an epistemological reflexivity, simultaneously modeling the processes of cinema and those of cognition itself. See Annette Michelson, "Film and the Radical Aspiration," in Adams P. Sitney (ed.), *Film Culture Reader* (New York: Film Culture, 1970).

12 Tsvetan Todorov, *Mikhail Bakhtin: The Dialogical Principles* (Minneapolis: University of Minnesota Press, 1985).

13 Andrew Bergman, *We're in the Money: Depression America and its Films* (New York: Harper and Row, 1972).

14 For more on Assayas, see the interview conducted by Richard Porton, "Portrait of the Artist as a Young Radical: A Interview with Olivier Assayas," *Cineaste*, Vol. 38, no. 2 (Spring 2013).

15 See Stuart Hall, "Encoding and Decoding in the Television Discourse," Birmingham: Centre for Cultural Studies, University of Birmingham, 1973.

16 Wollen, 1982, op. cit., p. 88, and quoted in Pam Cook, *The Cinema Book* (London: British Film Institute, 1985), p. 9.

17 Claire Johnston, "Women's Cinema as Counter-Cinema," in Claire Johnston (ed.), *Notes on Women's' Cinema* (London: Society for Education in Film and Television, 1975).

18 Laura Mulvey, "Visual Pleasure and Narrative Cinema," in *Visual and Other Pleasures* (London: Macmillan, 1989), p. 16.

19 Quoted in Fabien Danesi, *Le Cinema de Guy Debord* (Paris: Paris Experimental, 2011), p. 87.

20 David E. James, *Allegories of Cinema* (Princeton: Princeton University Press, 1989), p. 278.

21 See Robert Stam, *Reflexivity in Film and Literature: From Don Quixote to Jean-Luc Godard* (New York: Columbia University Press, 1992).

22 See "Entretien avec Christian Metz," *Ca 7/8* (May 1975), p. 23.

23 Bruno Latour, "The Politics of Explanation: An Alternative," in Steve Woolgar (ed.), *Knowledge and Reflexivity* (London: Dage, 1988).

24 Brenda Longfellow et al., op. cit., p. 9.

25 See Linda Williams, *Hardcore: Power, Pleasure, and the Frenzy of the Visible* (Berkeley: University of California Press, 1989).

26 See Linda Williams, *Hardcore: Power, Pleasure, and the Frenzy of the Visible* (Berkeley: University of California Press, 1989).

27 Vivian Sobshack, *Carnal Thoughts: Embodiment and Moving Image Culture* (Berkeley: University of California Press, 2004), p. 63.

28 Steven Shaviro, *The Cinematic Body (Theory Out Of Bounds)* (Minneapolis: University of Minnesota Press, 1993), pp. 255–256.

29 Brian Massumi, "The Autonomy of Affect," *Cultural Critique*, 31 (Autumn 1995), p. 104.

30 Corinn Columpar and Sophie Mayer, *There She Goes: Feminist Filmmaking and Beyond* (Detroit: Wayne State University Press, 2009), p. 6.

31 Thomas Elsaesser and Malte Hagener, *Film Theory: An Introduction through the Senses* (New York: Routledge, 2010).

32 See Jacques Ranciere, *Le Partage du sensible: Esthetique et Politique* (Paris: La Fabrique, 2000).

33 Deleuze, *Cinema 2: The Time-Image* (Minneapolis: University of Minnesota Press, 1989), p. 159.

34    See Vivian Sobchack, *Carnal Thoughts: Embodiment and the Moving Image* (Berkeley: University of California Press, 2004).

35    Vivian Sobshack, *Carnal Thoughts: Embodiment and Moving Image Culture* (Berkeley: University of California Press, 2004).

36    Lauren Berlant, *Cruel Optimism* (Durham: Duke University Press, 2011).

37    See M. M. Bakhtin and Pavel Nikolaevich Medvedev, *The Formal Method in Literary Scholarship: A Critical Introduction to Sociological Poetics* (Baltimore: John Hopkins University Press, 1991).

38    Belinda Smail, *The Documentary: Politics, Emotion, Culture* (London: Palgrave-Macmillan, 2010).

39    See Frank Rose, "Movies of the Future," *New York Times* (June 23, 2013), Opinion Section, 5.

40    Andreas Huyssen, *After the Great Divide: Modernism, Mass Culture and Postmodernism* (Bloomington: Indiana University Press, 1986), p. 53, 49, 61.

41    See Michele Aaron (ed.), *New Queer Cinema: A Critical Reader* (Edinburgh: Edinburgh University Press, 2004), p. 54.

42    See Jackie Stacey, "Queer Theory and New Queer Cinema" in Pam Cook (ed.), *The Cinema Book* (London: British Film Institute, 2007), p. 506.

43    Richard Dyer, *Now You See It: Studies on Lesbian and Gay Film* (New York: Routledge, 1990), p. 182.

44    Columpar and Mayer (eds.), op. cit, p. 31.

45    Ibid., p. 83

46    See Ruby Rich, *Chick Flicks: Theories and Memories of the Feminist Film Movement* (Durham: Duke University Press, 1998).

47    Rainer, in Camera Obscura Collective, 1976, 89, quoted in Alison Butler, "Avant-Garde and Counter-Cinema," in Pam Cook (ed.), *The Cinema Book* (London: British Film Institute, 2007), p. 94.

48    Blaetz, op. cit., p. 221.

49    Blaetz, p. 314.

50    Blaetz, p. 231.

51    For a very insightful collection of essays by major Kluge specialists (notably Miriam Hansen, Anton Kaes, Thomas Elsaesser, Carol Flynn, Gertrud Koch, and Andreas Huysse), see Tara Forrest (ed.), *Alexander Kluge: Raw Materials for the Imagination* (Amsterdam: Amsterdam University Press, 2012).

52    Douglas Kellner, *Cinema Wars: Hollywood Film and Politics in the Bush-Cheney Era* (Malden, MA: Blackwell Publishing, 2010), p. 132.

53    See Ortner, op. cit., p. 249.

54    Sianne Ngai, *Ugly Feelings* (Cambridge: Harvard University Press, 2007).

55    See Jane Gaines, "White Privilege and Looking Relations: Race and Gender in Feminist Film Theory," in Cultural Critique, 4 (Autumn, 1986).

56    See Yann Moulier-Boutang, *Cognitive Capitalism* (Cambridge: Polity, 2012).

57    See David Harvey, *The New Imperialism*(Oxford: Oxford University Press, 2003), p. 116.

# 4

# The Transmogrification of the Negative

A recurrent leitmotif in certain strands of subversive aesthetics consists in the **transmogrification of the negative**. Within the *longue durée*, this transmogrifying strain can be traced back to the perennial traditions referenced in earlier chapters, for example, to writers such as Rabelais who valorized the grotesque body and the lower social and bodily stratum. In the modern period, the spirit of irreverence went underground only to reemerge in plays such as Jarry's *King Ubu*. Later, movements such as Surrealism and Dada took over in displaced form the grotesque bodily symbolism, which had once formed a more central part of culture. Yet, the Mennipea and carnivalesque traditions reassert themselves in the films of Bunuel, Dali, and Vigo, in the travesty revolts of Genet's plays, and in various contemporary radical artistic and counter-cultural movements.

For romantic poets such as Coleridge, *transmogrification* conjured up the alchemical powers of the imagination, or more broadly the processes of metamorphosis, conversion, transformation, and transmutation, or, in later Deleuzian terms, "becoming." The artistic *transmogrification of the negative*, which rubs against the grain of the Platonic ideal of the beautiful, and even against the idea of aesthetics as an analysis of the beautiful and the harmonious, has, since the advent of *artistic modernism*, formed a noble and distinguished tradition. This trend responds to what Ben Highmore calls the "almost complete suppression of the fullness of human creaturely life within much aesthetic discourse," the elision of the "negative feelings" that "saturate our social, sexual, political, and private lives."[1] Turning classical aesthetics on its head, many of these transfigurative

*Keywords in Subversive Film/Media Aesthetics*, First Edition. Robert Stam with Richard Porton and Leo Goldsmith.
© 2015 John Wiley & Sons, Inc. Published 2015 by John Wiley & Sons, Inc.

aesthetics share the structuring trope of the strategic redemption of the low, the despised, the imperfect, and the "trashy" as a multi-leveled metaphor that evokes all sorts of redemptions, both social and aesthetic. If trash is artistically redeemable, so the socially "trashed" might be redeemable as well. Linking the theory of the commons to these underground trends, Stefano Harney and Fred Moten speak of the **undercommons** to characterize a shared underground space, a kind of **heterocosmos**—etymologically a "world of otherness"—in which the artist/intellectual can exist ambiguously with respect to capital and established institutions, within a parallel field of operations.[2]

   In the era of the *historical avant-gardes*, the transmogrifying trend blurred the borders between art and non-art. It was this impulse that fuelled the Dadaist and Cubist penchant for "found objects" and "papiers collés," summed up as **collage**—from the verb "to glue" to refer to reassemblage of scrap materials into art. (In a negation of the negation, some surrealists, such as lacerated-poster artists Raymond Hains and François Dufrêne, spoke of **décollage**, which consisted in the tearing, the scraping away of images and layers to disinter the beauty beneath.) In the realm of theory, we find the *transfiguration of the negative* in Bakhtin's exaltation of "redeeming filth" and the "bodily lower stratum"; in Benjamin's figure of the "ragpicker" and the "trash of history"; in Bataille's "excremental" fondness for the defiled and transgressive; in Derrida's recuperation of textual marginalia and the **socially-downgraded poles** of essentialist **hierarchical** binarisms; in Arthur Danto's "transformation of the commonplace"; and in Deleuze and Guattari's recuperation of "*minor literature*" and of stigmatized psychic states such as schizophrenia. In this chapter, we will explore the manifold aesthetic strategies that redeem hunger, garbage, failure, mistakes, and even cannibalism for the social purposes of art.

## An Aesthetic of Mistakes

One strand in *the transfiguration of the negative* is what might be called an **aesthetic of mistakes**. The history of art, after all, is a history of transgressions, that is, inventive violations of supposedly sacrosanct "rules," and, in the case of filmmaking, the violations of a set of normative procedures—smooth camera movements, suave transitions, the image always in focus, and so forth. The various New Waves violated cinematic decorum through "mistakes"—jiggly camera movements, deliberately incorrect edits, and sound–image disjunctions—techniques that later came to be seen as expanding the repertoire of film's expressive resources.

The *aesthetic of mistakes* eschewed the glamorous production values of the well-made industrial film, favoring instead the awkward, the transgressive, and the non-finalized. This aesthetic practices "**anticanonicity**"—that is, it deconstructs not only the canon as a reified set of masterpieces, but it also disassembles the generating matrix that creates canons and grammaticality. Rather than a disciplined mastery of canonical forms, it throws up an anti-canonical challenge to mastery itself.

Bakhtin invoked the literary equivalent of an *aesthetic of mistakes* when he spoke of Rabelais's **gramatica jocosa** ("laughing grammar"), in which artistic language was liberated from an asphyxiating correctness. The concept of "*laughing grammar*" is extremely well-developed within Afro-diasporic music and film, wherein the violation of aesthetic decorum goes hand in hand with a critique of social, aesthetic, and racial hierarchies. The **blues vernacular** tradition eschewed *bel canto* in favor of the dappled beauty of gravelly imperfection, rooted in a communal African aesthetic where everyone sang, including the raspy-voiced. Not coincidentally, the manifesto-song of the Bossa Nova movement, in parallel to Cinema Novo's defense of an "aesthetic of hunger," defended the artistic dignity of the *desafinado* (out-of-tune). We are reminded of how black musicians have historically turned noise into music, and "lowly" instruments (washboards, tubs, oil drums, plungers) into vibrant musicality—stretching the "normal" capacities of European instruments by playing the trumpet, *à la* Louis Armstrong, a few octaves "higher" than was usually deemed acceptable; or by playing three horns at the same time (similar to Rahssan Roland Kirk); or by composing concertos for pigs, and ram's horns, similar to Hermeto Paschoal—all as part of a high-flying aesthetic of tension and dissonance.[3] (In his DVD *L'Abcededaire*," Deleuze expressed his appreciation for Edith Piaf's way of hitting "false notes," and then setting them right.) Miles Davis sometimes advised musicians to "play as if you don't know how to play"; Godard, in this sense, changed cinema by acting as if he did not know how to film. The brilliant "errors" of such artists ended up changing both music and cinema, transforming the very criteria of taste.

Many of the "new cinema" movements, revealingly, cultivated an artistic dialogue with jazz. Apart from cinema having often featured jazz, the two arts manifest analogous processes of creation. They have in common a capacity to "eternalize" a lived moment of improvisational time. While classical scriptwriting and storyboarding imply planning, the idea of the shoot itself as what Jacques Rivette calls a "shared adventure" implies a jazz-like improvisation.[4] Much as John Coltrane spun the popular song "My Favorite Things" into a whirling dervish-like improvisation, so Jacques Rivette spun a few pages from Balzac's *L'Histoire des Treize* into a

12-hour film. While some films merely "include" jazz on their soundtracks, others, such as Shirley Clarke's *Harlem Story*, or Cassavetes' *Shadows*, or Rivette's *L'Amour Fou*, or Kiarostami's *Ten*, are formally jazzistic.[5] Certain artistic homologies link jazz with the new cinema movements: (1) the lack of a written script; (2) the emphasis on performative improvisation; and (3) the ironic relation to the canon, whether through jazz riffing on popular "standards," or Godard's riffing on standardized plots. With its polyrhythmic editing and swift changes of emotional pulse, *Breathless* is a seminal example of a jazzistic film. Larry Clarke's *Passing Through*, for David James, "translates [s] the sonic properties of jazz into visual expression."[6] Occasionally, directors have experimented with a jazz-like **apart-playing**, or **multi-track improvisation**, where individual collaborators, similar to jazz soloists, briefly shine by showcasing their "thing." Glauber Rocha attempted this kind of cinematic *apart-playing* in his big-budget avant-garde film *Idade da Terra* (1980), where he encouraged the actors, the cameraperson, and the crew to improvise alongside him.

Although sometimes exploited to camouflage lifeless acting or stodgy *mise-en-scène*, music at its best can imbue film with symbiotic intensities and social resonances. In William Greaves' *SymbioPsychoTaxiPlasm: Take One* (1968), we find actual **filmic improvisation**, with an "aesthetic of mistakes" as its corollary. Here, the anarchist-tinged refusal to take charge on the part of the black filmmaker-in-the-film becomes the catalyst for a revolt (devoutly desired by the director) on the part of his actors and crew. Using the annoyingly endless reshooting of the same scene of marital breakup from the fictitious film *Over the Cliff*, the director provokes the crew and cast to film themselves kvetching about his (manipulative) refusal to direct. With Miles Davis' *In a Silent Way* on the soundtrack, the film is built, in the jazzistic manner, on the agile recuperation of "mistakes"—the film runs out, the camera jams, the actors become restless, the director does not direct—to be recuperated as part of a new synthesis. In a *tour de force*, the film analogizes jazz's critical relation to the European mainstream by subverting dominant cinema conventions while also subtly evoking multiple insurgent energies against diverse authoritarianisms.

## Third Cinema: From Hunger to Garbage

The radical and anti-imperialist 1960s and 1970s were rich in examples of the *transmogrification of the negative*. In a 1965 manifesto essay, Rocha called for an **"aesthetics of hunger,"** expressed in "sad, ugly films" that treated hunger not only as theme but also as low-cost production strategy, elevating misery, as Deleuze put it, "to a strange positivity.[7] In a displaced mimesis, the material poverty of a low-budget style came to form the two-dimensional filmic correlative of poverty and the bodily pangs of hunger in the three-dimensional world. Latin America's originality, Rocha argued, was inseparable from its hunger and violence. In what Ismail Xavier sees as a kind of **aesthetic Fanonianism**, social violence would be allegorized through aesthetic violence to the stylistic and production norms of dominant cinema.[8] (Decades later, Ivana Bentes signified on Rocha's *aesthetics of hunger* by coining the term **"cosmetics of hunger"** to excoriate populist entertainment films such as *Eu, Tu, Eles* that departed from Rocha's radical vision to produce prettified versions of Brazilian poverty.)

While Rocha expressed his radical politics in auteurist fiction films, Fernando Solanas and Octavio Gettino rejected both the **"first cinema"** of Hollywood (and its imitators around the globe), and the **"second cinema"** of the auteurist art film (including in the "Third World"), favoring instead an insurgent **third cinema** consisting of militant documentaries made in close collaboration with activists. Aesthetically eclectic, the *third cinema* movement drew on currents as diverse as Soviet montage, Surrealism, Italian neo-realism, Brechtian *epic theater*, *cinéma vérité*, and the French New Wave, all alongside the rich legacies of national cultural practices. The Cuban filmmaker–theorist Julio Garcia Espinosa, meanwhile, eviscerated the "frozen forms" of **socialist realism**, the Soviet-style aesthetic that exalted idealized worker heroes (and sometimes Stalin himself) in an illusionist style. In his 1969 essay "For an **imperfect cinema**" (**cine-imperfecto**), Espinosa argued that a technically and artistically perfect cinema was almost always reactionary. A genuine popular art, he argued, could be energized by the "low" forms of popular culture. Rather than a self-sufficient, contemplative cinema, *imperfect cinema* proposes art as an endless critical process. Art, he concluded, will not disappear into nothingness; rather, "it will disappear into everything."[9] In a similar move in the context of *la Raza* and the Chicano movement, meanwhile, Tomas Ybarra-Frausto argued for **rasquachismo**—from "*rasquache*," or "lowly, miserable, person"—as a popular vernacular manner to make "have not" art out of impoverished resources.[10]

We find a shining example of the transfigurative redemption of the low and the filthy in the **aesthetics of garbage**. If the early 1960s trope of hunger signaled the desperate will to dignity of the famished subject as metonym for the Third World nation, the trope of garbage is more decentered, postmodern, and transnational. In social terms, garbage represents the diasporized, heterotopic site of the promiscuous mingling of rich and poor, center and periphery, the local and the global. As the ideal postmodern and postcolonial metaphor, garbage is mixed, syncretic, and a radically decentered social text. As congealed history, garbage is coagulated sociality, a gooey distillation of society's contradictions. A great social leveler, garbage forms the trysting point of the funky and the shi shi. As the lower stratum of the socius, the symbolic "bottom" of the body politic, garbage signals the return of the repressed; it is the place where used condoms, infected needles, and unwanted babies are discarded—the ultimate resting place of all that society both produces and represses, secretes and makes secret. Garbage is society's id; it steams and smells below the threshold of ideological rationalization and sublimation.[11]

At the same time, garbage forms the dark underside of globalization, a very material reality rooted in societies permeated by artificially stimulated consumption. Americans, for example, create 50% more garbage per capita than other similar Western economies, and double the trash output of the Japanese.[12] In many of the major cities in the world, as Arjun Appadurai points out, large "cities of disposal" literally live on mountains of compacted trash that "constitutes the earth beneath their feet and the sky that defines their horizons."[13] Waste is intimately connected to issues of health, pollution, wealth distribution, providing, in Edward Humes' words, "the ultimate lens on our lives, our priorities, our failings, our secrets, and our hubris."[14] Garbage also plays a central role in global economics. In what has become a locus classicus of neoliberal callousness, then World Bank head Larry Summers explained in an infamous memo (December 12, 1991) on trade liberalization that the Global South deserved to be literally "dumped on." An "impeccable logic," Summers argued, favored "dumping a load of toxic waste in the lowest wage country," since "health-impairing pollution" would have little effect on countries where many people already die young." Many African countries, he argued, "are vastly under-polluted."

It is one of the utopian, recombinant functions of art to work over dystopian, malodorous, and socially revelatory materials. Brazil's underground filmmakers of the 1960s, to our knowledge, were the first to speak of the "*aesthetics of garbage*" as a formalized artistic strategy with radical overtones. (Sganzerla used the phrase in 1968, an year before John Waters' film *Mondo Trasho*, and a half-decade before Water's *Trash Trilogy*.) The garbage metaphor conveyed an aggressive sense of marginality, of surviving within scarcity, of being condemned to recycle the materials of dominant metropolitan culture. For Brazilian filmmakers, a garbage style was seen as perfectly suited to a Third World country picking through the leavings— including in the form of "dumped" pharmaceuticals, TV programs, and nuclear waste—of a rigged international system. Bunuel's *Los Olvidados*

(1950) anticipated the *aesthetics of garbage* by concluding with the depositing of the corpse of its slum-born protagonist on a garbage dump. Almost two decades later, Rogerio Sganzerla's *Bandido da Luz Vermelha* ("Red Light Bandit," 1968), an example of what was variously called **marginal cinema**, **dirty-screen cinema**, **mouth of garbage**, and **udigrudi cinema** (Brazilian pronunciation of "underground"), begins with black slum children dancing around garbage-dump fires on the outskirts of São Paulo and ends with the protagonist's demise in a garbage dumpster.

When middle-class spectators think of people who work with and even feed themselves from garbage, they are likely to think of them metonymically as "garbage people," as those who live the bare animal existence of what Agamben calls **"zoe,"** as opposed to the **"bio"** of the self-aware individual endowed with subjectivity. Many garbage films, in contrast, stress the humanity of those who work with garbage to survive and the inhumanity of those who exploit them. Eduardo Coutinho's video *Boca de Lixo* ("Mouth of Garbage," but translated as *Scavengers*) centers on impoverished Brazilians who work and live at a dump outside Rio, all against the iconic–ironic backdrop of the outstretched arms of the Christ of Corcovado. The collectors ferret through whatever is thrown up by the daily lottery of ordure, sorting out plastic from metal from food for animals. Rather than take a miserabilist approach, Coutinho shows us singular individuals who are poor in resources but rich in inventive resilience, who at first hide their faces and resist being filmed at all. Indeed, Claudia Mesquita calls it a **negotiation film**, in that it "shows the negotiation that made its own existence possible."[15] The *catadores* fearlessly tell the filmmakers what to look at and how to interpret what they see. Instead of the suspect pleasures of a condescending pity, the spectator is confronted by vibrant hardworking people who dream, create, talk back, and reflect. Gradually, the film creates what Mesquita calls **"singularization,"** as we start to see brave individuals rather than sociological types. A homespun philosopher named "Whiskers" tells the filmmakers that garbage is a beginning and an end within a cyclical principle of birth, death, and rebirth. The film reveals garbage to be a form of stored energy, as containing in itself the seeds of its own transformation, the site of a deferred rendezvous between those who enjoy the luxury of wastefulness and those who cannot afford not to save what would have been wasted. Within the squalid phantasmagoria of the dump, the same commodities fetishized by TV commercials are shorn of their aura.

Since the money wasted in the production of mega-blockbusters might have financed thousands of less expensive films around the world, one might speak of a Hollywood **aesthetics of gluttony**. As Richard Maxwell and Toby Miller point out, Hollywood, as the biggest producer of pollutants in the Los Angeles area, is profoundly complicit in the ecological crisis. While *The Beach* was touted by its producers as raising environmental consciousness, its actual production ended up bulldozing any South Pacific scenery that did not "fit the company's fantasy of a tropical idyll; sand dunes were relocated, flora rearranged, and a 'new' strip of coconut palms was planted."[16] The Atelier Varan in Paris, launched by Jean Rouch to train international documentarians, in this sense, offers a counter-model in the form of a **sustainable cinema**, whereby each production leads to other productions, with equipment left for others to use, with ex-trainees becoming trainers who launch other ateliers. Zoe Graham speaks in this context of a **"sustainable documentary ecosystem"** to refer to films meant to be "passed on to future generations; as 'ecosystems' that thrive in different ways in different locations."[17] Fernando Cony Campos' *Ladroes de Cinema* ("Cinema Thieves," 1977), in this sense, takes advantage of **filmic leftovers** as a solution to scarcity. Set during Rio's carnival pageant, the film shows slum-dwellers, dressed up as carnival "Indians," stealing filmmaking equipment from American filmmakers documenting the carnival. Subsequently, they decide to make a film within the *samba-pageant style*. A visiting French ethnographer named Claude Rouch, in a transparent allusion to the French director, offers film stock and an initiation into film theory and technique. In the anthropophagic tradition, the *favelados* devour the colonizer's *savoir-faire* for their own purposes, making films off the stolen leavings of dominant cinema.

Coutinho's *O Fio da Memoria* ("The Thread of Memory," 1991) reflects on the sequels of slavery in Brazil through a fragmented history based on disjunctive scraps of garbage-like fragments. One strand consists of the diary of Gabriel Joaquim dos Santos, an elderly black man who constructed his own dream house as a work of art made completely out of cracked tiles, broken plates, and empty cans. (Now a tourist site, the house is considered a masterpiece of popular architecture.) As the film shows us Gabriel's house, the voice-over relays Gabriel's own words about the paradoxical "power of poverty." Garbage becomes an ideal medium for those impoverished people who themselves have been cast off, who have been "down in the dumps," who feel, as the blues line had it, "like a tin can on that old dumping ground." The trash of the haves becomes the treasure of the have-nots; the dank and unsanitary is transmogrified into the sublime and the beautiful.

Although such popular art is not usually seen as "avant-garde," this random piling up of *objets trouves* as a place of surprising juxtapositions is clearly reminiscent of the aleatory collages typical of the *historical avant-gardes*.[18]

Gabriel's artistic procedures thus evoke the Formalists' **"defamiliarization,"** the Cubists' **"found objects,"** Brecht's **"refunctioning,"** and the situationists' **"*détournement*."** This Afro-diasporic redemption of detritus also evokes the more specific tradition of the ways in which New World blacks, in a situation of extreme scarcity, have managed to quilt together communities and transmogrify waste products into art. Shorn of freedom, education, and material advantage, Afro-diasporic peoples have teased beauty out of the guts of deprivation, whether through the musical use of discarded oil barrels (the steel drums of Trinidad), the culinary use of throw-away parts of animals (*feijoada* and soul food), the textile use of throwaway fabrics (quilting), or the digital use of sampling in hip-hop.[19] Not coincidentally, black filmmakers Noel Carvalho and Jefferson De entitled their cinema manifesto **"Dogma Feijoada,"** in a play on the Dogma film collective and the Brazilian national dish thrown together from scraps by enslaved cooks and maids. In aesthetic terms, such **hand-me-down aesthetics** embody an art of discontinuity, whence their alignment with artistic modernism as an art of jazzistic discontinuity and "breaking," and with postmodernism as an art of recycling and pastiche.

In *Postmodernism, or, The Cultural Logic of Late Capitalism*, Fredric Jameson argues that, given the difficulty of subjects to grasp social totality or to organize past and present into a coherent whole, cultural productions are likely to be composed of "heaps of fragments" marked by "the randomly heterogeneous and fragmentary and the aleatory."[20] His words aptly define the aesthetic of Jorge Furtado's *Isle of Flowers* (1989) as a brilliant example of **postmodern Marxist garbology**. Described by its author as a "letter to a Martian ignorant about the earth and its social systems," Furtado's 15-minute short film exploits Monty Python-style animation, archival footage, and parodic–reflexive documentary techniques to indict the global distribution of food and wealth. In fact, the film, which begins with the image of a revolving globe, can be seen as one of the first films to denounce the social violence of the then widely touted phenomenon of globalization.

The film's protagonist is an allegorical tomato—planted, harvested, exchanged, refused, and then dumped—which makes its way from a Nisei farmer to a São Paulo supermarket to a bourgeois home to its final destination—the titular "Isle of Flowers." The structure of *Isle of Flowers* is **rhizomatic** in the Deleuze–Guattari sense, in that it develops through a series of lateral associative moves, such as a plant that grows horizontally, sending out shoots. An **aleatory technique** superimposes an arbitrary yet orderly structure on apparently random materials, revolving around definitions of terms such as "money," "island," and "human being." The first inkling that the film is not merely farcical comes when the word "progress" segues to the image of an atomic mushroom cloud. Modeled as a parody of TV educational programs for children, the film charts the history of capitalist exploitation in relation to human sustenance. A landowner allows the famished poor exactly 10 minutes to scrounge for food inside a fenced-in refuse pile. In this social anatomy of garbage, the truth of a society is revealed through its detritus. The urban bourgeois family is linked to the rural poor via the sausage and the tomato within a web created by the center–periphery system. Furtado shows the endpoint of an all-permeating logic of capitalist commodification, logical telos of the consumer society, and its ethos of planned obsolescence. Showing the seamy underside of globalization, the film exposes the transnational capitalist system as generating a world of wasteful immiseration. Garbage reveals the hidden face of a global system that had been idealized through the euphoric nostrums of "globalization." (In 2007, Furtado revisited the garbage theme in a fiction feature entitled *Basic Sanitation, the Film*. In this exercise in **metacinematic garbology**, issues of basic sanitation intersect with issues of basic filmmaking, all against the backdrop of the government measures meant to encourage film production.)

## Sublime Detritus

A sub-genre of the garbage film consists in those films that reveal the recondite beauty born of ordure, in an aesthetic of **sublime detritus**. Kant's discussion of the **sublime** takes place precisely where representation breaks down, where mimesis no longer simply registers the external world but rather conveys something intensely subjective and uncanny. Marcos Prado's *Estamira* (2004), in this sense, brings the *transmogrification* of garbage into art to a kind of paroxysm. Many of the accreted meanings of the *sublime*— from Longinus through Kant to Lyotard and Deleuze—have in common the idea of a surprising beauty, found in ineffably grand phenomena such as oceans or in objects or situations not conventionally seen as beautiful. In his *Critique of Judgment*, Kant argues that the *sublime* can only be occasioned by ungraspable natural objects that overwhelm the self and create "an abyss in which the imagination is afraid to lose itself."[21] While artistic mimesis generally has the power to beautify that which is displeasing or ugly in real life, Kant points to one exception—the ugliness that generates disgust—since our real corporeal nausea overwhelms whatever aesthetic pleasure we might feel. Lyotard describes the sublime as part of a **negative aesthetics** of formlessness, that "denies the imagination the power of forms,"[22] while Derrida calls disgust the absolute "other" of the conventional system of taste.[23]

The idea for *Estamira* first emerged when Prado decided, in 1994, to locate the ultimate destination of the garbage that he himself produced. His search led him to Jardim Gramacho, an immense garbage dump that received 85% of Rio's waste. Shocked by the sea of garbage and the fetid smell of putrefaction, Prado was even more horrified by the masses of desperate people working to glean some source of revenue from the dangerously unsanitary trash. After spending 6 years photographing the everyday life of the dump, Prado met a remarkable woman—Estamira— who told him that her mission in life was to reveal the truth, and that his mission was to reveal her mission.

As a poor mestiza/black/indigenous, single, and unemployed woman suffering from schizophrenia and residing in a garbage dump, Estamira at first glance constitutes a quintessentially marginalized figure, a veritable palimpsest of social stigmata, a case of *bare life* biding the pelting of pitiless storms that literally blow the garbage around her and the dump. Yet, as a vibrant and madly eloquent person, Estamira remains self-confident within her restless psyche. Her very refusal to see herself as a victim undercuts the potential paternalism of audiences accustomed to sanctimonious documentaries that provoke pity for the poor and self-congratulation on the part of the middle-class spectator. Rather than a "positive image," the film confronts us with an ill-tempered personality who belches, walks around naked, and declares, in Tourette-like bursts, her absolute hatred for religion, especially in its Pentecostalist iteration. Instead of a pitiable victim, we find a proud, complex, charismatic, and even arrogant individual who tells people that "*you* are common, I am not common."

Literally schizophrenic and "hearing voices," Estamira instantiates Bakhtin's idea that, as persons, "we are the voices that constitute us." As a "generator of concepts," Estamira is a kind of philosopher in the Deleuzian sense, one with a penchant for oxymoronic formulations (she speaks of "castles of garbage") and provocative abstractions: "Creation is abstract. All of space is abstract. Water and fire are abstract. Estamira is also abstract." Oscillating between abjection and megalomania ("no one can live without me"), she expresses both with equal force of conviction. Claiming to be "perturbed, but lucid" she often makes perfect sense: "Not wasting any-thing is wonderful. Whoever doesn't waste has what they need… what I most love is to work." She points out that Brazil abolished slavery, but failed to provide education and employment for the newly freed blacks, and that "everyone should be a communist, which is to say equal." She speaks of the "human format," and of the human being as the "only conditional," and envisions imaginary machines such as the "sanguine recorder" and "the superior natural remote control." Within her gendered mathematical theory, mothers represent the even numbers, while fathers represent the odd. And rather like a Bazinian theorist, she distinguishes between the "natural" and the "unnatural" camera.

A frequent objection to films such as *Estamira* is their supposed **"aestheticization of poverty."** The charge has two components, one ethical and the other aesthetic. The first, ethical component, alleges that the artist has instrumentalized misery for narcissistic or careerist purposes. This charge is often accurate; the aestheticization of poverty does indeed occur, especially when filmmakers exploit their human subjects as a pretext for a self-aggrandizing *exercise de style*. A tell-tale sign of opportunism, in such cases, is the failure to collaborate with the subjects of the film, or to screen the finished film for the participants, or to turn the film into an activist instrument, in short any failure to "give back." In the case of *Estamira*, Prado helped Estamira with her medicine, respected her wishes about the filmmaking, and tried to avoid a paternalistic stance. At the same time, the film explains the causes of her madness: the loss of her father at the age of two, a schizophrenic mother, her schizophrenic medical condition, dreadful experiences of rape, a philandering husband, and unrelenting poverty. Furthermore, Estamira's voice completely dominates the film, whether through her direct address to the camera, or in her role as the "voice-of-God-narrator." No narratorial voice explains her; she explains herself. At no point in the film does she become an object of derision.

The second, more properly aesthetic component of the *"aestheticizing poverty"* charge has to do with assumptions about the appropriate style for treating social misery. The *aesthetic of hunger* was one answer to this question: a film about hunger should be aesthetically "hungry." But while dos Santos in *Vidas Secas* consciously eschewed the picturesque, Prados seeks after beauty in an unlikely place. But this "beauty" does not preclude social usefulness; in fact, it is the film's beauty that enhances its social efficacity.

The aesthetization charge, in this sense, brings up a revelatory contrast between the critical reception of literature and of film. Literary theorists have long critiqued the **"mimetic fallacy,"** the idea that a film about boredom must itself be boring, and a film about poverty aesthetically poor. In literary studies, it has been established, at least since Auerbach's 1949 classic *Mimesis*, that a degraded milieu can be portrayed through an aesthetically pleasing style. For Auerbach, the entire world-historical drift of Western literature consisted in a melioristic process by which the Hebraic concept of the "equality of all souls before God" came to corrode the class-based hierarchies of classical Greek theater. It thus became possible to treat a "low" topic in a "high style" and turn abject subjects into scintillating prose. In *Madame Bovary*, Flaubert transformed the bovine inertia of provincial life into the *mot juste* of aesthetic exhilaration, just as Faulkner, in *The Sound and the Fury*, treated the mentally impaired simpleton Benjy with stylistic flair. But while in literature treating poverty in a dignified style elicits praise, similar treatment in film often elicits rebuke.

But what if the sublime style of *Estamira*, by aestheticizing its subject, actually honors it? The *aestheticizing poverty* charge forgets that art aestheticizes virtually by definition, in that it gives pleasurable, or at least communicative, form to the raw stuff of existence. One could as easily accuse tragedy of aestheticizing the travails of Oedipus, or melodrama of aestheticizing female suffering, or *noir* of aestheticizing crime. Behind the aestheticization charge lies the legitimate assumption that film, and even more documentary, must respect the dignity of the subject. What is less clear is why aestheticization would signify a *lack* of respect. While beautiful, Prado's film does not prettify anything; it shows the dump in all its horror, with rotting corpses and a witches' brew of steaming filth that Estamira poetically describes as a "broth of crumbs and poisons." At the same time, Kant pointed out that the sublime is best enjoyed from a situation of safety. Our encounter with Estamira, in this sense, is a sheltered one. Our experience is exclusively audiovisual, not haptic or olfactory; we see the garbage, but we do not experience the dump's nauseating smell or wound ourselves with hypodermic needles.

On another level, *Estamira* provides an exemplum of what philological literary critics such as Leo Spitzer, thinking of Flaubert, called "**free indirect style**," to refer to a kind of grammatical–stylistic procedure, an adroit modulation of tenses by which the slow abandonment of pronominal antecedents evokes a slow gliding into an internalized subjectivity. The effect is of a "dolly in" to consciousness, an indeterminacy of voice that mingles distance with intimacy, molding a sense of access to a character's mind but without abandoning authorial agency. Film theorists such as Pasolini, Deleuze, Andre Parente, and Ismail Xavier have argued that filmmakers, in a filmic version of Flaubert's "*Emma Bovary, c'est moi*," can deploy an artistic technique whereby authorial style becomes "contaminated," as it were, by the psychic processes of a perturbed or exalted or even delirious character. Prado films Estamira in a modernist–sublime style that turns the phenomenal surfaces of the garbage dump into images of incandescent splendor, thus rendering Estamira's own vision of the garbage dump as a thing of wondrous beauty. The modernist, dissonant music, meanwhile, colors and enriches the image, while image, sound, and music fuse in a transcendent whole that defies facile analysis. In a brilliant touch, Prado superimposes the ecologically minded music from Antonio Carlos Jobim's 1976 album *Urubu* (literally, vulture) on footage of Estamira surrounded by swirling vultures. In *Estamira*, the virtuoso stylistics render homage to the force of Estamira's personality, without ever presenting her either as mere social symptom, on the one hand, or as heroic exemplar on the other. Rather, her overflowing persona "conducts" the cinematic expression of her existential being, as if to say to the spectator: "here is a singular person, shaped by harsh circumstances, but not reducible to those circumstances, whom we recognize as one shape of what she calls the 'human format', in some ways opaque to us yet at the same time strangely moving, our fellow, our double."

## The Recombinant Sublime

Another Brazilian film offers the **recombinant sublime** of an artist who transforms garbage into iconic art, ultimately transfiguring the garbage, the artistic canon, and the participants in the project. The artist in question is Vik Muniz, whose artistic trajectory has carried the transmogrification of the negative to the extreme of making art out of "inappropriate" materials such as dirt, sugar, and tires. In this instance, Muniz worked with the *catadores* of the Jardim Gramacho garbage dump outside Rio de Janeiro, a city described by Muniz as "St. Tropez surrounded by Mogadishu." As celebrated in the Oscar-nominated film *Lixao* (translated as "Wasteland," 2010), Muniz restages canonical paintings such as Jacques-Louis David's *The Death of Marat*, using the *catadores* as human models and the trash as the privileged material of expression. As with *Boca de Lixo* and *Estamira*, *Wasteland* introduces us to witty, ironic, and intellectually curious *catadores*: Tiao Santos, president of the *catadores'* cooperative; Zumbi, the intellectual collector of trash-heap treasures such as Machiavelli's *The Prince*; and Suellem, a teenage mother. Muniz uses the scavenged garbage to fashion classical portraits. Suellen, posing with her two children, becomes a Renaissance Madonna; Zumbi becomes Millet's "Sower"; Tiao, his body draped over a trash heap bathtub similar to that of the dying Marat, surrounded by a photogenic sea of plastic bottles and abandoned toilet seats.

In the end, the reconstituted and re-photographed Marat is sold at an auction, netting US$50,000 for the workers' cooperative and facilitating the purchase of 15 computers, a truck, and a daycare center. Seeing their own portraits in Rio's Museum of Modern Art, the human models weep copious tears at the realization that the visitors to the museum see them as beautiful and worthy subjects of literally larger-than-life artistic representation. "We see ourselves as so small," they say, "but people out there see us as so big, so beautiful." While some critics were irritated by the heroicization of the artist, the social pleasure of the film derives from its emphasis on the convivial process that generates the art, from its demonstration of the possibilities of cross-class collaboration, and from the potentially transformative power of art for everyday people.

Just 2 years after *Wasteland*, another garbage-artist bio-documentary, *Bel Borba Aqui*, celebrates the Bahian artist Bel Borba, the "people's Picasso," who has been injecting chromatic joy into Salvador's cityscape for more than three decades. With the help of the local citizens, Bel Borba refunctions rotting buildings and abandoned vehicles to foster what might be called, following Mike Davis, **magical urbanism**. Trash becomes raw material for **Ovidian metamorphoses**: Coke bottles transformed into a giant dog; a plane repainted as a fish; and the steel hulk of a building turned into a façade of faces. (In the fall of 2012, Bel Borba was invited to work his form of **magical urbanism** [Mike Davis] in New York City, using only found and recycled materials from the city streets.)

Muniz's garbage version of Millet's *The Sower* reminds us that another artist, Agnes Varda, made her own belated entrance into the garbage genre with a film whose title—*Les Glaneurs et la Glaneuse* ("The Gleaners and I," 2000)—also alluded to a Millet painting. The Varda film treats "**gleaning**," originally the act of gathering leftover crops after the harvest. (John Keats referenced "gleaning" when he wrote of his dread that death might overtake him before his pen could "glean [his] teeming brain.") Once a collective, feminine, and rural practice, contemporary gleaning now tends to be more individual, masculine, and urban. While Muniz ennobles his subjects by placing them within remediated versions of classical paintings, Varda ennobles her subjects by juxtaposing their gleaning with classical paintings of gleaners by artists such as Millet, Van Gogh, Rembrandt, and Breton. Along the way, we meet a veritable aristocracy of gleaners—the rural poor, the homeless, gypsies, artists, chefs, and even the psychoanalyst Jean Laplanche—gleaning very diverse objects, from vegetables in the countryside to metal debris and appliances in flea markets.

Philosopher Alain Badiou has compared filmmaking to the purification of trash: "In the beginning, you take off from a pile of different things, a kind of confused industrial material. The artist makes a selection, works the material, concentrates it, gets rid of things, and reassembles them in hopes of producing moments of purity."[24] As if in illustration of Badiou's thesis, Varda's gallery of ragpickers culminates in the figure of the cineaste herself as a self-described **artistic gleaner** of images, fragments, and paintings, and whose credo is to film "rot, leftovers, waste." Varda reaffirms the connection between gleaning and filmmaking by shooting herself holding a gleaned stalk of wheat next to Breton's *La Glaneuse* (1877). Varda's cinematic gaze turns scraps of waste into abstract paintings. Close-ups of her own ageing throwaway skin are juxtaposed with rotting vegetables, evoking a continuum of sentient beings living out the cycles of vegetative and human life. As if serenely staring at death in the face and in the hand, she refuses to airbrush her own skin, and reveals its wrinkles and sun-browned dead spots. Within an *aesthetic of mistakes*, Varda even includes "defective" images in the form of footage normally destined for the trash can, for example, material inadvertently filmed showing the dangling lens cap moving over the shifting ground as she walks. The editing subtly aligns the literally marginalized figures in the film with the symbolically marginalized director of the film as the facilitator who constructs virtual connectivities between persons and communities that do not (yet) know each other, but which cohabit within the film, as a space for people to harvest what they have "in common."

Of all the garbage films, *Les Glaneurs et la Glaneuse* comes closest to linking the *literal commons*—in its original meaning as forest land available for purposes of gathering food, wood, and other necessities—to the *cultural commons*—reminding us of the common roots of the word "culture" with "cultivate" and "agriculture." Although less aggressively political than the Brazilian garbage films, *Les Glaneurs et la Glaneuse* practices what Virginia Bonner calls **"eco-feminist subversion."**[25] Varda gets the berobed male and female legal authorities to explain the complex laws regarding gleaning. We also meet the contemporary advocates of *enclosure*, in the form of a parsimonious landowner eager to prohibit gleaning; "grapes must be left on the ground to rot," he argues, because "one has to protect one's capital." (A sequel titled *Les Glaneurs et la Glaneuse ... Deux Ans Après* [*"The Gleaners and I: Two Years Later,"* 2002] solicits, *à la* Jean Rouch, the reactions and reflections of the participants in the first film.)

At this point in film history, garbage has become a transnational trope. In 1986, Ken Jacobs used discarded material found in a Canal Street dumpster—a 1965 newscast about Malcolm X—to make his *Perfect Film*, where the found footage, with minimal intervention on Jacob's part, functions in its own "perfect" way. Yo Barrada's *Hand-Me-Downs*, meanwhile, is constructed out of home movies shot by French tourists in North Africa, combined with Barrada's own voiceover recollections about growing up in Morocco in the years after World War II. In the realm of cultural critique, David Harvey speaks of the "throwaway society" generated by accelerationist late capitalism, while David Clarke speaks of "the junkspace" of postmodernity. Finally, in the domain of film criticism,

Kenneth W. Harrow, in his remarkable book *Trash: African Cinema from Below*, looks at African cinema through the analytical template of garbage.[26] Harrow finds literal and metaphorical garbage to be ubiquitous in African cinema: in Sembene's metaphor of cinematic *megotage* (cigarette-butt cinema); in the children framed between garbage cans in Sissoko's *Nyamanton* (1987); in the passage of The Man through the pits of an outhouse in Armah's *The Beautyful Ones Are Not Yet Born; a Novel* (1969); in the field of plastic bags, residues of Chad's civil war, in Haroun's *Daratt* (2006); in the *dechets humains* or "human garbage," chased away by El Hadji in Sembene's *Xala*; in the broken-down obsolescent machines in Sissoko's *La Vie Sur Terre* (1999); and in the used tires and dead bodies washed up on the beach in *Heremakono* (2002). All this trash, for Harrow, metaphorically points to the insidious process by which the Global North is the locus of commodity capitalism, and Africa the site where the waste of consumerism is dumped. While raw materials—agricultural products, oil, human labor—flow north, the "slag" created by producing goods for consumption remains in the South to foul the lands.[27]

## Anthropophagic Modernism

The Brazilian "**anthropophagy**" movement in the 1920s, for its part, transfigured the ultimate negativity—the cannibal as the horrific name of Europe's other. In the wake of the classical Greek fascination with the *anthropofagi*, the Christian crusades demonized infidel cultures as cannibalistic. But the trope became more ambivalent with the conquest of the Americas, when the cannibal became the avatar both of savage barbarity and of utopian desire. With the Brazilian modernists, we find a conflation, already implicit in Montaigne's essay *des Cannibales*, between the idea of cannibalism and what could be called the discourse of **radical indigenous egalitarianism**. The Brazilian modernists, centuries later, referenced Montaigne as they drew on cannibalism as a metaphor for artistic renewal, all part of a call for an indigenous-inflected art that would devour European techniques in order to better struggle against European domination. Rather than the good, pacific, noble, well-tempered and well-catechized Indian of romanticism, the modernists transformed the ill-behaved cannibals into cultural heroes. Just as the Tupinamba devoured their enemies in order to appropriate their strength, the Modernists argued, Brazilian artists and intellectuals should cannibalize imported cultural products and exploit them as raw material for a new synthesis, thus turning the imposed culture back, transformed, against the colonizer.

The Brazilian movement saw itself as conceptually allied with European avant-garde movements such as Futurism, Dada and Surrealism, but with an anticolonial thrust. In two manifestos, "Manifesto of Brazilwood Poetry" (1924) and "Cannibal Manifesto" (1928), Oswald de Andrade— the *cacique* of anthropophagy, as Breton was the pope of Surrealism— pointed the way to an artistic practice that was at once nationalist and cosmopolitan, nativist and modern.[28] The artistic audacity of the Brazilian modernist movement casts doubt on the diffusionist narrative whereby European modernism is seen as inspiring Latin American modernism in a unidirectional manner. The fashionable talk of "hybridity" and "syncretism" usually associated with the *postcolonial theory* of the 1970s and 1980s forgets that artists/intellectuals in Latin America and the Caribbean were theorizing hybridity over half a century earlier. In a sense, the Brazilian modernists "**tropicalized**" the European *avant-gardes*. De Andrade, who once signed a manifesto with the name "Marxillaire"—a combination of Marx, Apollinaire, and "maxillary" (as pertaining to the jaw)—linked the derisive laughter of the Brazilian Indian to the Enlightenment and even to Marxism. Whereas a certain ethnocentric discourse had projected the Carib as a ferocious cannibal and diacritical token of Europe's moral superiority, de Andrade invoked the cannibal as a revolutionary figure, linked to the French Revolution but also surpassing that revolution.

The literary critics of Brazilian modernism have largely focused on the rather sensationalist trope of cannibalism, downplaying Oswald's other focus on the socio-political superiority of egalitarian native societies without coercion, without police, army, puritanism, and inequality. It was in this sense that Andrade called for a revolution infinitely "greater than the French Revolution"—that is, the "Carib revolution"—without which "Europe would not even have its meager declaration of the rights of man."[29] As Alessandra Santos points out, anthropophagy was at once a historical reference, a creative process, a critical method, and a form of transtextuality *avant la lettre*.[30] Implicitly, Oswald was lauding the indigenous commons, promoting a gregarious and festive *communitas* as opposed to the individualist capitalist conception of individual rights centered on property and inheritance. Rejecting capitalist productivism, Oswald lauded a **sacerdocio** (sacred leisure) that preferred festive *rites* to individual *rights*, that valued idleness and the sheer happiness of a gregarious existence to generating profit, and that preferred to work only to live rather to live only to work. In a witty upturning of the usual "progressive" stagism, de Andrade declared Surrealism, with self-mocking solemnity, "the most important *pre*-Anthropophagic movement."[31]

Of the two poles of the cannibalism metaphor, the positive pole of indigenous communality and equality, and the negative pole of capitalist Social Darwinism, Joaquim Pedro de Andrade's 1969 adaptation of *Macunaíma* clearly emphasizes the negative pole.[32] Fusing what he knew of Oswald de Andrade's anthropophagical movement with the theme of cannibalism that runs through *Macunaíma*, the director turns **cannibalism** into the springboard for a critique of repressive military rule and of the predatory capitalist model of the short-lived Brazilian "economic miracle." In a preface written for the Venice Film Festival, the director provided a cannibalistic hermeneutic to help spectators decode the encrypted allegories of the film, suggesting that the "traditionally dominant, conservative social classes continue their control of the power structure—and we rediscover cannibalism..."

> The present work relationships, as well as the relationships between people— social, political, and economic—are still, basically, cannibalistic. Those who can, "eat" others through their consumption of products, or even more directly in sexual relationships. Cannibalism has merely institutionalized and cleverly disguised itself. Meanwhile, voraciously, nations devour their people. *Macunaíma* is the story of a Brazilian devoured by Brazil.[33]

In the film, the cannibalist theme announced in the preamble is treated in all its variations: people so hungry they eat themselves; the cannibal–giant–capitalist Pietro Pietra who cooks up an anthropophagous soup; the capitalist's wife who wants to eat him alive; and finally the man-eating siren who lures him to his death. The film shows the rich devouring the poor, and the poor, in desperation, devouring each other. In a coded reference to the dictatorship, the Left, devoured by the Right, purifies itself by eating itself, "an example of the "cannibalism of the weak."[34] The film outwitted the dictatorship's dull censors and became a hit, thanks to what might be called a **neo-Shakespearean synthesis**, that is, the provision of variegated pleasures for a differentiated audience—slapstick and bawdy innuendo for the contemporary "groundlings," literary allusions for the cultural elite, and political barbs for those ready to decipher them.

The modernists distinguished between degraded hunger "cannibalism" and "anthropophagy" as spiritual ritual practiced by a community that affectionately devours and incorporates the admirably courageous enemy. Two years after *Macunaíma*, Nelson Pereira dos Santos' pursued **cinematic anthropophagy** in his 1971 film *How Tasty was my Frenchman*. Based on dos Santos' own research into the history of *France Antartique*, the short-lived (1555–1560) French colony in Guanabara Bay near what is now Rio de Janeiro, the film subverts the conventional identification with the European protagonist of the captivity narrative. The title's first-person pronoun—*How Tasty was my Frenchman*—asserts identification with the cannibalistic point of view, and specifically that of the Tupinamba wife (Sebiopepe) shown in the penultimate shot, nibbling in close-up on her delicious French husband. The film portrays a strangely generous form of communal ritual, wherein the captured enemy is given a wife and treated well until the time of his ritual slaying, in which the victim, within a festive atmosphere, proudly vows vengeance for his people. The film offers a **cross-cultural initiation**, a kind of lesson in cultural relativism, indirectly posing Montaigne's question: "who are the real barbarians?" The film banalizes nudity by treating it in a non-voyeuristic manner, making it the cultural norm for the duration of the film. Systematically cutting off the conventional escape routes, the film maintains an ironically neutral attitude toward the protagonist's deglutition. Here, the European is the protagonist, but not the hero, and romantic love is less important than tribal loyalty.

If we substitute "dominant" and "alternative," or "mass" and "popular," for "Europe" and "Brazilian," we begin to glimpse the contemporary relevance of the modernists' **cannibalistic critique**. By appropriating an existing discourse for its own ends, *anthropophagy* assumed the force of the dominant discourse only to deploy that force, through a kind of artistic jujitsu, *against* domination. Such an **"excorporation"**—John Fiske's term for the ways in which subaltern populations produce culture out of the resources of the dominant system—steals elements of the dominant culture and redeploys them in the interests of oppositional practice.[35] The trope of cannibalism has become a kind of cultural dominant in Brazilian popular music, expressed in songs such as "Let's Eat Caetano," by Adriana Calcanhoto. Performance artist Guillermo Gomez-Pena, meanwhile, speaks of a **techno-cannibal aesthetic**.

Indeed, many of the subversive aesthetics discussed in this book—from Rocha's "*aesthetic of hunger*" to the underground "*aesthetics of garbage*"; from Claire Johnston's "*feminist Counter Cinema aesthetic*" to Henry Louis Gates' "*signifying-monkey aesthetic*" and Paul Leduc's "*salamander aesthetic*" (as opposed to dinosaur); from Jean Rouch's *cine-transe aesthetic* and Teshome Gabriel's **"nomadic aesthetics"** to Kobena Mercer's **"diaspora aesthetics"**; from Deleuze/Guattari's "*minor aesthetic*" to Espinosa's *cine imperfecto*—have in common the twin anthropophagic notions of revalorizing what had been seen as negative within colonialist discourse and of turning strategic weakness into tactical strength. (Even "magic realism" inverts the traditional condemnation of magic that opposes science against superstition.)

## Situationist *Détournement*

The transfiguration of the negative reached its European apotheosis with the **situationists**. Indeed, many of the aesthetic concepts already mentioned in this chapter can be seen as either anticipating or following in the wake of the *situationist* movement. (Brazilian anthropophagy, in this sense, was a proleptic *détournement* of the European avant-garde.) Credited as a crucial influence on the revolutionary currents of May 1968, **the Situationist International** formed as a group in the 1950s, and ultimately developed links to such cities as Brussels, Copenhagen, Amsterdam, and Paris. In a heady mix of libertarian Marxism and the French avant-garde, the situationists derived obvious inspiration from their precursors in Dada and the Lettrist International, as well as from the concepts of the philosopher/sociologist Henri Lefebvre. A film by the Lettriste Isidore Isou, *Le Film est Deja Commence* (1951), according to Maurice Lemaitre, had as its goal "the breaking, the explosion into pieces of the normal frame of cinematic representation."[36] Major situationist motifs include the Rimbauldian transformation of everyday life; the critique of commodity fetishism; the cognitive value of politicized *flânerie*; and the promotion of provocative "situations." The situations proclaimed the value of the **derive**—or the rapid passage or aimless drifting through varied neighborhoods and social ambiances—both as a means of critical examination of urban society and as an alternative model of narrative. (The *slackerism* in Richard Linklater's films, as Paul Cooke and Rob Stone point out, is very much linked to the director's admiration for Debord—who appears as Mr. Debord in *Waking Life* [2001]—and his ideas of revolutionary idleness.[37]) Debord also preached, and practiced, the art of *détournement*—that is, a guerrilla action by which pre-existing artistic elements were recombined into a provocative new ensemble, with the purpose of lifting the ideological veils that obscured social reality.

In their "User's Guide to *Détournement*" in 1956, Guy Debord and Gil J. Woman privileged cinema as the site where revolutionary art could attain its greatest effectiveness. It would be better, they wrote, "to detourn [*The Birth of a Nation*] as a whole, without even altering the montage, by adding a soundtrack that made a powerful denunciation of imperialist war and of the activities of the Ku Klux Klan."[38] (Decades later, DJ Spooky literally carried out the situationist project in his hip-hop remix of the Griffith film—*Rebirth of a Nation*.) *Détournement* could take many forms: the resignifying of clips through commentary and juxtaposition; the staging of subversive forms of spectatorship in the movie theater itself; and even the hijacking of an entire film through offscreen narration. At the height of the

Algerian War, in May 1956, the situationists created a provocative cover for the journal *Levres Nues*, consisting of a map of France in which all the French names of cities were replaced by Algerian names, that is, an anticolonial inversion of what France itself had done in Algeria. McKenzie Wark has identified a whole arsenal of *détournement* strategies, including **parodic-serious** *détournement* (Craig Baldwin's *Tribulation 99* [1992]); **algorithmic** *détournement* (as in DJ Rabbi's multimedia work *Society of the Spectacle: The Remix*); **bio-***détournement* (e.g., Critical Art Ensemble's *détournement* of lab techniques to counter the commercialization of the genetic code); and **recuperative** *détournement* (the recuperation of *détournement* back into the spectacle).[39] Situationist principles were, in some ways, opposed to those of the contemporaneous French New Wave, in that they were not invested in the romantic idea of the auteur as the sole proprietor of his film, preferring to subvert the ideas both of property and originality by reworking pre-existing texts, without asking permission, taking all of cinematic history as their raw material, in a form of artistic communism.

The prickly French theorist Debord gradually became famous for his oft-cited, but frequently misunderstood, concept of "**the spectacle**." With polemical succinctness, Debord asserted in his influential treatise *Society of the Spectacle* (1967) that "(I)n societies where modern conditions of production prevail ... (E)verything that was directly lived has receded into a representation." In certain respects, this indictment of ideological mystification updates Marx and Lukacs' notion of reification as retrofitted for post-war consumer society, while also anticipating Baudrillard's notion of the **simulacrum**—that is, pure simulation bearing no relation whatsoever to the real. Yet, commentators who reduce the *spectacle* to "bourgeois ideology," "one-dimensionality," or mere propaganda overlook Debord's belief that the spectacular society has invaded and permeated every nook and cranny of everyday social life. Since Debord evinced an equal contempt for both contemporary capitalist and bureaucratic Leninist societies, he delineated two offshoots of the spectacle: the "**diffuse spectacle**" pertinent to globalized corporate capitalism that entails "fragmentation" and "specialization" in the marketplace, and the "**concentrated spectacle**" that suffuses totalitarian, state socialist societies with "a totalizing self-portrait of power that masks its fragmentation."

While Debord's unabashedly experimental films eschew the conventions of commercial cinema, they nonetheless display a rather jaundiced affection for the same Hollywood movies being subjected to *détournement*. The potpourri of found footage and hectoring voice-over that typifies Debord's most famous film, the 1973 adaptation of his book *Society of the Spectacle* betrays a queasy ambivalence about film itself. Since the spectacle is described as the "concrete inversion of life"—the false consciousness that results when the commodity "completes its colonization of social life"—cinema cannot be exempted from the critique of the spectacular economy. Unfortunately, the didactic drone of Debord's narration imbues the film with the soporific feel of a tedious classroom lecture. Considered as an essay film, *Society of the Spectacle* is most intriguing when the appropriation of pop culture artifacts inadvertently subverts and complicates the film's supposed argument.

Although on one level merely an in-joke, René Viénet's and Gerard Cohen's *Do Dialectics Break Bricks?* (1973) performs (metaphoric) jujitsu on (literal) jujitsu in the form of a hijacked Korean martial arts film (Doo Kwang Gee's *The Crush*)—a story of conflict between Korean heroes and Japanese occupiers—that replaced the dialogue of the original soundtrack with post-synchronized paeans to council communism. Reputedly the first completely *détournement* film in history, the film is notable for its acerbic wit and reflexivity. The film's dedication expresses sympathy for the poor Korean filmmaker who has no knowledge of the violence done to his film. The offscreen narrator says of the film's protagonist that "he looks like an asshole, I admit, but it's not his fault. It's the producer's fault ... the actor has no control over his life." The film's hero reassures the heroine not to worry about the capitalists, because "the film is not over yet." One off-screen bit bids a character to "put away [his] phallic symbol"—that is, his sword. An odious bureaucrat threatens the workers with a structuralist onslaught: "I don't want to hear about class struggle. I'll send in my sociologists! And if that's not enough, my psychiatrists! My Foucaults! My Lacans! My structuralists!"

Another heir of situationism, Emile de Antonio, deployed "collage, compilation techniques, and imaginative soundtracks to create," as Douglas Kellner and Dan Strieble put it, "a distinctive documentary corpus."[40] As a brilliant director of **collage junk**, De Antonio broke with *cinéma vérité* and other observational traditions through a self-defined Brechtian sense of intervention.[41] De Antonio compared his work to **art brut**—Dubuffet's term for the raw work of psychotics and graffiti artists. Describing himself as a **radical scavenger** reinterpreting TV footage as the "outtakes of history," De Antonio purchased the rights of CBS-owned kinescopes of the McCarthy Hearings to make *Point of Order* (1963), a consequential denunciation of Joseph McCarthy composed out of found materials. Bypassing voice-over narration, De Antonio proved that even collage could have a point of view—in this case, relaying a passionate denunciation of hysterical anti-communism. In films where not a single sequence was staged and filmed by the director, the filmmaker becomes a

Bakhtinian **orchestrator of citations**, borrowed from others, yet where a creative personality and innovative perspective has clearly shaped the whole.

As a Marxist, De Antonio was a logical heir to Eisenstein's principles of *montage*. De Antonio's satirical documentary about Richard Nixon, *Milhouse: A White Comedy*, combines montage and *détournement*. One particularly effective **sound–image–montage** counterpoints Nixon extolling "law and order" against a black voice denouncing police abuse during the Republican convention. The ensuing images then decode Nixon's grand phrases about "law and order," revealing their racist "Southern strategy" subtext that promises to suppress any hint of black rebellion. Another *sound–image–montage* sequence pits Nixon's inane "I See a Day" speech against Martin Luther King's stirring "I Have a Dream" oration— the rhetoric and syntax of which Nixon transparently borrows— communicating clear sympathy for the eloquent urgency of the latter while exposing the mediocrity of the former. Nixon's voice, promulgating myths of success and equal opportunity through lower taxes, gradually give way to the resonant authority of King denouncing the barriers to equality while evoking a distant-yet-imaginable promised land of racial harmony.

In *Mr. Hoover and I* (1989), aka "A Middle-Aged Radical as Seen through the Eyes of His Government," De Antonio turned a very personal negative— his own harassment by the FBI—into a radical work of art. His **contrapuntal auto-bio-pic** placed in ironic relation two lives—that of J. Edgar Hoover as the scourge of human rights and black activism, and that of the courageous yet self-mocking radical himself. De Antonio performed **documental jujitsu** by turning his own surveillance file into an indictment of the FBI. In *In the Year of the Pig* (1968), meanwhile, De Antonio seduces establishment figures into inadvertent self-indictment, or what he called "getting the establishment to undress for you."[42] De Antonio also constantly used sound and music to ironic effect, for example, by superimposing "La Marseillaise" on Vietnamese instruments or overlaying "Chiquita Banana"—a reminder of the imperial role of United Fruit—over footage of then vice president Nixon's tour of Latin America. Thus, De Antonio counterpoints official idealizations—what Joseph Conrad called the "redeeming ideas"—and the "Heart of Darkness" realities being masked and euphemized.

## Culture Jamming

The situationist method generated a rich progeny of **textual hijacking**, where film bits or entire films were kidnapped for comic or political purposes. *Do Dialectics Break Bricks?*, in this sense, anticipates relatively apolitical *textual hijackings* such as Woody Allen's *What's up, Tiger Lily?* (1966) and *Dead Men Don't Wear Plaid* (1982), not to mention the various mash-ups and samplings that proliferate on the Internet. In *Tribulation 1999: Alien Anomalies under America* (2001), Craig Baldwin superimposes an absurdist narration about actual CIA interventions on found footage materials. Baldwin's *¡O No Coronado!* (1992), meanwhile, is framed as a historical flashback within the mind of the conquistador as he falls off his horse—an apt metaphor for the carnivalesque dethroning that the film performs. To relate the calamitous epic about one of the more deluded of the conquistadores, whose desperate search for the chimerical Seven Cities of Cibola led him into a fruitless, murderous journey across what is now the American Southwest, Baldwin deploys not only costumed dramatizations but also the detritus of the public domain archive: swashbucklers, pedagogical films, and industrial documentaries. Found footage from diverse costume epics takes us back to the Old World origins of New World conquest in the Crusades and the *reconquista*. Through the "prior textualizations" of tacky costume dramas and sci-fi films—Vincent Price (incarnating the Inquisition), the Lone Ranger, Charles Bronson—Coronado is portrayed as a Eurotrash scout for colonial power.

Meanwhile, the **high-tech** *griots* of hip-hop—foregrounded in early fiction films such as *Wild Style and Krush Groove* and later in documentaries such as *Corporate Criminals*—also root their art in the recycling of pre-existing materials. Initially the creation of black and Latino working-class teenagers in the United States, hip-hop and rap music have become a planetary *lingua franca* reflective of the Africanization of global culture within the trans-Atlantic dialogism of the **Afro-diasporic artistic commons**.[43] The explosion within hip-hop of what is variously called the **"sampling aesthetic"** or the **"cut 'n' mix" aesthetic** brings up the issue of copyright and the *enclosure* of creativity by corporate power. In an early phase, hip-hop authorized free-wheeling raids on the **intertextual commons**, bypassing the bourgeois proprieties of copyright. Found bits from soul ballads, radical speeches and advertisements were placed in mutually enriching relationships. Rap music videos, at least in the 1980s, recycled the voices and images of black martyrs such as Malcolm X and Martin Luther King in a **"versioning"** or remediation that sets up a direct line to African culture heroes, to the African-American intertext, and, as "Black Folks' CNN" (Chuck D's term), to the Afro-diasporic communities. Chuck D, who describes Public Enemy's music as an "assemblage of sounds," asks if one can "own a beat." (Is it a coincidence that those whose ancestors were stolen and turned into property should display a deep skepticism about private property and the morality of stealing?) How, one wonders, could the infinitely rich legacy of Afro-diasporic polyrhythms come to be "owned" by a corporation, as if one could "enclose" a few drops in the ever-churning ocean of circum-Atlantic musicality. Unfortunately, as corporate predators saw the possibility of new revenue-streams derived from musical property rights, the policing of sampling managed to partially dam the flood of hip-hop creativity.

Skating on the thin ice of the legalities of copyright and intellectual property, these various *cut' n' mix* projects bring us back to the "*aesthetic commons*" evoked in our first chapter, and to the resistance to contemporary forms of "*enclosure.*" The argument, once again, is about access to the *artistic commons* and the nature of legality. The original *enclosures* of land involved the transformation of customary practices into illegal acts: hunting became "poaching"; foraging became "trespassing"; and the gathering of firewood became "timber theft." Intellectual copyright, by analogy, turned the knowledge commons into alienable property. The issue of copyright brings up extremely complex questions. The fact that the debate is not simple is reflected in the fact that Chuck D, the originator of sample-based hip-hop, has instigated copyright-infringement lawsuits of his own, less in the name of profit than as a protest against those who would use his work for political messages that went against his principles. The debate pits those Taylor calls "intellectual property dogmatists," who believe that culture can be owned, against the free-culture enthusiasts, who believe that everything should be free.[44] While one group argues that "piracy and downloading are theft," the other, in an updating of Proudhon, argues that "intellectual property itself is theft." The *Steal This Film* series articulates the latter view in the "warning" that opens their films, the precise opposite of the usual caveats:

> Do not seek permission to copy this film. Anyone who fails to distribute this work, or impedes others from doing so, will be ostracized. All devices capable of being used to share this film should be so deployed. We ask the audience to remain vigilant in promoting such actions and to report docile consumption to cinema staff.

The issue, however, is about making sure that artists–intellectuals are credited, rewarded, and protected from cynical forms of appropriation while also making the cultural commons available to everyone on an equal basis. The paradox is that the commons is being opened up and fenced off simultaneously, and that the same corporate interests that spread content also want to profit from it through exclusive copyright and the invisible fences of trademark and patent law. Can we speak of **top-down** appropriation *à la* Disney and **bottom-up appropriation** *à la* Public Enemy? Can artistic creation in non-capitalist indigenous societies be treated in the same way as art in capitalist societies? In what only seems to be a paradox, some Native American tribes are buying land to augment their land-base as communal property. How can art belong only to its creator? Can the silence in a John Cage performance or Miles Davis improvisation be protected by copyright? Should Godard have patented his jump cuts? Can a corporation monetize the Torah, the Qu'ran, and the Christian Bible, or the praise songs of Vodun and *candomblé*? While artistic sources and influences deserve recognition, it is crucial to remember that artistic language always comes, as Bakhtin would put it, from the "mouth of the other." The corporate repo men, in this sense, are literally depriving artists of their means of subsistence by foreclosing their right to forage in the artistic woods. The goal, for Astra Taylor, is to construct a sustainable culture, within an **ethics of stewardship**. where creators can sustain themselves in conjunction with the collective self-sustaining as part of a broader social ecology, where we are not treated only as targeted consumers but rather as members of a "true cultural commons where we are nurtured as citizens and creators."[45]

## Neo-Situationism and the Aesthetics of Failure

The contemporary "sequel" to Debord's *Society of the Spectacle*, perhaps, is Slavoj Žižek's *Pervert's Guide to Ideology* (2013), directed by Sophie Fiennes. Both the Debord and the Žižek films treat the subject of ideology and film, but Žižek unpacks them with more carnivalesque brio and a deeper and more lively sense of the interrelated appeals of both spectacle and ideology. *Pervert's Guide to Ideology* emphasizes Žižek's forte—the phantasmatic dimension of ideology. Žižek invokes the term "**the Big Other**" (Lacan's "*Grand Autre*")—that unacknowledged phantasmatic figure that orients our thinking within bourgeois society, an allegorical figure for the unwritten rules, the force that makes us complicit with oppression (including our own) and lurks behind the sounds and images of popular films. The vagueness of the concept is the point. As an empty signifier, an obscure object onto which we project our desires (rather similar to the striped box in *Chien Andalou*), the *Big Other* is the ontological real of Coca-Cola, the magic in the commodity. It is literally nothing, like the invisible barrier that prevents the aristocrats from leaving the mansion in *Exterminating Angel* (1962).

*Pervert's Guide* begins with a film that is quite explicitly about ideology—John Carpenter's *They Live* (1988), where the protagonist's magical sunglasses reveal the sinister interpellations lurking behind feel-good advertisements, the mandate "to obey" hidden in the computer commercial, or the diktat to "marry and reproduce" underlying an ad showing a couple on a beach. In a way, *They Live* does what the situationists did through the *détournement* of ads in the metro through graffiti, but in staged, cinematic form. *Pervert's Guide to Ideology*, meanwhile, constitutes an instance of **film analysis as ideology-critique**, exploiting the charisma of blockbuster films such as *Jaws* or art films such as *The Last Temptation of Christ* to expose the operations of ideology. In what might be called a Keatonesque **site-gag**, the film places Žižek in the same similarly-lit decors of the films that he analyzes. When he speaks, with clownish dead seriousness, about *Triumph of the Will*, we see him gazing out of the window seat of a Nazi-vintage plane, and when he speaks of *Taxi Driver*, he occupies the cot in Travis Bickles' funky magazine-littered apartment.

Besides making the analysis visually interesting, this *mise-en-scène* conveys a truth about cinematic identification. Žižek becomes the portly embodiment of spectatorship itself, a performative illustration of the ways that films induce what Metz called "**secondary identification**"—identification with characters, with their milieu, and even with their costumes. As with the projectionist played by Buster Keaton in *Sherlock Jr.*, we project ourselves into the tantalizing world of the film. Nazism would not have worked without getting millions of people to identify with Hitler. *Triumph of the Will* (1935) places us, thanks to Žižek as our surrogate, in Hitler's seat, descending like a god on Nuremberg. While discussing *The Sound of Music*, Žižek occupies the Mother Superior's Office. Since male spectators can identify with woman characters thanks to **cinematic transvestitism**, Žižek can even don a nun's (bad) habit.

Scrutinizing the film through our own magical-intertextual sunglasses, we can discern behind Zizek's analyses the unacknowledged echoes of the concepts and themes of a wide array of thinkers-such as philosopher Althusser on ideology as unconscious and spontaneous; psychoanalyst Lacan on **ideology** as an unconscious fantasy that structures reality; film theorist Raymond Bellour on Hollywood films as axiomatically revolving around "the constitution of the couple;" literary theorist Rene Girard on the unifying function of the scapegoat as a fundamental trait of all religions; and historian Richard Slotkin on the "regenerative violence" of the frontier western. When one looks at the film through magical–intertextual sunglasses, one discerns behind Žižek's analyses the unacknowledged concepts of Althusser on ideology as spontaneous; Raymond Bellour on Hollywood films and the "constitution of the couple"; and Rene Girard on the unifying function of the scapegoat. Žižek's readings are allegorical in the classical religious sense, in that they decipher plots to find a single deep meaning. Perversely, Žižek recommends Christianity as a path to atheism—perhaps in the spirit of Bunuel's "Thank God I'm an atheist"—much as Socialist Bloc intellectuals jokingly defined communism as the "longest path to capitalism." At the end of the film, spectators are left unsure whether they should (1) join the Occupy and Arab Spring–style revolutions in the streets; (2) go to a Lacanian analyst; (3) commit themselves to "atheistic Christianity"; or (4) do a PhD in film studies.

Adam Curtis's BBC documentaries, for their part, employ found footage in the service of cleverly honed political arguments in what might be called a **neo-situationist** manner. Many of Curtis' films rely upon paradoxical rhetorical juxtapositions. *The Power of Nightmares* (2004), for example, constructs ideological links between two uncanny doppelgangers: Leo Strauss, the late philosophical guru of the neoconservatives, and Islamic fundamentalists. *The Trap: What Happened to Our Dreams of Freedom* (2007), meanwhile, foregrounds points of convergence between another set of improbable secret-sharers—in this case, between R. D. Laing's seemingly anti-authoritarian brand of anti-psychiatry and Margaret Thatcher and Tony Blair's neoliberal bromides. *It Felt Like a Kiss* (2009), in contrast, abandons the systematic interlinking of historical paradoxes that animate Curtis' earlier films and instead pours a number of cultural and political contradictions into a kind of cinematic Cuisinart. Energized by feverish montage, the film attempts to unravel how the post–World War II dream of infinite American plenitude—for example, the unnamed yet tacitly present "American Dream"—curdled into shadowy conspiracies and the dystopian apogee of the Manson murders.

If the desire to participate in **archival foraging** is both a constructive and a destructive impulse, sifting through the archives often functions as a radical act of criticism. Already in 1927, Russian filmmaker Esfir Shub foraged in the czarist archives, including the despots' home movies, to forge a devastating account of Czarist rule in *The Fall of the Romanov Dynasty* by juxtaposing czarist decadence against images of terrible poverty. Archival scavenging as a form of radical intervention informs other examples of radical found footage films, including Thom Andersen's and Noel Burch's *Red Hollywood* (1996) and experimental filmmaker Bill Morrison's *The Miners' Hymn* (2011). Andersen and Burch invert conventional wisdom by celebrating the work of blacklisted Hollywood writers and directors as being in fact just as subversive as their right-wing foes always maintained. Using this modus operandi, Nicholas Ray's *Johnny Guitar* (co-written by Phillip Yordan, a "front" for writers during the blacklist era) is recast as an anti-HUAC film; Abraham Polonsky, in discussing his famous noir film *Force of Evil* (1948), argues that "all films about crime are about capitalism because capitalism is about crime." Since the most exemplary found footage documentaries are committed to both the revivification of historical memory and the evisceration of outmoded ideas, they both preserve and reconstruct the archival legacy while capitulating to what Derrida terms *"archive fever"*: "a compulsive, repetitive, and nostalgic desire for the archive, an irrepressible desire to return to the origin ... the most archaic place of absolute commencement."

In recent years, a new form of *transfiguration of the negative* has emerged, in films where personal, even confessional, preoccupations rub shoulders with pressing political concerns. Some year ago, Paul Arthur christened a new strain in contemporary documentary as representing "**the aesthetics of failure**"—wherein a filmmaker's project is undone by the hazards of actual film production.[46] Building on the heritage of the Beckett-like *Waiting for Fidel*, the most famous instance of the *aesthetics of failure* is perhaps Michael Moore's *Roger and Me* (1989), where Moore's tragi-comic attempts to meet with Roger Smith, the CEO of General Motors, end up composing a strong indictment of a neoliberal globalization that exploits cheap labor in the Global South while dispossessing workers in the Global North. Moore's fondness for failed confrontations with a pedagogical thrust is downplayed in Moore's hugely successful *Fahrenheit 9/11* (2004). Much of the film engages in an effective variant of *media jujitsu* by administering strategic jabs at the blunders and crimes of George W. Bush against a sonic backdrop of rock tunes that evokes the wall-to-wall use of pop tunes employed on now-forgotten TV reality shows such as *Punk'd*, *Pop Up Video*, and *Newlyweds: Nick and Jessica*. Yet, the plangent tone of the film's opening sequence recalls, paradoxically enough, Chris Marker's more leisurely, intro-spective style of narration. Recapitulating the 2000 election debacle, Moore's voice-over—intoning "Was it Just a Dream?" as Ben Affleck, Robert DeNiro, and Stevie Wonder celebrate a chimerical Gore victory—succinctly sums up the equally illusory chasm between a far-from-Edenic but apparently more "normal" pre-9/11 phase and a paranoid postlapsarian America.

Exemplified as well by the self-reflexive films of Nick Broomfield and Ross McElwee, among others, these *aesthetics of failure* documentaries usually take the form of staged confessions highlighting the inability of earnest but clumsy directors to fulfill a particular journalistic or personal goal, resulting in a Xenon-like goose-chase after an elusive subject. The ironic homage to failure goes counter to the mystification of success in American cultural life and in mainstream fictions. Yet, the films, such as Fellini's *8½*, finally do exist, despite the portrayal of failure, and are therefore not failures at all. Israeli documentarian Avi Mograbi, meanwhile, has fashioned his own idiosyncratic form of failure aesthetics. Initially bent on making straightforward, committed films, he soon encountered practical and bureaucratic frustrations, and mock-autobiographical elements eventually surfaced. Sometimes called "**semi-documentaries**," Mograbi's films are, however, not postmodern pranks or fabulist conceits; rather, they are anchored in the gritty here and now of Middle Eastern politics, and specifically in two spaces: his own home as a place of lively political discussion and his own domestic film production company. In a kind of **processual reflexivity**, Mograbi ironically ponders the psychic risks of falling under the seductive spell of his political/ideological enemies while filming them, for example, his nemesis Ariel Sharon, as he details in *How I Learned to Overcome My Fear and Love Ariel Sharon* (1997), where the nod to Kubrick already signals an ironic intention.

The extent of Mograbi's assault on both conservative and "liberal" (i.e., Labor) Zionist shibboleths is apparent in his 2006 film *Avenge But One of My Two Eyes*. The film stages **ideological antiphony**—heated screamfests between antagonistic political perspectives—not to promote a spurious "balance" but rather to demystify some of his homeland's most cherished myths. For example, *Avenge But One of My Two Eyes* intersperses footage of students being ushered around the ruins of Masada under the aegis of the Labor Zionist youth group "Birthright"; classroom scenes featuring a lesson on the significance of the Biblical story of Samson; an extended telephone conversation between Mograbi and an actor impersonating an anguished Palestinian friend; and sequences focusing on ordinary Palestinian citizens being harassed by the Israeli military. In an unusually low-key polemic, a frequently self-lacerating form of historical critique provides the film's guiding structural principle, inasmuch as the legacy of Masada and the Samson story are clearly two of the Israeli state's foundational myths.

## Media Jujitsu

*Media jujitsu* refers to a kind of **asymmetrical semiotic warfare**, whereby media-makers draw from the arsenal of domination in order to turn the power of the dominant media against domination itself, turning strategic weakness into tactical strength. By re-accentuating pre-existing materials, *media jujitsu* re-channels energies in new directions, generating a space of critique outside the binaries of hegemony and resistance. In contexts of right-wing hegemony, *media jujitsu* becomes crucial, especially in an age where the new media technologies open up novel possibilities. Rather than an "aesthetic of hunger," the new media allow for **cybernetic minimalism**, that is, no-budget or low-budget *digital blockbusters*—such as Alex Riveira's 90-second "trailer" for his "forthcoming" film *Independence Day*, a Latino parody of the Roland Emmerich film that replaces the alien invasion of the original with a re-conquest of North America by Mexicans. Instead of July 4, the piece is set on Mexican Independence Day (September 16). Turning the US militarization of the border on its head, the film has nine air-borne sombreros fly over the obnoxious fence between the United States and Mexico to ultimately vaporize Washington landmarks such as the United States Capitol. "The next time you call them 'aliens'," a final intertitle warns ominously, "might be your last." In another video, *Why Cybraceros?*, Rivera creates a minimalist indictment of racist labor policies, combining archival footage showing the original bracero program, with animation that shows cyber-braceros guaranteeing the agribusiness utopia, of enjoying the benefits of the work of the undocumented workers, without the annoying presence of the workers themselves.

A number of texts perform *media jujitsu* by coaxing Hollywood films and commercial TV into indicting themselves, deploying the power of the dominant media against their own retrograde premises. Such works "mine" the mainstream in order to undermine it by, for example, turning the trash of stereotype into ironic artistic gold. The ludicrous catalogue of media Arabs (assassins, terrorists, fanatics), drawn from cartoons, newscasts, fiction films, and even game shows, in Elia Suleiman's *Muqaddimah Li Nihayat Jidal* ("An Introduction to the End of an Argument," 1990), hilariously deconstructs mass media Orientalism. Set against more critical materials, the sheer repetition of the caricatural images—from Rudolph Valentino to Elvis Presley—makes the stereotypes fall of their own weight. The performances of Spiderwoman Theatre, a group of three Native American (Cuna/Rappahanock) sisters, as documented in *Sun, Moon and Feather* (1989), carnivalize Hollywood stereotypes by having two of the sisters mimic and sing along with Nelson Eddy and Jeanette MacDonald performing "*Indian Love Call*" in such a way as to "re-Indianize" a Hollywood caricature.

A contemporary master of *media jujitsu* is Canadian filmmaker John Greyson, perhaps most notably in his **satiric-activist music videos** supporting the Palestinian-led Boycott, Divestment and Sanctions (BDS) movement, which calls for artists to boycott Israel as a protest against the occupation of the West Bank and Gaza. In two of the videos, Greyson deploys the charismatic force of a popular genre (music video) and a medium (video-sharing websites), together with the commodified charisma of some of the world's most popular performers, as a form of support for BDS. While lauding those such as Bjork and Santana who have refused to play in Israel, the videos use parodic humor to mercilessly shame those such as Diana Krall, Elton John, and Metallica who have ignored the boycott.

It is their mix of shock, humor, and outrage that makes Greyson's satirical music videos so audacious. *Hey Elton* (2010) directly addresses Elton John and pleads with him to respect BDS. A split screen juxtaposes the singer in concert with footage of the Israeli bombing of Gaza. Singer/composer David Wall, in an act of **satirical mimicry**, skillfully imitates the rather sentimental style of Elton John's greatest hits, but injects new lyrics supporting the boycott: "Goodbye Yellow Brick Road" becomes "Good Bye Settlement Roads"; "Sorry Seems to be the Hardest Word" becomes "Boycott Seems to be the Hardest Word"; and "I Guess That's Why They Call It the Blues" becomes "I Guess That's Why They Call It Apartheid." *BDS Bieber* (2011) extends similar treatment to Justin Bieber, mingling atrocity footage with revised lyrics. *Vuvuzela* (2010), finally, offers an activist equivalent of the Monty Python routines treating philosophers as soccer players, by deploying images from the FIFA World Cup to address the decision of artists to respect or not respect the boycott.

A final form of media jujitsu consists in **camcorder activism**—the use of video cameras in an earlier period, and digital cameras later on, to record and publicize the abuses of the police. Contemporary anarchist video activists fuse pedagogy with active resistance in the form of **counter-surveillance**. A prototypical example is "Cop Watch LA," a collective with considerable anarchist input. Cop Watch LA goes well beyond the role of media watchdog and demonstrates how the line separating filmmaking and direct action can be permanently effaced. Armed with video and cell phone cameras, volunteers monitor police harassment of poor and minority communities in Los Angeles. Clint Henderson, meanwhile, has released onto the Internet "ten top videos" revealing police abuse, including the unwarranted abuse of special-ed children, homeless men with schizophrenia, and defenseless grandmothers. While outside the realm of "art" usually assessed by film critics and historians, what Richard Modiano labels a burgeoning "cinematic record of police transgression" also performs an archival function for our era that parallels the aspirations of participant–observers such as the journalist Henry Mayhew and the photographer Jacob Riis in the nineteenth and twentieth centuries. Since anarchist pedagogy is so closely aligned to self-emancipation, Cop Watch LA's efforts to unmask police malfeasance efface traditional boundaries separating spectators, filmmakers, and educators. The Rashomon Project, meanwhile, has developed an online toolkit for creating **multi-perspectival video chronologies** to help activists to document demonstrations of police abuse that can then be posted on social media sites. In what might be called **subversive Aristotelianism,** activists synch up multiple video perspectives, thus respecting the Aristotelian unities of place, time, and action in a portrayal of, for example, a protest demonstration.

In the late 1990s, amateurs wielding camcorders recorded horrific abuse by the Brazilian police in various favela neighborhoods—notably Cidade de Deus (in Rio de Janeiro; the scene of the famous 2002 film *City of God*) and Diadema (in São Paulo; also ironically the home of the actor Fernando Ramos da Silva who played the title character in Babenco's *Pixote: a Lei do Mais Fraco,* himself subsequently killed by the police). The camcorder footage, subsequently shown on Brazilian TV, showed police sadistically humiliating, beating, and robbing favela residents, and, in one case, murdering a man simply for the crime of trying to talk to them. In a bitterly ironic essay entitled "Diadema—Never Again," journalist/filmmaker Arnaldo Jabor anointed the camcorder *témoignage* the year's "Best Brazilian Film." In an acid mimicry of academic exegesis, an example of **film criticism as social critique,** Jabor pointed out the film's cinematic virtues as an exceptionally powerful "horror film." The police chief, dubbed "Rambo" by his underlings, Jabor speculates, was perhaps trained by the Actor's Studio, although he explodes like a Charles Bronson character. While the uniformed "actors" brilliantly played their role as sadistic policemen, the *favelado* "extras" effectively played their role as oppressed victims. Without cranes, dollies, or even tripods, the amateur cameraman achieved an "elegant alternation of zoom-ins with long shots and pans," within a single-shot aesthetic recalling Antonio's *The Passenger* or Straub's *Nicht Versohnt.* Through the brilliant use of offscreen space, both policeman and victim remain behind a wall as we hear the man's desperate plea followed by a gunshot, followed by an eerie silence. Jabor also notes the homosocial and homoerotic overtones of the scene, where men bond through sadism in a "symbolic gay orgy." "Some men," Jabor concludes, "are being punished in our place."

## The New Kino-Eye: Vision Machines

Digital media bear the paradoxical "double logic of *remediation*" suggested by Bolter and Grusin—the strange, contradictory way in which diverse digital media promise both a greater degree of *im*mediacy, an authentic experience of the real, and a *hyper*mediated experience of interconnectivity, multiple perspectives, and networked affiliations.[47] But while Bolter and Grusin make a distinction between "transparent" and "opaque" media— that is, between those media that are more immediate, and those that are more hypermediated—the increased interconnectivity and interdependence of digital media makes such contrasts less and less distinct. In Harun Farocki's 2007 video installation *Deep Play*, the soccer match between France and Italy in the 2006 FIFA World Cup Final is represented on 12 different screens, each visualizing a different aspect of the game: television camera feeds, data visualizations of the players' movements, video game simulations of the match, and even security camera feeds from in and around the stadium. In some ways, Farocki's piece already blurs boundaries by bringing soccer into the art gallery—but his work primarily serves to point out the hypermedial interconnectedness inherent in all of these modes of digital visualization, regimes of visualization that are easily overlooked amid—or assimilated into—the spectacle of the public space of a soccer stadium.

To be sure, all of these examples subtly index one of digital moving-image media's greatest distinctions from their analog predecessors: their immense, seemingly inexhaustible capacity for image recording and storage, and their ability to process and render what often seems like a parallel virtual world of images rendered as meta-data. In Farocki's installation—as in others of his works, including *Eye/Machine I–III* and *I Thought I Was Seeing Convicts*—the spectator enters Paul Virilio's **vision machine**, that sightless mechanical–industrial kino-eye that encodes real time and real space into the objective virtuality of the computer.[48] In the face of mass surveillance and data collection, the matter of the ontology of the digital image seems less pressing than its deployment as an instrument of social control or a weapon of war. This became abundantly clear when, in November 2012, the Israeli defense forces released images of their drone assassination of Hamas military commander Ahmed al-Jabari, posting the video clip on YouTube and linking to it via their Twitter feed. (Hamas responded with its own threats, also issued via Twitter.[49])

Digital technology's role in the proliferation—and now, inevitability—of round-the-clock monitoring has resulted in a range of aesthetic strategies to contend with and counteract the surveillance state. The modes of *counter-surveillance* discussed in the preceding text have been in place long before the digital turn, though there seems to have been a significant uptick in **surveillance art** in the late 1990s: practitioners such as the Surveillance Camera Players and the artist Deni Beaubois (in his 1996 video *In the Event of Amnesia the City Will Recall...*), both of whom staged impromptu performances in front of security cameras, performing for the "audience" at the other end of the CCTV camera.[50] What distinguishes much of this work in the digital era is its sense of the inevitability of surveillance—its acceptance of 24/7-recording as a fact of twenty-first-century life and its desire to return this surveillant gaze as a way of addressing the politics of visualization and control. This is a practice that scholars Steve Mann, Jason Nolan, and Barry Wellman have dubbed "sousveillance"—that is, surveillance from below—and more recent artists and filmmakers have taken up the practice of a **sousveillance art**.[51] Canadian photographer Jon Rafman's ongoing web project *9 Eyes* collects odd images inadvertently captured by Google Street View's mobile nine-lensed camera unit—found images from the *digital sublime* documenting all manner of strange sights, beautiful compositions, and crimes in progress.

Also making strategic use of the encroaching Googlization of everyday life, the installation video series *Lugares que no existen: Goggle Earth 1.0* (2009), by Spanish filmmakers Isaki Lacuesta and Isa Campo, points to mysterious blank spots within the all-seeing, surveillant interface of Google Earth. In countries as diverse as Columbia, Ecuador, Russia, Australia, and Spain, these are "special places excluded from this vision," protected areas (military facilities, government buildings, and nudist beaches), or those transformed by property speculation whose locations have been blurred on Google Earth. Similarly, Iraqi-born artist and photographer Jananne Al-Ani's video series "Shadow Sites" (2012) takes on the aesthetic of aerial photography to explore the ways in which the Middle Eastern landscape was viewed by the military and news media during the Iraq War. In Al-Ani's work, the desert topography of Jordan (used as a geographical stand-in for Iraq), viewed from a distance, appears as a depopulated abstraction of rough geometric lines and textures. Evidence of human activity is everywhere in the form of architecture and agriculture, but the people themselves are too far away to be visible, enabling Al-Ani to restage wartime news media's conditions of spectatorial disengagement from the human subjects on the ground. Similarly, in response to the proliferation of drone technology, many artists have realized the *vision machine* in more literal form. The first example of this is probably Bureau of Inverse Technology's *B.I.T. Plane* (1999), which takes a drone's-eyed view of Silicon Valley, and has been updated more recently by Alex Rivera's *Low Drone* (2013), in which the artist customizes a consumer-grade drone to look like a low-rider, the flamboyantly painted, hydraulically elevated vehicle that's a staple of Mexican–American communities in Southern California.[52] Via the artist's website, users can simulate the *Low Drone*'s patrol of the fence that separates Tijuana from San Diego in a sly subversion of US immigration policy and border control.

Other artists have taken up the *sousveillant* gaze in more intimate ways, further implicating themselves in patterns of surveillance. Iraqi–American artist Wafaa Bilal's *3rdi* (2010–2011) is a project in which the artist actually implanted a small surveillance camera on the back of his own head and transmitted the video to his website via a small portable hard-drive and a wireless 3G Internet connection. According to the artist, *3rdi* "arises from a need to objectively capture my past as it slips behind me from a non-confrontational point of view," but it also coyly addresses the obsessive self-documentation that the Internet allows and even encourages (not to mention, perhaps, the need for an Iraqi–American to watch his back during the so-called War on Terror).[53] This suggests an extreme form of *autoethnography* for the digital age: a cinema of the selfie in which self-portraiture becomes increasingly intimate, even **auto-surveillant**.

Although it might be objected that jujitsu tactics place one in a perpetually reactive posture of merely deconstructing or reversing the dominant, we would argue that media jujitsu is not merely defensive. By defamiliarizing and re-accentuating pre-existing materials, they re-channel energies in new directions, generating a third conceptual space of negotiation (Bhabha) outside of the binaries of domination, in ways that convey specific cultural and even autobiographical inflections. In a context of marginalization, jujitsu becomes a necessity. Since radical discourse has historically been placed in a defensive position by the hegemonic culture, it is virtually obliged to turn the dominant discourse against itself. All media and systems of domination, as Hans Magnus Enzensberger suggested, are **"leaky"**[54]; our responsibility is to turn such leaks into a flood. We can therefore create and support subversive popular culture along a wider spectrum, which would include a flexible gamut of strategies: infiltrating the dominant, corroding the dominant, transforming the dominant, kidnapping the dominant, and, at times, simply ignoring the dominant—in order to create fresh and viable alternatives.

## Notes

1   Ben Highmore, *Everyday Life and Cultural Theory: An Introduction* (London: Routledge, 2002), p. 122.
2   See Stefano Harney and Fred Moten, *The Undercommons: Fugitive Planning and Black Study* (Wivenhoe: Minor Compositions, 2013).
3   See chapter by Arthur Jafa, "69," in Gina Dent (ed.), *Black Popular Culture* (Seattle: Bay Press, 1991).
4   See interview with Rivette, *Cahiers du Cinema*, 204 (September 1968): 8.
5   On jazzistic film, see Gilles Mouellic, *Improviser Le Cinema* (Crisnee, Belgium: Yellow Now, 2011).
6   David E. James, *The Most Typical Avant-Garde: History and Geography of Minor Cinemas in Los Angeles* (Berkeley: University of California Press, 2005), p. 325.

# 182 *Keywords in Subversive Film/Media Aesthetics*

7 Deleuze, *Cinema 2, The Time-Image* (Minneapolis: University of Minnesota Press, 1989), p. 222.

8 Ismail Xavier, *Sertao/Mar* (1983), São Paulo: Cosac Naify, 2007 (Second Edition).

9 Julia García Espinosa, "For an Imperfect Cinema" (1973), in Michael Chanan (ed.), *Twenty-Five Years of the New Latin American Cinema* (London: British Film Institute, 1983), p. 33.

10 Tomas Ybarra-Frausto, "Rasquachismo: A Chicano Sensibility," in Richard del Castillo (ed.), *Chicano Art: Resistance and Affirmation, 1965–1985* (Los Angeles: Wright Gallery UCLA, 1991), pp. 155–162.

11 This passage revisits material first published in Robert Stam's essay "Palimpsestic Aesthetics: A Mediation on Hybridity and Garbage," in May Joseph and Jennifer Fink (eds.), *Performing Hybridity* (Minneapolis: University of Minnesota Press, 1999).

12 See Edward Humes, *Garbology: Our Love Affair with Trash* (New York: Penguin, 2012), p. 5.

13 Arjun Appadurai, *The Future as Cultural Fact: Essays on the Global Condition* (London: Verso, 2013), p. 125.

14 Ibid., p. 6.

15 See Claudia Mesquita, "Stretching the Borders," in Arlindo Machado (ed.), *Made in Brasil: Tres Decadas do Bideo Brasileiro* (São Paulo: Itau Cultural, 2007).

16 See Richard Maxwell and Toby Miller, "Film and the Environment," in Mette Hjort (ed.), *Film and Risk* (Detroit: Wayne State University, 2012), p. 272.

17 Zoe Graham, PhD thesis proposal at NYU Cinema Studies, provisionally entitled "Transnational Pedagogy: Film School without Borders."

18 For a survey of recycled art from around the world, see Charlene Cerny and Suzanne Seriff, *Recycled, Reseen: Folk Art from the Global Scrap Heap* (New York: Harry N. Abrams [in conjunction with the Museum of International Folk Art, Santa Fe], 1996).

19 In his fascinating intervention at the "Hybrid Cultures and Transnational Identities" Conference, Teshome Gabriel showed slides of the salvage art of African-American artist Lefon Andrews, who uses paper bags as his canvas and dry leaves for paint. Teshome demonstrated the method by showing the audience a paper bag and some leaves, revealing them to be the basic materials that went into the beautiful artifacts pictured in the slides.

20 Frederic Jameson, *Postmodernism, or, The Cultural Logic of Late Capitalism* (London: Verso, 1991), p. 25.

21 Kant, *Critique of Judgment*, quoted in Daniel Morgan, op. cit., p. 74.

22 J.-F Lyotard, *Lessons on the Analytic of the Sublime* (Stanford: Stanford University Press, 1994), pp. 44–45.

23 Jacques Derrida, "Economimesis," in *Diacritics* 11(2) (Summer 1981): 3–25, cited in Ngai, *Ugly Feelings*, p. 334.

24 Alain Badiou, *Cinema* (Paris; Nova, 2010), pp. 363–364.

25   Columpar and Mayer (eds.), op. cit., p. 122.

26   Kenneth W. Harrow, *Trash: African Cinema from Below* (Bloomington: Indiana University Press, 2013).

27   Ibid., p. 84.

28   See Maria Eugenia Boaventura, *A Vanguarda Antropofágica* (São Paulo: Attica, 1985), p. 114.

29   For an English version of the "Cannibalist Manifesto," see Leslie Bary's excellent introduction to and translation of the poem in *Latin American Literary Review*, 19(38) (July–December 1991).

30   See Alessandra Santos, *Cannibal: Arnaldo Antunes* (São Paulo: Versos, 2013).

31   The "Indians" of North America, meanwhile, have also deployed the cannibal trope for their own purpose. In *Columbus and other Cannibals* (New York: Autonomedia, 1992), Native American historian Jack D. Forbes uses the Cree term "*wetico*"—roughly "cannibal," or more broadly the evil person or spirit that terrorizes other creatures—to designate the "unimaginable death, destruction, exploitation and greed" brought by Europeans to the Americas.

32   Joaquim Pedro de Andrade made many films related to the Modernist movement: *O Poeta do Castelo*, a short film about the modernist poet Manuel Bandeira (with whom Mário de Andrade exchanged letters); the feature *O Padre e a Moça*, which adopts a poem by Drummond de Andrade; and *O Homem do Pau Brasil*, inspired by the other monstre sacre of Modernismo, Oswald de Andrade.

33   The full preface is included in Randal Johnson and Robert Stam, *Brazilian Cinema* (New York: Columbia University Press, 1995).

34   Ibid.

35   See John Fiske, *Understanding Popular Culture* (Boston: Unwin Hyman, 1989).

36   Quoted in Vincent Deville, *Les Formes du Montage dans le Cinema d'Avant-Garde* (Rennes: Presses Universitaires de Rennes, 2014), p. 162.

37   See Paul Cooke and Rob Stone, "TransAtlantic Drift: Hobos, Slackers, Flaneurs, Idiots and Edukators," in Lucia Nagib and Anne Jerslev (eds.), *Impure Cinema* (London: I.B. Tauris, 2014).

38   Quoted in Ken Knabb (ed.), *Situationist International Anthology* (Berkley: Bureau of Public Secrets, 2007), p. 9.

39   McKenzie Wark, "Détournement: A User's Guide," *Angelaki: Journal of the Theoretical Humanities*, 14(1) (2009): 147–150.

40   See the invaluable anthology by Douglas Kellner and Dan Strieble (eds.), *Emile de Antonio: A Reader* (Minneapolis: University of Minnesota, 2000), p. 2.

41   Ibid., p. 31.

42   Ibid., p. 35.

43   See David Tooop, *The Rap Attack: African Jive to New York Hip-Hop* (London: Pluto Press, 1984).

44    Taylor, op. cit., p. 150.
45    Astra Taylor, op. cit., p. 232.
46    See Paul Arthur, "Jargons of Authenticity: Three American Moments," in Michael Renov (ed.), *Theorizing Documentary* (New York: Routledge, 1993).
47    Jay David Bolter and Richard Grusin, *Remediation: Understanding New Media* (Cambridge, MA: MIT Press, 1999), p. 19.
48    Paul Virilio, *The Vision Machine* (Bloomington: Indiana University Press, 1994), pp. 59–77.
49    Noah Shachtman and Robert Beckhusen, "Hamas Shoots Rockets at Tel Aviv, Tweeting Every Barrage," *Wired*. Retrieved November 15, 2012. <http://www.wired.com/dangerroom/2012/11/gaza-social-media-war/?utm_source=Contextly&utm_medium=RelatedLinks&utm_campaign=MoreRecently>
50    See <http://www.notbored.org/the-scp.html> and <http://www.denisbeaubois.com/Amnesia/In%20the%20event%20of%20Amnesia%20copy%202.html>
51    Steve Mann, Jason Nolan, and Barry Wellman, "Sousveillance: Inventing and Using Wearable Computing Devices for Data Collection in Surveillance Environments," *Surveillance & Society*, 1(3): 331–355.
52    <http://lowdrone.com>
53    <http://wafaabilal.com/thirdi>
54    See Hans Magnus Enzensberger, *The Consciousness Industry: On Literature, Politics and the Media* (New York; Seabury Press, 1974).

# 5

# Hybrid Variations on a Documentary Theme

Although often assumed to be polar opposites, documentary and fiction are, in fact, theoretically and practically intermeshed, just as history and myth, also conventionally seen as opposites, are symbiotically connected. Poststructuralist historian Hayden White argued in *Metahistory: The Historical Imagination in Nineteenth-Century Europe* (1973) that the myth/history distinction was arbitrary and of recent invention.[1] In words that apply to film as well as to historiography, White pointed out that it matters little whether the world that is conveyed to the reader/spectator is conceived to be real or imagined; the manner of making *discursive* sense of it through tropes and emplotment is identical. In this chapter, we will examine the ways in which the hybridization of documentary and fiction has been mobilized as a radical aesthetic resource.

## The Fiction–Documentary Continuum

Poststructuralism, in its broad assault on essentialist binarisms, also has the effect of undermining the documentary/fiction dichotomy. Conventional historical narrative, for Roland Barthes, is but "a particular form of fiction," where the historian tries to give the impression that the past "is speaking for itself."[2] Derrida's claims about genre in general in "The Law of Genre" apply equally to documentary and fiction: "The trait which marks membership inevitably divides, the boundary of the set comes forth, by invagination, an internal pocket larger than the whole; and the outcome of this division and of this abounding remains as singular as it is limitless."[3]

*Keywords in Subversive Film/Media Aesthetics*, First Edition. Robert Stam with Richard Porton and Leo Goldsmith.
© 2015 John Wiley & Sons, Inc. Published 2015 by John Wiley & Sons, Inc.

As **trans-genres** incorporating myriad subgenres, documentary and fiction allow for an infinity of permutational crossings and variations. It is revealing, in this sense, that some spectators misrecognize films such as *City of God* (2002) or *Entre les Murs* (2008) as "documentaries," when in fact they are staged films that deploy **documentary effects**—that is, the mimicry of the documentary style through the use of non-actors, handheld camera, and blurred footage. The proliferation of syncretizing coinages such as **documenteur** (the title of an Agnes Varda film), **"fiction documentaire"** (Jacques Ranciere), and **"reality fictions"** (Frederick Wiseman) also testify to the burgeoning hybridization of the two modes.[4] Furthermore, the hybridizations are multifarious, not simply in intercourse between documentary and fiction, but rather in a polyandrous flirtation between documentary and music video, documentary and installation art, documentary and literary adaptation, documentary and experimental video, as well as between formats, platforms, and media.

Christian Metz famously argued that all films, insofar as they all involve arrangement, editing, and mediation, are fiction films. Yet, the converse is also true; all films are arguably documentaries, in that they document *something*, even if only the changing modes of production and performance at a given point in time. In a generic aporia, just as space is inevitably conceived as both finite and infinite, so all films are inevitably analyzable both as fictions and as documentaries. Rather than see documentary and fiction as distinct generic essences, we might better distinguish, with Roger Odin, between **fictionalizing** and **documentarizing modes**, and between **documentary** and **fictive operations**, as characterizing many, if not most, documentary and fiction films.[5] In a sense, all films form what David James calls **allegories of cinema**—filmic registers of their own modes of production, their own staging practices, and their own shaping of social relations.[6] What, then, constitutes the documentary difference? For some, a higher coefficient of **ethical responsibility** distinguishes the two modes: documentary representations, existing on a continuum with real life, have more serious practical and ethical consequences for the "characters." For Vivian Sobchack, documentary is "constituted and inscribed as ethical space: it stands as the objectively visible evidence of subjective visual responsiveness and responsibility for a world shared with other subjects."[7] For Jean-Louis Commoli, documentaries submit to the **"risk of the real,"** that is, they are shadowed and nourished by the vicissitudes of production, actuality, and shifting human relationships. That risk can take lethal form, as with the *coup d'etat* that interrupted the filming of *The Battle of Chile* (1973–1976) and led to the murder of the film's cameraman.[8] The risk can also take the less dramatic form of mutual insecurity, whereby the anxieties of the filmmaker at the moment of filming meet the anxieties of the filmed subject at the moment of being filmed, while each side risks, as Commoli puts it, "becoming 'other' to themselves."[9] *5 Broken Cameras*, by Palestinian Emad Burnat and Israeli Guy Davidi, concretizes *the risk of the real* in the most literal sense through its story of five cameras literally broken by Israeli soldiers and police during protests against the "separation wall." The film's final, as-yet-unbroken sixth camera, conveys a kind of cautious optimism that ultimately the risks are worth the trouble.

The hybridization of documentary and fiction is hardly new. Apart from filmmakers such as J. Stuart Blackton, who filmed the Spanish–American War in the Caribbean (1898) in New Jersey bathtubs, even a cursory look at film history reveals a wide spectrum of practices, with gradations rather than fixed lines between the two modes. *Citizen Kane* (1941) was based on a historical prototype (Hearst) and begins with a semi-parodic fake newsreel ("News on the March"). Both Hitchcock's *The Wrong Man* and Bunuel's *Los Olvidados* were based on journalistic reportage and filmed in black-and-white documentary style. While aesthetic practices of the 1960s and 1970s such as **expanded cinema** sought to destabilize hierarchies and boundaries of medium specificity,[10] the various New Waves—Neo Realism, the Nouvelle Vague, Cinema Novo, New German Cinema—injected documentary elements into fiction films as a means of formal renovation. Conversely, the French ethnographer/filmmaker Jean Rouch injected fictive elements into documentary leaving, as Rouch put it, "almost no boundary between documentary film and films of fiction."[11] His *La Pyramide Humaine* stages a fictive psychodrama about racial divisions in a French lycee in Abidjan, but the fiction generated very real consequences in the form of friendships and quarrels, love affairs and breakups. For Rouch, advance-plotted psychodramas were a way of "lying to tell the truth," using a fictional premise to open up reality to risk and adventure. Rouch wielded the **camera as a catalyst**, capable of provoking personal transformations through the filmic experience.[12] Initially contrived psychodramatic situations, in his view, could become **filmic therapy**, triggering positive changes in the form of more equal and convivial social relations.

Edgar Morin, together with Rouch, coined the term *cinéma vérité*—a translation of Vertov's *Kino Pravda* ("cinema-truth," but, in the Russian context, also "cinema-newspaper")—to refer to a documentary process that reflexively foregrounds the actual processes of filmmaking. *Cinéma vérité* was often contrasted with **direct cinema** (also known as **observational cinema**)—that is, non-reflexive "fly-on-the-wall" filmmaking taking advantage of lightweight cameras and synchronous sound to record social life as accurately as possible. Yet, Frederick Wiseman, the filmic anatomist of what might be called **institutional micropolitics**—observational critiques of social institutions such as asylums, prisons, hospitals, and universities— has long labeled his films *reality fictions*, where documentary is "just another form of fiction."[13] Linda Williams, meanwhile, has proposed the term "**anti-*vérité***" to refer to films that eschew realistic recording life-as-it- is in favor of "a deeper investigation of how it became as it is."[14]

Cinema, then, has been endlessly enriched by the cross-play of fiction and documentary. Through **reciprocal chameleonism**, the two trans-genres come to resemble one another. Just as to fictionalize documentary is to enliven it, so to documentarize fiction is in some ways to democratize it, given that documentary, more likely to be filmed *in loco*, has historically been more socially inclusive than the fiction feature, more likely to be filmed in studios or their equivalent. Mutual enrichment occurs when directors mingle the two modes through **thespian hybridity** or the insertion of actors into the stream of real life and real-life situations. Haskell Wexler's *Medium Cool* plunged its actors into the maelstrom of the protests at the 1968 Democratic Convention in Chicago. The Brazilian film *Iracema* (1975), set in the Amazon region, meanwhile, pairs two players of very different status and experience, one a famous white actor (Paulo Cesar Pereio) playing a truck driver, the other an unknown indigenous beginner (Edna de Cassia) playing a prostitute, as a strategy for charting unequal relations of power in the pre-existing footage.

Eduardo Coutinho's *Jogo de Cena* ("Playing"), meanwhile, has both actresses and "real people" recite the very same lines of dialogue, within a strategy of disorientation where the spectator loses track of what is performative enactment and what is individual recollection. Both actresses and non-actresses "break frame" and comment on their "performance." In a transpersonal continuity, one "performer" picks up where the other left off. The manufactured tears of the professional actress (Marilha Pera) turn into real tears when she remembers difficult situations with her own daughter. Coutinho facilitates the **self-fabulation of character**, a process that Deleuze, in a different context, calls "the becoming of real characters when they begin to fictionalize themselves…"[15] Within Coutinho's *theatrum mundi* ("theater of the world"), the limits of theater and world, as in Brechts's "everyday theater of the street," become subject to a provocative destabilization.

The melding of fiction and documentary can generate non-fiction films every bit as suspenseful as the best fiction films. Through a stratagem that might be called **sequestering suspense**, the José Padilha documentary *Bus 174* (2002) turns the real-life hijacking of a Brazilian bus by a homeless street person named Sandro into a **sociological thriller**. Since Brazilians knew the outcome from the media due to saturation coverage—police mistakenly killed one of the passengers, and later killed Sandro—the film downplays suspense in the conventional sense, exploring instead the human "backstories" and social implications of the event. What would make a *person* like Sandro sequester a bus? In a kind of **outtake jujitsu**, Padilha used outtakes from Globo Networt reportage—re-invoiced through commentary and supplemented with interviews—to expose the superficiality of Globo's own portrayals. Repeatedly abused by the police, Sandro, we learn, had been an eyewitness to the notorious 1995 Candelaria police massacre of street children. Directly addressing the police, he shouts "Look at my face! Take a good look!" and denounces police violence. Sandro becomes the disturbed yet eloquent spokesperson for the victims of the police and the prison system. Rather than merely register violent events, *Bus 174* exposes the ideological blinders through which the media usually relay them. But, even more remarkably, the film **hijacks Hitchcock**, as it were, in that its narrative structure strongly resembles that of certain memory-based Hitchcock films that proceed via a double and contradictory temporal movement—a narrative forward-zoom combined, as it were, with a backward dolly—in that the story simultaneously moves forward in terms of the unfolding events in the sequestered bus, and backward, toward the origin of a trauma. Much as Hitchcock traces the origins of Gregory Peck's amnesia in *Spellbound* (1945), or of Marnie's kleptomania in *Marnie* (1964), Padilha traces the social origins of Sandro's trauma.

## Murderous Reenactments

The ever-more audacious mixing of fact and fiction in documentaries becomes especially striking in the realm of reenactment. A number of recent documentaries, such as *S-21: The Khmer Rouge Killing Machine* (2003) and *El Sicario, Room 164* (2010)—get murderers to reenact their crimes. Joshua Oppenheimer's *The Act of Killing* (2012), co-directed with an Indonesian who has chosen to remain anonymous for self-protection reasons, is especially daring in this sense, in that the director induced mass-killers, in a kind of **reenactment as self-indictment**, to restage their own acts of murder. The most powerful and irrefutable indictment, after all, is that which comes not from the prosecutors but from the perpetrators. The protagonist of the film is Anwar Congo, a thug deeply involved in the 1965–1966 Indonesian genocide that slaughtered 1 million–3 million people and swept General Suharto into power, all with the knowledge and complicity of the United States, Great Britain, the Netherlands, and

Australia. (Most Western news agencies treated the massacres as "good news" for the West.) As the head of the "Frog Squad," Anwar killed roughly 1,000 souls with his bare hands. Since the current government has not completely severed its links to this genocidal past, no one has been jailed for these crimes; in fact, people such as Anwar have been feted as national heroes, and even applauded, as we see in the film, on an Indonesian talk show. Since such acts had been rendered heroic by the official narrative, Anwar had every reason to believe that the film would celebrate his "feats."

The death squad members offer a toxic brew of racism (toward the Chinese), machismo (toward women), phobic anti-communism (toward political enemies), homoerotic homophobia (through bellicose male bonding), sadism (toward everyone), and sheer love of orgiastic mayhem. To gain access to his subjects, the filmmakers exploited the gangsters' love of Hollywood-style entertainment. Using **strategic flattery**, Oppenheimer proposed a fiction film where the murderers would play their own roles, within the sensational codes of their most adored genres—the Western, the gangster film, and Elvis Presley musicals. (The thugs were known as "movie theater gangsters" due to their penchant for hanging out in their favorite cinemas.) The result is the film-within-the-film "Arsan and Amina," where Anwar performs innumerable reenactments, while his friend Herman, dressed as a "communist" drag-queen, threatens to devour Anwar's simulacral liver. In what is very probably a historical first, the filmmakers induce the killers to not only confess their crimes, but also to reenact them in a style and genre of their own choosing. In a perverse version of Commoli's "*auto-mise-en-scène*," where the desire of the filmed subject informs the staging of the film, **style itself becomes a form of confession**. It is as if Hitler not only confessed his genocidal acts, but filmed them in the style of *Nosferatu*, or *Triumph of the Will*, or *Scarface*.

By inviting the gangster–cinephiles to recreate the murders in Hollywood style, Oppenheimer highlights the role of mass-mediated phantasy informing both the crimes themselves and the reenactments of those crimes. Various sequences are staged in the manner of a Western (with the killers in cowboy hats) or as a horror film, or as a musical, such as when dancers writhe by a waterfall to "Born Free." For these movie-fed gangsters, Hollywood offered an ethos, an acting school, and audiovisual training in torture techniques. Yet, Hollywood-genre films were not the only "film school" that shaped the imaginary of the killers. An Indonesian propaganda film— *Pengkhianatan G30S/PKI* ("the September 30 Movement Treason," 1984)— which we briefly glimpse on a TV monitor—also blended documentary and fictionalized reenactments in a style inflected by melodramas and horror films. Televised annually and made mandatory viewing for school children for decades, the film, marked by morbid sensationalism and perverse sexuality, left Indonesian children traumatized by its imagery of bloodthirsty communists killing mild-mannered general fathers in their homes in front of their children. The propaganda of Suharto's "New Order" regime, as Intan Pramaditha points out, was built on a "spectacular violence" that coexisted with its "invisible double," the "spectral violence" of secret assassins such as Anwar.[16] In a kind of narrative striptease, "terror was produced by the oscillation of what Indonesians could see and were unable to see."[17] Government propaganda portrayed the communist-affiliated *Gerwani* women as literally castrating Amazons, and, in *Pengkhianatan G30S/PKI*, one of them slashes a "good" general with a razor blade. The cross-dressing of Anwar's friend Herman, as what Pramaditha calls "a scantily-clad liver-eating woman whose sexual monstrosity overemphasized through Herman's unruly body," clearly alludes to the junta's portrayals of the *Gerwani*.[18]

There is, of course, a canonical precedent for this kind of *theatrical self-indictment*, in the **mousetrap strategy** of the play-within-the-play in *Hamlet*, set to "catch the conscience of a king." Similar to Hamlet observing Claudius during the play, Oppenheimer observes Anwar's looks. But, in this instance, it is as if Claudius had set the mousetrap himself and had himself reenacted his murder of Hamlet's father. (The film's title also recalls *Hamlet*'s incessant play with theatrical metaphors—for example, "you who are witnesses to this act" and "hold the mirror up to nature.") As in *Hamlet*, the "something rotten" in the ambient polity turns everyone into actors—the Chinese merchants who have to pretend they enjoy being extorted; the victims pretending not to hate their torturers; and the bought electorate pretending to support their candidate. The same thug who boasts about raping numerous women hypocritically assumes a posture of prayer when interrupted by the call to prayer of the muezzin. Even Oppenheimer himself tells lies of omission by pretending that he is not a leftist.

Giving voice to the **hauntologies** (Derrida) of dictatorship, their film proliferates, similar to an Elizabethan tragedy, in severed heads, nightmares, and specters. Anwar reenacts his misdeeds with gusto and a strange pride. In a kind of fascist *lehrstucke*, he demonstrates, on the very roof that formed the décor of his crimes, his favored technique of wire-strangling as a way of avoiding too much blood. Out of some inverted narcissism or some Dostoyevskian impulse to revisit the scene of the crime, Anwar acknowledges all his misdeeds—the false charges against the victims, the gratuitous cruelty, the imaginative sadism—and seems eager for everyone, including his grandchildren, to see the reenactments. Generally, he seems cheerful, supposedly exulting in his 90 minutes of movie fame.[19] But he is not the only one who confesses. Avoiding the trope of the "rogue element," the film repeatedly shows that the social rot begins at the top, with the heads of a 3-million-member gang, with media moguls, corrupt landowners, heads of film festivals, and even a vice president!

Many aspects of *The Act of Killing* are very disturbing—for example, the lack of poetic–historical justice; the idea that anyone can become a fascist; and the fact that the killers are socially accepted. But perhaps the most disturbing elements are the utterly banal normality of the killers, and the Tarantino-style nonchalance with which they reenact their killings. While lacking in cultural capital, these *lumpen ubermenschen* are not stupid: they use words such as "sadistic" and exhibit a knowledge of Hollywood-genre films worthy of a film scholar. (We do not usually associate the word "cinephile" with the word "assassin.") Instead of the "banality of evil" that Hannah Arendt discerned in the insipid bureaucrat Eichmann, *The Act of Killing* reveals the **charm of evil**, that of a dapper *bon vivant* who loves his pets, his grandchildren, and the cha-cha-cha. The film leaves the spectator dizzy and squirming, suffering from an acute case of moral vertigo, without a comfortable haven. Within the film's *immanent critique*, no one directly voices the humanistic values we assume to undergird and animate the film; no one in the film gives voice to ethical normativity. While the film could be faulted for a number of political errors—not providing sufficient context, not emphasizing the perspective of the victims, not showing resistance to the regime, not providing a subject position for progressive Indonesian viewers—its **entrapment strategies** ultimately serve the interest of the victims.[20] The film immerses us in Anwar's upside-down world of sanctioned immorality—extortion is normal, murder is divine, rape is fun—while making clear that, as with a Hitchcock villain or with Tony Soprano, we are tempted to like him. Nor are enlightened Western spectators so safely distant from the perpetrators' misdeeds as they might like to think. For decades, American citizens indirectly supported, through their taxes and their compliance, many such "anti-communist" regimes in places such as Chile, Argentina, Vietnam, South Africa, and Iran. The still-living architects of those policies, such as Henry Kissinger, are still treated reverentially on American TV talk shows.

Tacit norms of humanity do emerge in subtle ways in the film. Some of the "extras," who reenact the massacres that took place in their own villages, look absolutely terrified even after the "director" says "cut!" A neighbor recalls with nervous laughter that, as a boy, he buried his own stepfather, murdered by Anwar's death squads. The technicians in the talk show studio, on hearing Anwar boast of his killings, wonder how he can sleep at night. Certain questions in Javanese from Oppenheimer himself, who the thugs seem to assume is just another anti-communist American supportive of their cause, similarly, imply a certain moral standard. When Anwar asks Oppenheimer if his former victims would have felt what he felt now while playing their role in the film, the director answers that it would have been much worse, since for them it was not acting.

Many of the most important cues, however, are non-verbal, having to do with the arc of emotion as revealed by the **symptomatic body**. Anwar's body language and expression move almost imperceptibly from exuberance to doubt to a certain melancholy, depression, and even nausea. A clear crack in his psychic armor appears when he briefly plays the victim of torture and is thus obliged to imagine a tiny portion of the pain and humiliation suffered by his own victims. "Do you think I have sinned?," he asks. Even more dramatic is the near-final scene where Anwar, subject to a kind of visceral karma, doubles over with a severe case of the dry heaves. It is hard not to read the retching as an instance of bodily mourning or even **failed catharsis**, an abortive attempt to purge massive guilt. Without these ephemeral glimpses of doubt and answerability, the film would have been quite simply intolerable, resulting in a kind of triple horror: the horror of the crimes themselves, the horror in knowing that the criminals were never punished, and the horror of knowing that they felt little remorse. Although one death squad member points out that "history is written by the winners," Oppenheimer has, at least for one moment, tricked one of the "winners" into imagining—however briefly—the feelings of history's "losers." (Oppenheimer is putting the finishing touches on his film about the victims(*The Look of Silence*), and activists in Indonesia are currently using *The Act of Killing* to raise consciousness about the massacres.)

## The Mediatic Spectrum

One way to demonstrate the overlapping of genres is by examining different portrayals of the very same event as mediated across a broad **mediatic spectrum**. The event in question is the massacre in Carandiru Penitentiary in São Paulo on October 2, 1992, when 325 military police, firing 515 shots, slaughtered at least 111 inmates. Although the Brazilian police made the standard claim of a "cross fire" between inmates and police, no police were killed or even seriously wounded. Most prisoners were killed in their own cells, many shot in the back. Frightened at the prospect of contracting AIDS from the blood of their victims, the police forced the surviving inmates to clean up the deluge created by their own bloodbath. The case of Carandiru, as with the earlier Attica Prison massacre in the United States (1971), exemplifies the state-of-exception situation lived by those who are reduced to what Agamben calls **bare life**, subject to the raw power of the state, where the incarcerated, in a racialized state of exception, are defined as outside the pale of humanity, and where the authorities have the power of decision over life itself.

As a manifest instance of Weber's concept of "the state's monopoly on violence," the prison is also the place where Althusser's idea of **"interpellation"**—the process by which ideological apparatuses address individuals and endow them with a social identity, constituting them as subjects—becomes terribly literal. No longer an abstract ideological "hailing," *interpellation* now takes the very concrete form of an intercom voice heard ordering "prisoner number 347" to "strip naked and come to the yard!" In post-slavery societies such as Brazil and the United States, incarceration is inevitably racialized, so that prisoners are disproportionately drawn from an "undercaste" of people of color.

The Carandiru massacre generated a substantial **discursive afterlife** in the form of the written, performative, and audiovisual texts, all along what might be called the **discursive/mediatic/artistic continuum**, that is, the entire spectrum of audiovisual and mediatic practices treating the event, including official reports, first-hand *témoignages*, memoirs, novels, poems, songs, and films. Here, we will examine four accounts of the same event representing different points along the spectrum including: (1) TV network news (Globo Reporter, 1992); (2) a feature fiction film (*Carandiru*, 2002); (3) a music video ("Diary of a Prisoner," 1998); and (4) a feature documentary (*Prisoner of the Iron Bars*, 2003). Although all of the various mediatic renderings of the Carandiru massacre manifest certain media specificities—TV's direct transmission, the primordial role of music and lyrics in the music video, etc.—they also all mingle documentary and fictive procedures.[21]

Although much of the news is no longer directly transmitted, the Globo Reporter account foregrounds the contagiously "viral" sense of **liveness** that surrounds TV generally with an aura of vivacity and simultaneity. Thanks to direct transmission, TV news can shape mass emotion and opinion on a moment-to-moment basis. The Globo Reporter summation of the Carandiru massacre displays TV news' vocation as a conduit, a literal "channel" for national emotion—in this case, the grief and shock provoked by the massacre. Yet, this channeling is marked by clear eruptions of fiction and staging. The most strikingly fictional shot—a close-up, against a blue backdrop, of a gun firing directly at the spectator—can be traced back to a similar shot almost a century earlier, in *The Great Train Robbery* in 1903, where the sheriff character fires his pistol directly at the spectator/camera. Globo Reporter has the pistol shot immediately follow an inmate's claim of "summary executions";

the effect is to suture the spectator into the experience of the prisoners being directly fired upon. In terms of the cinematic logic of continuity editing and eyeline matches, the spectator too is subjected to a simulacral version of a "summary execution."

As TV news has increasingly transformed itself into infotainment, it has drawn more on more on the formal and aesthetic codes of the fiction film. In *Carandiru*, the fiction effect passes also through the sound and music tracks. Globo Reporter, for example, uses various forms of music and sound effects, each with its own generic overtones: (1) a musical percussive logo, an electronic tick-tack that evokes the typical sounds of a (rather archaic) newsroom, serving as a kind of sonic establishing shot; (2) a music piece in the style of an action movie or horror film, meant to evoke the terror of the massacre; (3) an ominous monochord, first used in *The Battle of Algiers*, meant to evoke (and create) a sense of fear; and (4) a more lachrymose music meant to evoke the sadness of the grieving relatives and loved ones of the victims.

Carandiru was again the subject of the Hector Babenco fiction feature *Carandiru* (2003), which also hybridizes forms, genres, and media. A scrupulous reenactment of the massacre by the auteur–director of *Kiss of the Spider Woman* (1985), the film adapts a memoir by a doctor (Drauzio Varela), who had worked at Carandiru Penitentiary combating the AIDS epidemic. The film's major achievement is its careful reconstruction, partly within the very same prison, of precisely that which the state intended to hide—the massacre itself. Babenco performed an immense public service by reconstructing the sounds and images of the slaughter, making visible that which the authorities had intended to keep off-stage and offscreen, literally "ob-scene."

*Carandiru* illustrates the concept of "**intermediality**"—that is, the interconnectedness of the various media of communication that draw from and inflect one another in an interactive manner. Instead of emphasizing any singular medium specificity, the concept of *intermediality*—associated in media studies with Andre Gaudreault—stresses overlapping and mutually impacting specificities across the mediatic spectrum. *Intermediality* forms the basis of a theory or analytic as a way of talking about the complex *remediations* across media, including the technological and economic realms of convergence and conglomeration. Henry Jenkins' coinage "**convergence culture**," in this sense, designates the accelerating collisions and interactions between old and new media, the transmedial co-presence of multiple interconnected screens within a more participatory digital paradigm.[22] In the case of *Carandiru*, *intermediality* serves to buttress the *reality effect* of the film through **reciprocal authentification**, as the on-screen neighboring of TV footage, placed alongside staged scenes, implies that both forms of representation exist as part of a continuum of veracity.

At the same time, the film is marked by Hitchcock-style **techniques of subjectification**. As Varela wanders through the prison corridors, less a character than an ambulatory sensorium, he peeps in on the prisoners in their cells. He becomes an eye, literally privileged in outsized close-ups reminiscent of the opening shots of Hitchcock's *Vertigo* (1958). With the inmate patients, meanwhile, Varela functions as a giant ear; he is the listener, the secular priest/analyst who listens to their confessions but who withholds judgment. *Carandiru* in this sense offers an interesting variation on the **panoptical situation** described by Foucault. The Benthamite prison system fostered a non-reciprocal gaze; the inmates are hyper-visible from the central viewing point of the tower, completely exposed to relentless observation, never knowing when and if they are being watched. In *Carandiru*, in contrast, the visual field is not organized around the centralized gaze of authority but rather around the mobilized gaze of the middle-class doctor–*flâneur*. Varela exercises his panoptical powers benevolently, in favor of the prisoners. The result is an oxymoronic figure—a humanized panoptical observer, a **simpaticon**, as it were, the empathetic bearer of an institutionally sanctioned gaze.

The choice of music in film is often ideologically laden, conveying a distinct perspective on the social relations between the director, the narrating character, and the characters. In *Carandiru*, the music is non-diegetic, commentative, atmospheric, and, in stylistic terms, modernist and dissonant. It relays not only a normative social ethos of the middle-class spectator but also the normative cultural ethnos of both the white middle-class author of the memoir (Varela) and the middle-class director of the film (Babenco). In this sense, the music indirectly reinforces the social divide separating the filmmakers from the prisoners, conveying a social vantage point from which the prisoners are being pitied but also judged from what is, in the end, a position of **ethical panopticism**.

Carandiru is also the subject of the rap music video "Inmate's Diary," by Mauricio Eca and featuring Racionais MC, one of the most politically radical of the Brazilian rap groups. Although the *minor* genre of music video is rarely seen as creating "subversive cinema," "Inmate's Diary" shows the genre's radical possibilities by offering a scathing 8-minute critique of Brazilian prisons, one ultimately more effective than the big-budget Babenco film. The video stages the lyrics of a poem by a former inmate named Jocenir, here played by the leader of Racionais MC, named Mano Brown (after James Brown). The music video reflects the social dynamics linking Brazilian prisons to the world of rap as the favored genre of music among the inmates, who not only consumed rap but also produced it in names such as "Rap Inmates" and "509e" (after their cell number).

The title heralds a literary genre—the prison diary—part of a venerable tradition of prison literature that includes the Russian Dostoevsky, the Brazilian Graciliano Ramos (*Prison Memories*); the Frenchman Jean Genet (*Journal d'un Voleur*); the Italian Gramsci (*Prison Notebooks*); and a host of African-Americans (Malcolm X, George Jackson, and Mumia abu Jamal). Through lyrical poetry, the prisoner writes himself into the dignity of a virtual freedom. Dated "São Paulo, Oct 1, 1992"—that is, the day before the massacre—the poem conveys the eerie calm before the storm, as Mano Brown/Jocenir writes his poem in his cell:

> here I am, another day
> under the bloody eyes of the guard
> you can't imagine what it's like
> with your head in the sights of an HK
> or a German or Israeli machine gun
> it rips up a thief as if he were made of paper

The poem conveys the uneasy sensation of living literally "under the gun." In a tense crossing of gazes, the poet even projects himself through Keat's "negative capability" into the mind of his guard, seeing him as an exploited nobody whose mass-mediated fantasies lead him to fancy himself as the hero in an action movie:

> meanwhile, up against the wall, standing,
> just one more average Joe
> serving the state, the guard,
> a military policeman
> is hungry, but he thinks he's Charles Bronson

The following verses bring us close to Foucault's modern prison, based not on the disciplinary spectacle of the scaffold but rather on the slow-grinding "*emploi du temps*," or daily routine: "the days are all the same/I light a cigarette, watching the day go by, killing time so time doesn't kill me. After evoking the soul-killing ennui of internalized prison routines, the next segment conveys what might be called a **cross-class shot/counter shot**, where the exchange of looks is less between individuals than between social classes—in this case, between the Carandiru prisoners and the passengers in the passing train, and symbolically between margin and center. Sound-punning on the similarity of the sounds of the train and a machine gun and directly addressing the reader/spectator, the poem continues:

> ratatattat—one more train goes by
> full of respectable people, in a hurry,
> Catholic, reading their newspaper,
> self-satisfied and hypocritical
> moving toward the city center.
> looking at us, full of curiosity
> but we're not in some zoo
> for you, our lives have less value than your cell-phone
> …

The garbage imagery of the finale becomes more frankly denunciatory:

> In Brazil, human beings are disposable, like a used tampax or a Brillo pad.
> Then, in an apotheosis: corpses in the well
> and in the inner yard Hitler smiles in hell.
> the state robocop is cold and feels no sympathy, only hatred, laughing like a hyena.

The words "Hitler smiles in Hell" cue a devastating montage of photographs of the piled-up corpses of the Holocaust edited together with photographs of the gathered corpses of the murdered inmates. Here, garbage is beyond redemption and transfiguration. The intention is not to create an obscene equation of two incommensurable catastrophes, but rather to point to the murderous mechanism of otherization undergirding both.

"Inmate's Diary" obeys an aesthetic mandate specific to the music video—what might be called the **music-as-dominant principle**; the music and lyrics, almost by definition, occupy the command position, providing *anchorage* for the diverse materials. The raspy, metallic music perfectly suits an existential reality dominated by guns and metal, a place where even the psyche, to survive, has to be "armed and dangerous." Through **percussive mimesis**, the repetitiveness of the rhythm echoes the iterative solitude of prison life. The harshness of Mano Brown's voice and music break with the middle-class *douceur* of musical styles such as *bossa nova*, just as the incendiary lyrics break with the myth of the cordial Brazilian "racial democracy."

At the same time, the music video cinematizes a literary genre. The supposedly *minor* genre of the music video enjoys equal access to the riches of cinema's aesthetic legacy. The low-budget video manifests the distant influence of Italian neo-realism through a style where technical inadequacies—shaky camera, grainy images, blurred shots—become an index of authenticity. In a symbiotic match of style and subject reminiscent of the *"aesthetics of hunger,"* a gritty imperfect style renders a gritty, even abject, situation. At the same time, the expressionist lighting has a police-style spotlight play menacingly over the face of Jocenir/Mano Brown behind the bars of the cell. Throughout, an electric current of sympathy moves between various figures and identities: between the rapper and the inmates; between the prisoners and rap music itself; and between the video and its public, expressive of the mediated solidarities of a community coming into voice.

# From Representation to Self-Presentation

A final film addressing Carandiru Penitentiary—Paulo Sacramento's feature documentary *Prisoner of the Iron Bars* (2003)—brings up key political/aesthetic issues of voice and representation. While preparing to make the film, Sacramento realized that his pampered background did not prepare him for the task. To find collaborators and get to know the prison, he offered filmmaking training to both the guards and the prisoners, but since only the latter were interested, they ended up being the co-directors of the film. Bakhtin's characterization of literary texts as **"hybrid constructions"** taking place on "interindividual territory," while true of all films as involving collaboration, is even more apt for a film such as *Prisoner of the Iron Bars*. The subtitle reveals the film's intention: rather than **portraits** of the prisoners, we have **self-portraits**. Instead of characters in search of an author, we have prisoner characters as co-authors of their own portrait. The film is premised on a kind of **subject–director contract** based on complementary knowledges; while the filmmaker initiates the prisoners into the trade secrets of filmmaking, the prisoners initiate the filmmaker into the secret codes of the prison. The film thus breaks with what Jean-Claude Bernardet calls the **"sociological documentary,"** where "experts" speak in "voice-of God" narration about the socially excluded while reaffirming their own power and authority.[23]

Sacramento avoids the trap of the **appropriation of speech** through a strategy of **hybrid authorship** or, in Foucauldian terms, "speaking together" instead of "speaking for." It was in conjunction with his work with the GIP (Prison Information Group), after all, that Foucault came to speak of "the indignity of speaking for others."[24] The film in this sense partially undermines the usually asymmetrical power relations between director and subject, a relation that becomes even more overwhelmingly asymmetrical in the case of those suffering the "social death" of incarceration. *Hybrid authorship* becomes a partial answer to Spivak's famous question—"can the subaltern speak?"—where she points to the aporias of **subaltern speech**, or the problematic nature of authentic, unmediated self-representation by oppressed and marginalized groups imagined as powerless to shape their own representation.[25]

*Prisoner of the Iron Bars* practices **authorial self-relativization**, or the subversion of directorial power through a suggestive array of mechanisms: (1) the **transfer of expertise** by which the prisoners themselves become the real experts, those best equipped to reveal the secret codes, power arrangements, and political economy of the prison; (2) **the dispersive delegation of** *mise-en-scène*, by which the prisoners register scenes that Sacramento could not possibly have filmed, such as scenes from inside the cells at night; and (3) the **inversion of the panoptical gaze**, so that we do not look *at* the prisoners through the peephole as do the guards (or as with Varela in the Babenco film); rather, we look with the prisoners looking *at* the guards looking through the peephole.

Finally, the film practices **social normalization through domestication** by showing the prisoners in the cells that they have remodeled into a simulacra of home through their own *mise-en-scène* of personal artifacts. Centralizing the peripheralized, the film creates a kind of **self-subjectification** through carceral phenomenology. Rather similar to Juliette Jeanson in *2 ou 3 choses que je sais d'elle* ("Two or Three Things I Know About Her"; 1967), the prisoners become the phenomenologists of their own lives. As they reflect on the most routine events (falling asleep, preparing coffee), the spectator comes to partially inhabit their circumstances and their subjectivity. The film thus fuses two points of enunciation usually separated—that of the subjects/objects of the film, those who supposedly experience without reflection; and that of the directors, who are "supposed to know" and positioned to reflect with a distanced intelligence.

In a kind of *mise-en-abyme* of collective authorship, *Prisoner of the Iron Bars* foregrounds **subaltern agency** by showing the prisoner–filmmakers in the act of filming, often in pairs. The prisoners are so much at ease, so convinced that the director is *not* an agent of the state, that they proudly display even their illegal activities, such as making rum, planting marijuana, and fabricating weapons. (If Babenco's perspective is creepily *voyeuristic*, that of the prisoner–cineastes is proudly *exhibitionistic*.) *Prisoner of the Iron Bars* offers a strong case of what Comolli, borrowing from Claudine de France, calls "*auto-mise-en-scène*," the process by which the desire of the filmed subject comes to inform the *mise-en-scène*. Yet, the prisoners are not angelized either by the director or by themselves; rather than heroes, they are complex, fully human subjects. At the same time, the film makes us aware of the limits of "giving voice," since, at any given moment, due to what Consuelo Lins and Claudia Mesquita call the **imbrication of perspectives**, we are often not completely sure who actually filmed what we are seeing.[26] Hence, Sacramento gives the camera to the prisoners, but also reveals the limits of this democratizing gesture.

*Prisoner of the Iron Bars* can be seen as a culmination of an inexorable trend toward the **democratization of filmic authorship**. Although filmmaking, historically, has usually been in the hands of middle-class directors equipped with access to literal and symbolic *"cultural capital"* (Bourdieu), many countervailing projects have tried to place the camera in the hands of the disempowered. Although this (partial) transfer of power was extremely difficult when filmmaking equipment was cumbersome and expensive, the various technological advances—from lightweight cameras and sound recording equipment in the 1960s to video cameras in the 1980s up through the various digital revolutions—have made it infinitely easier. Digital cameras and smartphones, especially, allow for an immediacy, intimacy, and mobility far beyond what earlier technologies could achieve.

Jean Rouch was an early key figure in this mutation toward more egalitarian film production. Although Rouch-style collaboration now seems somewhat limited in the light of subsequent developments, it still constituted a major change in approach. Rouch spoke of **shared anthropology**—that is, a dialogic collaboration between filmmaker–ethnographer and the ethnographic subject (a sharing both reciprocated and reversed in Manthia Diawara's wittily titled film portrait *Rouch in Reverse*). With Rouch, democratization took many concrete forms, beginning with **improvisation by the filmed subjects**—for example, Oumarou Gando as "Edward G. Robinson" improvising his commentary for *Moi Un Noir* ("I, a Negro," 1958), which reportedly inspired Belmondo's nonchalant *bavardage* in Godard's *À Bout de Souffle* ("Breathless," 1958). Another major democratizing change consisted in **participant feedback** in the form of screenings where the subjects offered their commentary and critiques—some included, for example, in *Chronique d'un Été* ("Chronicle of a Summer," 1960), in the final film itself.

Many of the "rules" articulated in Rouch's 1973 book *The Camera and Man* work toward the same democratizing effect. Rouch's goal of **cohabitation**—living with the subjects prior to filmmaking—fosters more intimacy with the filmed subjects. The production ideals of **minimal crew** and **handheld equipment** make film productions less intimidating by minimizing intrusion into the subjects' everyday lives. Rouch's option for **minimal voice-over**, meanwhile, downplays omniscient commentary in favor of the words of the actual participants, while the **rejection of the zoom lens** was designed to minimize the symbolic predatory violence of ethnographic voyeurism. (Some of the Dogme 95 rules—location shooting, direct sound, handheld camera—follow Rouch's 1973 recommendations, but without their cross-cultural anthropological underpinnings.)

More thoroughgoingly radical attempts at democratization go back to the many leftist collectives of the late 1960s—be it Cine-Liberation in Argentina; Third World Newsreel in the United States; or Society for the Creation of New Works (SLON), Cine-Lutte, and Groupe Medvekine in France. We find a precursor in the form of the **cine-tracts**, or militant, 16-mm, black-and-white, short films by anonymous collectives treating the 1968 "events of May" in France. The *cine-tracts* orchestrated still photos of demonstrations, the recorded sounds of militancy, voice-over commentary, and the slogans of the day. One of the most famous *cine-tracts*—dubbed **imagetexts** by W. J. T. Mitchell—featured a Parisian graffito equating the CRS (de Gaulle's militia) with the Nazi SS.[27] Chris Marker was a key figure in the largely student-led *cine-tract* movement, and a guiding force in the attempts to "put cameras in the hands of the workers," through his efforts with SLON in collaboration with French factory workers.

Cinema was intimately involved in May 1968, in the near-revolution in France largely led by young people, beginning with *L'Affaire Langlois*, the February protests against the government's removal of Henri Langlois as head of the French cinemateque. In May 1968, many French filmmakers called for the closing of the Cannes Film Festival to express solidarity with the striking students and workers. Calling up the memory of the French Revolution and the "three estates" (nobility, clergy, and the people), leftist filmmakers tried to create a cinematic equivalent through the short-lived *Etats Generaux du Cinema*, which audaciously proposed the complete abolition of censorship, free movie screenings, state support for non-commercial films, universal education in filmmaking, and, more generally, a cinema unencumbered by the profit motive. (Long thought to be utopian, some of these measures have been realized in the French school system.)

A shift in attention from texts to their authorship and their collaborative production triggers a theoretical shift. The question of the mimetic real gets displaced onto the very different register of who is empowered to *represent*, or stage, interrogate, or even deconstruct the real. Rather than verisimilitude, the issue becomes one of who is actually producing the film, holding the camera, and doing the editing. This process of empowerment is more multi-faceted than might at first appear, and could involve something as minimal as the appearance of an extra of color, or the casting of a person of color in minor and then major roles, or of actually involving a person of color in directing or producing the films. At the same time, the act of **"giving voice"** is very complicated. The phrase implies that one person or group possesses voice and then delegates it to an oppressed person or group. The concept is rooted in a charitable conception: the haves "give" to the representational have-nots, while the haves maintain their economic dominance, cultural capital, and paternalistic superiority.

The real challenge, to use terms from Spinoza, is to turn **potenza** (power over) into **potere** (power as agency). In cinema, it has never been simply a question of handing over the camera to representatives of the disempowered group. In the 1970s, different directors took different positions on the question of voice. For Chris Marker, placing cameras in the hands of workers would inevitably lead to a more accurate and politically coherent representation that would reveal, if not *the* truth, at least the provisional truth of a working-class perspective. For the more skeptical Godard, such a handover would result only in a kind of pathetic mimicry rooted in false consciousness, whereby, in a circular mimesis, worker–filmmakers would produce films where workers themselves would imitate those actors— as with Jean Gabin, who had incarnated workers on the screen—and thus produce an imitation of an imitation.

In Japan, meanwhile, the films of Shinsuke Ogawa also have a place in this history of democratization. Ogawa's roughly 25 films, made between the 1950s and 1990s, are embedded documents of the postwar Japanese left, from radical student movements, to the violent resistance of farmers to the construction of the Narita Airport in the early 1970s, and then to Japan's rural north, where Ogawa and his crew learned farming techniques and taught filmmaking, initiating a hybrid collective practice in which the documentary subject and filmmaking crew become all but indistinguishable.[28] The Kurdish actor–writer–director Yilmaz Guney also deserves mention as someone who managed to write and even direct films while in prison, at a time when Kurdish activism and even the Kurdish language were taboo in Turkey.

But it is perhaps the post-war history of Brazilian cinema that most dramatically exemplifies this dramatic shift **from representation to self-representation**. While the Cinema Novo directors were all white middle-class heterosexual male intellectuals "speaking for" the marginalized masses, now Brazilian directors are female, gay, lesbian, black, and indigenous. This paradigm shift is not only reflected in the trajectories of individual directors such as Coutinho, but also revealed through a comparison of two versions of the same film project, one from 1962 and the other from 2010. The initial project, called *Five Times Favela*, was a five-episode film centered on the Rio favelas, directed by Cinema Novo directors such as Leon Hirszman and Carlos Diegues. The 2010 remake, in contrast, was produced by Diegues but filmed by directors from the favelas (Manaira Carneiro, Wagner Novais, Rodrigo Felha,

Cacau Amaral, Cadu Barcelos, and Luciana Bezerra). The revelatory new title was *Five Times Favela: This Time by Ourselves.*

Many zigzags marked the slow movement toward self-representation. First came a theoretical critique of documentary itself. In 1972, Arthur Omar published a manifesto defending the concept of **"anti-documentary,"** or films that problematized the paternalism of the leftist documentaries of the time, while Hélio Oiticica proposed a **quasi-cinema**, or a merging of the plastic arts with experimental cinema. Eduardo Coutinho's *Cabra Marcado para Morrer* ("Twenty Years After," 1984) registered the representational shift toward agency as it stood at the time of the political "opening" of the mid-1980s. Coutinho's initial plan, conceived in the optimistic left-populist years before the 1964 *coup d'etat*, was a kind of **cine-rescate** or recovery of history, which would dramatically reconstruct the real-life political assassination, in 1962, of peasant leader João Pedro Teixeira. In a gesture of **actantial self-representation**, the actors were to be the actual participants (João Pedro's comrades), the locale was to be the actual site of the events, and one of the "actors" would be the deceased leader's widow Elizabete, playing herself. Interrupted by the "risk of the real" in the form of the 1964 *coup d'etat*, the filmmakers and the peasant participants were dispersed, and the material already shot had to be hidden from the dictatorship. With political liberalization 20 years later, Coutinho sought out the footage and the participants. Thanks to the film, Elizabete emerges from underground, re-encounters her family, and recomposes her identity as a person, a mother, and an activist.

*Cabra Marcado para Morrer* reflexively charts a dramatic mutation in representational practice. Between the two versions in 1964 and 1984, a radical change in filmic treatment exemplifies what one might call the **historicity of film stylistics**. The 1960s meeting with the widow is rendered in the didactic manner of the period—a mélange of *Salt of the Earth*-style socialist realism, stilted performance, over-explicit dialogue, and the heroicized image of the "people" promoted by the leftist Centers for Popular Culture. The 1980s meeting, in contrast, takes place in the era of network TV and the evolving style of Brazilian TV reportage. Coutinho shows photographs to his subjects, where their own image provokes recollections and emotions. In a kind of **experiential photogenie**—Jean Epstein's phrase for the fascination of the filmed face—the film shows the conflicted emotions of love and loss and anger as they play across Elizabeth's face. The filmic language, two decades later, is less inclined to discourse omnisciently about the other, more inclined to listen and learn.

In the wake of *Cabra Marcado para Morrer*, Coutinho continued his unending search for more open and democratic forms of filmmaking, in which all filmic subjects are created equal. Consistent with his refusal of paternalism, miserabilism, and moralism, Coutinho distinguishes between the **interview**—premised on formal distance and social hierarchy—and the **conversation**, premised on intimacy, relative equality, and openness to digression. Rather than make films *about* others, Coutinho makes films *with* others. His constantly developing capacity for listening intensifies the desire of the filmed subjects to speak. In this sense, Coutinho develops what might be called, playing on Bakhtin, a **filmic grammar of listening**, or what Comolli synaesthetically calls the **listening camera**.[29] Here, Bakhtin's and Medvedev's notion of "**speech tact**" can help illuminate the social dynamics of conversational exchange in Coutinho's films. Against the grain of "film as a visual medium," Coutinho demonstrates that tremendous intellectual excitement and emotional feeling can be generated simply by people speaking to one another. The Russian authors define *speech tact* as the "ensemble of codes governing discursive interaction," determined by "the aggregate of all the social relationships of the speakers, their ideological horizons, and, finally, the concrete situation of the conversation."[30] Coutinho's work, in this sense, explores the various dimensions of *speech tact*. Within what Carlos Alberto Mattos calls **the dramaturgy of speech**, the goal becomes, as Coutinho himself puts it, "an experience of a provisional and utopian equality."

For Consuelo Lins, Coutinho's films constitute **embodied theory**, where theorization is consubstantial with and tested by filmic praxis.[31] The search is less for story and character than for a novel premise or provocative concept. Brazilian analysts such as Lins have noted certain general traits within Coutinho's alternative *poiesis*, including: (1) **spatial concentration**, an option to explore a single locale (the favela *Babilonia*) or even a single apartment building (*Edifício Master*); (2) the on-screen *display of the apparatus* and the filmmaking team; (3) **aesthetic minimalism** (no non-diegetic music, sparing use of montage and voice-over); (4) **leisurely duration**, sufficient for the subject to be at ease, and expose his or her (5) **hidden transcripts** (proscribed non-official thoughts and feelings);[32] (6) **no prior scripting** to avoid pre-set agendas; (7) **single encounters** with the filmed subject, to avoid the temptation of "rewriting"; (8) the **option for listening** as opposed to directorial assertiveness; and (9) the **refusal of totalization**, an emphasis on singular human subjects traversed by contradictory social forces rather than on individuals as specimens of pre-existing sociological or ideological categories ("the working class," "typical *umbanda* practitioner").[33] The result of all these procedures is what Xavier calls the "**aesthetically-inflected auto-construction of the character**."[34]

Indigenous media in Brazil also merits mention as part of this trajectory of democratization, although in this case the *auto-construction* has been more collective than individual. Indigenous films challenge the dominant Western aesthetic, not in the sense of producing films that are more avant-garde in the usual sense, but rather in the sense of making manifest the communal cultural assumptions that undergird indigenous *poieses*. Indigenous media begins from a taken-for-granted communalism where the filmmakers are assumed to be speaking not for themselves but for their communities. Ginsburg speaks of **embedded aesthetics**, in which the imperatives of the community overwhelm individual artistic distinction, a "system of evaluation that refuses a separation of textual production and circulation from broader arenas of social relation."[35] Unlike the French New Wave, with its Oedipal *ressentiment* against "*le cinema de papa*," the indigenous filmmakers, within a kind of **tribal auteurism**, see themselves as primarily accountable to family and clan rather than to producers or sponsors. They consciously seek the approval of the elders, who insist on certain civilities—for example, that the "characters" not be interrupted in mid-speech. Both the elders and their juniors see film as a way to preserve the traditional corpus of songs and stories.

## The Strategic Advantages of Hybridization

The early years of the twenty-first century, according to critic Robert Koehler, form a golden age of **cinematic "in-betweenness**," in films that concertedly slip through the cracks of the border fences between fiction and non-fiction and represent a "byproduct of our collective hyperconsciousness regarding cinema and its effects, so that the filmmaker knows that the audience knows the tricks the filmmaker is playing, and that intention is written in high relief."[36] For Koehler, a quintessential example is Lucien Castiang-Taylor and Illisa Barbash's *Sweetgrass* (2009), a nearly uncategorizable film that evokes affinities with disparate genres—the ethnographic film, the nature documentary, avant-garde installation work, and the Hollywood Western. The film's essential thrust is dryly summed up in the final title card: "In 2003, over three months and one hundred and fifty miles, the last band of sheep trailed through Montana's Absaroka-Beartooth mountains." Yet, this chronicle of several "penultimate" sheep drives—culled from 200 hours of footage—is, despite the filmmakers' status as "visual anthropologists" ensconced in academia, far from clinical or austere. Bleating furiously, while careening up hills and down valleys with abandon, the sheep, in a case of **animal stardom**, are unquestionably the scantily clad vedettes of *Sweetgrass*.

Quite remarkably, the film functions as both fieldwork and a spectacular visual and aural experience that engages the viewer's sensoria in a truly *immersive* fashion. On one level, the film exemplifies **"experimental ethnography"**—Catherine Russell's term to denote films, such as those by filmmakers such as Maya Deren, Peter Kubelka, Kidlat Tahimik, and Tracey Moffatt, that combine the concerns of ethnography and the formal strategies of the avant-garde. While the film's rigorous brand of "observational" cinema mitigates against the inclusion of talking heads or voice-over narration that might fully explain the economic or historical factors that has made the annual trek of thousands of sheep to pasture a relic of the past, the film does provide a wealth of opportunities for aesthetic innovation and historical and sociological inquiry.

For much of its duration, *Sweetgrass* keeps its distance from mere humans, while toying with an anthropomorphism that never degenerates into whimsy. In a by-now-legendary shot, the pre-credits sequence concludes with a passive, cud-chewing sheep staring into the camera. The hilariously endearing shot effects a **return of the animal gaze**. In a subsequent sequence, the casual brutality of "nature red in tooth and claw" comes to the fore as a mama sheep casually tosses away one of her less-favored newborn lambs. Without sentimentalizing the animal world, the sheep are depicted as a surprisingly volatile mixture of innocence, venality, and irascibility. Unapologetically interventionist, Koehler even points to the filmmakers' decision to use microphones for the animals—**animalic** *point d'ecoute* (point of hearing)?—in an effort to enhance the film's aural texture.

Nikolaus Geyrhalter, meanwhile, is a non-fiction filmmaker whose political impetus is linked to a self-consciously aestheticized approach, where the absence of commentary and non-diegetic music coexists with ostentatious camera movements and recherché camera set-ups. Geyrhalter's *Our Daily Bread* (2005) depicts the antiseptic world of factory farming and functions as a critique of what Henri Lefebvre termed **everyday life**, defined as "...dull routine, the ongoing go-to-work, pay-the-bills, homeward trudge of daily existence." Geyrhalter's intricately choreographed tableaux illustrate the peculiarly ingenious practices endemic to the behemoth of agribusiness. *Our Daily Bread* is preoccupied with Rube Goldberg–like contraptions for slaughtering animals, as well as massive operations involved in harvesting fruits and flowers, that are familiar only to selected workers and the corporate cognoscenti. The film forms part of an ongoing documentary tradition— Wiseman's *Meat* comes to mind—that explores a subject usually left out of fiction films because of being seen as the opposite of "entertainment"—that is, routinized work in all its minute particulars. Of course, in addition to exploring the twenty-first-century version of what Marxist theorist Harry

Braverman once termed "the degradation of work in the twentieth century" through "de-skilling" and the replacement of local "craftsmanship" with homogenized mass production, Geyrhalter's documentary can also be easily aligned with recent documentaries and features such as Wang Bing's *West of the Tracks* (2003), Jennifer Baichwal's *Manufactured Landscapes* (2006), and Jia Zhangke's *Still Life* (2006), which explore how workers have become expendable fodder in the age of globalization. Unlike Wang, Baichwal, or Jia's films, however, Geyrhalter's emphasis is less on the scourge of environmental devastation than the complicity between our everyday lives—specifically the need for fast, consumable food—and corporate efficiency. Geyrhalter's deadpan gloss on the food industry portrays the agribusiness version of what Lefebvre termed the "**bureaucratic society of controlled consumption.**" Geyrhalter does not offer panaceas or stopgap solutions, suggesting that changing our personal habits cannot alleviate this malaise; even vegetarians and vegans are complicit with the banalization of the Western diet graphically delineated in *Our Daily Bread*.

The documentaries of Brazilian filmmaker Sergio Bianchi, meanwhile, practice what João Luiz Vieira calls a "**cinema knife**" whereby cinema becomes both an instrument of aggression and a social scalpel performing surgery on the body politic.[37] Bianchi's **deconstructive documentary** *Mato Eles?* (Should I Kill Them, 1983) critiques the usual sentimental approach to the Brazilian Indians, beginning with the title, where the shifter pronoun "I" could refer either to the director or to the Indians—"Should I (the white) kill the Indians? Or should I (the Indian) kill the whites?" The very formulation mocks white Brazilian sentimentality about "our Indians." The relationship is no longer cordial; rather, it is a struggle to the death. Instead of the customary depiction of the local habitat, interspersed with talking-head interviews and disembodied voice-overs expressing the enlightened humanism of middle-class white filmmakers, Bianchi mocks both the official discourse concerning the Indian and the bourgeois *bonne conscience* of the denunciation documentary. As a form of **parodic pedagogy**, *Mato Eles?* is structured around a series of apparently whimsical multiple-choice quizzes addressed to the spectator. The Brechtian call for the *active spectator* who "renders a verdict" is tinged here with bitter irony. One question reads:

> Very few Indians remain from the once-numerous Xeta tribe. What happened to the others? Choose one of the following: (1) they all intermarried with the white population and are living in the cities; (2) they all died due to infection, diseases, and litigation concerning land rights; (3) they are all on vacation in Europe; (4) the Xeta never existed, this documentary is false; and (5) all of the above are correct.

Another quiz poses three unpalatable but hardly impossible outcomes: "The extermination of the Indians should be: (a) immediate; (b) slow; or (c) gradual." Leaving little space for spectatorial self-satisfaction or false optimism, the quiz confronts the audience with the reality of extermination in a manner that initially provokes laughter yet subsequently elicits reflection and self-doubt.

*Mato Eles?* mocks the traditional romantic–Indianist exaltation of the "disappearing" Indian by revealing that the "brave warriors" of the nineteenth-century romantic poets are now trapped in a dreary twentieth-century cycle of impoverished powerlessness. At one point, Bianchi gives us a **satiric trailer** announcing an Indianist epic entitled, in homage to James Fenimore Cooper, *The Last of the Xeta*. The lush strains of the Brazilian Indianist opera *O Guarani* (1870), by the "Brazilian Verdi" Antônio Carlos Gomes, swell our expectations for an epic romantic spectacle. Instead, Bianchi shows us a series of photographs of the sole surviving member of the tribe. The brave warrior of romanticism has become the object of police-style mug shots coldly registering the human remainders of genocide. Nor does Bianchi exempt himself from criticism. In a case of *financial reflexivity*, a gnarled-face Guarani asks Bianchi how much money he will make on the film, an unflattering question that would normally have found its way to the editing-room trashcan. An authorial voice-over then speculates about the myriad ways of financially profiting from the Indians—anthropological scholarships, coffee-table photo albums, indigenous arts and crafts shops, and European tours for the films. Here, voice-of-God commentary mocks the filmmaker–God himself, in an act of self-desacralization directed at the power structure, the canonical documentary, and the cineaste himself.

Eyal Sivan's and Michel Khleifi's *Route 181: Fragments of a Journey in Palestine–Israel* (2004), for its part, offers **road-movie documentary as ideology-critique**. Co-authored by a Christian Palestinian and a Jewish Israeli sharing virtually identical political positions, this politically courageous and aesthetically innovative film treats the history and actuality of Israel–Palestine. Here, a form of *hybrid authorship* with geopolitical overtones impacts the very methods of filmmaking. The film's **binational-authorship** defies the conventional prejudice that assumes an *a priori* animosity of "Jew against Arab" and "Israeli against Palestinian." *Route 181: Fragments of a Journey in Palestine–Israel* is carefully structured around a Quixotic pursuit of the phantasmatic border line proposed by the UN's 1947 Partition Plan, along which the filmmakers interview the Christian and Muslim Palestinians, Jewish Israelis, Zionists and non-Zionists, Ashkenazim, and Mizrahi living along that imaginary line. With mordant irony, the film captures the grim origins of the ongoing crisis. The trek—from the south of Israel near Gaza to the north near the Lebanese border—evokes an ambiguous historical past as the film unearths the repressed memories of interviewees who lived the events associated with the founding of Israel. While all nation-states are on some levels anomalous, Israel, as Ella Shohat points out, is more anomalous than others, in that the state, rather than give expression to a pre-existing nation, created a nation by engineering a transplanting of Jews ingathered from the four corners of the globe while displacing the Palestinians. Thus, Israel is simultaneously an attempt at national liberation for an oppressed Jewish people, a settler–colonial state, and a remnant of nineteenth-century nationalism.[38]

In a situation where one nation was founded on the ruins of another (potential) nation, the argument about Israel–Palestine is less about facts than about interpretative and ideological grids. In this sense, the film offers a **perspectival counterpoint** between the Zionist perspective, within which the foundation of Israel constitutes a "war of independence," and the Palestinian perspective, within which that same foundation of Israel constituted a *Nakba* ("catastrophe") of dispossession, dispersal, and ethnic cleansing. Sivan and Khleifi explore the ways that many Israelis appear to both affirm and disavow this legacy of Palestinian dispossession, and the relationship of this apparent political schizophrenia to the ongoing historical impasse. The film conducts this exploration through an **ambush technique** earlier used in Marcel Ophul's *Le Chagrin et la Pitie* and in Claude Lanzmann's *Shoah*. It consists in creating a seductive atmosphere of camaraderie that facilitates **inadvertent self-indictment**. This technique emerges in a sequence where an Israeli veteran talks about what for him is the "war of independence." The marked "Euro-Israeliness" of one of the filmmakers, Sivan, prods the veteran to imagine a danger-free zone of confession.[39] Given that Sivan's Israeli citizenship and Ashkenazi appearance and manner clearly mark him as "one of us," the veteran proudly recounts how the army provoked the flight and diasporization— or what Israeli historian Ilan Pappe calls the "ethnic cleansing"—of Palestine. After listening calmly to the veteran's boasts, Sivan poses a simple question—"Did you ever think about the Palestinians?" The question triggers a dramatic reversal in attitude, as the veteran's amiable manner mutates into suspicious outrage and authoritarian postures. In this sense, *Route 181: Fragments of a Journey in Palestine–Israel* reveals what might be called the **power dynamics of interlocution**. The veteran wrongly assumed a shared "ideological horizon" with the filmmakers, but learned that his assumption was mistaken, with revealing and (for him) painful consequences.

# Performative Films

Documentary theorist Bill Nichols' concept of **"blurred boundaries"** allows him to argue that the legal controversies that ensued from examination of the Rodney King tape, as well as new developments in avant-garde documentary, call into question any received ideas concerning the monolithic "nature of reality." Although Nichols does not invoke Ludwig Wittgenstein's concept of **family resemblances**, the term does suggest an exit of sorts from the taxonomic cul-de-sac that sometimes plagues scholars attempting to distinguish between closely aligned and overlapping documentary subgenres. The term *family resemblances* derives from Wittgenstein's formulation of the notion of **language games**—an important component of his opposition to metaphysical conceptions of language that tether it to a rigidly ontological conception of reality. Instead, the more provisional and elastic category of language games emphasizes the disparate ways in which language is *used* in conjunction with a constantly changing, almost Heraclitian "flux of life." Wittgenstein's anti-essentialism makes it possible to highlight how language games overlap and intersect, an approach well suited to the loosening of the boundaries between fictional narrative and non-fiction that surfaces in both experimental documentary and the fiction–documentary hybrids of art cinema directors such as Jia Zhangke, Pedro Costa, and Abbas Kiarostami.

Nichols codifies increasingly popular deviations from standard non-fiction formulas as **"performative"** avant-garde works that "deflect our attention from the referential quality of documentary altogether," films that exemplify "a deflection of documentary from what has been its most commonsensical purpose—the development of strategies for persuasive argumentation about the historical world." Elaborating on Nichols, Stella Bruzzi points out that *performative documentaries* actually bifurcate into two types: those that happen to feature performative subjects, and those that are filmically performative and feature "performer–directors."[40] Shirley Clarke's *Portrait of Jason* (1967), in this sense, offers an early example of the first category of **performative self-representation**. The film captures, with startling vividness, the response to a filmmaker's provocations on the part of a representative of the era's underground gay subculture. Clarke's dapper hustler protagonist overwhelms the viewer with a stream-of-consciousness cascade of words recounting his sexual exploits and antipathy toward the straight world. Despite his dissolute persona, Holliday retains his charm and fragile integrity. As a sterling example of minority self-representation, *Portrait of Jason* exemplifies what Thomas Waugh terms **"the right to play oneself."** Waugh wisely laments the fact that the practice of the interview "has long been shunned by the purist inheritors of the noninterventionist American school of *vérité*, macho fetishists of untempered visual surfaces; it has been denounced by critics muttering about 'talking heads' as if they had never seen *The Sorrow and the Pity* or *Portrait of Jason*."[41]

Marie Losier's debut documentary feature, *The Ballad of Genesis and Lady Jaye* (2011), features protagonists whose *joie de vivre* both sums up the garden-variety definition of "**performativity**," as well as illuminates Judith Butler's more specialized elucidation of the "**instability of gender**" masked by the "false coherence" of normative sexual roles. Losier gently subverts the standard reflexes of documentary portraiture by invoking a playful avant-garde tradition—the ribald strain of experimentalism associated with figures such as the Kuchar Brothers and Guy Maddin. As with Losier's short films on Richard Foreman and Tony Conrad, *Ballad* is literally a participatory documentary since the filmmaker constantly demonstrates her affection for her subjects by creating amusing dreamscapes that enhance the homemade *mise-en-scène*. In *Tony Conrad, DreaMinimalist* (2008), for example, the diminutive filmmaker, dressed in an inflatable pumpkin suit, bounces around on a bed with Tony Conrad, courageously decked out in a demure pink negligee. In the new film, Genesis Breyer P-Orridge explains her musical process while dressed in a fanciful bird costume.

Such films offer, on the one hand, a marriage of the Bazinian immediacy of "the aesthetic of discovery" proffered by both documentary and neorealism, and, on the other hand, the fragmenting tradition of **montage**.[42] They exemplify what might be called **global neorealism**, a loosely defined aesthetic or group style of filmmakers who fuse neo-realism's devotion to the contours, if not the literal replication, of reality with a nuanced sense of political commitment. Politicized versions of this group style mark the work as of such disparate directors as, among others, Lisandro Alonso, Jia Zhangke, Apichatpong Weerasethakul, Abbas Kiarostami, Nicolas Pareda, Miguel Gomes, and Pedro Costa.

Abbas Kiarostami's *Close-Up* (2000) constitutes a seminal example of this international predilection. The film focuses on the case of Hossein Sabzian, a working-class man and passionate film-lover who successfully impersonates the well-known director Moshen Makhmalbaf. Although ultimately condemned by the Iranian authorities as a con-man, Sabzian himself plays the lead role in the story of the plight of a man who dupes a middle-class family into using their home as a location for his bogus film. The tale is heart-wrenching primarily because the protagonist's ruse is not a cruel deception but rather a wish-fulfillment fantasy of **auteur-impersonation as homage**, a case of desperate cinephilia, at once abject and glorious, motivated partly by Sabzian's intuition of a homology between his own sufferings and those of Kiarostami's heroines.

The extant critical literature on *Close-Up* offers both aesthetic and ideological rationales for Kiarostami's decision to fictionalize what many considered an unremarkable incident. The film's structure is frequently compared to the *faux*-**fictional techniques** of Orson Welles' *Citizen Kane* (1941), described as a deconstruction of traditional documentary techniques. After explicating how Sabzian's real-life humiliation is transformed into triumph through Kiarostami's fictional embellishments, Ivone Margulies hails the director's methodology as a form of "pedagogic humanism" contingent upon a process of "**redemptive reenactment**."[43] Restaging and manipulating events reinforces this humanistic and redemptive agenda. Re-scripting the trial allows for a perspective on Sabzian's hoax that is more empathetic than the harsh tone that prevailed at the original proceedings. Filming the protagonist's benign transgressions from his vantage point, and from that of his nominal "victims," serves to demarcate crucial class distinctions as well as the aspiring director's moving devotion to a craft that he is unable to practice. The plunge into fiction also enables Kiarostami to fashion a touching meeting between Sabzian and his idol Makhmalbaf, something that would have been impossible if a Gradgrindian adherence to "the facts" was observed— "not the inscription of reality but the reality of the inscription."

Yet, what is the impetus for these filmmakers' decisions to abjure straightforward documentary and embrace documentary/fiction hybridism? When documentaries are subject to the dictates of the state, as is true both in Kiarostami's Iran and Jia Zhangke's China—a fiction/non-fiction hybrid allows for a more multi-layered investigation of multiple "truths" than is usually possible in undiluted non-fiction. For Jia and Kiarostami, moreover, storytelling takes precedence over information. Walter Benjamin's claim in "The Storyteller" that the storyteller is associated with teachers, sages, and "righteousness" has great resonance in both the Iranian and Chinese contexts. By aligning himself with storytelling instead of with journalism or even with documentary, Jia can unravel the innumerable historical lacunae and contradictions that characterize contemporary China. Jia's *24 City* (2008), for example, masterfully interweaves actors portraying workers, with interviews with actual workers at Factory 420 in Chengdu, a munitions factory scheduled for demolition to make way for luxury condominiums. The eradication of historical memory is one of the film's primary motifs, even though the state capitalist veneer of the current regime made it necessary for Jia to ask the condominium developers for funding to sponsor his critique of modern blight. In addition, the testimonies included in the film by ex-workers and their impersonators do not eulogize an idealized proletarian past but rather score the hardships and displacements wrought by Mao's disastrous and repressive hyper-industrialization and forced collectivization of the late 1950s—the "Great Leap Forward."

As the critic Zhang Xudong explains, Jia's films enact a "**cognitive mapping**"—a term taken from Edward Tolman and picked up by Fredric Jameson to refer to the mental maps and cognitive templates through which individuals decode their spatial environment—of *xiancheng*, the "county-level" cities that, unlike huge metropolises such as Shanghai and Beijing, become an "in-between area" where the daily reality of contemporary China is laid bare, a terrain without "clear-cut boundaries or sharp distinctions between rural and urban, between industrial or agricultural...."[44] By making ordinary workers heroic (although not in the clichéd style of socialist realism) and shooting film stars such as Joan Chen prosaically (Jia slyly has Chen play a character who her workmates maintain looks similar to Joan Chen), the mundane becomes both epic and strangely opaque; the unpalatable past, the devastation wreaked by the Great Leap Forward, and the unsavory present, intent on suppressing the residue of those hardships, are conjoined and placed in a tenuous state of suspension.

The open-ended, poetic-narrative documentaries of the Portuguese director Pedro Costa are also concerned with endowing poor protagonists with newfound dignity. His *Letters from Fontainhas* trilogy focuses on a community of Cape Verdean immigrants in a poor neighborhood of Lisbon that is slowly being destroyed by bulldozers as the inhabitants are transferred to a sterile housing development. For Thom Andersen, *aestheticizing poverty* is Costa's "greatest virtue" since the poor are no more bereft of beauty than the rich. Andersen celebrates Costa for being a master of what Deleuze has called "**affective framing**," a manner of forming images usually associated with contemplative close-ups, but that can "also be applied to large spaces by rendering them as if they were faces [so as to bring] the feeling intrinsic to an action out of the action itself."[45] *Affective framing*'s ability to evoke what Lefebvre labeled the **production of space** makes it more than a formalist rubric. Lefebvre maintains that "an existing space may outlive its original purpose and the *raison d'etre* which determines its forms; it may thus in a sense become vacant and susceptible of being diverted, reappropriated, and put to a use quite different use from its initial one."[46] Although Lefebvre cites the utopian transformation of public spaces (e.g., the brief metamorphosis of the Halles Centrales from a place of work into an ongoing festival from 1969 to 1971), the dystopian erosion of formerly viable, if problematic, communities, in *24 City and Letters from Fontainhas* is also intimately linked to the manner in which the urban landscape become a topos for the politicization of space.

Kiarostami, Jia, and Costa's doc/fiction hybrids provide fodder for what has almost become a received modernist truism: that realism is a highly stylized construction. The nausea Barthes felt when confronted with the **veristic malady**, that is, mimesis's "conservative reproduction of already existing signs," was an implicitly left–libertarian response to the aesthetic conservatism of leftists, of whom Lucács remains the most sophisticated representative.[47] Walter Benjamin's concept of the **mimetic faculty** proposes a very different definition of the impulse to imitate or re-present that is delineated in the work of writers and theorists from Plato to Erich Auerbach. For Benjamin, the mimetic faculty is what Miriam Hansen calls a "**relational practice**—a process, comportment, or activity of 'producing similarities' (such as astrology, dance, and play); a noncoercive engagement with the other that resists dualistic conceptions of subject and object..."[48] (Aware of the darker reservoirs within the mimetic faculty, Adorno brooded over the pitfalls of **controlled mimesis**, a term that more or less describes fascist efforts to achieve a "totally administered society." The most successful fusions of fiction and documentary strive for the "noncoercive engagement with the other" embedded in the highly idiosyncratic interstices of the mimetic faculty. Sylvain George alludes to Benjamin's "Critique of Violence" at the outset of *May They Rest in Revolt* (2011). George evokes Benjamin's **messianic materialism** before launching a grim account of impoverished immigrant workers' lives in an unwelcoming France—hinting at a provisional hope that Benjamin's radical eschatology can stave off despair.

## The Essay Film and Mockumentaries

The essay film is, in Deleuzian terms, **doubly minor**: first, in the sense of being a documentary, and thus seen as ontologically inferior as parasitic on reality and therefore not a "real film"; and, second, in the sense of being the filmic counterpart to a minor literary genre—the essay—inferior in canonical prestige to the poetry, tragedy, and the novel. Yet, for theorists such as Lyotard, the essay genre is the quintessential and aesthetically liberating form of postmodern thought, while, for Adorno, the essay tends to subvert "totalities of truth" through heresy.[49] In *The Essay Film: From Montaigne to Marker*, Timothy Corrigan argues that the essay from the Enlightenment to the present complicates "... the very notion of *expressivity* and its relation to *experience*, the second cornerstone of the essayistic." For Corrigan, "essayistic expression (as writing, as film, or as any other representational mode) thus demands both loss of self and the rethinking and remaking of the self."[50] In this sense, the essay film "renegotiates assumptions about documentary objectivity, narrative epistemology, and authorial expressivity...."[51]

One of the salient characteristics of the classical essay from Montaigne to Adorno is a *freedom of invention* that allows for indulgence in a **digressive aesthetic** where preoccupations superficially peripheral to the topic on hand become foregrounded. A *dialogic* fondness for digression often entails a qualified approval of what Montaigne's biographer Sarah Blakewell identifies as **Pyrrhonian Skepticism**, which goes beyond "ordinary dogmatic Skepticism ... summed up in Socrates' remark: 'All I know is that I know nothing' ... by "adding ... 'I'm not even sure about that'...."[52]

Essay films often generate digressive aesthetic and contrarian skepticism by juxtaposing ostensibly dissimilar preoccupations. Oscillating from topic to topic without frivolously losing focus is one of the essay film's dexterous balancing acts. Formulating interconnected elective affinities recalls Benjamin's nuanced embrace of "*flânerie*," that is, the practice of artists who register in literary form their slow-paced promenades through modern city streets to become the "philosophers of modernity." At once aesthetic consumerism and socially critical observation, *flânerie* is situationist *derive* and contemporary slackerism *avant la lettre*, a form of redemptive meandering. For Benjamin, artist–*flâneurs* construct "**dialectical images**"—that is, flashes where the past is illuminated at the moment of its disappearance into the present. Sifting through the archive to create a kind of dialectical frisson can simulate a similarly dialectical process.

The films of Chris Marker, acknowledged master of the essay film, operate on, between, and across the borders of past, present, and future, as well as across the interstices of documentary, experimental cinema, and fiction. Marker's career combined a search for radical convergences between politics and the arts, linked with a search for political utopias—(Fidel's Cuba? Mao's China? The Paris May? Allende's Chile?, the US anti-war movement?)—and technological advances, all tempered by his lucidity about the limitations of actually existing political projects. Revolutionary nostalgia notwithstanding, a barely submerged vision of anti-authoritarian socialism is the specter haunting many of Marker's films, especially *A Grin Without a Cat* (1977; screened in France as *Le fond de l'air est Rouge*). Hewing to a left perspective without deliquescing into dogmatic sloganeering, the film pulls off the remarkable feat of achieving a first-person identity that is neither confessional nor stolidly didactic. Compiled primarily from found footage, the film draws from a huge reservoir of materials (including discarded excerpts from little-known films). The film begins with snippets from *Battleship Potemkin's* (1925) Odessa steps sequence, but the voice-over, as lyrical and meditative as it is militant, tempers Eisenstein's revolutionary brio without diluting it. The decision to intercut the famous climactic shots of *Battleship Potemkin* with moments of insurrectionary fervor from the 1960s infuses new life into Eisenstein, demonstrating that this revered classic is not merely a hoary film-school chestnut, but a living document.

Marker's vision often surfaces, quite incongruously, in the film's evocation of authoritarian figures such as Mao, who nevertheless helped place a wedge between the Manichean, Cold War opposition of capitalism and state socialism. This accretion of political incongruities cements Marker's orchestration of collisions between the contradictory "bounded verbal–ideological belief systems" (Bakhtin) characteristic of **intra-left heteroglossia**. For example, even though Mao's "cultural revolution" constituted a reshuffling of power from above rather than a spontaneous surge of power from below, Marker reveals Maoism to be a *situated utterance* (Bakhtin), read differently in different locations as it becomes inflected by local social and discursive conditions. Marker's cinematic scavenging unearths footage of French Maoist cadres as well as US Black Panthers, all brandishing Mao's *Little Red Book*. In these instances of **political remediation**, the iconography of the cultural revolution involves strategic displacements and adaptations encompassing, respectively, the European concern with class struggle and the North American focus on racial injustice, as when the Black Panthers refashioned the imperious Mao to fit their ideal of a pugnacious street fighter who spurned the accomodationist rhetoric favored by moderate civil rights leaders.

Marker coined the phrase *"cine ma vérité"* ("cinema my truth") to emphasize the personal dimension of his films, not as an index of narcissism but rather as a gesture of perspectival modesty. The two parts of *Grin Without a Cat* (1977) bear witness to the melancholy descent from the utopian hopes of the 1960s to subsequent disenchantments. Shuttling between decades in a kind of **transhistorical montage**, Marker threads together scenes of revolt from different periods in France, Chile, Germany, and the United States. Graphic and kinetic matches between gestures and movements—including literal gestures such as throwing objects at the police—link rebellions in the various periods. With seamless dialectical finesse, the elusive dream of a left untethered to either Washington or Moscow reaches critical mass in a wistful homage to May 1968, that fleeting historical moment when France—convulsed by wildcat strikes and student unrest—seemed on the verge of revolution. By gleaning images of rebellion from around the world, *Grin Without a Cat* can be seen as creating what

Deleuze, in the context of Resnais' films, calls a **"world memory,"** where the different levels of the past no longer relate to a single character, a single family, or a single group, but to quite different characters so as to link unconnected places in a kind of "world memory."[53]

Adorno's abhorrence of "enduring truths" and bogus universalism leads us back to the etymological origins of "essay" as "a try" or "attempt" and suggests affinities with literary and cinematic essays that set out to subvert the political status quo. Certain directors fuse a personal voice with political critique through **synecdochic strategies**, where a single object or site comes to stand in for a broader socio-historical phenomenon. To cite a notable political essay film, in Noel Burch and Allan Sekula's *The Forgotten Space* (2010), the cargo ships that carry 90% of the world's goods represent "globalization and the sea," which constitutes the forgotten space of our modernity. Alternately, Frank Gehry's Guggenheim branch in Bilbao, which unites consumerism and the veneration of modernity in an old port city, encapsulates a parodic "neo-maritime baroque ambiance." In *Jaffa the Orange's Clockwork* (2009), Eyal Sivan chronicles how Jaffa, once known as a Palestinian city, metamorphosed into a brand of orange, and how this "branding" became emblematic of the Israeli–Palestinian conflict.

Academic writing—on what Jane Roscoe and Craig Hight call the **mock-documentary** in *Faking It: Mock-documentary and the subversion of factuality* (2001); what Alexandra Juhasz and Jesse Lerner call the **fake documentary** in *F Is for Phony: Fake Documentary and Truth's Undoing* (2006); and what others call the **mockumentary** (and **rockumentaries** such as *This Is Spinal Tap* [1984])—suggests that a host of sub-genres with marked family resemblances—docudramas, parodic non-fiction, "reality TV"—implicitly undermine the **indexicality** of the photographic image and its claim to represent the real. Mockumentaries form part of the very respectable tradition of **reenactment** and **restaging**, as when De Antonio restages a trial of anti-war protestors in his film *In the King of Prussia* (1983), starring actual protestors such as the Berrigan Brothers, with Martin Sheen as the judge. "Indexicality," as Peter Hughes argues, "can be faked."[54] In fact, as we have seen, fake documentaries have been an integral part of film, going back to filmmakers such as Thomas Edison and J. Stuart Blackton "documenting" imperial wars in the fields of New Jersey. Although many *faux*-documentaries are little more than frivolous stunts, films that self-consciously undermine documentary's apparent transparency and verisimilitude perform a critical function. For Juhasz and Lerner, fake documentaries challenge three interconnected documentary norms: (1) the technologies of truth telling; (2) the authority granted to or stolen by those who make such truth claims; and (3) the need to assert untold truths that have fallen outside the register of these norms.[55]

Fake documentaries foster an **anti-hermeneutics of suspicion**. Indeed, it is now difficult for the cine-literate to watch the History Channel (aka the Hitler Channel) without thinking of *Zelig*, or watch a rock band profile without thinking of *This is Spinal Tap*. The most intriguing *mockumentaries* have more affinities with films such as *F for Fake* (1973) or *Land Without Bread* (1933), which combine earnestness and playfulness, than with a number of gimmicky non-fiction pranks (e.g., Russ Hexter's *Dadetown*, 1995) mainly intended to pull the wool over the eyes of unsuspecting audiences. Australian director Anna Broinowski's ingeniously structured *Forbidden Lie$* (2007) reveals the Orientalist impetus of Norma Khouri's literary scam by combing intricately choreographed reenactments with traditional documentary staples such as interviews and investigative research. Fusing elements of the mockumentary, the crusading documentary exposé, and confessional cinema, Broinowski's film pinpoints the appeal of Khouri's best-selling, fabricated memoir, *Forbidden Love*, by detailing how her deception reinforces Western preconceptions concerning Muslim women. *Forbidden Lie$* (2007) deploys **unreliable narration**, a device (literary in origin) where the challenge for the viewer/reader is to ferret out the narration's inconsistencies and aporias. The film's opening gambit involves a **tongue-in-cheek adaptation** of Khouri's fraudulent memoir, which incorporates many of her ideological shibboleths that the film will subsequently demystify. An image of a veiled woman traversing the desert, for example, crystallizes the Orientalist fantasy that permeates Khouri's fanciful mode of autobiography.

In *Archive Fever*, Derrida points out that "There is no political power without control of the archive."[56] Given the importance of cinema in gay culture, David James points out, the archeology of the Hollywood film has especially engaged gay and lesbian filmmakers.[57] Cheryl Dunye's *The Watermelon Woman* (1996), in this sense, raids the film archive in the name of lesbian feminism. In the film, an African-American lesbian filmmaker (Cheryl, played by Cheryl Dunye herself) exercises her **archival fever** by "discovering" (i.e., creating) documentary evidence of the existence of a silent-era lesbian actress named Fae Richards, who we see in **pseudo-archival footage** that shows her as everything from an extra to a lead actress, as a mammy archetype, as a mobster, and as "Watermelon Woman" in a film-within-the-film entitled *Plantation Memories*. Explicitly **"signifying"**—Henry Louis Gates' term for the interactive dialogism within the African-American literary tradition—on Melvin van Peebles' *Watermelon Man* (1970), the film offers its own queer-feminist response to that film.

Yet, here too, the "imaginary" neighbors with the "real," as *pseudo-archival footage* mingles with real archival footage, faked photos with real photos. As a case of do-it-yourself historiography, the film gives a sense that if Fae Richards did not exist, she would have to be invented. The film, in this sense, is an accurate representation of what might have been.

One of the most politically incisive of the mockumentaries is Kevin Willmott's *C.S.A.: The Confederate States of America* (2004), a mock-serious *Zelig-like* account of an alternative history in which the Confederacy has won the Civil War. Presented as a British documentary broadcast on "Confederate Network Television," the film begins with a fictitious disclaimer warning the viewer that the film might not be suitable for "children and servants." The Ken Burns–style commentary alternates between two fake-talking head historians, the white conservative Southerner Sherman Hoyle, and black Canadian Patricia Johnson. Mingling *faux* newsreel materials, parodically racist commercials, and TV shows, and genuine footage with ironic voice-over commentary, the film's highlights include: a fictional D. W. Griffith silent film (*The Hunt for Dishonest Abe*) in which Harriet Tubman helps a black-faced Abraham Lincoln escape to Canada—"We both niggers now," she tells Lincoln. History is mediated through a racist filter: the Civil War is now "The War of Northern Aggression," while the "Washington Redskins" have become the "New York N…s." What is most disturbing in this counterfactual exercise, perhaps, is that, in some ways, the film is *not* a phantasy. If one listens to right-wing Southern (and Northern) politicians and hate radio, it becomes clear that white supremacist ideologies and confederate thinking (states' rights, nullification, etc.) are alive and well, and not only in the South.

In more general terms, almost all of the films discussed in this chapter break down the customarily inviolate boundaries separating two orders of filmic discourse, replacing the usual wall with a permeable membrane, leading to documentary-inflected fictions and fictionalized documentaries. **Intermedial hybridization and cross-fertilization**, the exchanges of energies between the various trans-genres, have been key factors in creativity in the media arts. For Adorno and Horkheimer, modernity, meanwhile, emanating from the Enlightenment, "has always aimed at liberating men from fear and establishing their sovereignty. Yet the fully enlightened earth radiates disaster triumphant."[58] The other side of the coin is Benjamin's assurance that "In every true work of art, there is a particular point at which someone who is able to put himself in that position can feel a cool wind blowing, as if from a coming dawn. From this it can be seen that art, which has often been thought to obscure any relation to progress, can in fact help to define progress *genuinely*. Progress does not lie in the continuity of the course of time, but in interferences with it, at home, or wherever something truly new makes itself felt for the first time with the soberness of the dawn."[59]

## Notes

1   See Hayden White, *Metahistory: The Historical Imagination in Nineteenth-Century Europe* (Baltimore: John Hopkins University Press, 1973).

2   Roland Barthes, "Historical Discourse," in Michael Lane, (ed.), *Introduction to Structuralism* (New York: Basic Books, 1970), p. 145.

3   Jacques Derrida, "The Law of Genre," *Glyph: Textual Studies*, 7 (Spring 1980).

4   The phrase *"fiction documentaire"* is in Ranciere, *La Fable Cinematographique* (Paris: Le Seuil, 2001), p. 201.

5   See Roger Odin, *De la Fiction* (Bruxelles: De Boeck, 2000).

6   David E. James, *Allegories of Cinema: American Film in the Sixties* (Princeton: Princeton University Press, 1989).

7   Vivian Sobshack, *Carnal Thoughts: Embodiment and Moving Image Culture* (Berkeley: University of California Press, 2004), p. 248.

8   On risk in cinema, see Mette Hjort, *Film and Risk* (Detroit: Wayne State University Press, 2012).

9   Jean-Louis Comolli, *Voir et Pouvoir* (Paris: Editions Verdier, 2008).

10   See Gene Youngblood, *Expanded Cinema* (New York: P. Dutton & Co., Inc., 1970) and Allan Kaprow, *Assemblage, Environments & Happenings* (New York: H. N. Abrams, 1966).

11   Quoted in Patricia Auferdeide, *Documentary Film: A Very Short Introduction* (New York: Oxford, 2007), p. 112.

12   Brian Winston calls *Chronique* the "totemic ancestor" of reality TV shows such as *Wife Swap* (Brian Winston, "Rouch's 'Second Legacy': *Chronique d'un Ete* as Reality TV's Totemic Ancestor," in Joram ten Brink, *Building Bridges: The Cinema of Jean Rouch* [London: Wallflower, 2007]).

13   David Stewart, "Fred Wiseman's Novelistic Samplings of Reality," *Current* (February 1998). Available at: <http://www.current.org/doc/doc802wiseman>

14   Linda Williams, "Mirrors without Memory: Truth, History and the New Documentary," quoted in Amber Day, *Satire and Dissent: Interventions in Contemporary Political Debate* (Bloomington: Rolan University Press, 2011), p. 112.

15   Gilles Deleuze, *L'Image-Temps* (Paris: Minuit, 1985), pp. 195–196.

16   Intan Paramaditha, "Tracing Friction in *The Act of Killing*," forthcoming in *Film Quarterly*. (Robert Stam thanks Intan Paramaditha for sending him the essay prior to its publication.)

17   Ibid.

18   Ibid.

19   Oppenheimer had to become a bit of an actor himself by maintaining his composure in the face of the crimes being reenacted. Were his ruse to be discovered, he could easily be expelled from the country, while the collaborating technicians—listed in the final credits as "anonymous"—could suffer terrible consequences.

20   Robert Stam expresses his appreciation to Yemane Demissie for his critical insights concerning the film.

21   The following section forms an altered and shortened version of an essay that appeared in Jens Andermann and Álvaro Fernández Bravo (eds.), *New Argentine and Brazilian Cinema: Reality Effects* (New York: Palgrave, 2013).

22   Henry Jenkins, *Convergence Culture: Where Old and New Media Collide* (New York: New York University Press, 2008).

23   Jean-Claude Bernardet, *Cineastas e Imagens do Povo* (São Paulo: Cia das Letras, 2003), p. 15.

24   "Intellectuals and power: A conversation between Michel Foucault and Gilles Deleuze," in Michel Foucault (ed.), *Language, Counter-Memory, Practice: Selected Essays and Interviews* (Ithaca, NY: Cornell University Press, 1980), pp. 205–217.

25   Spivak, Gayatri, "Can the Subaltern Speak?" in *Marxism and the Interpretation of Culture* (Urbana: University of Illinois Press, 1988), pp. 271–313.

26   Consuelo Lins and Claudia Mesquita, *Filmar O Real* (Rio: Zahar, 2008), p. 40.

27   Quoted in Andre Habib, *Chris Marker et l'imprimerie du regard* (Paris: L'Harmattan, 2008), p. 76.

28   See Abé Markus Nornes, *Forest of Pressure: Ogawa Shinsuke and Postwar Japanese Documentary* (Minneapolis: University of Minnesota Press, 2007.)

29   In a 2012 interview with Daniel Fairfax, Jean-Louis Comolli explained, "As we filmed, we also listened to the speech of our interlocutors. Shots showing people listening are very numerous in this series. They show that listening is very important, that it is essential to film with a camera as if it were an ear. The camera is there to listen, not just to film. The active sense, when it comes to filming, is hearing, not sight"—Daniel Fairfax, "Yes, we were utopians; in a way, I still am…": interview with Jean-Louis Comolli (Part 2), *Senses of Cinema* 64 (September 2012), available at: <http://sensesofcinema.com/2012/feature-articles/yes-we-were-utopians-in-a-way-i-still-am-interview-with-jean-louis-comolli-part-2/>. Access date: December 15, 2013.

30   Mikhail Bakhtin and Pavel Medvedev, *The Formal Method in Literary Scholarship: A Critical Introduction to Sociological Poetics*, trans. Albert J. Wehrle (Cambridge: Harvard University Press, 1985), p. 95.

31   Ibid., p. 8.

32   James C. Scott, *Domination and the Arts of Resistance: Hidden Transcripts* (New Haven: Yale University Press, 1990), p. 34.

33   The noteworthy analysts of Coutinho's work include Consuelo Lins (*O Documentario de Eduardo Coutinho: Televisao, Cinema, e Video* [Rio de Janeiro: Zahar, 2004]); Carlos Alberto Mattos (*Eduardo Coutinho: O*

*Homem que caiu na Real* [Portugal: Festival de Cinema Luso-Brasiliero de Santa Maria da Feira, 2004]); and Luiz Zanin Oricchio (*Cinema de Novo: Um Balanco Critico da Retomada* [São Paulo: Editora Estação Liberdade Ltda., 2003]). On Brazilian documentary in general, see also the excellent essays by Andrea Franca, Cesar Guimaraes, Claudia Mesquita, Ivana Bentes, José Carlos Avellar, Miguel Pereira, and Mariana Baltar in Cezar Migliorin, (ed.) *Ensaios no Real* (Rio de Janeiro: Beco Do Azougue Editorial Ltda., 2010); and also Jens Andermann and Álvaro Fernández Bravo (eds.), *New Argentine and Brazilian Cinema: Reality Effects* (New York: Palgrave, 2013).

34 Cezar Migliorin (ed.), *Ensaios no Real* (Rio de Janeiro: Azougue, 2010), p. 78.

35 Ginsburg, "Embedded Aesthetics," *Cultural Anthropology*, 9(3) (1994): 365–382.

36 Robert Koehler, "Agrarian Utopias/Dystopias: The New Nonfiction," *Cinema Scope*, 40 (Fall 2009): 1.

37 See João Luiz Vieira, *Camera-Faca: O Cinema de Sergio Bianchi* (Portugal: Festival de Cinema Luso-Brasiliero de Santa Maria da Feira, 2004).

38 See Ella Shohat, *Israeli Cinema: East/West and the Politics of Representation* (Austin: University of Texas Press, 1989).

39 See the expanded edition of Shohat's *Israeli Cinema* (I. B. Taurus, 2010), p. 281.

40 Stella Buruzzi, *New Documentary: A Critical Introduction* (London: Routledge, 2000), p. 163.

41 Thomas Waugh, *The Right to Play Oneself: Looking Back on Documentary Film* (Minneapolis: University of Minnesota Press, 2011), p. 24.

42 Dudley Andrew, *What Cinema Is!* (London and Malden, MA: Wiley Blackwell, 2011), p. 33.

43 Ivone Margulies, "Exemplary Bodies: Reenactment in *Love in the City, Sons, and Close-Up*," in Ivone Margulies (ed.), *Realism; Essays on Corporeal Cinema* (Durham: Duke University Press, 2002), p. 238.

44 Zhang Xudong, "Poetics of Vanishing: The Films of Jia Zhangke," *New Left Review*, 63 (May–June 2010).

45 Thom Andersen, "A Band of Outsiders" (Criterion booklet accompanying *Letters from Fontainhas* DVD set), p. 27.

46 Henri Lefebvre, *The Production of Space*, trans. Donald Nicholson-Smith (Oxford and Cambridge, MA: Blackwell, 1991), pp. 68–168.

47 This paraphrased description of Barthes's position comes from Martin Jay. See his *Cultural Semantics: Keywords of Our Time* (Amherst: University of Massachusetts Press, 1998), p. 120.

48 Miriam Hansen, *Cinema and Experience: Siegfried Kracauer, Walter Benjamin, and Theodor W. Adorno* (Berkeley: University of California Press, 2012), p. 147.

49 Timothy Corrigan, *The Essay Film: From Montaigne, After Marker* (Oxford and New York: Oxford University Press, 2011).

50 Ibid., p. 21.

51 Ibid., p. 6.

52    See Sarah Blakewell, *How to Live: A Life of Montaigne* (New York: Random House, 2010).

53    Deleuze, *Time-Image*, p. 11

54    <http://www.latrobe.edu.au/screeningthepast/reviews/rev_16/PHbr16>

55    Alexander Juhasz and Jesse Lerner, *F Is for Phony: Fake Documentary and Truth's Undoing* (Minneapolis: University of Minnesota Press, 2006), pp. 10–11.

56    Jacques Derrida, *Archive Fever: A Freudian Impression* (Chicago: University of Chicago Press, 1998), p. 4.

57    David E. James, *The Most Typical Avant-Garde: History and Geography of Minor Cinemas in Los Angeles* (Berkeley: University of California Press, 2005), p. 367.

58    This passage from *Dialectic of Enlightenment* is quoted in Rolf Wiggershaus, *The Frankfurt School: Its History, Theories, and Political Significance*, trans. Michael Robertson (Cambridge, MA: MIT Press, 1994), p. 327.

59    From Benjamin's *Passagen-Werk*, quoted in Rolf Wiggershaus, op. cit., p. 327.

# 6

# Hollywood Aristotelianism, the Fractured Chronotope, and the Musicalization of Cinema

This book, *Keywords in Subversive Film/Media Aesthetics*, has embraced throughout certain features of political modernism while questioning aspects that seemed elitist, Western-centric, and aesthetically exhausted. As with the sociology of "modernization," the trope of a modernist *avant-garde* implies a stagist telos of progressive change moving inexorably in a linear direction within a single temporal sequence, defining some as "ahead" and others as "behind." But social and aesthetic innovation is not always forward-looking; the artist, as we have seen, can also look to culturally alternative modalities of storytelling from the past for inspiration. Cinemas in both the Global North and the Global South, in this sense, have explored a wide spectrum of alternative aesthetics featuring other historical rhythms, other narrative structures, and other views of the body, spirituality, and the collective life. In this sense, subversive aesthetics can go beyond both conventional realism and political modernism. After questioning the **orthodox chronotope** within mainstream media fictions, this chapter will highlight a wide array of alternative cinematic forms.

## Hollywood Aristotelianism: the Orthodox Chronotope

Fusing Kant's ideas about time and space as fundamental categories of cognition with Einstein's theories of time as the fourth dimension of space, Bakhtin defines the **chronotope** ("time space") as the "intrinsic

*Keywords in Subversive Film/Media Aesthetics*, First Edition. Robert Stam with Richard Porton and Leo Goldsmith.
© 2015 John Wiley & Sons, Inc. Published 2015 by John Wiley & Sons, Inc.

connectedness of temporal and spatial relationships within artistic representation," where time "thickens, takes on flesh, becomes artistically visible" and space becomes "responsive to the movements of time, plot and history."[1] Mediating between the historical and the artistic, chronotopes materialize time in space and provide fictional environments whereby constellations of power become visible.[2] In Rancièrean terms, they distribute, share, and parcel out the space–time of the sensible world. Correlated with the real world but never equatable with it, these chronotopic structures are mediated through history, medium, genre, and authorship.

The "orthodox chronotope" denotes the dramatic realist aesthetic that still dominates much of mainstream media, however refurbished through the *frisson* of new technologies. As a way of telling stories through the cinematic organization of time and space, the orthodox chronotope has as its aesthetic cornerstone the reconstitution of a coherent fictional world. While filmmaking is a highly discontinuous process, these techniques mold the impression of a seamless diegetic continuity through elaborate etiquettes for introducing scenes, evoking the passage of time and movement in space, while also rendering imperceptible the transitions from shot to shot. Devices of **subjectification**, meanwhile, suture the spectator into the fiction through point-of-view editing, shot/reverse shots, and eye-line matches.

Some of the undergirding principles of this representational system can be traced back to latter-day schematizations of Aristotle's account of tragedy as involving: plausible stories, believable (but flawed) characters, rising action, plot turnabouts, and final catharsis. It is no coincidence that Aristotle's *Poetics* is considered "the Bible of Hollywood producers," while one standard guidebook is called *Aristotle's Poetics for Screenwriters: Storytelling Secrets from the Greatest Mind in Western Civilization* (2002). Thus, manuals advise prospective screenwriters to start a story at the beginning and proceed to the end; to clarify the primary cause triggering the action; to follow a three-act structure and to build the story around a character's desires, all within an organically complete story that moves logically toward a climactic finale generative of emotional release. The Charlie Kaufman/Spike Jonze film *Adaptation* (2002) alludes to this model by having the actor playing script guru Robert McKee (author of the best-selling *Story: Substance, Structure, Style, and the Principles of Screenwriting*) mouth the doxa—artists should never call attention to their art; films should create strong, noble characters, and catalyze catharsis—doxa that the film itself both flouts and respects.

Most of the popular guides, including Syd Field's canonical *Screenplay: the Foundations of Screenwriting* (2005), lay out rigid rules: the first act must be 30 minutes long, the second 60 minutes, the third 30 minutes, and so forth. *The Portable Film School: Everything You'd Learn in Film School (Without Ever Going to Class)* (2005), by D. B. Gilles, decrees "12 storytelling musts"—virtual Proppian "functions"—comprising: (1) a story; (2) a trigger event; (3) a major dramatic question; (4) a "want" propelling the character's actions; (5) obstacles to the "want"; (6) an ally aiding the main character; (7) a failure on the way to success; (8) a "middle-of-act-two" event that exacerbates tension; (9) an "end-of-act-two" turning point or **peripety** involving a sudden reversal of fortune; (10) a third-act climax; (11) an overall arc of character change from ignorance to knowledge, prejudice to tolerance, and so forth; and (12) an ending that is, if not happy, at least "satisfying."[3]

But each "must" triggers a "why? Why must there be only *one* hero, and *one* ally? Why not a dispersed or collective protagonist? Why a single "want" rather than multiple and even contradictory "wants?" What about characters who imagine themselves to be pursuing one "want" when they are actually pursuing another? What about marginalized characters who know what they want but have to "defer their dreams" because of material, social, and even racial constraints? Why must the hero fail, and then succeed, rather than the reverse? Does not the obligatory progression from failure to success encode the "cruel optimism" (Berlant) of an "anyone-can-make-it" mythology out-of-synch with the fantastically unequal societies shaped by neoliberal economics? What about all the great works whose power does not depend on dramatic actions, those **hypofictions** that pursue what Rancière calls "**the splendor of the insignificant**"?[4] Why must endings be "satisfying" as opposed to provocative, or even disturbing? Are the mushroom clouds shown at the end of *Dr. Strangelove or: How I Stopped Worrying and Learned to Love the Bomb* (1964) "satisfying?" Would *Caché* (2005) be more successful without its ambiguous final shot? If literary and filmic artists had been constrained by such "musts," there would be no *Don Quixote* (1605), no *The Life and Opinions of Tristram Shandy, Gentleman* (1759), no *Ulysses* (1922), no *One Hundred Years of Solitude* (1967), and no *Breathless* (1960), *Hiroshima Mon Amour* (1959), or *Caché* (2005).

The dictates in these manuals embed covertly elitist assumptions. In innumerable trailers, an insistently breathy male voice, rising stentorian above the din of sonic-boom soundtracks, calls up some outsized noble savior figure: "In a moment of danger, when all had abandoned hope, *one man...*" The orthodox schema, in this sense, is premised on a "one-man" (or woman) **heroic individualism** of the kind excoriated by Brecht: first, in terms of stories revolving around individual success and domination;

second, in terms of the competitive capitalist-style relations assumed to hold between characters; and third, in terms of personalist assumptions about authorship. Moreover, screenwriters are urged to find *their* personal story and to "stick to what they know"—a sure formula for banality. Michael Tierno's *Aristotle's Poetics for Screenwriters: Storytelling Secrets from the Greatest Mind in Western Civilization* even decrees that screenwriters "move [their] audience by teaching them what they already know," advice that precludes from the outset any aesthetic epistemological leaps. What disappears in the orthodox schema is not only the collaborative poesis of media-making but also everything a media-maker might learn through reading or watching films, everything that makes the director less a godlike demiurge creating *ex nihilo* than a (still highly personal) **orchestrator of pre-existing texts**, images, and discourse.

At its most authoritarian, neo-Aristotelian cinema becomes a filmic deputy of what Rancière calls **the police**, that is, the totalizing force that apportions social power and recognition, praise and blame, and glory, which enforces the distribution of the sensible social order against the **sans-part**, those having no role or share in the socius. Ivana Bentes offers the treatment of the *favela* in Padilha's *Elite Squad* as an example of such policing: not only are the favela-dwellers literally policed within the story, but so too are the spectators virtually dragooned into identifying with the police. Through a kind of **spectatorial hostage-taking**, an overpowering narrative logic makes it "impossible *not* to desire what the narrative desires, and impossible not to justify the [police] actions [in a way] that reaffirms the absolute authority of the power that will normalize chaos and contain catastrophe."[5]

Speaking more broadly, the problem-solving mode of the classic narrative—analyzed by Bordwell, Thompson, and Staiger—instantiates a competitive and pseudo-progressive *Weltenschauung*.[6] Within the double-meaning of *histoire* as both story and history, a partial isomorphism links the progressive arc of stagist history to the optimist arc of story. Dominant cine-aesthetics relays time as a linear succession of events related through cause and effect based on individual purposes, rather than conveying an associative **transpersonal time** linked to rituals and festivals. In an ethos where "time is money," dominant cinema monetizes time in carefully measured doses of commodified excitement. A thrill-a-minute blockbuster style mandates that every filmic moment produce its quantum of spectacular effect. In contrast, **"slow cinema,"** by analogy to "slow food," favors a more leisurely and non-productivist approach. Alessandra Raengo speaks of the alternative **"hanging out" aesthetic** of films such as *Fruitvale Station*, where the spectator and the character share quality-time, at an unhurried and unglamorous pace.

Of course, we cannot saddle Aristotle with all that is banal in film, just as we cannot condemn Hollywood cinema in its totality. "Hollywood" here serves as a synecdoche for the blockbuster aesthetic (launched by *Jaws* and *Star Wars*) and for conventional storytelling. Completely legitimate as one *possible* aesthetic, the neo-Aristotelian schema has generated thousands of marvelous and even socially progressive films. The problem is less the schema itself than its formulaic character and its inhibiting effect on creativity. Yet, it is noteworthy that so many radical artists and theorists invoke Aristotle as a kind of nemesis: Brecht detested the overpowering constellation of Fate, Pathos, and Catharsis intrinsic to the Aristotelian theory of tragedy; Jean-Pierre Bekolo parodically linked Hollywood to Aristotle in his self-reflexive *Le Complot d'Aristotle* (*"Aristotle's Plot,"* 1996); and Native American writer Sherman Alexie eviscerated Aristotle in a preface to a screenplay: "Aristotle was not a Spokane Indian ... Fuck resolutions, fuck closure, fuck the idea of story arc. Embrace the incomplete, embrace ambiguity, and embrace the magical and painful randomness of life."[7]

Admittedly, the orthodox chronotope no longer holds sway as it once did. The model has been relativized not only by the new digital media but also by the New Hollywood of the late 1960s (*Bonnie and Clyde*, 1967) to the early 1980s (*One from the Heart*, 1981), by the Sundance Indie alternative, and by an international wave of art films. Popular films such as *Chungking Express* (1994), *Run Lola Run* (1998), *City of God* (2002), and *Babel* (2006) feature fresh ways of staging, framing, and editing.[8] Although some scholars speak of a **"post-classical" cinema**, Bordwell and Thompson have disputed that notion. While acknowledging innovations, such as "multiple protagonists" and "network narratives," they argue that the dominant storytelling mode never abandons the tacit norm of prodding the spectator to identify with individual characters pursuing individual goals. Bordwell points to fundamental continuities in the way that filmic continuity itself is treated. In *The Way Hollywood Tells It: Story and Style in Modern Movies* (2006), Bordwell points to an array of novel strategies, including: Tarantino-style **"allusionism,"** Noel Carrol's term for insider "winks" to the cine-literate; hyperkinetic "run and gun" camerawork (*à la The Bourne Ultimatum*, 2007); **"hyperclassicism,"** Kristin Thompson's term for stylishly, maximally classical films such as *Jerry Maguire* (1996); **paradoxical time schemes** (*à la Eternal Sunshine of the Spotless Mind* [2004] and *Memento* [2000]); the interplay of colors and formats in *JFK* (1991); and the puzzle plots of *House of Games* (1987). (While Bordwell speaks of **"intensified continuity,"** Thomas Elsaesser speaks of **"classical plus" cinema**.[9])

Bordwell wittily pinpoints some of the stylistic pyrotechnics that accompany intensified continuity: "bipolar extremes of lens lengths," "whiplash pans and jerky re-framings," "bombastic crane shots," a "goulash of stocks and gauges," and virtuoso "flying-cams." For Bordwell, these innovations represent a case of intensified continuity rather than of ruptured or fractured continuity, since most fiction films merely fine-tune classical dramaturgy. (The same gradualist continuity also applies, one might argue, on a political level, where Hollywood films display occasional signs of a risk-free liberalism but precious few of genuine radicalism.) Within a *plus ca change* paradigm, most dramatic films maintain as their "default framework" the neo-Aristotelian mode of plausible story (*mythos*), believable characters (*ethos*), plot turnabouts (*peripiteia*), and spectatorial catharsis.[10] The engine gets overhauled, as it were, but the chassis remains, or, to switch to a culinary register, the same old hamburger has gained a patina of *nouvelle cuisine*. New techniques still serve the old goal of telling stories in "a clear, arousing way"[11]—non-linear editing fashions linear plots.

In *Post-classical Cinema: An International Poetics of Film Narration* (2009), Eleftheria Thanouli, meanwhile, argues against Bordwell that there has indeed been a significant mutation in aesthetics that justifies the term "*post-classical.*"[12] (The argument boils down to the perennial issue of when a series of deviations from a stylistic norm crystallizes as a new, alternative norm.) Drawing on films such as *Lola Rennt* (1998), *Magnolia* (1999), *Fight Club* (1999), *Amélie* (2001), and *City of God* (2002), and on the "smart cinema" (Jeffrey Sconce) of Ang Lee, Atom Egoyan, and Hal Hartley, she notes a revisionist cinema characterized by what Bolter and Grusin call *hypermediacy*—that is, a modality of representation that "acknowledges multiple acts of representation and makes them visible."[13] In a kind of naturalized reflexivity, such films maintain the ideal of realism while also foregrounding the artifice of the natural, the constructed character of filmic space and time, and the mutual relativization of formats and genres. Although post-classical film "does not eliminate the classical rules and conventions," Thanouli argues, it does introduce "new norms that become the technological and aesthetic dominant of this new narrative paradigm."[14] For the purposes of this book, however, the new hypermediated cinema, which might be called post-auteurist as well as post-classical, makes cinema much more interesting and formally innovative, but not necessarily more radical in political terms.

Our objections, in any case, are to the formulaic and conservative nature of Hollywood neo-Aristotelianism rather than to realism per se. Many classically realistic films transcend descriptive realism to develop a **social**

**analysis**. *The Battle of Algiers* (1966), for example, went beyond simply being a realistic representation of the anticolonial struggle, to become a **Fanon-informed analysis** of the very revolution about which Fanon wrote in *The Wretched of the Earth* (1961). Quite apart from depicting the struggle with painstaking accuracy, Pontecorvo "reads" it through Fanonian ideas about the "two cities" and the violence of the colonized as the reciprocal response to the violence of the colonizer. Pontecorvo performs an innovative **mediatic mimesis**—that is, the deployment of the protocols of mass media reportage (handheld cameras, zooms, long lenses) combined with the identificatory mechanisms of the fiction film—on behalf of colonized people. Pontecorvo thus hijacks "objectivity"—which for Fanon "always works against the native"—to express anticolonialist views usually anathema to the dominant media.

Contemporary **metarealist films**, meanwhile, "tweak" and stylize the real into a broader kind of social demonstration, where realism is a question rather than answer. Borrowing from Patricia Osganian, Martin O'Shaughneessy speaks of an **aesthetic of the fragment** to refer to a "sea-change in the cinematic face of social–political struggle represented by the passage from a universalizing, discursively mediated vision to one marked by a newly raw and near mute corporeality."[15] The aesthetic of the fragment "emerges from the shattering of something larger, from the loss of social connectivity, shared values, and intergenerational continuity."[16] European directors such as the Dardennes Brothers or Laurent Cantet, for example, foreground extreme forms of social exclusion and class domination, pinning "down the real through the collision of a hard core of exploitation and the struggles of an individual moved by his or her desire for autonomy."[17] In such films, sustained proximity fosters identification, as socially marginalized characters, pursued by moving cameras with skin-close intimacy, form what Raengo, in a different context, calls the **physiological centers of the film**, where the spectator feels, unaided by any explicit commentary, the working of oppression through the body.[18]

In films such as *Investigation of a Citizen Above All Suspicion* (1970), meanwhile, realism is deployed as **social-systemic demonstration**, in what amounts to a quasi-mathematical proof of the reality of class justice. The murderer–protagonist played by Gian Maria Volonte simply takes full advantage of the impunity enjoyed by those at the top of the state power hierarchy. In an act of bravado, the protagonist even points toward himself as the guilty party. The investigators are obliged by the imperatives of the system to ignore the overwhelming evidence of his guilt. An inexorable systemic logic mandates that he *not* be guilty, just as an inexorable systemic logic mandated that the Wall Street figures responsible for the 2008 financial crisis *not* go to prison.

Fredric Jameson famously argued that all Third World texts form **national allegories**, where "the story of the private individual destiny is always an allegory of the embattled situation of the public third-world culture and society."[19] (We find a classic filmic visualization of national allegory in Mehboob Khan's *Mother India* [1957] where peasants working in fields literally form together the shape of the titular country.) Rather than a mere illustration or rhetorical figure, allegory becomes a cognitive instrument or trans-epochal way of thinking. Building on the work of Ismail Xavier, we can distinguish further between the various types within *national allegory* in cinema: (1) the teleological **Marxist-inflected allegories** that reveal history as the progressive unfolding of an immanent historical design (Rocha, Sembene); (2) **modernist self-deconstructing allegories** where allegory is deployed as an instance of language-consciousness in the context of a felt loss of historical purposes (Sganzerla); and (3) **strategic allegories** where indirection becomes a means of subversion under dictatorial regimes (dos Santos' *A Very Crazy Asylum* [1970]).[20]

What all the variants have in common is that they go beyond conventional realism by constructing an oblique or synecdochic utterance that solicits hermeneutic completion or deciphering—evoking the past (or future) to address the present, evoking a "there" to suggest the "here," or the "small" to evoke the "large," the personal to evoke the political, or the microcosmic to evoke the macrocosmic. Matteo Garrone's *Gommorah* (2008), for example, constructs a **transnational allegory** by linking organized crime and neoliberalism. Similar to Coppola's *The Godfather* (1972), often seen as an allegory of corporate and governmental malfeasance in the Watergate era, *Gomorrah* offers an **anti-capitalist parable** of convergence between the Neapolitan Camorra mafia and global capitalism. The Camorra sees itself not as an adjunct of the Italian state, but as a malleable multinational corporation. Quoting the book's exegesis of the machinations of the Casalesi Mafioso clan: "Alliances with Nigerian and Albanian clans meant that they no longer had to be involved in direct peddling and narcotrafficking operations. Pacts with clans in Lagos and Benin City, alliances with Mafia families in Pristina and Tirana, and agreements with Ukrainian Mafiosi in Leopolis and Kiev liberated the Casalesi from bottom-rung criminal activities."[21] This depiction of the dark underbelly of globalization reveals a world that has become "flat" in a manner that makes Thomas Friedman's pro-globalization bromides seem ludicrous.

## Alternatives to Aristotle: the Menippean Strain

The neo-Aristotelian schema limits radical aesthetic possibilities by declaring stylistic heterodoxy out of bounds, much as the dominant political system declares radical political alternatives out of bounds. Yet, cinema can construct **fractured chronotopes** that explode the diegetic continuum of the orthodox chronotope by mingling contradictory spatiotemporalities. Jacques Rancière, interestingly, also cites Aristotle as nemesis, as he traces his own radical engagement with film to Jean Epstein's fond hope that cinema *abandon* the Aristotelian fable as "the arrangement of necessary and verisimilar actions that lead the characters from fortune to misfortune … through careful construction of the intrigue and denouement."[22] Picking up on Epstein's cues, Rancière argues for a **cinema of situations**: "life is not about stories, about actions oriented toward an end, but about situations open in every direction [that are part of] a long and continuous movement made up of an infinity of micro-movements."[23] Against the exaltation of the plot (*mythos*), Rancière defends the materiality of the image (**opsis**) and the fracturing of the **thwarted fable** (*fable contredite*). Alexander Kluge contests the dramaturgy of tragedy's ineluctable suffering by happily spoiling the conclusive final acts of tragic operas.

Deleuze, in a similar vein, indirectly questions neo-Aristotelian plotting by downplaying **movement-image cinema**, the sensory-motor-based, organically unified schema in which the images conform to the necessity of action—reminiscent of the Aristotelian "unity of action"—in favor of **time-image cinema**, which frees time from narrative causality. (Updating Deleuze for the digital era, Patricia Pisters has proposed a third term, the **neuro-image**, which highlights the omnipresence of media and its neurological interconnectedness with our consciousness.[24]) Deleuze's preference for sinuous Leibnizian *folds* over straight Cartesian lines, along with his emphasis on **pure optical and sonorous situations** that do not arise from or issue out into purposive actions, also points to the supercession of teleological causality. At the same time, Deleuze favors serial and **atonal montage** relayed through **irrational cuts** (a term borrowed from "irrational numbers" in mathematics), that is, editing discontinuities that open up **interstices** or gaps through an act of combination: "The interaction of two images engenders or traces a frontier which belongs neither to one nor the other."[25] Deleuze's formulations about the recalibrated temporalities of post-war cinema— "crystals of time," "sheets of the past"—also move away from the dominant model, even if usually only into the realm of auteurist subjectivism. The Deleuze–Guattari concept of the **rhizome**, finally, points to a form of plotting that is less "rooted" in characterological depth than embedded in decentered non-hierarchical networks.

The manuals' elision of any non-realist alternative forms is all the more surprising, given that cinema, if sometimes seen as progressing inexorably toward Bazin's **"myth of total cinema"**—the complete adequation between filmic copy and real-world model—has also sometimes been regarded by theorists as the most illusory, artificial, and magical form of art, historically linked to sideshow legerdemain and the conjuring of illusion. In his call for a **"shamanic cinema,"** Raul Ruiz traces cinema back to "magical" events that prefigure it: "a caveman's hand pressed against a lightly colored surface ... simulators (half-transparent demons of the air, described by Hermes Trimegistus); shadows, pre and post-Platonic; the Golem ...; Robertson's Fantascope; [and] the magic butterflies at Coney Island."[26] Cinema thus realizes its greatest potential when it deploys both the indexical realism of what theoreticians such as Andre Gaudreault call **"monstration"**—the act of "showing forth" the pro-filmic materials— and the "magic" facilitated by animation, montage, and superimposition. (Digital media exponentially expand the possibilities for both realism and magic.) Films, in sum, are potentially "*magical realist*"; they conjugate the realistic and the fantastical, making dreams realistic and reality dreamlike, making documentaries fantastic and fictions veridical.

Alternative filmmakers have developed myriad ways of breaking away from the linear, cause-and-effect conventions of neo-Aristotelian narrative poetics in order to defy the "gravity" of chronological time, literal space, and conventional realism. These high-flying strategies include: (1) **palindromic narrative**, deployed in Todd Solondz' *Palindromes* (2004), which defies conventional realism by having the same character (Aviva, whose name is itself a palindrome) played by eight different actors, across lines of age, race, and gender; (2) **the pluralization of the self**, high- lighted by Todd Haynes in *I'm Not There* (2007), a **multi-bio-pic** where six actors, across lines of race and gender, enact different facets of Bob Dylan's life. In his synopsis of the film, Haynes cited Rimbaud's famous aphorism—"*je est un autre*"—and explained, in language close to that developed in this book, that the "breadth and flux of a creative life" cannot be contained "within the tidy arc of a master narrative" but only in a "fractured" narrative featuring a "multitude of voices"[27]; (3) **genre bifurcation**, practiced in Todd Solondz' *Storytelling* (2001), which combines two unrelated stories, one designated "Fiction," about a college writing class, the other designated "Non-Fiction," about a high school student applying to college, with different actors but sharing a link to the broad subject of schooling; (4) **character bifurcation**, as in Sally Potter's *Thriller* (1979), where Mimi I, the female character drawn from Puccini's *La Bohème* (1896), is placed outside the narrative in which Mimi II is the heroine, and where Mimi I analyzes Mimi II's construction as a melodramatic heroine; (5) **intermedial proliferation**, as when Godard multiplies TV monitors and their stories in *Numero Deux*; (6) **disjunctive narration**, as in Cozarinsky's *One Man's War* (1981), which superimposes text from the Nazi officer Ernst Junger's intimate diary with Nazi newsreels from the period; (7) **displaced vocalization**, for example, Kluge's use of a "speaking knee" as narrator in *The Patriot* (1979); (8) **subjunctive interpolations,** as when Chris Marker's voice-over in *Letter from Siberia* announces "If I were to make such a film," followed by an actually-existing animated segment; and, finally, (9) **trickster figures**, as in some African films that promote magical transformations—for example, in Jean-Pierre Bekolo's *Quartier Mozart* (1992), where a sassy young woman (Chef de Quartier or "Queen of the Hood") is transformed into "Montype" ("my guy") by Maman Thekla, the sorceress who takes the shape of "Panka," familiar from Cameroonian folklore, blessed with the capacity to make a man's penis disappear with a handshake. These non-linear potentialities are dramatically enabled of course by the internet and digital media that allow for **collective storytelling** in the form of interactive web-based projects such as "Hollow," where more than thirty residents tell the story of one impoverished country in rural West Virginia.

A number of radical films opt not for systematic magic but rather for intermittent **magical eruptions**. Tanner's *Jonah who will be 25 in the Year 2000* (1975) disrupts its narrative continuity with sepia-tinted segments, ushered in by minor jazz chords heralding a shift in mode. All the interludes bear some oblique or fantasmatic relations to the story, often showing life-as-it-should-be rather than as it is: the worker gets to look at the boss's books; the adults get to play in the mud like children; and the home-bound mother in front of her TV set is personally addressed by the TV newscaster. Palestinian filmmaker Elia Suleiman, for his part, sprinkles the stylized yet ultimately realist narratives of his films with counterfactual gestures, many offering self-declaredly magical solutions for the intractable challenges set up by the Israeli occupation. In *Divine Intervention* (2002), the director endows a tossed apricot pit with the power to blow up Israeli tanks, a pink balloon with the ability to cross checkpoints, and a Palestinian woman with the martial skills of a Ninja. In a pastiche of Kubrik, the equally Palestinian Larissa Sansour's *A Space Exodus* (2009) has the director herself, wearing a white spacesuit, against the sonorous background of an Arabized version of *The Blue Danube*, plant a Palestinian flag on the moon, declaring: "A small step for a Palestinian, a giant leap for mankind." In a situation where Palestinians are rendered progressively more homeless and exiled on earth, space provides a fantasy homeland.

If we are looking toward classical Greece for ideas, we might just as well turn not to Aristotle but rather to the broad tradition of the Menippea as exemplified by Aristophanes and Ovid. Bakhtin posits the following taxonomy of traits for **Mennipean satire**: (1) the **presence of the comic**; (2) **freedom from historical limits**; (3) **liberty of thematic/philosophical invention**; (4) a focus on **the adventures of the idea** in the world; (5) the fusion of **philosophical dialogue, high symbolism, fantastic adventure, and *bas-fonds* naturalism**; (6) **contradictory points of view** on essential questions; (7) a **three-plane structure** (earth, sky, and hell); (8) **fantastic experimentalism**; (9) **abnormal psychic states**; (10) the **violation of decorum**; (11) **violent contrasts and oxymoronic representations**; (12) **social utopia**; (13) **intercalary genres**; (14) **pluristylism and pluritonality**; and (15) **political relevance**. If media-makers were to turn for inspiration not to the Hollywood version of Aristotle's *Poetics* but rather to the *Menippea*, they might easily conjure up a more radical, open, digressive, and nomadic range of diverse points of view; the violation of decorum possibilities. While the Aristotelian model privileges organic unity and the number One—a *single* purpose; *individual* characters; *unity* of time, space, and action—the Mennipea practice systematic pluralization. This option for the multiple, the heterogeneous, and the centrifugal informs many of Bakhtin's key terms: "pluristylism," "polyphony," "polivocality," "pluritonality," "polyglossia," "*multiple* points of view," "*excess* seeing," etc. Moreover, many of the aesthetic options characteristic of the *Mennipea*; elements of social utopia; topical relevance—resonate with radical politics, in that they *socialize* the personal rather than personalize the social *à la* Hollywood. Indeed, Ovid's *Metamorphoses* proliferates in social utopias with commons and ecological overtones, a world without "threatening laws, "fear of punishment," "no sword nor helmet," and "no town enclosed with wall."[28]

Literary critics have deployed the Menippean schema to shed light on fictions that might otherwise be dismissed as "flawed." Mário de Andrades's *Macunaíma*—arguably the unrecognized "mother" of all magical realist novels—was sometimes labeled an "artistic failure" (and un-filmable) because of its astonishing juxtapositions and magical transformations. The novel's putative "mistakes," however, as Suzana Camargo has convincingly argued, actually reflect the "essential characteristics" of the Menippea.[29] To linger on just a few traits (many carried over into the 1969 film of same name), the novel flaunts the freedom from historical limits by having its "scene" bound improbably and without transition from the Amazon to the backlands of São Paulo in an impossible zigzag, and by having its characters magically change skin color or die and come back to life, while animals metamorphose into buildings and telephones. Here the anachronistic mingling of historical periods facilitates what Bakhtin calls "*the dialogue of the dead with the living*," so that seventeenth-century historical figures rub elbows with contemporary counterparts. This freedom of invention rhymes not only with the Menippea and with modernist trans-realism but also with the chronotopically fractured character of the Amazonian legends themselves. A totemic imaginary generates what one might call the **cross-species dialogue** of the animal and the human. "Fish used to be people just like us," Macunaíma tells his brothers, confirming the view of some anthropologists that, for some Amazonian peoples, all sentient beings were originally human, but some later became animal, as opposed to the Western view that all beings began as animals, but some later became humans. Rather than the high-modernist stripping down of narrative, the fractured chronotope of the Menippea explodes the representational continuum through **narrative proliferation**, a centrifugal multiplication of improbably juxtaposed stories drawn from an incommensurably heterotopic set of times and spaces.

Far from the Amazon, the veritable poet–laureate of *threshold encounters* in the Global North is perhaps Canadian filmmaker John Greyson, who for decades has been promiscuously cross-breeding documentary and fiction, reality and fantasy, the queer and the straight, the national and the transnational, and the activist and the academic. Greyson's minor cinema foregrounds not only the theme of "*becoming minoritarian*"(Deleuze) but also of assembling *minoritarian becomings* in conjunction with an aesthetic of *gay relativity*. A number of Greyson's films revive the Mennipean tradition of *threshold encounters* between characters from different historical epochs, a process Greyson calls "**recruiting the dead**" (for the sake of the living). The threshold encounter in Greyson's *Urinal* (1989) takes the form of an imaginary meeting of historically closeted gay, lesbian, and bisexual artists who never actually met—Frida Kahlo, Sergei Eisenstein, Langston Hughes, Yukio Mishima, Florence Wyle—all gathered to discuss the police repression of gays in present-day Toronto. Compounding the implausibilities, Greyson adds a literary character (Dorian Gray) as an undercover police agent. Each narrator presents a mini-documentary: Eisenstein, for example, offers tips not on intellectual montage but rather on corporeal connection in the form of cruising men in "Toronto's hottest tearooms." In an atmosphere of lively contestation, the resurrected artists constantly challenge one another's opinions, manifesting a kind of **queer heteroglossia** or the multi-discursivity of a dissensual gay community.

Greyson's posthumous **transhistorical "gay outing"** retrospectively "corrects" a platitudinous factual history by having the artists, in a retroactive fantasy of transnational activism, protest an event—police entrapment in Ontario—that took place long after their death. Hyperbolizing what Roger Hallas calls **queer anachronism**, Greyson has the characters read their own biographies, deploy poststructuralist terminologies, and screen videos of their own lives. In a polystylistic manner, this unstable generic amalgam of a film is part fictive documentary *à la Zelig*, part musical, part melodrama, part animation, part multi-biopic, part an exercise in **anatomic** (in Northrop Frye's sense) **comic erudition** (in the form of pedantic commentary dedicated to the history of the toilet), and part a talking-heads exposé of homophobia in Ontario. The characters coexist in a kind of **essayistic temporality** where the author/director can freely bring to the foreground any time or text, whether through intertitles, verbal allusion, or staged scenes. Queer anachronisms also proliferate in Derek Jarman's period pieces, where the fracturing and reassembling of historical epochs completely contradict the very definition of the "period piece" as a film set in a precisely delineated historical past. For example, Jarman's 1991 film *Edward II* inserts the **queer futurity** (Muñoz) of the gay rights movement into the Elizabethan period, while his 1977 film *Jubilee* has Ariel from *The Tempest* transport Queen Elizabeth I into the punk rock scene in 1970s London.[30]

Mark Rappaport's **mockumentary bio-pic** *From the Journals of Jean Seberg* (1995) offers a different kind of threshold encounter. In the tradition of novels based on "letters-found-in-an-attic," Rappaport invents a fictitious journal by Seberg herself, thus facilitating a **posthumous dialogue** between Seberg, as mummified in film clips, and herself as played by an actress (Mary Beth Hurt). In an example of **filmic metacommentary**, the cited clips are reworked through the superimposition of alien soundtracks, through voice-over narration unpacking the sexism of the period, and through mini-essays on Godard, the Kuleshov-effect, and other topics. Another kind of *threshold encounter* has Seberg meet her actress–peers Vanessa Redgrave and Jane Fonda, whom Seberg never actually met but who share with her a history of victimization by male producers, directors, and husbands. This political radicalism led, in Seberg's case, to persecution by the FBI for her support for the Black Panthers. In *Rock Hudson's Home Movies* (1992), meanwhile, Rappaport deploys a strategy of **posthumous resuscitation** where he has Eric Farr appear as Rock Hudson himself, analyzing the homoerotic aspects of his own performances. Alexander Kluge's mixed-mode opus *News from*

*Ideological Antiquity: Marx/Eisenstein/The Capital* (2008), finally, hosts a threshold encounter between culture heroes Karl Marx, James Joyce, Sergei Eisenstein, Bertolt Brecht, and Kluge himself, against a backdrop of archival photos, music recitals, animated films, staged scenes, operas, telephone conversations, and a festival of brightly colored intertitles. Here, the **internal monologue** a la James Joyce meets the **external monologue** of Eisenstein as filtered through the transtextual dialogism of Kluge. More dialogic than dialectical, the film's multilateral conversation does not move toward any clear conclusion. The telos is the conversation itself, and the relation between the film's dialogism and the spectators who rework the materials of the film into their own synthesis.

## Pop Culture Anachronism and the Chronotope of the Road

As a corollary of the fractured chronotope, an **aesthetic of anachronism** is common both to the avant-garde and to certain "low" forms of popular culture such as sketch comedy and standup. An *aesthetic of anachronism* animates the work of Mel Brooks, for example, rooted in his background as a Catskills tumbler and stager of manic absurdities for *Your Show of Shows*, the NBC variety show of the early 1950s. In *History of the World, Part I* (1981), Brooks has ancient Romans fly El Al Airlines, while his portrayal of the Spanish Inquisition features Esther-Williams-style swimming pool numbers where cavorting nuns entice orthodox Jews into embracing the Christian faith ("Convert! Don't be boring..."). Even before the Brooks films, however, the oft-censored radio comic Stan Freberg deployed anachronism to powerful political purpose. The album *Stan Freberg Presents the United States of America, Volume One: The Early Years* (1961) offers an anachronism-riddled version of history that raises provocative questions about the European conquest of the misnamed "New World." The first episode, narrated by Orson Welles, links the two 1492 events (the Inquisition and the Conquest of the Americas) by having Columbus and his lover Isabela take amorous advantage of Ferdinand's absence while the king is "off working at the Inquisition." When Columbus first arrives in the Americas, an Indian asks him if he is "on a Fulbright?" Columbus responds: "No, I'm on an Isabela." Anticipating the later anti-quincentennial protests, Freberg even casts doubt on the "discovery narrative." In response to Columbus' claim of "discovery," the Indian protests: "You discover me? No, I discovered you, right here on this beach!"

Three decades later, a *post-Brechtian* sketch by the performance group Culture Clash also deploys an aesthetic of anachronism by fusing the historical Columbus with Don Corleone, the mafia boss character played by Marlon Brando in the Coppola film *The Godfather* (1972). Here, the Great Discoverer wants to "get out of the shipping business," but it keeps "pulling him back." To the strains of the film's famous score, the sketch portrays Columbus as a heavily accented mafioso who kills and plunders the indigenous people. In the end, Columbus is slain by his own mestizo son for having killed his native mother, America. As he lies "dying," Columbus quibbles about historical inaccuracies—"I didn't die like this!"—while his son crosses himself and wishes him: "Happy Columbus Day, Papa!" Another Culture Clash sketch has a radical Chicano and his Puerto Rican friend invoke the *orixas* of Santeria to raise Che Guevara from the dead. Miraculously conjured up in full guerilla regalia out of the image from the famous poster, Che requests a briefing on world trends since his death. He is informed about the fall of communism, the rise of *Chicanismo*, and the corporate cooptation of revolutionary symbols, including his black beret and red star.

Culture Clash's deployment of *Santeria* as a form of time travel traces its roots to a Latin American tradition that might be schematically summed up in the term **"magic realism."**[31] Unlike other artistic movements characterized by manifestoes and explicit position-taking, *magic realism* was less an avant-garde movement than a "literary current linking various writers who practice an expanded notion of realism."[32] The **non-synchronous temporality** typical of magic realism mingles past, present, and future time. In an aesthetic of impossible simultaneity, Isabel Allende has her Eva (in *Eva Luna*, 1987) tell us that "While you and I are speaking here, behind your back Christopher Columbus is inventing America, and the same Indians that welcome him in the stained-glass window are still naked in a jungle a few hours from this office, and will be there a hundred years from now."[33] Thus, magic realism encodes a malleable superimposability of **sheets of time** (Deleuze) conceptualized as more spiral than linear, reminiscent of the simultaneous temporalities of trance-religions. It is no accident that Foucault derived his notion of **heterotopia**—or the juxtaposition in a "single real place of several spaces, several sites that are themselves incompatible"—from the writing of Borges, one of the precursors of magic realism.[34]

Magic realism turns conventional realism on its head; instead of Defoe's inventories of objects and animals, wielded as "reality effects," we find Márquez' **irreality effects**, or the strange mingling of fact and fancy. The Defoe-like precision of "four years, eleven months, and two days" of rain is made in Márquez's *One Hundred Years of Solitude* (1967) to generate magical flowers popping out of the "driest of machines."[35] In Carpentier's *The Lost Steps* (2001), the mere smell of mushrooms induces hallucinations, and swarms of butterflies darken the sky. Yet, this magic is not so distant from the literal truth: some mushrooms **are** powerful hallucinogens, and, in the Brazilian *Pantanal*, butterflies **do** suddenly darken the sky. Rui Guerra's *Erendira* (1983), one of the more compelling examples of **magical cine-realism**, mobilizes the fantastic in the service of an underlying realism. When the film begins, 14-year-old Erendira (Claudia Ohana) is living with her autocratic grandmother (Irene Papas) in a lugubrious mansion, where the girl serves as maid, cook, and confidante. When Erendira forgets to extinguish the candelabra, the mansion catches fire and burns to the ground. "My poor dear," the matriarch tells Erendira, "your entire life will hardly be sufficient to repay me." After informing Erendira of the crippling extent of her debt, she stipulates prostitution as the means of repayment. Thanks to Erendira's natural beauty and the grandmother's entrepreneurial skills, Erendira soon becomes the most sought-after courtesan in the region. At times, Guerra composes particularly telling equivalents for the magical mango world of Márquez's Macondo, where the sun rises at night and sets at dawn, not through Spielbergian pyrotechnics but rather through **magical minimalism**. With anachronistic abandon, the décor commingles mythic time with World War II planes and contemporary trucks, reinforcing the feeling of a transtemporal tropical nowhere land. In a style at once historical and fabulous, Márquez and Guerra use fantasy to expose the real. While the events seem fantastic, they point to recognizable social realities, such as Erendira's unpayable debts, for example, become a figure for the IMF-style "debt traps" plaguing the Global South.

In "Forms of Times and the Chronotope in the Novel," Bakhtin speaks of the **chronotope of the road** as the site where "the spatial and temporal paths of the most varied people—representatives of all social classes, estates, religions, nationalities, ages—intersect...."[36] and where the most various destinies collide and interweave with one another.[37] Bakhtin's account illuminates a number of Latin American/Latino films that treat allegorical voyages. Alex Rivera's video *Papapapa* (1996), for example, exploits the pun in the Spanish title (potato/father) as a trampoline for historical counterpoint, In a kind of **vegetative picaresque**, the film counterposes two incommensurable voyages: that of the director's Peruvian father as an immigrant to the United States, where he ultimately becomes a metaphorical "couch potato," consuming junk food imported from Peru; and that of the literal potato, globalized by the "Columbian

Exchange," which moves from the position of sacred object in Peru to saleable commodity in the world. Rivera mines the lowly tuber for its complex colonial history (and even its skin color), drawing hilarious connections between cross-national citizenship and cross-border commodification.

Artur Omar's proto-mockumentary *Triste Tropico* (1974), meanwhile, offers a kind of parodic–cannibalist take on *magic realism*. Its title, transparently inspired by *Tristes Tropiques* (1955), Lévi-Strauss's ethnographic memoir about Brazil, triggers an evocative chain of cultural associations. While the French ethnographer left France in the 1930s to flee anti-Semitism and discover indigenous Brazil, the "protagonist" of *Triste Tropico*, similar to countless Brazilian intellectuals, goes to Europe only to rediscover a Brazil that he thought he had left behind. The film disorients the viewer by its constantly mutating relation to spectatorial expectations. The opening shots—family photos, traffic in 1920s São Paulo—lead us to expect a home-movie-style documentary. The offscreen narrator tells us that the film concerns a certain Arthur Alvaro de Noronha, known as "Dr. Arthur," who returned from studies in Paris to practice medicine in Brazil. As with most mockumentaries, *Triste Tropico* relies on the spectator to fill in the lacunae of the representation. Some period footage shows us a man with his family; we infer that the man is the aforementioned Dr. Arthur. In Paris, the voice-over informs us, the doctor became friendly with Andre Breton, Paul Eluard, and Max Ernst, our first clue that a truly surreal biography awaits us.

As it proceeds, the film develops a kind of **hallucinatory narration**. The doctor becomes involved with Indians, is venerated as an indigenous Messiah, and finally degenerates into cannibalism and sodomy—an exclamatory intertitle ("the horror!") underlines the Conradian dimension of the story. The narrated descent into an Amazonian heart of darkness coincides with the spectator's descent into a tangled undergrowth of cinematic disorientation. As the offscreen narration becomes progressively more detached from the image track, we begin to suspect that we have been the dupes of an immense joke, as if Borges had slyly rewritten Conrad. The illustrious Dr. Arthur now appears to be a figment of an overexcited authorial imagination. The central anti-Aristotelian procedure of *Triste Tropico* is to superimpose a linear (albeit absurd) offscreen narration on extremely discontinuous materials—amateur movies, shots of carnivals, book covers—that together form a kind of serial chaos. Within this audiovisual bricolage, we find certain Lévi-Straussian motifs and binary oppositions: "raw Brazil" and "cooked Europe"; Apollonian order and Dionysian frenzy; and *la pensee sauvage* and *la pensee civilisee*.

Fernando Solanas' **radical road movie** *El Viaje* (1972), for its part, fuses the course of an individual life with the course of history by following a single 17-year-old character's five-century-long journey from Patagonia to Mexico in search of Latin American identity. The film's style of **cartoon irrealism** is dictated by an intermittently appearing comic strip supposedly left behind by the young man's absent father. The opening classroom sequence—where a windy cataclysm rips presidential portraits off the wall and sends them flying on a stone horse bearing the Argentinean national hero San Martin—suggests a Benjaminian explosion of the continuum of history. Through *magical-realist* meteorology, snow falls indoors, and Chilean floodwaters invade the streets of Buenos Aires, evoking perhaps the tsunami of dictatorships rippling around the Southern Cone from Brazil (1964) to Chile (1973) to Argentina (1976). Transformed by his voyage, the protagonist does not find a single, univocal identity, but rather a **dissensual polyphony** of race, religion, and ethnicity.

George C. Wolfe's play/PBS performance *The Colored Museum* (1986) offers a different kind of fractured chronotope and a different kind of voyage. Riffing on the tradition of colonial expositions, the play is structured as a series of "exhibits," each dramatized as a museum piece in which mannequin-style figures come to life to enact an aspect of African-American history. The opening "exhibit" ("Git on Board") recasts the slave ship as a transatlantic flight with "Celebrity Slaveship" Airlines. Within a Brechtian minimalist staging combined with percussion and illustrative archival materials, a single actress manages to evoke a plane full of people. Through the **spatialization of time**, the sketch has the plane fly over Black History. The flight attendant, the very perky and well-spoken "Miss Pat," reminds the passengers to "fasten their shackles" as she shepherds them through the turbulent patches of Black Atlantic history. Assuring them that the airline will not be throwing passengers overboard to collect the insurance, she promises to make their "Middle Passage" as pleasant as possible. (Her sugary words are undercut by engravings of packed slave ships and the lacerated backs of whipped slaves.) Looking out the window, the passengers behold the American Revolution, the Civil War, the Great Depression, and the Civil Rights struggles, all in tandem with a mutating black popular culture of star athletes and Supremes-style girl groups. All the while, Afro-style percussion evokes the possibility of revolt. Reminding black passengers how lucky they will be to be celebrities on the basketball court and characters in Faulkner novels, she issues a stern warning to the restless underclass "natives" traveling coach: "drums and rebellion will not be tolerated!"

## Baroque Modernism and the Marvelous American Real

The Franco-Cuban novelist Alejo Carpentier first coined the phrase "**the marvelous American real**" in his preface to *El Reino de Este Mundo* (in 1949). Although its precise meaning is somewhat elusive, the phrase gestures toward a number of thematic leitmotifs: the botanical/meteorological sublime of the natural commons of rainforests, hurricanes, and volcanoes; the continent's syncretisms of indigenous, African, and European cultures; and the tragic heroism of rebel figures such as Montezuma in Mexico and King Henri Christophe in Haiti. Although the phrase "*marvelous American real*" locates this aesthetic in Latin America, at times Carpentier finds its aesthetic antecedents in earlier periods—in the archaic past of mythological texts such as *Popol Vuh* and *Chilam Balam*, for example—or in distant locations such as Hindu and Persian literature.

It has long been commonplace to speak of **the baroque**, conceived as a loose constellation of aesthetic traits such as irregularity, assymmetricality, excess, the grotesque, and the melancholy—as a cultural dominant in Latin America. As a critical term, the baroque classically evokes voluptuous spirituality, labyrinthian curvature, the cohabitation of contraries, the exaltation of the senses, and the mingling of the sacred and the profane. Despite its elite origins, many left theorists and artists have discerned radical possibilities in the baroque, from Walter Benjamin's view of the baroque as the piling up of fragments, to Gilles Deleuze's discussion of a "**new baroque**" where "the figure and the ground are in movement in space," to Severo Sarduy's embrace of the baroque as a revolutionary form.[38] Angela Ndalianis has spoken of "**neo-baroque aesthetics**," while Timothy Murray has invoked the "**digital baroque**."[39] All of these figures transfigure the baroque, though once considered merely a chronological period within the taxonomies of art history to make it a contemporary form of social–historical–artistic thinking in a decentered world.

Carpentier invoked the baroque in the title of his *Concierto Barroco*, first conceived in 1936, when he learned that the Italian composer Vivaldi had written an opera on the conquest of the Americas (*Montezuma*). Carpentier sees "America" itself as a baroque concert counterpointing European, African, and indigenous elements, a cut-n'-mix of highly elaborated melodies and complex African polyrhythms, set in a landscape whose lush vegetation hides the gold and silver that financed *crioullo* luxury and European capitalism. Within an aesthetic of anachronism, Carpentier has the novel's musical jouissance climax in a jazzistic romp at the Venetian festival where Carpentier has musicians from different historical epochs meet in a Menippean "dialogue between the dead and the living." A conga-line procession, propelled by a percussive Afro-Cuban chant, generates Scarlatti's complaint about "cannibal music!" Carpentier's fantastic Venetian symphony points through proleptic anachronism to the later-to-be-realized Africanization of world music, the trend whereby Afro-diasporic musical forms such as jazz, salsa, samba, reggae, and hip-hop have come to dominate popular culture, providing anticipatory forms of what Paul Gilroy calls **"planetary conviviality."**[40]

Paul Leduc's *Barroco* (1988), for its part, is less an adaptation than a **baroque tone-poem** or extended music video "inspired" by the Carpentier novella. Leduc politicizes the novella by inserting new scenes evoking the horrific toll of conquest, colonialism, and slavery, while at the same time celebrating the artistic creations generated by that very same conquest. Adopting the **musical structure** of the novella, the Leduc film is structured like a *baroque* concert divided along classical lines into four musical (and thematic) movements: (1) *Andante* for the autonomous freedom of indigenous peoples before the Conquista; (2) *Contradanza* for the asymmetrical syncretisms of the colonial period; (3) *Rondo* for the Moorish and European musical currents mingling in Flamenco; and (4) *Finale* for the fantasy opera of social counterpoint and conflict. Running through the film's soundtrack is the *clave* (key) rhythm, the 1-2-3, 1-2 staccato beat familiar from salsa and *son*. But the music syncretizes this Afro-Caribbean rhythm with a prestigious Euro-descended instrument—the cello—setting up a musical base-line for the film's many musical styles, ranging from opera and flamenco to rumba, bolero and danzon.

Leduc's *Barroco* develops an aesthetic based on what Nestor Garcia-Canclini calls **"multi-temporal heterogeneity"** or the fusing of incompatible times.[41] In the film's harlequinade tapestry, an encyclopedic orgy of musical performances and citations, mingling Bach, Vivaldi, Rossini, Schubert, Moorish songs, French chanson, flamenco, salsa, bolero, mariachi, and indigenous and African religious music, forms the pliable musical matrix of the film. The diverse musics modulate into one another, so that Rossini's "Barber of Seville" gives way to a rhumba on the same topic (*"El barbero de Sevilla loco se volvio"*), reminding us of the reciprocal feedback effects between the erudite culture of opera and the popular culture of carnival. As in the novella, Louis Armstrong and Groucho Marx appear in the form of wax dolls, and in a grand transhistorical apotheosis, the characters/groups dance together at the Tropicana, Havana's kitschy 1950s-style nightclub. A strategy of **thespian anachronism**, meanwhile, casts the same players for different roles representing different historical periods. An eighteenth-century Mexican *señorita* becomes a *criolla* Cubana and a flamenco-dancing gypsy becomes a murdered Spanish *anarquista*, only to return as an international *roqueira*.

## Trance-Modernism

While adaptations of magical realist novels are often trite, some films not based on novels incarnate "magic realism" by mingling the realism of *cinéma vérité* with the fantasy of baroque allegory. (Playing on the Spanish word for "south," Rocha called for "**sur-realismo**" or a surrealism appropriate to the Global South.) *Terra em Transe* (Land in Anguish, 1967), Rocha's **baroque allegory** about the "tragic carnival" of Brazilian politics is deeply imbued with the spirit of *sur-realismo* . Literally allegorical, the film is set in an imaginary country called "Eldorado" that closely resembles Brazil. A fantasy sequence, presented as a dream of the agonizing narrator-protagonist Paulo Martins, demonstrates the potentialities of the Benjaminian baroque modernism. The right wing figure of the film—named Porfirio Diaz after the Mexican leader who massacred Indians and solicited foreign investment—arrives from the sea, in a scene redolent of a myth of national origins.

The sequence brilliantly exemplifies Benjamin's suggestion, in his *Theses on the Philosophy of History*, that the historical articulation of the past did not involve representing it "the way it really was" but rather of seizing hold of a memory as it "flashes up at a moment of danger." Within Benjamin's **dialectical image**, repressed aspects of history take on fresh meaning in the light of contemporary crises. Here, in the wake of the "moment of danger" of the 1964 *coup d'etat* which overturned the populist government of João Goulart, Rocha conjures up the memory of Pedro Cabral, the Portuguese "discoverer" of Brazil. In a **transhistorical fusion**, Rocha conflates the twentieth-century *putschiste* Diaz with a stylized and satiric version of Cabral's "First Mass," celebrated with the Indians in 1500. Within official Brazilian historiography, the "First Mass," (like Thanksgiving) evokes pacific Christianization and the putatively "cordial" relations between whites and Indians. The sequence's fractured chronotope orchestrates impossibly multiple temporalities—the millennial inheritance of Yoruba praise-songs, the 1500 date of Cabral's arrival on Brazilian shores, the turn-of-the-century period of Porfirio Diaz' rule, and the 1964 *coup d'etat*—in order, finally, to stress the continuities between the conquest and contemporary oppression by portraying the present-day right-winger as the heir of the conquistadores.

While Brechtian theater deploys disjunction between image and sound, Rocha goes farther by staging the historical disjunctions between vast cultural and ecological matrices—European, African, and Indigenous—existing in frazzled relations of conflict and domination. The mass is accompanied not by Christian music but rather by Yoruba religious chants, thus evoking the "trance" religion historically suppressed by Christianity. Instead of the austere minimalism typical of hyper-Brechtian staging, moreover, we find a multi-layered saturation of image and sound, a hysterical *trauerspiel* linked both to carnival and to *candomblé*. The scene's fractured and discontinuous aesthetic stages life in the colonial "**contact zone**," defined by Mary Louise Pratt as the space in which "subjects previously separated" encounter each other within "conditions of coercion, radical inequality, and intractable conflict."[42] In Rocha's self-described "**dialectical–materialist–structural–psychic–linguistic**" method, social contradictions are manifested on various planes. Each character is associated with a discourse, a music, and an architecture as manifestations of a **social psyche**. The intellectual protagonist, for example, is associated with modernist architecture and the music of Villa-Lobos, while the populist politician is associated with samba.

The aesthetic of the "First Mass" sequence draws heavily from the Africanized forms of Rio's yearly samba pageant, with its bricolage historicism, its sacred polyrhythms, and its delight in extravagant *allegorias* (floats) and *fantasias* (costumes). The dazzling formal originality of the sequence exemplifies **trance-Brechtianism**, that is, it uses trance to go beyond Brecht by simultaneously tropicalizing, Africanizing, and carnivalizing Brecht's theories through the possession-trance of West African religions. While Brecht invoked the metaphor of "transe" in an ethnocentrically negative way to refer to a passive, narcoleptic audience, Rocha recognized the positive centrality of trance as a structuring element in the film. Rocha's "**cinema of agitation**," for Deleuze, puts "everything into a trance, the people and its masters, and the camera itself, pushing everything into a state of aberration...."[43] Some scholars have spoken of trance itself as characterized by multi-temporality. Scholar Awam Ampke, who worked with trance techniques in collaboration with the Nobel Prize–winning playwright Wole Soyinka in Nigeria, speaks of trance as a "multi-sensory form of knowledge-making offering a liberatory sense of transcendence through an awareness of simultaneous times and spaces."[44] Deleuze, meanwhile, links trance to popular becoming: "the trance, the putting into trances, are a transition, a passage, or a becoming ... [Rocha] puts the parties in trance in order to contribute to the invention of his people...."[45] In a case of **style as mimesis**, Rocha's neo-baroque

Afro-avant-gardist aesthetic here figures the discontinuous, dissonant, fractured history of the Latin-American multi-nation through equally dissonant images and sounds.

It is not often that a single film inspires a prodigiously influential multi-art movement, but such was the case with *Terra em Transe* (1967) and Tropicália. Caetano Veloso credited the Rocha film with catalyzing the Tropicalist movement: "all of that Tropicalia thing was formulated inside me on the day that I saw *Terra em Transe*."[46] According to Caetano himself, "my heart exploded during the opening sequence, when, to the sound of a *candomblé* chant, an aerial shot of the sea brings us to the coast of Brazil." Without that "traumatic moment," Caetano writes, "nothing of what came to be called tropicalism would have ever existed."[47]

Since the aerial shot taking us across the Atlantic to the shores of the Americas recapitulates the Middle Passage, one might argue that the Tropicalia movement was born in an epiphany of African-ness, literally under the sign of the **Black Atlantic** (Farris Thompson, Paul Gilroy), that is, the world impacted by the slave trade with its horrible sequels as well as its splendid artistic offshoots. In the late 1960s, *Terra em Transe* was a major catalyst for the radical anthropophagic theater of Ze Celso, the provocative installations of Hélio Oiticicca, and the endless mutations of Tropicalia, all of which inaugurated a new matrix for the arts during the ensuing decades.

The Africanized "First Mass" sequence in *Terra em Transe* reminds us that, far from "saving" the artistic patrimony of the non-European world, colonizing versions of Christianity (similar to some militant versions of Islam) have in fact often been *destroyers* of the religious artistic patrimony. Much of the *indigenous artistic commons* of Africa and indigenous America was suppressed by colonial authorities because it was seen as "pagan," "idolatrous," and "polytheistic." Through a superimposed set of misinformed hierarchies, West-African spirit religions were seen as: (1) oral rather than written, unlike the "religions of the Book"; (2) polytheistic rather than monotheistic; (3) superstitious rather than scientific; (4) disturbingly corporeal and ludic (danced, entranced) rather than abstractly theological; (5) insufficiently sublimated (involving actual animal sacrifice rather than symbolic or historically commemorative sacrifice); and (6) as drowning the unitary, bounded individual self in the transpersonal fusions of trance. The ideal of self-control is threatened by the conflation of selves—as the medium as horse and the orixa as rider become indistinguishable.[48]

In a less Eurocentric perspective, all these "deficiencies" might be seen as bringing intellectual and especially artistic advantages: the lack of a written text discourages fundamentalist dogmatism; the multiplicity of spirits allows for artistic creativity; and dance and music form a powerful basis for an **Afro-diasporic aesthetic**. As a spiritual *fiesta*, *candomblé*, similar to carnival, can be seen as an exercise in **performative alterity**. Just as carnival *"fantasias"* (costumes) can transform an impoverished slum dweller into an aristocrat, so spirit possession can turn a maid into the ruler of seas and storms, into an Iemanja or an Iansa. Both carnival and *candomblé* set in motion a complex dance of positionalities and identities, fostering a creative dialogue, often transgendered and transracial, between self and other. When transposed into the narrative arts, these transmutations help artists move beyond the assumptions of the unified rounded characters of dramatic realism.

While Rocha actually filmed *candomblé* trance in *Barravento*—the title refers to the stormy vertigo that precedes the onset of possession—in *Terra em Transe*, he turned trance into a structuring trope. Rocha was one of the many artists who combined anti-racist and anticolonialist politics with an informed affection for West African trance-religions, with jazz often serving as the "gateway drug" leading to Afro-artistic ecstasy.[49] This transnational movement led to various outbreaks of **trance-modernism**, including on the part of many major white artist/intellectuals: first, Orson Welles, whose all-black "Voodoo Macbeth," staged in Harlem in 1936, featured religious drummers from Sierra Leone (legend has it that the drummers staged a curse ceremony against hostile critic Percy Hammond and that the critic died soon thereafter); second, Maya Deren, the American avant-garde filmmaker who was initiated into Haitian vodun and who created books and entrancing films on the subject (*Divine Horsemen: The Living Gods of Haiti*, 1985); third, the French "ethnographic surrealist" filmmaker Jean Rouch, who not only filmed African trance-religions, but also coined the term **"cine-trance."** For Rouch, the trance phenomenon constituted essential engines both of spirituality and of artistic creation. Theatrical directors such as Julian Beck, Peter Brook, and Grotowski, Rouch pointed out, all used the ethnography of religious possession in their training of actors.[50] In *Les Maîtres Fous* (1955), Rouch filmed trance rituals that functioned metaphorically as a coded mockery of the British colonial authorities. By drawing on African religious culture for his trope of *cine-trance*, Rouch was equating his own filmmaking practice with possession, in order to evoke a sense of danced and kinetic alignment between the filmmaker and the possessed subject of religious ecstasy.[51]

While every religion arguably opens up a **religious–aesthetic field** that stimulates certain arts, senses, and faculties, in the case of Afro-diasporic religions, the arts form the energetic matrix of a multi-sensory religion characterized by a complex and dynamic *mise-en-scène*. As with cinema, these religions form **multi-art practices**; they engage all the arts, high and low, temporal and spatial—including music, dance, poetry, narrative, costume, and cuisine. Rather than mere decorative accouterments, the arts form an integral part of the religion as a synaesthetic system of belief. As a form of performative spirituality where "soul claps its hands and sings," the faithful are also performers—above all, the priests and priestesses and mediums, but also the community as the addressee of the performance, those for whose benefit the ritual is performed. The artist–gods, meanwhile, shape the very atmosphere of worship. Olodumare, as creator of the universe, can be seen as a cosmic artist, and many of the *orixas* are not only artists or artisans (Ogum being the patron saint of metal smiths), but also have artistic preferences in terms of colors, ornaments, and cuisine. Nor is the meaning of the *orixas* static. Associated with the spread of iron-making technology in sub-Saharan Africa millennia ago, Ogum has been recoded in films such as *Antonio das Mortes* (1969) and *Amuleto de Ogum* (1974) as a New World warrior for social justice.

A number of Afro-diasporic films—from Nigeria (*A Deusa Negra*, 1979; *Sàngó: The Legendary African King*, 1998) and Cuba (e.g., *¡Patakín! Quiere Decir ¡Fábula!*, 1981; *Oggun: the Eternal Present*, 1991) to the United States (*I & I: An African Allegory*, 1991), and Brazil (*A Forca de Xango*, 1977)—deploy the **Yoruba pantheon as an artistic resource** by having the *orixas* participate directly in the characters' lives. Eduardo Coutinho's documentary *Santo Forte* ("The Mighty Spirit," 1999) engages with the spiritually multiple worlds of the inhabitants of a Carioca favela where Catholicism, *Umbanda*, Kardec-style spiritism, and Pentecostalism coexist in ecumenical conviviality within the same community and even within the same person.[52] The *orixas*, as with Greek gods, actively intervene in the interviewees' lives, resulting in scrambled **pronominal "shifters"**—the "I" of the speaker might refer either to the speaker or to the *orixa* by whom the speaker has been possessed—and the pluralization of the self. *Je*, in Rimbaud's memorable phrase, becomes *autre*.

Brazilian filmmaker Vera Figueiredo promotes an encounter between Rio's carnival pageant and Yoruba cosmologies in her *Samba of the Creation of the World* (1989). As an example of ***candomblé* feminism**, the film celebrates the gender egalitarianism of Yoruba cosmologies—within which the universe is created not by a patriarchal God but rather through dialogic collaboration between the feminine principle (incarnated by *Odudua*) and the masculine principle (*Obatala*). A number of non-Brazilian artists have paid homage to the aesthetic power of Afro-diasporic music and religion, as evidenced in the odes to *candomblé* in Sandra Barnhard's *Without You I am Nothing* (1990), in David Byrne's film *Ile*

*Aye* (*House of Life in Yoruba,* 1989), in Paul Simon's album *Spirit of the Saints,* and in Michael Jackson's song in collaboration with the Afro–Brazilian cultural group Olodum, "They Don't Care About Us."

## Contrapuntal Variations

The various arts, as we have seen throughout, have a capacity to potentialize one another by releasing innovative energies in the other arts, including through borrowed metaphors. Many theorists and practitioners of the arts, in this sense, have drawn on music and musical metaphors. In the 1920s, both Mário de Andrade and Mikhail Bakhtin, unknown to each other, drew on the musical trope of **polyphony** to elaborate their aesthetic theories. For Bakhtin, *polyphony* refers to the coexistence, in any textual or extra-textual situation, of a plurality of voices that do not fuse into a single consciousness but rather generate dialogical dynamism among them-selves.[53] Mário de Andrade, in a similar key, spoke of "**polifonismo**" as "the simultaneous artistic union of two or more melodies whose temporary effects of sonorous conflict collaborate to create a total final effect."[54] Although music is often seen as a temporal art, it also evokes spatial relations and is thus chronotopic. In cinema, music can form its own alternative **musical chronotope**, not necessarily subordinated to the chronotope developed on the other tracks. Musical chronotopes can also be juxtaposed and orchestrated polyphonically to suggest new levels of meaning.

Deleuze's claim that cinema is philosophical, in that it "*generates concepts*" in non-verbal form, also applies to music, which *generates concepts* in sensuous–affective–intellectual form. Many theorists have either anti-cipated or echoed Deleuze's ideas about the conceptual power of music. Film theorist/filmmaker Jean Epstein spoke of **lyrosophy** or the singing of thought and knowledge.[55] Robert Farris Thompson calls African music and dance "**nonverbal formulations of philosophies of beauty and ethics**,"[56] much as Clyde Woods spoke of **blues epistemology** as expressing an African-American self-awareness about its own space and time.[57] Combining "acoustics" with "epistemology," Steven Feld speaks of "**acoustemology**" as a sonic way of knowing and being in the world.[58] To paraphrase Nietzsche's words about dance, music relays the very movement of thought itself.[59] In the context of Afro-diasporic art, Farris Thompson speaks of the "**aesthetic of the cool**" to refer to "balance in the midst of daunting difficulty."[60] In a formulation reminiscent of our own *archaic innovation*, Thompson speaks of the **antiquity of the cool** as a "means of putting innovation and tradition, invention and imitation, into amicable relations with one another."[61] Cinematographer Arthur Jaffa, meanwhile, speaks of the cinematic possibilities of "**Black visual intonation**," whereby "irregular, nontempered (nonmetronomic) camera rates and frame replication ... prompt filmic movement to function in a manner that approximates black vocal intonation," forging the filmic equivalent of the tendency in Black music to "treat notes as indeterminate, inherently unstable sonic frequencies rather than ... fixed phenomena."[62]

Although both cinema and music generate concepts, they do so in media-specific ways. In the general absence of a metonymic link between a configuration of musical notes and some pro-musical object, music is less anchored in veristic representation. As what Susanne Langer called "the **tonal analogue** of emotive life," music is communicative without being discursive; its intelligence is trans-trance discursive, at once emotional and architectonic.[63] At the same time, music can be seen as a *tonal analogue* to thought. In his **Afro-diasporic intellectual bio-pic** *The Stuart Hall Project* (2013), John Akomfrah counterpoints the changing musical moves of Miles Davis with the changing intellectual moves of Stuart Hall, as the two figures "play" in a kind of musical–philosophical duet. With his music, Stuart Hall tells us, "Miles Davis put his finger on my soul," so that "the various moods of Miles Davis matched the evolution of my own feelings." Thus, Akomfrah interlaces the historically shaped alterations in structures of feeling as refracted within two different registers of thought, emotion, and modes of creating and thinking.

Music has an immediate appeal to the senses, going directly to what might be called the "emotional jugular." Indeed, no aspect of cinema exemplifies better than music what affective corporeal theory variously calls bodily knowledge, sensory thought, and affect as that which is felt immediately rather than understood intellectually. For José Miguel Wisnik, music "acts on individual and collective life, interlacing social representations and psychic forces."[64] Since music is structured, but not in itself "plotted" in terms of any causality other than the musical, it can reinforce the dramatic realist model or subvert it through an alternative aesthetic logic. Plots provide the narrative skeleton of a film, but music often forms an integral part of its affective interstitial tissue. In a film, music can develop a parallel "plot" or sonorous logic based on the accords, harmonies, tensions, and dissonances of the music itself, in a parallel narrative that can run support, comment on, contradict, or ignore the other plot, in such a way as to generate creative tensions and novel intensities and potentialities.[65] Michel Chion speaks of **a-empathetic music** and the **unrelated score**, that is, film music characterized by a calculated indifference toward the image and the dramatic moment.[66] Through **musical–sonorous emplotment**, a film's sound design can tell a different and parallel story through melody, harmony, and rhythm.[67] Within a jazzistic structure, according to David James, a narrative can progress "like cascading shards of scenes separated by large ellipses, so that the overall plot is essentially a frame, equivalent to a referential melody in a bebop composition."[68]

Although music is not directly political, it has clear political implications. In Hollywood films about Africa, such as *Out of Africa* (1985), the choice of European-style symphonic music tells us that the "heart" of the film is not in Africa but in Europe. In the 1949 Hollywood film *Christopher Columbus*, the commentative (non-diegetic) music virtually proclaims the film's Manichean schema: the religiously connoted choral music "blesses" Columbus; that associated with the "natives" curses them as ominous, provoking an acoustic sense of threatening encirclement. Music can, at times, overwhelm narrative, or, conversely, be "instrumentalized" by extra-musical forces. In an extremely witty sequence in *Pervert's Guide to Ideology* (2012), Slavoj Žižek, seated in a simulacrum of the Korova Milk Bar in *A Clockwork Orange* (1971), explains that the "Ode to Joy" from Beethoven's Ninth Symphony is not only a favorite of the Alex character in the Kubrick film, but has also been enlisted to support extremely diverse ideologies and institutions—Soviet communism, white Rhodesian Independence, Sendero Luminoso, the European Union, and Maoist China. The open-ended nature of what Barthes called **"polysemy"** (multi-semanticality) in relation to music—for Žižek, reminiscent of the "empty shell of ideology"—allows it to dramatically change its political valence as it is successively re-contextualized through mutating discursive–musical–social forms of **anchorage**.

While music cannot create a revolution, it can provide its sound track. Paul Gilroy, drawing on Ernst Bloch's notion of the "*not yet*," speaks of Afro-diasporic music as **"anticipatory"** in its power to proleptically model social change and movement.[69] One major formal innovation of the already discussed *Les Stances à Sophie* (1971) is the diegetically unmotivated musical presence of the Art Ensemble of Chicago, whose members appear in cameos but whose free-jazz has no clear link to the story. The Ensemble's music forms an **autonomous track**, suggesting a twist on Brecht's separation of the elements as suggestive counterpoint rather than causal sequence. While untethered to the image, the music resonates, on another level, with the experimental feminism of the film and its characters. Since the Art Ensemble was known for carnivalizing musical decorum through found instruments such as bicycle horns, gongs, and metal objects, the film hints at a **cross-practice homology**—an isomorphic structure of form and content—between the Ensemble members as experimental free-music

254    *Keywords in Subversive Film/Media Aesthetics*

pioneers going beyond the harmonic structures of bebop, the "unruly women" as experimental sexual and gender pioneers, and the Mizrahi film as a critique of cinematic language. At the same time, the film evokes homologies between jazz as a critique of conventional musical language, and the Celine/Rochefort novel as a critique of conventional literary language. The current of sympathy that connects the rebellious white women and the insurgent black artists, meanwhile, reminds us of Simone de Beauvoir's highlighting, in *The Second Sex* (1949), of the subterranean affinities and analogies between white women and black men as two oppressed and infantilized groups. Celine's search for personal freedom reverberates with the film's aesthetic search within the arts as a realm of freedom. The Ensemble music, alongside the mini-communes forming throughout the film, figure alternative "ensembles" of creative solidarity.

If conventional film music usually psychologizes the story by adding a sense of emotional depth to characters, music can also "socialize" a film by injecting a social–cultural–political dimension. The African music "covering" shots of Nanni Moretti on his Vespa riding through Rome in *Caro Diario* (1993) "re-Africanizes," as it were, a city in millennial contact with Africa. The sounds of Raï music "covering" images of Paris in Zemmouri's *100% Arabica* (1997), similarly, engender an **acoustic take-over** of filmic urban space, a musical Africanization. The ouverture Raï song accompanies three Maghrebi-French characters roller-blading from the touristy Place de la Concorde to a funky *banlieu* Raï concert. The very cityscape of Paris, as heard and seen as if "through" Raï music, is "Arabized" by the music.

Henri Lefebvre entitled a collection of essays *Rhythmanalysis* to refer to the rhythms of urban spaces and their effects on the inhabitants. Josh Kun, meanwhile, speaks of **"audiotopias"** that foster "a possible utopia for the listener … a space that we can enter into, encounter, move around in, inhabit, be safe in, learn from…."[70] Music can open up worlds of alterity and possibility. For James Baldwin a kind of "salvation," music arguably provided black people in the diaspora with a **percussive principle of hope** (Ernst Bloch) that salved the psyche and enabled survival despite slavery, segregation, and chain-gangs. In Brazil, the Afro-Reggae cultural group combined the words *"batucada"* (percussion) and *"cidadinia"* (citizenship) to form *"batidania"* (percussive citizenship). Deleuze speaks of the deterritorializing power of *la ritournelle*, the tra-la-la refrain that serves as a kind of ambulatory emotional home.

The films of Eduardo Coutinho, in this sense, offer a kind of **audiotopian** *auto-mise-en-scène* by having his filmed subjects, often poor and socially marginalized people, sing their favorite songs, as occurs in the touching scene in *Boca de Lixo* (1993), where the daughter of one of the garbage *catadores* sings a beloved Brazilian "country" song, or the scene in *Babilônia 2000* (1999), where a woman from the favela sings her idiosyncratic version of Janis Joplin's "Bobbie McGhee," where she mangles the English lyrics yet conveys the throbbing pulse of the song. The process culminates in Coutinho's *As Canções* (2011), in which a very diverse array of people, ranging from celebrities to ordinary people, talk about the songs that have marked their lives, thus revealing music's power to release repressed emotions and synthesize the intimate feelings and memories of a lifetime.

As a "host" for the full panoply of the arts, cinema is a place where we go not only to follow stories and meet characters but also to see paintings, hear poetry, and listen to music—"affective-turn" theorists might add "to touch" and "to smell"—and to do it all at the same time. In a kinesthetic interplay, the senses, and the filmic tracks, do not operate in isolation but rather intersect, mingle, fuse, and synergistically play together. Music and sound are tactile; they give us chills, affect our pulse, and trigger our tears. Music is historical, in that it intertwines private and public memory. At once highly technical, even mathematical, while also philosophical and spiritual, music is mysterious, in that it is difficult to explain why we can absolutely love a mere configuration of notes. Music evokes worlds of desire, possibility, and pain. With music, to cite the synaesthetic phrase from *King Lear*, "we see it feelingly."

Film sound theorist Michel Chion speaks of **sound–image synchresis** to evoke the "spontaneous and irresistible weld produced between particular auditory phenomenon and visual phenomenon when they occur at the same time."[71] The ways that we are moved by music, and by the synchresis of music and image, often transcend "plot" in any conventional sense. Thanks to the mysterious multiplier effect of synchresis, the music becomes more than music and the image more than image. The conjunction of the bluish planet "Melancholia" slouching toward Earth in Lars von Trier's *Melancholia* (2011), combined with a dark bass rumble and a chord transition from the prelude to Wagner's *Tristan & Isolde* (2006), is, for many spectators, deeply moving. Music and image together conjure up, in a kind of proleptic nostalgia, the boundless tragedy that would be the destruction of our common planet and the end of our collective species-being. The music of *Tristan & Isolde*, Manohla Dargis reminds us, was meant, by Wagner's own account, to evoke "endless yearning, longing, the bliss and wretchedness of love; world power, fame, honor, chivalry, loyalty and friendship all blown away like an insubstantial dream." In the context of a planetary ecological crisis, a "mere" harmonic shift, in conjunction with the image of a planet, conjures up a cosmic sadness at the thought of a galactic splintering of planet earth and its transformation into an insubstantial dream, all faded into thin air, with no human dreamers left as witnesses.

The arts are not always in synch; indeed, the gaps between them have often served as spurs for innovation. The auteurs of the French New Wave wanted to bring cinema in synch with modernism in the other arts such as music (Varese, jazz), theater (Ionesco), and the novel (Claude Simon). At times, popular music has been more adept at crystallizing an alternative aesthetic than film. In Brazil, music has often developed an aesthetic synthesis that is at once Brazilian and transnational, popular and avant-garde, accessible and erudite, a synthesis rarely achieved by Brazilian cinema in the same way. Brazilian music is confidently cosmopolitan, fully capable of constructing strong stylistic and cultural counterpoints. Afro-diasporic music generally displays an anthropophagic capacity to absorb a wide array of influences, Western and non-Western, while still being driven by a culturally African bass note. Although this relative confidence partly has to do with a relatively low-cost medium and distinct insertions into the global economy, it also has to do with aesthetic models. There is no equivalent in the field of popular music to the institutional/aesthetic hegemony of Hollywood; music is not obliged to either conform to or reject a powerful institutionalized aesthetic norm. In popular music, hegemony is loosened, since in much of popular music, the "dominant" *is* Afro-diasporic. One wonders, then, what would happen if films went beyond "including" music to "**becoming music**," by creating the counterpart in cinema of the rich synthesis of touching melody, complex harmony, poetic lyrics, and polyrhythmic percussion offered by popular music at its best?

The metaphor of "counterpoint" as extrapolated to aesthetics, is drawn, obviously, from the world of music. In *Culture and Imperialism* (1993), Edward Said proposes the **contrapuntal readings** of literary texts, that is, the mutual haunting of different spaces, histories, and perspectives within the larger arc of colonial domination.[72] One set of histories—for example, colonial slavery in the Caribbean—is induced to haunt another set of histories—for example, Jane Austen's England. But counterpoint often structures films themselves. The already-mentioned *Even the Rain* (2010) practices **contrapuntal history** by juxtaposing sixteenth-century debates about the Conquest with contemporary debates about globalization, thus illuminating the transtemporal connectivities between the two issues. The film stages the same *contraversia*—between the neo-Aristotelian Spanish jurist Gines de Sepulveda, who argued that a "just war" against Indians was justified because of their horrific practices, and the more open-minded priest

Bartolome de las Casas, who argued that the Indians would have a more-than-equal right to wage a "just war" against the European invaders. (The debate is portrayed as well in the Mexican film *Fray Bartolomé de las Casas* [1993], and in the film of the Jean-Claude Carrière staging of the very same debate in *La Controverse de Valladolid* [1992].)

In a much less radical way, the Brazilian TV Series/film *Caramuru: A Invenção do Brasil* ("*Caramuru: The Invention of Brazil*," 2001) counterpoints indigenous and European views of the "discovery of Brazil" through the Pocahantas-like real-life love story of the Portuguese Diogo Álvares Correia and the Indian princess Paraguaçu in sixteenth-century Brazil. The opening sequence attempts what might be called **polyperspectival narration** by having the narrator–host recount the mutual discovery of Europeans and indigene. One view, from the caravelas, shows the Portuguese amazed at the (relative) nakedness of the natives and the variety of their adornments, while the other view, from the shore, shows the Indians amazed at the gigantic ship and heavy clothing of the hairy and ill-smelling Portuguese. Each civilizational group projects its myths on the other; the Portuguese imagine they have happened upon the Biblical Eden, and the Indians think that the Europeans have come from their own mythical "Land without Evil."

The indigenous-authored (Guarani) film *Two Villages, One Path* (2008), meanwhile, offers a historically anchored **cultural counterpoint**. Against the backdrop of the ruins of the São Miguel Jesuit Missions in the South of Brazil, the film counterpoints two versions of conquest history—that of the official white tour guides, and that of the Guarani Indians, who, in order to survive, sell trinkets to the tourists visiting the ruins. While the official guides mystify the Jesuit "protectors" of the Indians, the Guarani remember the Jesuits as those who enslaved them and worked them to death. Indirectly alluding to a form of colonial enclosure, one Guarani explains: "the whites demarcated our territory. Imposed boundaries. Put up this fence for us to obey." The counterpointing of winners' and losers' history reminds us again of Walter Benjamin's call for the **dialectical image** that wrenches the past of the oppressed from history as a continuum of empty time defined by the victors.[73]

If *Two Villages, One Path* offers a perspective counterpoint related to the *Red Atlantic*, Sergio Bianchi's idiosyncratically titled film *Quanto Vale Ou É Por Quilo?* ("*How much is it worth, or is it by the Kilo?*," 2005) offers a **transhistorical counterpoint** related to the Black Atlantic. The film counterposes two historical periods—eighteenth-century slavery, and twenty-first-century class/race divisions and NGOs—in order to disinter common patterns of exploitative hypocrisy. Mingling past and present, fiction and documentary, the film's non-linear narrative highlights historical continuities and discontinuities. The pre-credit ouverture sequence, shot in the style of a historical costume drama, dramatizes an incongruous form of black protest. Based on an actual event in 1799, the scene shows a recently manumitted black woman named Joana (Zezé Motta) protesting loudly as armed men on horseback take away her own slave and hand him over to a white master. Shifting to the present, a sequence showing a black woman in a Rio favela, celebrating her 80th birthday, segues to a promotional video pleading for contributions to a humanitarian campaign dubbed "Smiles" sponsored by "Philanthropic Partners from Philadelphia." Thus, the film lampoons a narcissistic humanitarianism more concerned with the "brand" of the benefactors than with the well-being of the beneficiaries. Throughout, the film analogizes the old order of slavery with the new globalized order of racialized class oppression; the charitable *senhora* offering the slaves hand-me-down clothing morphs into an equally "charitable" contemporary NGO operative. One vignette condenses the logic of this *historical counterpoint.* Huddled with other prisoners in a suffocatingly overcrowded prison cell, the black actor Lazaro Ramos addresses us directly from behind bars: the Brazilian prison, he tells us, is the contemporary equivalent of the slave ship. Thus, the film gives voice to the **hauntologies** of slavery—a play by Jacques Derrida both of Marx's "specter of communism" and on the French pronunciation of "ontology"—the way in which slavery is both here and not here, totally surpassed and ominously present.

## Transformative Becomings

If the Bianchi film stresses the bitter legacies of the Black Atlantic, other films convey a more positive, or at least ambivalent, aspect of that same history in the form of the variegated modalities of cultural mixing generated by 500 years of uneven coexistence within the history of the Red (indigenous), the White, and the Black Atlantics.[74] In one of the most massively dramatic historical examples of what Deleuze calls "**becoming-other**," millions of indigenous people, Africans, Europeans, and Asians in the Americas were variously "othered," advantaged, hurt, and transformed by asymmetrical contact with people different from themselves. These power-laden encounters have found manifold expressions in cultural life, generating a wide range of terms for mixing, with diverse etymological–historical–disciplinary genealogies, whether religious (**syncretism**), biological (**miscegenation**), botanical (**hybridity**), linguistic (**creolization**), cultural (**indigenization**), or political–cultural (**assimilation**).[75] Each form of asymmetrical difference offers diverse and intersectional modalities, crudely summarized as top-down, bottom-up, and lateral.

Individual and collective self-shaping are arguably at the very kernel of world history generally—before the migration of peoples there was the migration of continents—but especially of the Americas with its unique mix of European, African, and indigenous cultures. From the beginnings, some Europeans "went native," married or raped native women, learned indigenous languages, and partially adopted indigenous ways. Geronimo de Aguilar joined the Mayans in the fight against Cortez and was killed by his fellow Spaniards. As a result of this very uneven history, very diverse people, as Guillermo Gomez-Pena puts it, "…fantasize about wanting to be of another race, about wanting to escape their own race and ethnicity … whites wanting to be Black or Latino, Latinos wanting to be blonde or Spanish, blacks wanting to be white, everyone wanting to be Native American. The desire to become Indian is a quintessential American desire … as much as they hate "real" Indians, they'd love to become Indian warriors or shamans."[76] One of Gomez-Pena's carnival-like practices is to invite audiences into **identity-makeover booths** where, with the help of make-up artists, they can choose to become a Mexican revolutionary, an Afrocentric activist, or to compose a designer hybrid identity. They then go out into the streets to provisionally "test run," as it were, what it means to take on one of these identities in the world. Partly mocking, partly endorsing, such experimental transformations of the self, Gomez-Pena speaks of "**ethnocyborgs**" who are "one-quarter human, one quarter technology, one quarter pop-culture stereotype, and one quarter audience projection."[77]

Nietzsche's words about the transformations of the theatrical spectator could easily be extended to cinema: "In the theater, one becomes a commoner, herd, woman, Pharisee, electoral mob, lord of patronage, idiot … there one becomes one's neighbor."[78] Audiovisual media are especially adept at staging and even shaping identity transformations. Through **cinematic chameleonism**, similarly, the mutable spectator comes to occupy a plurality of subject positions. What Edgar Morin calls cinema's "**polymorphous projection-identifications**" allow for ephemeral alignments with characters and situations in ways that both transcend and shape identity.[79] As in carnival, ordinary social positions are bracketed—as the poor confound themselves with the rich, the black with the white, the woman with the man, and so on. For Deleuze, "becoming-other" is at the core of cinema, in that filmmakers "must become others, with their characters, at the same time as their characters become others themselves."[80]

In *A Thousand Plateaus* (1980), Deleuze and Guattari become the theorists of a multitude of "becomings"—"**becoming animal**," "**becoming woman**," "**becoming Indian**," "**becoming minor**," and so forth. On the one hand, these formulations are very appealing because they seem to move beyond a paternalistic tolerance toward a real embrace of and identification with the other, to the point of partially becoming the other. At the same time, the concept has just a whiff of the **unilateral chameleonism** of the dominant, where white, male, heterosexual, middle-class, Western individuals play with identity in a way not available to the historically otherized. The empowered enjoy the privilege of "occupying" and "settling into" subaltern identities. The dominant pole is silenced but present; the empowered seem to masquerade as the disempowered— humans become animals, men become women, whites become minor, and so forth—in a one-way process that risks reproducing historical hierarchies and the *faits accomplis* of colonial domination. Historically, it is people of color who had to whiten themselves to become worthy subjects, women who had to internalize the male gaze, and so forth. Racially-advantaged global elites can easily traverse borders without suffering the usual real-world consequences. Hybrid and syncretic becomings, as Deleuze is doubtless aware, are therefore power-laden. It is no surprise, then, that some feminists (e.g., Luce Iragaray) have criticized the notion of "becoming woman," while some Native American scholars (e.g., Jodi Byrd) have questioned the notion of "becoming Indian."

Analysts such as Amy Herzog argue in defense of Deleuze–Guattari, however, that the obvious purpose is to dismantle binary notions of gender, race, and so forth. The valid point is that, for Deleuze, identity is always in a state of flux, always in motion, with a collective dimension of not simply representing pre-existing groups but rather of shaping new subjectivities, solidarities, affiliations, and identifications. For Deleuze, "becoming" (*devenir*) is not an imitation or reproduction of a pre-existing group but rather an exit from the dominant, not an arrival but rather a "movement toward." (An ambiguity in the hyphen in *devenir-minoritaire* creates doubts as to whether it should be translated as "becoming-minoritarian" or "minoritarian becoming"; the first implies one-way role-playing from above while the latter avoids unilateralism in favor of collective dynamism.) In a very evocative phrase, Deleuze speaks (in *L'Abécédaire de Gilles Deleuze*—his French television interview program with Claire Parnetin in 1988–1989) of the "**assemblage of all the minoritarian becomings**," a phrase that intimates a coalitionary alliance of social becomings in an emancipatory direction. In this sense, one might speak of catalyzing new constituencies of affiliation and solidarity.

For Deleuze, as for Rancière, it is not a question of representation of a pre-constituted group but rather a dynamic process of what Rancière would call **political subjectification**. At the same time, *bio-power* can create artificially cohesive groups who share little beyond their own victimization. The institution of slavery, for example, reduced extremely varied peoples to the common status of enslaved blacks, a historical situation which obliged the victims of slavery to act and resist as a group united in a common effort.

Deleuze's exhortation (in *What is Philosophy?*, 1991) that the philosopher "**become Indian**" calls for contextualization within the history of philosophy and the ongoing exchange of ideas between European and Euro-American thinkers and indigenous thought. Speaking generally, the figure and the reality of "the Indian" was a structuring presence in the Renaissance and the Enlightenment periods. The Indian question was disputed all around the Atlantic countries by Spanish jurists (Sepulveda, Vitoria), French humanists (Montaigne), British empiricists (Locke), American statesmen (Jefferson, Franklin), German metaphysicians (Hegel), and Brazilian writers from Pero Vaz de Caminha to Eduardo Viveiros de Castro, as well as by the indigenous themselves. The "Indian" got caught up in controversies about religion, property, sovereignty, and culture. Indeed, no in-depth analysis of modernity can bypass the indigenous peoples of the Americas, whether negatively, as the "victims of progress," or positively, as the catalysts for Western thinking and artistic production, discernible in the work of Shakespeare, Hobbes, Locke, Jefferson, Melville, Marx and Engels, Oswald de Andrade, Gilberto Freyre, and countless others.

However, in the French case, philosophers have been "**becoming Indian**" and Indians have been "becoming philosophers" for some five centuries, going back to Jean de Lery's sixteenth-century account of his experiences in Brazil and continuing up through Lévi-Strauss and Pierre Clastres in the twentieth century. When Montaigne, inspired both by his readings of Jean de Lery and by encounters with actual Tupinamba Indians, argued in the essay "Des Cannibales" that Indian ritual cannibalism paled in violence compared to the cruelties of European wars of religion, he was, in a sense, "becoming (philosophically) Indian." Indeed, French writers have conducted a five-century dialogue both with actual Indians and with the symbolic figure of the Indian as exemplar of freedom, moving from Jean de Lery to Montaigne to Rousseau, Diderot, and Voltaire in the eighteenth century to Chateubriand in the nineteenth century, to Lévi-Strauss, Pierre Clastres, and Rene Girard in the twentieth century.[81]

262 Keywords in Subversive Film/Media Aesthetics

Countless films from the Americas (and some from Europe) show white characters "becoming Indian," even if usually superficially and without much benefit to Indians themselves. Brazilian films such as *Caramuru: A Invenção do Brasil* (2001) and *How Tasty Was My Little Frenchman* (1971), Mexican films such as *Cabeza de Vaca* (1991), Venezuelan films such as *Jericó* (1991), and American films such as *Little Big Man* (1970) and *Dances with Wolves* (1990) feature "white Indian" characters. Such films give expression both to the historical reality and the phantasmatic white desire to "become Indian." The counterpart of the "white Indian" is the "red white man," or the Indian forced to assimilate into European culture. This "good Indian" has played a primordial role in the Brazilian national imaginary, in the form of the good Christianized Indian Peri in José de Alencar's novel *O Guarani: Romance Brasileiro* (1857), who also sacrifices himself for the whites. It is no accident that Brazilian modernists such as Oswald de Andrade despised Peri and all the other "Indian sons of Mary" and "Uncle Tom" Indians. The nineteenth-century Indianist movement, moreover, did not actually defend the actually existing Indian. Romantic Indianism coincided with the period of Indian annihilation. While indigenous people were forced to become white and Christian to survive, whites have always had the luxury of merely playing at being Indian.

As a transnational figure, the "white Indian" can be found all around the Red Atlantic, including in Europe, a product of 500 years of genocide, coexistence, racism, and romanticism. Various European countries have their own versions of the Indian. If the French Indian as object of projection was philosophical, the German Indian was literary and romantic. The specifically German fascination with the Brazilian Indian goes all the way back to the sixteenth century, with the bestselling travel account of Hans Staden, the German taken captive by the Tupinamba—and partial model for the Frenchman in *How Tasty Was My Little Frenchman*—the writer who, more than anyone else, disseminated the idea of the Brazilian cannibal Indian. Many Germans have claimed a special relationship to the Indian as a kind of cultural alter ego or benevolent *doppelganger* of the German people.[82] This flirtation with the Indian as a secret sharer of the German soul reached a paroxysm with the hugely popular Indianophile novels of Karl May (1842–1912), whose Apache hero Winnetou came to incarnate the German reader's desire to re-enchant the world through a vicarious "Native" experience.

One aspect of **intercolonial narcissism** is that colonizing nations often show immense sympathy for other peoples' victims.[83] Thus, the same nineteenth-century Germans who had little sympathy for internal others (such as the Jews) or external others (such as the nearly exterminated

Herrero), nonetheless, adored their Native American Winatoos. (Even Hitler loved Karl May novels.) More innocently, the many "Indian hobbyist clubs" active in Germany, which play at reenacting the "Indian life style" in teepees on weekends, trace their genesis to the cultural frisson engendered by May's novels as well as by carnivals, Wild West shows, and Hollywood films. Indeed, Karl May–style romanticism also generated an entire film genre—the German "Indianer Films" popular in both East and West Germany.

Various forms of transcultural "becomings" intersect in the remarkable documentary *The Master and the Divine* (2013), directed by Thiago da Costa as part of the Video in the Villages project in Brazil. The title refers to the two characters whose relationship structures the film—the "master," an eccentric German-speaking Silesian monk named Adalbert Heide who has been filming the story of his life with the indigenous Xavante for decades, and "Divine," a Xavante literally named "Divino," a former altar boy with Father Heide, and now a filmmaker and village leader. Doubly reflexive, *The Master and the Divine* is not only a film about filmmaking but also a film about the fraught yet friendly dialogue between two filmmakers representing very distinct and colliding cultures existing in relations of domination and subordination. Through **crisscrossed "becomings,"** the white European Heidi "becomes Indian" (while retaining his Western "positional superiority"), while a "Red" Indian Divino becomes "white" (while still remaining Xavante). The German master is a colonizer who Christianizes the natives and corrects their "primitive" and "pagan" ways and turns them into workers. Yet, his approach is in some ways dialogical; he learns about Xavante culture, is fluent in Xavante, has a Xavante name (*tsa amri*), knows and defends some Xavante customs, and is on some levels accepted by the Xavante as one of their own. Heide is, in short, the *colonisateur sympathique* who adores indigenous culture but only in what he regards as its ideal "primitive" and proselytizable *tabula rasa* form.

Commenting on Heide's films, the director notes that Heide "constructs himself as a hero." Heide sees himself as a mini-God, the self-described *factotum* (etymologically, he who "does everything") who teaches the Xavante the love of God and of labor. In his own mind, Heide embodies a series of Western cultural heroes: he is at once Prometheus and Prospero, leader, pedagogue, and boss. Presented on a German TV program as a white adventurer in the tropics, Heide is a self-declared "white Indian," a European who has "gone native" to the point of sporting war paint and a Xavante headdress. The dialogue between the master and Divino stages a battle of two cultures and two aesthetics. But rather than a Manichean struggle between a clearly defined colonizer and his colonized victim, this battle reveals a number of paradoxes and ambivalences. Ironically, it is the priest who cultivates a "positive image" of the Xavante—one steeped in primitivist images of the noble savage—while Divino has no qualms about showing negative Xavante behavior such as drunkenness and tribal dissension. While Heide sweetens everything in an epic-romantic style, Divino prefers a self-reflexive critical realism that foregrounds the tensions not only between the Xavante and the whites, but also among the Xavante themselves. While the priest prefers pastoral shots of traditionally attired Indians rowing canoes on pristine creeks, underscored by Andean flutes, the supposedly nature-loving Indian prefers talking heads, especially those elders similar to his father who can provide vital information about Xavante history. In a kind of phantasmatic indigeneity, the older European filmmaker, in a regime of **cinematic tutelage**, imagines himself as "protecting" the image of the Xavante, and seems obviously threatened by the indigenous upstart who might end his imagistic and cognitive monopoly. When Heide needles Divino for having forgotten traditional skills such as headdress making, Divino responds that although he has forgotten how to make them he can always relearn the practice by looking at his own film. As a high-tech Indian, Divino mocks Heide for his lack of mastery of Final Cut Pro. The Indians, we see, are answering back, giving as good as they get, as they probably always did, even if that backtalk did not usually make its way into the official histories.

Not only does the figure of Heide as a white Indian go far back into cultural history, so too does the Divino–Heide relationship. Overdetermined by a complex web of images and tropes, their relationship reincarnates the German Shatterhand's alliance with Winnetou in the Karl May novels (and their film adaptations); he even jokingly calls Divino "Winnetou." Their friendship recalls those cross-race homoerotic "bromances" between European and indigenous men that have marked literary and filmic history: Crusoe and Friday in *Robinson Crusoe*, Ishmael and Queequeeg in *Moby-Dick*, the Lone Ranger and Tonto in the TV Western. In the German Indianer film that Heide projects for the Xavante, the Winnetou character—obviously a white actor in redface—sacrifices his life for the German Shatterhand.

On Brazilian television, meanwhile, even Indians get to "play Indian," as we see in an astounding sequence that shows Divino as a child responding to the call of the blonde TV star Xuxa—wearing a Sioux warrior headdress—singing "*Vamos brincar de Indio*" ("Let's Play Indian"). To the accompaniment of "Indian war cries," Xuxa leads the children in a happy song:

> Let's play Indian, but without anyone to capture me!
> Come, join my tribe? I'm chief and you're my partner.
> …
> Come paint your skin so the dance can begin…

Similar to Heide, Xuxa is better at playing Indian than the Indians themselves; she has to teach the Indians to "become Indian." She is the *cacique* who makes pale homages to Indian dignity in fake Indian-speak ("Indian make noise. Indian have pride."). The lyrics honor the Indians even while demeaning them. As Xuxa drags the frightened-looking Xavante boys into her circle of fun, they look awkward and reluctant. With their body paint, they become Hollywood extras ("spearchuckers)," in a spectacle where she plays the starring role. Xuxa tries to teach them to be good little Indians, but they are not very good pupils, not really good at becoming Indian, and in a kind of sullen opacity, refuse to play her image of themselves.[84]

The "white Indians" represent only one version of the variegated **mutational fictions** typical of the Americas (and beyond). All these unpredictably mutating identities nourish a specific form of the fractured chronotope, this time characterological, as manifested in the trope of **racial metamorphosis**. In films such as *Macunaíma* (1969) in Brazil, and *Zelig* (1983) in the United States, chameleonic characters literally change color through **ethnic synchresis**. As an elusive protean entity in constant metamorphosis, perpetually *sous rature*, Mário de Andrade's oxymoronic protagonist, the "hero without any character" is born black and Indian, but subsequently becomes white, a Turk, and so forth. In the North American counterpart film, Woody Allen's "chameleon man" Zelig, similarly, is born white and Jewish but, in an orgy of becoming, transforms himself into a Greek, a Chinaman, a Black man and an Indian, leading to his denunciation by the KKK as a "triple threat" to American values.[85]

In a sequence of racial transformation, the black Macunaíma (Grande Otelo) turns into the white Macunaíma (Paulo José). When Macunaíma and Jiguê's girlfriend Sofará (Joanna Fomm) go into the woods to set a trap for a tapir. When Sofará gives Macunaima a marijuana joint, one puff turns him into a handsome prince. The pair romp and gambol in the woods as we hear an old carnival song—"Peri and Ceci"—that references the characters from the Indianist novel *O Guarani: Romance Brasileiro* (1857), where Peri is the noble savage Indian and Ceci the Euro-Brazilian woman with whom Peri is in love. The sequence, occasionally misread as racist by North American audiences, is in fact a satirical barb directed at the Brazilian "economic miracle" of the late 1960s. Sofará, the European "Ceci" of the allegory, is dressed in an "Alliance for Progress" sack. Her magic cigarette, that is, American intervention, has turned Macunaíma, hero of his people, into a papier-mâché prince, just as the "economic miracle" touted by the military junta supposedly turned Brazil into an apparently prosperous nation. (In fact, the prosperity was short-lived, consisting largely of a brutal transfer of wealth from bottom to top, and soon gave way to a record national debt and giveaways to transnational [mainly North American] corporations.) At the very nadir of the dictatorship, through **transnational allegory**, the film managed to outwit the censors and call critical attention to racism, militarism, and imperialism.

## The Shape-Shiftings of Popular Culture

The trope of racial metamorphosis renders literal, visible, and palpable a process that usually remains invisible—the ethnic synchresis that occurs when diverse populations brush up against and "rub off" on one another. The process of **asymmetrical chameleonism** that characterizes multi-racial societies in the Americas comes up in manifold ways in contemporary popular culture. At times, it emerges in regressive and racist forms such as blackface minstrelsy, where white men (usually) blackens up their faces and wears fright wigs in a performative caricature of blackness. The phenomenon of "passing" in such classical race melodramas as *Imitation of Life* (1959) or in contemporary novels/films such as *The Human Stain* (2000), meanwhile, embeds an assumption of white social advantage. "Passing for black," meanwhile, implies a social fall or at times a sociological experiment, as in *Black Like Me* (1964), where a white journalist passes as black in order to dramatize black oppression for a white audience. Another rather ambiguous version of what Deleuze calls **becoming minoritarian** has recently taken the form of "whigger" characters—whites who wear baggy pants and perform hip-hop style, who want a piece of blackness (except, as Greg Tate put in a title, "for the burden")—in such figures as Warren Beatty as a rapper in *Bullworth* (1998) or the hip-hop sexual groupies in James Toback's *Black and White* (1999), or in Dave Chappelle's unforgettable sketch about the blind black wizard of the Ku Klux Klan. Within the chiasmus whereby a black man hates black people but some white people love them, in the sketch's finale has the black Klan member call whiggers "niggas." While the black man misrecognizes himself as white, the whites respond with a high five to the honor of being inter-pellated as black.

Although these mutational fictions take myriad forms, they all point to the mutabilities of race and identity in a structurally racist society. A quick taxonomy of the more striking figures and genres would include: (1) the **racial *bildungsroman***, or whites blacken themselves to live, learn, and communicate the reality of racism to skeptical whites (e.g., *Black Like Me*, 1964); (2) **comic/didactic switcheroos**, where racial transformation triggers a pedagogical process for white racists—a rich white man in

*Watermelon Man* (1970), a racist Frenchwoman in *Agathe Cléry* (2008); (3) **allegorical power reversal** (*White Man's Burden*, 1995); (4) **surprise relative plots** that turn on the sudden appearances of an unknown new (white or black) member of a family thought to be racially homogenous; (5) **thespian transformation** (Robert Townsend as King Lear, Superman, and "Rambro" in *Hollywood Shuffle*, 1987); (6) **whiteface drag** (Shawn and Marlon Wayans in *White Chicks*, 2004); (7) **multi-actor characters** (*I'm Not There*, 2007); (8) **morphing race** (the racial kaleidoscope in Michael Jackson's "Black or White"); (9) **posthumous race-change** (Chris Rock turns white in *Down to Earth*, 2001); (10) **transracialized classics** (Orson Welles' 1936 "all-black *Macbeth*" play; *Carmen Jones*, 1954; *The Wiz*, 1978); (11) **transtextual/transsexual adaptation** (*Karmen Geï*, 2001, as a lesbianized and Africanized *Carmen*); and (12) **open-ended theatrical alterity** (Boal's "Theater of the Oppressed," where "spec-actors" can freely choose to enter into the spectacle across lines of race, gender, and sexuality).

The ubiquity of the theme of magical racial shape-shifting in popular culture is a clear index of widely shared desires, anxieties, and utopias of becoming. In earlier times, this desire for racial shape-shifting took the form of the Jewish Fanny Brice singing "I'm an Indian," or French singer Gilbert Bécaud singing "*Je suis Indien*," or simply of children playing "cowboys and Indians." It also takes the form of the **thespian chameleonism** of Anna Deveare Smith incarnating a wide gallery of ethnicities in her filmed one-woman performances in plays such as *Fires in the Mirror* (1992) and *Twilight: Los Angeles, 1992* (1994). Working from literal transcriptions, Smith makes others' words her own, constructing **hybrid characters** who are at once unmistakably her own African-American self and versions of a variety of ethnic "anothers." For Anne Anlin Cheng, Smith's strategy is based on **melancholic incorporation** by which the spectator is made to see conflictive views and groups as occupying a single stage and body.[86] By playing so many diverse roles, Smith hyperbolizes the **multiple-consciousness** (as an amplification of DuBois' **double consciousness**) and code-switching that are a virtual necessity for oppressed people managing conflictual demands in a racist society.

The humorous aspects of these various ethnic tensions and synchronicities form the basis of much of the sketch comedy of Richard Pryor, Whoopi Goldberg, Chris Rock, Wanda Sykes, Stephen Colbert, Key and Peele, and Dave Chappelle. While not necessarily radical in political terms, this work has the signal virtue of shattering the essentialist doxa of single, coherent "races." It also moves beyond the problematic trap notions such as "positive image" and "color blindness." Stephen Colbert mocks the idea of liberal color-blindness by claiming that he has no idea whether his guests are white or black. "I don't see color, even my own," claimed Colbert, adding "but they tell me I'm white, and I must be because I spend all my time denying that I'm a racist." Some of the new black comedy instantiates what Toure, borrowing from Thelma Golden, calls a **post-black aesthetic**, one that manifests a post-Obama confidence and an irreverent lack of concern with "positive images." In her "now-that-we-have-a-black-president" sketch, Wanda Sykes cheerfully reports that she can now carry giant watermelons out of supermarkets with pride. Even slavery can be grist for a comedy of racial inversion, as in the Key and Peele sketch where the duo complains at an auction-block that the slave owner is showing favoritism toward darker-skinned blacks; in an anachronic discourse, the slave owner accuses them of "racism."

A Chappelle's sketch, meanwhile, stages an athletic-league style "racial draft" for a multi-racial crowd segmented into ethnically-separated cheering sections, where the audience is asked to assign celebrities and politicians to a single "correct" racial team. Although the parodic draft supposedly aims at clarity of racial definition, it only reveals the utter impossibility of any such clarity in an irreversibly mixed society. "The Blacks" vote to give Colin Powell and Condoleezza Rice to "The Whites" (suggesting that politics trumps race); Tiger Woods rediscovers his blackness and mangles black slang (suggesting that food and language affect our perception of color); Lenny Kravitz joins the Jewish people (religion trumps race); the Wu Tang Clan come out as Asian (culture trumps race), and so forth. Ridiculing stable and essential identity as chimerical, the sketch indirectly mocks the infamous "one-drop black rule," which makes anyone, even of the most partial African ancestry, "black," and—the inverse—"one-drop white rule," which makes any Indian, of even very partially European ancestry, bureaucratically "white." The commonality is in the disempowerment of each group, one in terms of generating more slaves, the other in dispossessing Indians of their right to land.

## Metaphysical Cine-Poetry

In a more sober vein, the fractured chronotope has affinities with what might be called "**metaphysical cine-poetry**." The term "metaphysical conceit" was initially coined by critics such as Samuel Johnson to describe the artistic procedures of seventeenth-century "metaphysical poets" such as George Herbert and John Donne. In a literary anticipation of cinema's *montage interdit*, the metaphysical conceit consists in a provocative comparison between two unlike objects—lovers and saints, separated lovers and the legs of a compass—within a fused contradictory whole. In "Hymn to God in my Sickness," Donne analogizes his own deathbed agony by stressing the **disjunctive affinities** between two unlike situations: an orchestra tuning up for a concert before the king, and Magellan searching for a passage to the Pacific. In cinema, the juxtaposition of shots, or the superimposition of music or commentary on an image, allows for a kind of **metaphysical cine-poetry**, a linking of incongruous images where a *discordia concors* joins dissimilar entities and suggests occult resemblances. As a leading practitioner of *metaphysical cine-poetry*, Godard, in *Histoire(s) du Cinema*, Chapter 4(b), quotes poet Pierre Reverdy: "[The Image] cannot be born from a comparison but from a juxtaposition of two more or less distant realities. The more the relationship is distant … the stronger the image will be." The famous shot in Godard's *Two or Three Things I Know About Her* (1967) that superimposes whispered philosophic ruminations on successively closer shots of espresso coffee cup foam offers a splendid example. The evocative powers of language meet and channel the polysemic openness of the image, showing that we sometimes literally perceive the world *through* language. As the coffee cup disappears, the verbal evocation of "galaxies" induces us to imagine—almost *see*—drifting nebulae within the majestically swirling foam. That which is so sublimely immense as to defy human comprehension—the galaxies—emerges from the porcelain confines of an espresso coffee cup.

We find this same Renaissance play with extreme differences of scale in Guzmán's *Nostalgia for the Light* (2010). As with the Godard film, the Guzmán film too invokes the galaxies. The film's *discordia concors* meditates on the relationalities between three apparently discordant entities: (1) astronomers scanning the sky above; (2) archeologists exploring what lies beneath the earth below; and (3) indefatigable Chilean widows searching the desert's surface for the bones of relatives murdered during the dictatorship. Although astronomers, archeologists, and widows would not seem to have much in common, the film reveals their subterranean affinities. All three are exploring the past—the archeologists and the widows, obviously, but also the astronomers witnessing events that occurred light years earlier. All three are also linked to the space of the Atacama Desert, a moisture-free place resembling the surface of Mars. The site's dryness enables it to conserve the human and animal past—with untouched remains of fish, mollusks, Indian petroglyphs, and even mummified humans—while allowing unusual visibility for telescopes. The same lack of humidity that helps astronomers scrutinize the universe also helps archaeologists and Chileans trace the remainders of the past. The women scour the desert for calcium in the form of bones of their murdered relatives, while the astronomers look for calcium as a remnant of stars and the Big Bang. (One of the women, Vicky Saavedra, reports crying endlessly while clinging to the single relic of her brother's material being—a foot.) In a kind of **astronomical sublime**, the observer is overwhelmed by the unmasterable totality of an infinitely vast universe, as uncannily beautiful images of asteroids segue into extreme close-ups of asteroid-like bone fragments. A skull becomes a *paysage moral*. In a case of the **microscopic–astronomical sublime**, the closest of close-ups transition into the longest of long shots; we see the world in decaying bones, the universe in a grain of Atacama sand.

Guzmán's poignant **film essay-meditation** begins with a shot of a creakingly archaic German telescope and images of the moon, as Guzman as narrator recalls his childhood passion for astronomy. After astronomer Gaspar Galaz explains that astronomy helps us look into the past to understand our origins, archeologist Lautaro Núñez Atencio adds that archeologists too recreate the past on the basis of meager traces. Luís Henríquez, a survivor from Pinochet's Chacabuco concentration camp, describes how a cohort of about 20 prisoners, led by Doctor Alvarez, learned astronomical theory during the day and how to identify constellations at night. Studying the cosmos gave them a paradoxical feeling of freedom during imprisonment. What is prison when one has the freedom to wander among the stars? What is exile when one feels at home in the Milky Way? The military, fearing that the prisoners might use the constellations to guide an escape attempt, banned the astronomy lessons.

*Nostalgia for the Light* (2010) is multi-chronotopic in Bakhtin's sense. Quite apart from the film's adherence to the Menippean three-plane schema (earth, sky, underworld), the film orchestrates multiple chronologies—the human life span, the life of species, the life of planets and galaxies, the birth and death of a dictatorship—all emerging from a single topos. The Guzmán film also rhymes with Deleuze's reference in *Cinema 2: The Time-Image* (1989) to **sidereal time** as "a system of relativity, where characters would not be so much human as planetary, and the accents not so much subjective as astronomical, in a plurality of worlds constituting the universe."[87] Various lived temporalities converge with the buried histories of a desert that shelters ancient rock paintings, pre-Columbian mummies, dinosaur remains, Pinochet' victims, and the corpses of the first, aboriginal *desaparecidos*—the massacred indigenous people. Guzmán reminds us of the matter of memory, and the memory contained within matter itself. For Guzmán, those with memory are able to live in the fragile present moment, while those without memory are psychically homeless. Pinochet's victims remember the very same events that other Chileans, resisting the gravitational force field of memory, try to forget.

In the end, *Nostalgia for the Light* communicates a sense of **politicized mysticism**, a subdued tenderness for people and the universe, a Dantean wonder at the "love that moves the sun and the other stars." The film heralds what risks becoming a final form of politics rooted in a **galactic consciousness** of species vulnerability, a proleptic nostalgia for our not-yet-lost planet. In their lunatic search for the truth, the astronomer, the archeologist, the cineaste, and the widow, to borrow from Shakespeare, are "of imagination all compact." The filmmaker's eye, in a fine frenzy, "doth glance from heaven to earth, from earth to heaven," bodying forth the "forms of things unknown." As an intergalactic meditation on time and space, the film brings us back to the perennial conundrums of philosophy, where one asks with childlike wonder: "When did time begin? Where does space end? Why is there something rather than nothing? And what makes us care?" And what special capacities, finally, does film have to address such issues?

# Notes

1   See "Forms of Time and the Chronotope," in Mikhail Bakhtin, *The Dialogical Imagination: Four Essays* (Austin: University of Texas, 1981).

2   Ibid.

3   D. B. Gilles: *The Portable Film School: Everything You'd Learn in Film School (Without Ever Going to Class)* (New York: St. Martins, 2005).

4   Felicity Colman (ed.), *Film, Theory, and Philosophy: The Key Thinkers* (Montreal: McGill-Queens University Press, 2009), p. 345.

5   Ivana Bentes, "Global Periphery: Aesthetic and Cultural Margins in Brazilian Audiovisual Forms," in Jens Andermann and Álvaro Fernández Bravo (eds.), *New Argentine and Brazilian Cinema: Reality Effects* (New York: Palgrave, 2013), p. 114.

6   David Bordwell, Janet Staiger, and Kristin Thompson, *The Classical Hollywood Cinema: Film Style and Mode of Production to 1960* (New York: Columbia University Press, 1985).

7   Corinn Columpar, *Unsettling Sights: The Fourth World on Film* (Carbondale, IL: Southern Illinois University Press, 2010), p. 173.

8   See Eleftheria Thanouli, *Post-Classical Cinema: An International Poetics of Film Narration* (New York/London: Wallflower, 2009).

9   David Bordwell, *Minding Movies: Observations on the Art, Craft, and Business of Filmmaking* (Chicago: University of Chicago Press, 2011), p. 169.

10  Bordwell, *As Hollywood Tells It*, p. 12.

11    Ibid., p. 119.

12    Eleftheria Thanouli, *Post-Classical Cinema: An International Poetics of Film Narration* (London: Wallflower, 2009).

13    See Bolter and Grusin, *Remediation: Understanding New Media* (Cambridge: MIT Press, 1999).

14    Thanouli, p. 178.

15    Bordwell, *As Hollywood Tells It*, p. 3.

16    Ibid., p. 128.

17    Ibid., p. 25.

18    See Alessandra Raengo, "In the Shadow," *Camera Obscura*, 83(28) (2013).

19    Fredric Jameson, "Third World Literature in the Era of Multinational Capitalism," in *Social Text*, 15 (Fall 1986).

20    See Ismail Xavier, *Allegories of Underdevelopment: Aesthetics and Politics in Modern Brazilian Cinema* (Minneapolis: University of Minnesota Press, 1989).

21    Roberto Saviano, *Gomorrah: A Personal Journey into the Violent International Empire of Naples' Organized Crime System* (New York: Farrar, Straus, and Giroux, 2006).

22    Felicity Colman (ed.), *Film, Theory and Philosophy: The Key Thinkers* (Montreal: McGill-Queen's University Press, 2009), p. 340.

23    Jacques Rancière, *Film Fables*, quoted in Colman (ed.), *Film, Theory, and Philosophy*, p. 339.

24    Patricia Pisters, *The Neuro-Image: A Deleuzian Film-Philosophy of Digital Screen Culture* (Stanford: Stanford University Press, 2012).

25    Jacques Deleuze, *Cinema 2: The Time Image* (Minneapolis: University of Minnesota Press, 1989), p. 181.

26    See Raul Ruiz, *Poetics of Cinema* (Paris: Editions Dis Voir, 1995), p. 73.

27    Robert Sullivan, "This is not a Bob Dylan Movie," *New York Times*, October 7, 2007.

28    From Ovid's *Metamorphoses*, quoted in Roy Walker, "The Golden Feast," in John Zerzan, *Against Civilization* (Port Townsend, WA: Feral House), p. 199.

29    Brazilian critic Suzana Camargo explores *Macunaíma* in terms of the Menippea in her *Macunaíma: Ruptura e Tradição* (São Paulo: Massao Ohno/João Farkas, 1977).

30    See José Muñoz, *Cruising Utopia: the Then and There of Queer Futurity* (New York: New York University Press, 2009).

31    Material in the next section borrows, alters, and expands materials already published in Robert Stam, *Literature through Film* (Oxford: Blackwell, 2005).

32    See Jean Weisgerber, *Le Realisme Magique: Roman, Peinture, et Cinema* (Paris: Editions L'Age d'Homme, 1987), p. 27.

33    Isabel Allende, *Eva Luna* (New York: Bantam, 1989), pp. 300–301.

34    Michel Foucault, in Josh Kun, *Audiotopia: Music, Race, and America* (Berkeley: University of California Press, 2005), p. 23.

35 Gabriel García Márquez, *One Hundred Years of Solitude* (New York: Avon Bard, 1971), pp. 291–292.

36 Bakhtin, "Forms of Time and of the Chronotope in the Novel," in *The Dialogic Imagination* (Austin: University of Texas Press), p. 243.

37 Ibid., p. 244.

38 See Gilles Deleuze, "The Fold: Leibniz and the Baroque," quoted in Timothy Murray, *Digital Baroque: New Media Art and Cinematic Folds* (Minneapolis: University of Minnesota Press, 2008), p. 35.

39 See Timothy Murray, *Digital Baroque: New Media Art and Cinematic Folds* (Minneapolis: University of Minnesota Press, 2008) and Angela Ndalianis, *Neo-Baroque Aesthetics and Contemporary Entertainment* (Cambridge: MIT Press, 2005).

40 See Paul Gilroy, *After Empire: Melancholia or Convivial Culture?* (London: Routledge, 2004).

41 See Nestor Garcia Canclini, *Culturas Híbridas: Estrategias para Entrar y Salir de la Modernidad* (Mexico: Grijalbo, 1990), p. 14.

42 See Mary Louise Pratt, *Imperial Eyes: Travel Writing and Transculturation* (New York: Routledge, 2007).

43 Deleuze, *Cinema 2: The Time-Image* (Minneapolis: University of Minnesota Press, 1989), p. 219.

44 Personal e-mail to Robert Stam on January 30, 2013. Awam has a marvelous capacity to write print-ready, quotable e-mails.

45 Deleuze, *Cinema 2: The Time-Image* (Minneapolis: University of Minnesota Press, 1989), pp. 222–223.

46 Quoted in Chris Dunn, *Brutality Garden* (Chapel Hill: University of North Carolina Press, 2001), p. 77.

47 See Caetano Veloso, *Verdade Tropical* (São Paulo: Companhia das Letras), p. 99.

48 For a more extended discussion, see Robert Stam, *Tropical Multiculturalism: A Comparative History of Race in Brazilian Cinema and Culture* (Durham: Duke University Press, 1997).

49 On Rouch, See Steven Feld (ed.), *Cine-Ethnography: Jean Rouch* (Minneapolis: The University of Minnesota Press, 2003).

50 See Jean Rouch, *Les Hommes et les Dieux du Fleuve* (Paris: Artcom, 1997).

51 For an excellent study of Rouch, Rocha, and their use of possession religions, see Mateus Araujo Silva, "Jean Rouch e Glauber Rocha, de um transe a Outro," *Devires*, 6 (1) (January–June 2009). For an excellent analysis of Rouch's relation to trance, see Cecilia Sayad, *Performing Authorship: Self-Inscription and Corporeality in the Cinema* (New York: Macmillan, 2012).

52 For an excellent discussion of Santo Forte, and Coutinho generally, see Cecilia Sayad, *Performing Authorship*.

53 For more on the Bakhtinian conception of "polyphony," see Mikhail Bakhtin, *Problems of Dostoevsky's Poetics* (Minneapolis: University of Minnesota Press, 1984).

54 See Mário de Andrade, *A Escrava Que Não e Isaura*, in *Obra Imatura* (São Paulo: Livraria Martins Editora), p. 268.

55    See Jean Epstein, "Bonjour Cinema and other Writings" in *Afterimage*, 10 (Autumn 1981): 19.

56    Robert Farris Thompson, "Aesthetic of the Cool," *African Forum*, 2(2) (Fall 1966): 85.

57    See Clyde Woods, *Development Arrested: Race, Power, and the Blues in the Mississippi Delta* (London: Verso, 1998), p. 108.

58    Steven Feld, "A Rainforest Acoustemology," in Michael Bull and Les Back (eds.), *The Auditory Culture Reader* (Oxford: Berg, 2003).

59    Nietzsche, cited in Alain Badiou, op. cit., p. 35.

60    Robert Farris Thompson, *Aesthetic of the Cool: Afro-Atlantic Art and Music* (New York: Periscope, 2011), preface.

61    Ibid., p. 7.

62    Arthur Jaffa, in Gina Dent (ed.), *Black Popular Culture* (Seattle: Bay Press, 1992), p. 266.

63    See Susanne Langer, *Feeling and Form: A Theory of Art* (London: Routledge, 1953).

64    José Miguel Wisnik, *Sem Receita* (São Paulo: Publi-Folha, 2004), p. 200.

65    Kun, op. cit., p. 16.

66    Michel Chion, *La Musique au Cinema* (Paris: Fayard, 1995), p. 140.

67    For parallel ideas, see also Amy Herzog, *Dreams of Difference: Songs of the Same: The Musical Moment in Film* (Minneapolis: University of Minnesota Press, 2010).

68    See David James, *The Most Typical Avant-Garde: History and Geography of Minor Cinemas in Los Angeles* (Berkeley: University of California Press, 2005), p. 325.

69    See Paul Gilroy, *The Black Atlantic: Modernity and Double Consciousness* (Cambridge: Harvard, 1993).

70    Kun, op. cit., p. 2.

71    Michel Chion, *Audio-Vision: Sound on Screen*, trans. and ed. Claudia Gorbman (New York: Columbia, 1994), p. 63.

72    Edward Said, *Culture and Imperialism* (New York: Knopf, 1993). For an analysis of counterpoint in relation to Bakhtin's use of musical metaphors, see Robert Stam, *Subversive Pleasures: Bakhtin, Cultural Criticism, and Film* (Baltimore: Johns Hopkins, 1989).

73    See Walter Benjamin, "Theses on the Philosophy of History" in Walter Benjamin, *Illuminations* (New York: Schocken, 1969).

74    Robert Stam and Ella Shohat develop the concepts of the "Red Atlantic" and to a lesser extent the "White Atlantic," in their *Race in Translation: Culture Wars in the Postcolonial Atlantic* (New York: New York University Press, 2012).

75    Often the discussion takes a metaphorical form—as when members of various ethic groups perceived as being overly assimilated are dismissed metaphorically as "oreos" (black on the outside, white on the inside), "coconuts" (brown on the outside, white on the inside), "apples" (red on the outside, white on the inside), and "bananas" (yellow on the outside, white on the inside)— the commonality being the dominant power of the internalized racism of whiteness as the "inside" identity.

76 Guillermo Gomez-Peña, *Conversations across Borders* (London: Seagull, 2011), p. 43.

77 Ibid., p. 114.

78 "Nietzsche against Wagner," in *Nietzsche Werke*, Alfred Baeumer (ed.), vol. 5/2 (Leipzig: Alfred Kroner, 1930 (translation by James Stam).

79 See Edgar Morin, *Le Cinema ou L'Homme Imaginaire* (Paris; Gallimard, 1980).

80 Quoted in Michael Chanan, *The Politics of Documentary* (London: British Film Institute, 2008), p. 213.

81 These ideas are developed at greater length in Robert Stam and Ella Shohat, *Race in Translation* (2012).

82 Some have even argued that the ancient Germans had been the symbolic "Indians" of the Romans. See Feest, *Indians and Europe*, p. 612.

83 For more on this concept, see Robert Stam and Ella Shohat, *Race in Translation: Culture Wars in the Postcolonial Atlantic* (New York: New York University Press, 2013).

84 For an excellent analysis of the Xuxa show, and of the role of the Indian within the Brazilian imaginary generally, see Tracy Devine Guzmán, *Native and National in Brazil: Indigeneity after Independence* (Durham: University of North Carolina Press, 2013).

85 See Ella Shohat and Robert Stam on Zelig in "Zelig and Contemporary Theory," *Enclitic*, IX(4) (1987).

86 See Anne Anlin Cheng, *The Melancholy of Race: Psychoanalysis, Assimilation, and Hidden Grief* (New York: Oxford, 2000).

87 Deleuze, *Cinema 2: The Time-Image* (Minneapolis: University of Minnesota Press, 1989), p. 102.

# 7

# Aesthetic/Political Innovation in the Digital Era

In this final chapter, the conclusion, we will further explore the radical possibilities of digital media—already partially explored in previous chapters—and also offer some ideas about the future of subversive aesthetics. What unique possibilities—or challenges—do digital moving-image media pose for aesthetic subversion? For that matter, what does it mean to demarcate a set of aesthetics, separate from those of film, television, or analog video, particular to the digital technologies, computer interfaces, and other so-called "new media"? *Keywords in Subversive Film/Media Aesthetics* has argued throughout that the very newness of new media is itself a mirage. Scholars such as Siegfried Zielinski have challenged the notion of a linear progression of technological advancement, and have instead privileged a history of interruptions, dynamic moments, and turning points, while others such as Lisa Gitelman have sought ways to more deeply historicize emergent media, expanding our understanding of how media histories are written in the first place. These approaches further buttress our understanding of "new media" not as a faddish novelty, but as always embedded in a broadly defined *commons* with aesthetic traditions rooted in multiple cultures.

At the same time, it would be myopic to suggest that technological innovation in mediatic forms of representation do not present distinct challenges and opportunities. New modes of technological reproduction, exhibition, and dissemination prompt changed attitudes on the part of artists and call into being new modes of public address and audience formations. Within film and media studies, discussions of digital media have been particularly preoccupied with characterizing the ontological differences between the photochemical indexicality of celluloid and the

*Keywords in Subversive Film/Media Aesthetics*, First Edition. Robert Stam with Richard Porton and Leo Goldsmith.
© 2015 John Wiley & Sons, Inc. Published 2015 by John Wiley & Sons, Inc.

digital image's processes of algorithmic encoding.[1] While such questions of medium-specific ontology are important, we might nonetheless question the utility of a comparison between something so materially specific as celluloid and something so categorically diffuse as "digital media." Indeed, the sheer multiplicity of digital media—which, even if we speak only of digital video, arises in a vast array of forms, formats, and contexts viewed on a seemingly innumerable variety of screens and platforms (cinemas, handheld devices, monitors)—confounds easy categorizations of its origins, uses, and effects. Malcolm Le Grice's term "**hydra-media**" suggests the multi-functionality that digital technology brings to representational media. This diversity of forms and functions has led scholars such as Alexander Galloway to focus on the interface, not so much as a way of identifying the thing itself as a way of describing its modes of mediation and representation. Galloway calls this the "**interface effect**": a way of addressing the apparatus not as an object or specific technology but as a set of processes effecting certain results—"not media, but mediation itself."[2] Harun Farocki, in his 1995 film *Interface*, identifies it as "a point of relation to the actual world," thus *foregrounding the apparatus* by calling attention less to its mechanics than to its effects by underscoring the processes by which different technologies mediate and virtualize the real.

Consider just two seemingly different, but related digital examples: Wolfgang Staehle's *Empire 24/7* (1999–2004) and Phil Solomon's "*EMPIRE*" (2012). Both are *revisionist adaptations* of Andy Warhol's 1964 8-hour in long-take endurance and *in extremis* observational cinema. Staehle's work remakes Warhol's film using a live feed of streaming online video, simulating a *surveillant gaze* or a kind of **closed-circuit realism**. Solomon's work achieves similar results by simulating Warhol's portrait of the Empire State Building entirely within "Liberty City" (the virtual world based on New York City), of the PlayStation video game *Grand Theft Auto IV* (Rockstar Games, 2008), appropriating game space as a kind of **video game heterotopia** of impossible physics (including supernatural weather patterns and moon phases), the *digital sublime*, alternate temporalities, and virtual perspectives. However, while each work is clearly distinct in the precise digital technologies employed, what unites the two works is the way in which both foreground *not* the technological apparatus—the digital gadgetry so often fetishized in discussions of new media—but rather the very everydayness of their digital gazes. In both works, the materiality and technological innovations of the digital interfaces themselves seem less important than the ways in which the digital interface has, in a way, become simultaneously invisible, in the sense of being hidden within an infrastructure of surveillance and control, and omnipresent, in the sense of being seamlessly integrated into the patterns of our everyday consumption of advertising and media and interaction with networked social environments.

Access to a wider variety of tools for the making, manipulation, and dissemination of media has also occasioned new sets of social relations— new relationships between makers and audiences, users, and producers that often exist beyond the reach of the state and the mainstream media. Yiman Wang notes how the materiality of modern cameras—their portability; their use of small LCD screens in place of viewfinders; and their ubiquity as everyday objects that presume no authority, institutional backing, or professionalism—contributes to a process of "decoupling the documentary maker and the camera," thus allowing makers and subjects alike to regard the camera as a shared tool, representing alternate perspectives rather than those of narrative or semiotic authority.[3] This has enabled the already mentioned *democratization of voice and authorship*, which fuses these formerly hierarchized roles into the single figure of the "prosumer"—the producer–consumer subject—who generates and distributes his or her own media, and buys media generated by other prosumers via online communities centered around collaboration and mutual support.[4] Dan Harries coined the term **"viewsing"** to combine viewing the media and using it.[5]

In its ideal sense, **prosumer aesthetics** call forth a Brechtian critical spectator with a call to praxis that would overturn and reclaim the *aesthetic commons* and the industrial apparatus of image-making. For underserved and underrepresented populations, digital media has certainly offered greater access to moving-image technology, as evidenced by the proliferation of community-access media outlets, the rise of *indigenous media*, and the opening-up of new centers of cultural production outside of Western cultural centers or patterns of cultural philanthropy. This has especially been true in Africa, where the production of moving-image media has usually been supported by foreign funding (historically, from the Soviet Union; from former colonizers such as France and the United Kingdom; or, in rare cases, from Hollywood studios). The availability of digital cameras and modes of distribution has occasioned, among other things, the rise of the low-budget-big-business of **Nollywood** filmmaking in Nigeria, a multi-million-dollar industry that averages hundreds of productions each year and is now one of the largest film industries in the world, distributing its works across the continent and to diasporic communities throughout the world. As European austerity measures reduce funding sources for Francophone African *auteur* cinema, digital access allows local commercial industries to thrive, and Nollywood has served as a model for emergent film industries throughout the continent—for example, in Tanzania, Kenya, Uganda, and South Africa.[6] While Nollywood's products usually cleave to a range of familiar genres such as action movies, domestic melodramas, comedies, and the occasional horror film, the industry's resilience nonetheless provides an important means of cultural autonomy and an alternative to commercial infiltration from outside.

While it is not modeled on Francophone auteur cinema, Nollywood, despite its name, is also not really modeled on Hollywood in terms of its aesthetics or modes of production and distribution. The first major film industry to be founded *after* the advent of the Internet, Nollywood has adopted what Alessandro Jedlowski calls **"rhizomatic" production** arrangements, attributing the Nollywood video boom to two key factors: "the informality of the Nigerian economy and the adoption of digital technologies."[7] Nollywood offers a version of what John and Jean Comaroff call **"Afromodernity,"** which is not a "response to European modernity, or a creature derived from it" but rather a *sui generic* entity that is "actively forged … from endogenous and exogenous elements of a variety of sorts."[8] Unlike earlier minoritarian films in the West, but similar to the post–black wave in art, the films are not terribly concerned with presenting a "positive image" of Africa and Africans; rather, they exhibit the supreme confidence of presenting Africans, "warts and all," capable of 419 scams, bigamy, and green-card marriages. Although Nollywood films have been attacked as guilty of a new kind of "Tarzanism," critics such as Diawara argue that Nollywood should be saluted for telling African stories that everyone can identity with.[9] While technically imperfect, we must remember that some Third Cinema theorists called for an "imperfect cinema" that eschewed Hollywood production values. While usually not explicitly anticolonial or even critically postcolonial, the films at least have the virtue of resonating with the desires and curiosities of African and Afro-diasporic audiences. "By stealing from Hollywood the star system, the dress style, the music, by remaking Western genre films, and by appropriating the digital video camera as an African storytelling instrument," Nollywood is, as Diawara puts it, "a copy of a copy that has become original through the embrace of its spectators."[10]

While *camcorder activism* has been a feature of subversive aesthetics in many Western societies since at least the 1980s, the more recent proliferation of consumer video has occasioned a low-budget aesthetic of digital documentary, docu-realism, and citizen journalism in societies where independent media has been hitherto impossible or highly restricted. Such activities are not without risk: in Iran, blogger Sattar Beheshti was arrested, tortured, and murdered when his criticisms of the government on Facebook became classified as a "cybercrime." Filmmaker John Greyson, meanwhile, turned the lemon of his imprisonment in Cairo during the Tahrir Square events into the lemonade of a protest video concerning his 50-day detention. The video consisted of a retroactive diary, entitled *Prison Arabic in 50 Days*, showing Rosetta Stone–style flashcards illustrating key Arabic words related to their prison experience, beginning with words such as "investigation" and "prosecutor," moving through the word "enough," illustrated by a wristwatch, and ending with "you are free," "let's go," and "thank you," evoking their release after international protests.

Elsewhere, digital media have allowed alternative forms of journalism to thrive. One of the most prolific of such contexts is that of Chinese independent documentary production, which has quickly burgeoned into a mode of media resistance in the years since the 1989 Tiananmen Square protests and the introduction of consumer video cameras into the Chinese market. Engaged in the practice of *xianchang*, or "on-the-scene" shooting, Chinese digital or DV documentary has been a crucial medium through which to document and critique the widespread inefficiency, injustice, and oppression within the People's Republic.[11] Zhao Liang's 2009 documentary *Petition* uses hidden cameras to go inside the otherwise inaccessible enclaves of Beijing bureaucracy where petitioners for justice are repeatedly deferred and brushed off, if not manhandled, beaten, or arrested.

More recently, this kind of journalism has burgeoned via digital modes of distribution and collaboration—on microblogging sites such as Sina Weibo and video-sharing sites such as Youku-Tudou, as well as through efforts to circumvent government censorship initiatives such as the Golden Shield Project (also known as the Great Firewall of China). Huang Weikai's *Disorder* (2010) uses a form of *hybrid authorship* by drawing from more than 1,000 hours of footage from a Guangzhou video collective. The footage, taken by a dozen independent videographers on a mixture of video cameras and cell phones, captures uncanny, comical, and occasionally shocking moments of everyday life in urban China to portray the dysfunction of systems of urban order—pigs running loose on a highway; police busting black-market dealers of anteaters and bear paws; water flooding the streets and fire raging through buildings; a routine arrest devolving into police brutality and a civilian riot; a crocodile swimming down the Pearl River; and a baby lying discarded on a heap of garbage. These videos illustrate what Zhang Zhen has identified as a kind of **Chinese situationism**, through which "artists find the flexibility and anonymity of video extremely conducive to a direct critique of everyday life, resorting to elements of *cinéma vérité* and on-scene reportage."[12]

But they also exemplify the particular kind of decontextualized and distracted mode of reception of online movies that Huang is attempting to collage or even force together into a single work. The brevity of these clips; their offhand, improvised quality; and their low-grade camera phone resolution suggest a *cell phone cinema* aesthetic, often seeming similar to a collage or compendium of offhand, improvised videos captured on cell phones, or *e'gao* (Internet parodies) that might be accessed through Toudou or Youku, or circulated through email or MMS.[13]

Huang's film suggests digital documentary's renewed commitment to Jean Rouch's idea of **participatory camera**, in which filmmakers and subjects alike participate in a shared cine-anthropology that reclaims the terrain of everyday life from normative or hegemonic modes of discourse.[14] This collaborative practice is one that filmmaker Julie Perini calls "**relational filmmaking**," which locates reality through shared perspectives and co-creative strategies, rather than the usual top-down, privileged, professionalized points-of-view.[15] Mexican filmmaker Eugenio Polgovsky's work, in the same vein, frequently treats the camera as a participant in the action onscreen rather than an impartial observer. Both *Tropic of Cancer* (2004) and *The Inheritors* (2008) document the experience of Mexico's rural poor—the harsh lifestyle of bird and snake hunters in the desert region of Tamaulipas in the former, and the experience of child laborers in a diverse set of regions in the latter. Polgovsky's camera occupies an intimate yet oblique presence in each film, remarkably tactile and participatory, but one that frustrates our desire, as spectators, to intervene on the action and injustices we see onscreen. This creates an awkward space for the viewer, forcing into the foreground basic questions that have dogged the documentary form since its inception: problems of perspective, of veracity and transparency, of insider/outsider positioning, and of the role—social, political, aesthetic, entertainment—of the documentary artifice.[16]

In their interrogation of the positions of author, subject, and spectator alike, many of these digital documentaries seek to mobilize what Meg McLagan calls **witnessing publics**—that loose collection of individuals, constituted by and through the media, to act as observers of injustices that might otherwise go unreported or unanswered.[17] Expanding upon McLagan's idea, Leshu Torchin links this reconception of the public to the work of Benedict Anderson, Jurgen Habermas, and Arjun Appadurai in its constitution of an *imagined community* of conscientious witnesses. Digital video's enhanced mobility thus helps to forge new discursive spaces in which to bear witness to atrocity as an initial step to effecting change.[18]

Another kind of witnessing takes place with **FutARism**, a "movement," complete with a manifesto, led by Iranian–Canadian artist Amir Baradaran.

The project consists in discerning the radical potential of new technologies and apps. (The "AR" stands for **"Augmented Reality**," which superimposes digital effects on pre-existing images.) One of Baradaran's most provocative interventions was "Frenchising Mona Lisa," an AR app that allows the user to train his or her smartphone on Da Vinci's *Mona Lisa* and watch the mysterious Italian lady (superimposed on Baradaran's body) loosen her hair and wrap a French flag around her in the form of the (currently banned) Islamic *hijab*. AR alters perceptions but leaves the original artifact intact. Thus, Baradaran called attention to a number of paradoxes—Mona Lisa also wears a veil, but one that is socially approved; and, as an undocumented Italian model, she is an "illegal immigrant," yet allowed into the museum. The provocation defies the border separating the museum from the outside world; defies cultural borders by Gallicizing an Islamic icon demonized by the French right; and questions the rules of property and propriety in terms of who "owns" art. Mocking the Islamophobic hysteria of the right, a fake Daily Show-style news bit, available on Baradaran's website, shows putative riots in European capitals, protesting the "defacing" of the Mona Lisa by setting fires and destroying police cars. Newscasts speak of the "infamous **infiltration artist**" Baradaran, and hijacked archival footage shows the EU assembly denouncing him as the "assassin of European democracy." Through a split screen, we see Angela Merkel and David Cameron supposedly reacting with shock to the digital veiling, and yet other figures on the right seem more favorable to the gesture. Sarkozy is made to say that he "admires [Baradaran's] energy, courage, and extraordinary career," while Berlusconi adds a homo-erotic touch, calling him "young, handsome, and well-tanned." The result is a multiple *détournement*, of the technology, of the museum, and of news footage, having as its target both Islamophobia and the stuffiness of the museum.

## Beyond Accelerationism: Digital Montage and Duration

If digital photography's proliferation and mobility allow for new social formations to arise around the creation of moving images, the seemingly limitless possibilities offered by digital software and hardware for shaping and reconfiguring these images—what Philip Rosen calls digital media's **"infinite manipulability"**—suggests still more potentialities for subversive aesthetics.[19] Indeed, much of the recent scholarship on digital media has emphasized the ways in which the enhanced capacity for acquisition, storage, and manipulation of media has resulted in the widespread use—even standardization—of appropriation as an aesthetic practice. Practices that were once considered avant-gardist, such as *montage* and *collage*, become, Lev Manovich argues, mere industrial standards with the advent of computer software that automates operations of menu selection, remixing, sampling, synthesis, and open sourcing.[20] For Nicolas Bourriaud, the result of this proliferation of processes among cultural producers and consumers alike is an **art of postproduction**—as opposed to original artistic production—that attempts "to respond to the proliferating chaos of global culture in the information age."[21] This notion that culture is a collection of malleable, dissociated elements to be taken up and used at will makes *postproduction* a strategy that potentially subjects the aesthetic commons itself to a kind of *corporate avant-gardism*. Indeed, this immense and expanding battery of effects is usually put to use in the spectacular, uncanny verisimilitude of Hollywood CG animations, and many digital devices and operations, while still potentially radical, have become now commonplace in the industry: non-linear editing software, as well as in-frame combinations of spaces and temporalities through digital image compositing, and what Manovich calls "**spatial montage**" (also known as "**windowing**").[22]

There are acts of resistance to this grab-bag, to be sure: just as the *accelerationist aesthetics* of post-continuity prompt a counterstrike of *slow cinema*, digital media's enormous capacity for moving-image recording and storage has occasioned an aesthetic of the **digital long-take** in international art and documentary cinema. While Alexander Sokurov's *Russian Ark* (2002) deploys the *digital long-take* to summon the ghosts of the *chronotopic space* of Moscow's Hermitage Museum, *sensory ethnographers* Libbie Dina Cohn and J. P. Sniadecki push the device to the furthest extreme of direct cinema with *People's Park* (2012). In a 78-minute single-take tracking shot that floats and weaves through the Chengdu park of the title, the camera takes in a fluid succession of tiny sequences and portraits, as old folks dance, young children climb on rocks and run around, families drink tea, and people generally gaze back inquisitively or suspiciously into the lens. Here, the *digital long-take* serves as a canny way of addressing both the filmmakers' necessarily limited point-of-view, as well as a sly take on Bazin's anti-montagist notion of the long-take's capacity for spatiotemporal realism.

Even if the *art of postproduction* has largely served more commercial aims, with many more makers deploying its destabilizing techniques for apolitical (if frequently interesting) and spectacular images, there are nonetheless many artists whose experimentations with these media allow for meditations on *palimpsestic time*. In his *Decay of Fiction* (2002), the avant-garde filmmaker Pat O'Neill uses a combination of 35-mm film, time-lapse photography, and digital overlay to turn Los Angeles's Ambassador Hotel into a hallucinatory haunted house of Old Hollywood, with characters from old black-and-white movies stalking the halls of the hotel's crumbling present-day structure. O'Neill's own career bears the traces of this commercial/avant-garde schizophrenia, being split between the deeply personal experimental films he's been making since the 1960s and the for-hire visual effects work he has done for films such as George Lucas' *Star Wars* series.

While this box of digital tricks can be used to create expensive RealD simulacra to immerse the spectator in massive IMAX movie screens, they can also, at their most extreme, be used to create *critical utopias* that expand the possibilities of time and space, as well as individual and social identity. German–Canadian artist Oliver Husain's videos *Beau Mot Plague* (2001) and *Q* (2002) place live-action figures against green screens that transport them to **virtual heterotopias**—surreal, digitized versions of ersatz commercial zones and sterile super-malls—pointing out the inhuman banalities of the globalized present with wit and a flair for the bizarre. Similarly, Shana Moulton's works, including her ongoing video series *Whispering Pines*, explore themes of New Age renewal, domesticity, and the mutable, posthuman body through a barrage of digitally rendered tchotchkes and animated effects. More radical still is Ryan Trecartin, who harnesses a wealth of kitschy low-budget digital effects to make hallucinatory, hilarious, and frequently irritating videos that resemble both the shocking gender- and sexuality-bending John Waters' "Cavalcade of Perversions" (in his movie *Multiple Maniacs*, 1970) and the bubble-pop glossolalia of a teenager's Twitter feed, delivered at maximum volume, and all mixed through kaleidoscopic digital effects. In his videos, Trecartin and his friends appear in a variety of outrageous disguises and identities, screaming directly into the camera in preposterous accents, and completely taking over suburban environments. In the 2004 video *A Family Finds Entertainment*, Trecartin plays Skippy, a ghoulish, sexually ambiguous, psychopathic teenage boy who locks himself in his bathroom, playing with a knife. Shortly after he escapes, he is hit by a car and killed, only to be resurrected later in the video following a protracted and ornate ritual that culminates in a massive house party, featuring an enormous amount of body paint, glitter, lame, illegal fireworks, and wormholing scene transitions. The video is a catalog of Brechtian and Bakhtinian tropes— *gestus, distantiated acting, acting as quotation, the carnivalesque, transvestism, marketplace speech*, and the *bodily lower stratum*—placed in an intermedial blender, an amped-up version of Eisenstein's "montage of attractions." Trecartin's work creates not just a kind of manic queer utopia, but an expression of the kind of ADD-addled, polymorphous perversity and play of physical, racial, and gender identity found in the free, decontextualized space of the Internet and in utopic online spaces such as *Second Life*, which, as Vivian Sobchack has suggested, promise liberation from or malleability of identity.[23]

## Tools of Engagement: Interactivity and Digital *Détournement*

However, is the cyber–*Second Life*, in fact, the Bakhtinian *people's second life*? Perhaps Chris Marker thought so: in the last years of his life, the French filmmaker (along with his orange feline avatar, Guillaume-en-Égypte) was a sometime-inhabitant of the vast interactive virtual universe, where he "built" an online museum to house his photography and video work, reimaginings of famous paintings, and assorted curios, documenting it in his short video *Ouvroir*—named after the island that served as the location for the museum—which serves as a kind of travelogue of his surreal dreamscape.[24]

Of course, the openness and possibility of such spaces does not make them immune to regressive politics, especially in the form of racist and sexist pranks and aggression (instances of "griefer" culture). But this merely suggests the always-renewed need for intervention on the part of artists and activists in these putative utopias.[25] While the **myth of interactivity**, as Manovich has argued, may have been considerably overstated in the Internet's early years, the impulse to engage and interact has not shown signs of abatement in the digital era.[26] Indeed, the forms of distanced viewing that globalized digital telecommunications have normalized—what McKenzie Wark has called "**telesthesia**"—seem to engender a corresponding impulse to use newer media to destabilize the formal conventions and hierarchies of older ones.[27]

**Interactive documentary**, for example, reconfigures the linear organization of cinematic narrative to better match online interfaces and modes of engagement. Eline Jongsma and Kel O'Neill's expansive immersive documentary project titled *Empire* (2013), about the legacies of Dutch colonialism at several points around the globe, and Leanne Allison and Jeremy Mendes' *Bear 71* (2012), which follows a grizzly bear across Banff National Park, both deploy tools such as GPS tracking, multiple screens, and interactive interfaces that guide the user through variably complex amounts of information and narrative experiences. Whether *interactive documentary* actually represents a more truly "interactive" form than the supposedly more passive experiences of reading a book or watching a film in a cinema is perhaps less important than its attempt to seek more nuanced and adaptable approaches to narrative.

Even works that are not actually interactive can still borrow the **aesthetic of the interface** and its logic of comparison, data processing, and multiple displays. The work of Lebanese photographer, filmmaker, and "archival artist" Akram Zaatari often uses the visual schema of the computer interface to model interventions in the historical archives. In his 2005 video *In This House*, this interface aesthetic is used to literally dig up history. Using a multi-screen database-like frame, Zaatari's film provides documentation, photographs, and maps in various panes that support the main image—the laborious process of digging an enormous hole in the garden of a suburban home in order to find a letter buried there since the days of the Lebanon–Israel conflict. Zaatari's film makes tangible a project with which he, in his capacity as founder of the Arab Image Foundation, has long been concerned—unearthing those images that disturb rather than confirm dominant historical narratives. In an earlier film titled *Her + Him Van Leo* (2001), he conducts this search slightly closer to home, after discovering, in his mother's closet, a *risqué* photo of his grandmother taken in Cairo in 1959 by the famed portrait photographer Van Leo. What starts as an attempt to solve a family mystery (if not to satisfy a little prurient curiosity) soon becomes an affectionate portrait of an aging artisan, as photographer and video maker sit down for a series of discussions on the advent of video technology and photography's threatened future. Zaatari's work once again simulates computer processes to analyze Van Leo's images, with special attention given to his retouching techniques, but he also playfully editorializes with lush period songs and all-cap onscreen text, emblazoning his discoveries of Van Leo's nudes with the pithy epigram "GRANDMOTHER IS NAKED."

Many interactive operations are, of course, standard across digital media—Blu-ray menus, blockbuster tie-in websites, and online gambling portals boast much of the same interactive capabilities, if not more, in the service of synergizing and monetizing content across multiple platforms. This approach, which Henry Jenkins has labeled **"transmedia storytelling,"** is less concerned with the complexity and variability of narrative modes than with "creating a unified and coordinated entertainment experience" across as many delivery channels as possible, saturating markets and dominating attention.[28] In terms of subversive aesthetics, the trick is more to counteract than to merely interact—to take up the situationist practice of *détournement* in appropriating the materials of the digital and *occupying* the virtual commons.

In this way, this *sampling aesthetic* moves from music to other media and even theoretical conceptualizations of media. Extending often apolitical practices of cinephilia into the politicized realm of revolution, Patricia Zimmermann and Dale Hudson developed the concept of "**collaborative remix zones**" to define "zones where plural pasts, multiple temporalities, multiple artefacts, and polyvocalities can join together to reclaim public spaces" by adopting "strategies of radical historiography and reverse engineering."[29] Zimmermann and Hudson respond to the ways in which transnational media corporations (TMCs) "repurpose" classical and contemporary cinema as "classic," releasing films on special-edition DVDs and Blu-ray Discs, each purportedly offering an experience that is closer but still not the same as a film's original theatrical release on 35 mm or 70 mm. Rather than fetishizing the past as such singular and inaccessible moments, *collaborative remix zones* open the past to "fluid, multiple, polyphonic, and plural" moments that often look more toward the future than the past. They differ somewhat from the mash-ups of Hollywood blockbusters and hits that Barbara Klinger discusses in relation to media fandom.[30] Zimmermann and Hudson examine live remixes that take orphaned and amateur footage from national archives, alongside "pirated" media distributed on YouTube (such as the opening sequences to Mexican telenovelas) to describe ways that cinephilia can become subversively politicized. *Collaborative media zones* exercise a form of *anticanonicity* by incorporating "images and cinemas that have never circulated within transnational networks," so that cinephilia becomes a practice of "experience and exchange" in which film archives are not simply repositories for preservation but nodes in a network of cinephilic outreach.[31]

In Onward Project's *Trafficking in the Archives* (2006), for example, Technicolor's feature production of Chester M. Franklin's *The Toll of the Sea* (1922), starring Anna May Wong, becomes found footage, along with a Universal Newsreel documenting 1936 as a "bumper year" for ice harvesting, US Department of the Interior propaganda on Maine sardines from 1957, and James Knott's amateur feature film *The Tahitian* (1956). The curators, professional musicians, and filmmakers in Onward Project work with archivists from the National Film Preservation Foundation, the UCLA Film and Television Archive, Northeast Historic Film, and the Human Studies Film Archives at the Smithsonian Institution to "reconsider" early US cinema through its representations of "changes to the environment effected by humans in their quest for love and money."[32] (Onward Project's other collaborative remixes of early film include *Nanook Revisited* [2004] and "*Within Our Gates*" *Revisited and Remixed* [2004].[33])

In an era when TMCs exercise tight control over access to—and sometimes thoughts about—film, television, music, video games, and even the news, the power to provide a different "context" to the "content" of images through remixing collaboratively can subvert assumptions and expectations and politicize practices in ways that that extend those of the Grupo Cine Liberación and other revolutionary media-makers. The remixes by Onward Project perform critical interpretations of depoliticizing discourses used by TMCs to produce certain classical films as "classics" and filmmakers as "auteurs," accessing and reactivating an *aesthetic commons*.

## IRL Subversions: Tactical Media and Digital Materialism

Whether interactive or counteractive, these renewed means of engagement in the digital media on the part of the user are seen by many scholars as ways of challenging seemingly cold, inhuman digital perfectionism with a more human *aesthetic of mistakes*. Borrowing a term from filmmaker Harmony Korine, scholar Nicholas Rombes calls this human **"mistakism"**— seeking out and exploiting the flaws of digital media in order to disrupt its frequently smooth, shiny surfaces with humanism.[34] The *video game heterotopias* created with **machinima**—for example, Solomon's *"EMPIRE,"* which was "filmed" entirely within a video game's environment, often in ways parallel or contrary to the game's intended purpose—require just this kind of intervention, a reconfiguration of intellectual property for the artist's own ends, which frequently rub against the banal mass media protocols of the games' designers. More extreme in this regard, works such as Radical Software Group's *Prepared PlayStation 2* (2003), JODI's *Untitled Game (Modifications of Video Game, Quake 1)* (1996–2001), and *Max Payne Cheats Only 1* (2004) exploit the bugs and glitches mistakenly encoded in popular video games, **hacking** a popular skateboarding game in order to force it to malfunction, locking the skateboarding figure onscreen into jerky, flailing grooves and stuttering ruts. Film- and video maker Peggy Ahwesh has offered an even simpler *hack* with her 2001 piece *She Puppet*, which undermines the shoot-'em-up video game *Lara Croft: Tomb Raider*, exposing not only the glitches in code, but also the implicit gender relations of the game.

Programmer subculture frequently sees these *hacking* strategies as part of a tradition of resistance and innovation that reaches back long before the rise of digitality and extends much further in its disciplines and purviews. According to this definition, *hacking* lays claim to the whole *aesthetic commons* as a terrain for occupation, reuse, and reimagining—in both the virtual and physical spaces of the everyday, or in ways and spaces that blur the distinction between the two.[35] Thus, the *hack* may take the form of a virtual occupation and sit-ins conducted by activists in real space, and thus resemble other online forms of **tactical media**. Online activist groups such as Electronic Disturbance Theater (EDT) and Critical Art Ensemble, whose projects of **electronic civil disobedience** serve as **virtual sit-ins**, form updated versions of the long-practiced tactics of street-theater protests that use sheer numbers to block or barricade urban thoroughfares.[36] For the EDT, these strategies work just as well for inter-rupting the flow of networks as they do for physical spaces: repeatedly since 1998, EDT has deployed viral software to flood servers of websites run by the Mexican Government and anti-Zapatista organizations in response to an incident in December 1997 that resulted in the murder of 45 people at the hands of the Mexican Paramilitary in the remote Chiapas village of Acteal, Mexico. In response, EDT encouraged users around the world to download a type of software called FloodNet, which would swarm the servers of these websites with requests for website pages that did not exist, slowing and eventually shutting down the websites. Similar tactics were also used in 1999 against the website of the World Trade Organization, and in 2008 against a number of nanotech and biotech corporations said to be profiting from the war in Iraq.[37]

Where the ideology of wirelessness, cloud-computing, and mobile net-works promotes the idea of a dematerialization, diaphanousness, and intangibility of the digital, *tactical media* insists instead on **digital materialism**, encountering and taking hold of the virtual in its real-life forms and effects. These strategies work not just in the direction of immersive experiences such as **augmented reality**—in which apparatuses and projections enable interactions between digital devices and physical environments through the use of computer-generated sensory inputs such as GPS data or graphics—but also in more *mistakist* ways that seek to penetrate and take control of the smooth interfaces. In this way, then, countering the myth of the immaterial involves *revealing the apparatus* through interventions in its physical form.[38] This practice follows a long tradition of physical disruptions, including *Magnet TV* (1965) by Nam June Paik, and also the *glitch art* video clip *Digital TV Dinner* (1979) by Jay Fenton, Raul Zaritsky, and Dick Ainsworth, created using the Bally Astrocade video game console. At the start of the video, a voice explains "the absolute cheapest one can go in homemade computer art—this involves taking a US$300 video game system [and] pounding it with your fist so the cartridge pops out while it's trying to write the menu."

The DIY customization of cheap commercial electronic synthesizers via **circuit-bending**, pioneered by Reed Ghazala in the 1960s, meanwhile, has long been part of electronic music (and that practice too has older roots in John Cage's prepared pianos from the 1940s). Moving-image media *materialist* aesthetics, explicitly theorized by British filmmaker Peter Gidal in the 1970s, extend from a similarly extensive line of artisanal film and media practitioners.[39] More recently, the practices of **glitch** and **datamoshing** have utilized and exacerbated the artifacts, bugs, and errors of digital compression to create smeared, multi-colored distortions, in videos that exploit the effects of oozing, smearing, and disintegrating that occur once digital images are infiltrated and hacked.[40] Programmer Bertrand Planes' codec *DivxPrime*, developed in 2004, is often credited as the software that first enabled the exploitation of the realm of digital compression, but a wave of *glitch art* made by various means followed, including Takeshi Murata's *Monster Movie* (2005), a parade of morphing monsters ripped from Hollywood horror movies, and Simon Tarr's *Interruptus* (2011), a stroboscopic video of rainbow grids and blobs made from downloads of explicit adult videos that Tarr strategically halted mid-download (hence the title).

However, as Lisa Klarr reminds us, the project of *digital materialism* is not just about emphasizing the physical forms that technology takes, its objects, and interfaces. It is also a way of seeking out and exposing its material effects in the global chain of production. Klarr asks: "Might it then be possible to locate digital materialism in the body, be it the body manufacturing semiconductors or the body writing code?"[41] Some artists and programmers have taken up *digital materialism* as a means of implicating themselves within the patterns of production and consumption intrinsic to late capitalism, and perhaps trying to find ruptures, points of resistance, and ways out. Hito Steyerl's two (very) short videos, *STRIKE* (2010) and *STRIKE II* (2012), find the artist attacking moving-image apparatus with a set of tools: in the first video, Steyerl takes a hammer and chisel to an LCD monitor, and with a single but decisive "strike" smashes a jagged, abstract pattern onto the screen; in its sequel, she and her daughter attack the camera with a pair of hammers. Both videos find the artist "on strike" from representation, giving Glissant's *right to opacity* an extreme form, but do so via a highly performative act—the video art equivalent of punk-rock guitar-smashing. Similarly, JODI's hybrid performance-video project *Folksomy* (2008/2010) uses custom software to remix user-generated YouTube videos, most of which emphasize the users' ambivalent relationships with technology—from lovingly singing ballads to their iPhones to gleefully smashing laptops with hammers.

As these various approaches to *digital materialism* suggest, the strategies of digital subversion—indeed, of all such types of resistance—are concerned less with the interplay of media forms than with their real-world effects—the ways in which they bleed into and infiltrate the physical world. As we have suggested, the steady integration of digital technologies into the fabric of our everyday interactions in the form of small, mobile technologies has radically altered not only how we consume and perceive moving images, but also the social and cultural collectives that we form around them. For Paola Voci, "[s]maller screens' *individualized* (personal, portable, private) and at times clandestine acts of vision" have infiltrated everyday life, causing "(new) mediated cultures and web-based social networking and mobile cultures" to emerge.[42] Scholars Sean Cubitt, Nikos Papastergiadis, and Scott McQuire attribute this, in part, to digital media's "**transience**"—not its (temporal) ephemerality, but its material instability and spatial agility.[43] David Hogarth calls digital media "interlocal," in that they foster new communities and distribution channels for films and videos, as well as networks, that often skirt the restrictive broadcast parameters of nation-states and major media corporations.[44] Even if the "transience" of digital media makes them difficult to specify in any single material form, they nonetheless continue to shape physical and virtual collectivities, and physical and virtual spaces.

Nor is this shaping confined to the context of "smaller screens." During the 2011–2012 Occupy Wall Street demonstrations in Lower Manhattan, the "Bat Signal," Illuminator, and Occupy Cinema projects sought to make use of and democratize a distinctly "big screen" mode of exhibition: high-powered LED projectors that plaster slogans and moving images onto skyscrapers, visually "occupying" the skyline. Explicitly drawing upon a legacy of **radical exhibition**—from Russian Revolution's trains, which took artists such as Dziga Vertov and Vladmir Mayakovsky around Russia spreading multimedia agit-prop; to Polish projection artist Krzysztof Wodiczko; to international art group Graffiti Research Lab's use of open-source software and high-power laser technologies to throw large-scale "laser-tagging" of buildings—Occupy Cinema used car batteries and power inverters to power a mobile projection unit displaying videos—of Anna Pavlova performing *The Dying Swan*, Alain Resnais and Robert Hessen's *Guernica* (1950), Maya Deren's *Ritual Transfigured in Time* (1946), and some "Occupied" animated GIFs—onto buildings and surfaces, including an image of the famed local free-market mascot *Charging Bull*, a bronze sculpture by Arturo Di Modica.

In Brazil, meanwhile, **Media Ninja**, whose acronym in Portuguese stands for "Independent Narratives, Journalism, and Action," arose originally out of a 2005 collective of artists and cultural producers hoping to produce art, cultural events, and online content, but which came into its own when it began to use new media to plan, broadcast, and report on the demonstrations that swept over Brazil in 2013. With no central administration, the post-partisan collective broadcasts demonstrations via live-streaming channels on Twitcasting, and posts updates on Twitter, Facebook, Tumblr, Google+, and Flickr. Media Ninja is, as of this date, present in 200 Brazilian cities, constituting itself as an alternative form of media that records police brutality and spreads the word about demonstrations as they happen. The state voyeur is *vu*, recorded by hundreds of cameras and cell phones. The stunning success of Media Ninja has obliged politicians and the corporate media to deal with it, since the collective has far overtaken the conventional media in its capacity to perform on-the-spot moment-by-moment coverage of demonstrations on the spot, creating political action films in real time.

## In Guise of a Conclusion

The increased availability and mobility of technologies that enable projection and exhibition on a large scale, as Media Ninja demonstrates, hints at the possibility of a more widespread reclaiming of public space— not just the streets but the spaces around them—from advertisers and real-estate developers. But it also points toward digital media's capacity to offer new forms of resistance, which in turn might be deployed to shape new collectivities and public spheres. While it has become commonplace to speak of the end of innovation and the exhaustion of the avant-garde in a world where all the great works have already been achieved, the *fractured chronotopes* that we have discussed in the previous chapter, and the digital strategies examined here, do offer something that is simultaneously very old and very new. The aim of what Kluge provocatively calls the "**arrière-garde**" is not to "establish the new" but rather to "bring everything forward."[45] (According to philosopher Paul Feyerabend, even science, to advance, must return to older theories to overturn the scientific status quo.[46]) Against the postmodern nostrum that "all the stories have been told," many stories have in fact *not* been told, or perhaps, more accurately, have not been *heard*. The very availability of the *aesthetic commons* suggests that the elegiac "everything's-been-done" conventional wisdom of postmodernism was based on a monocultural premise. Once we open the lens toward the world's (multi)cultures—including indigenous cultures, simultaneous with the maximum use of digital chameleonisms of formats and media—the possibilities of fruitful interfecundations become infinite.

Aesthetic innovation arises, not exclusively but importantly, then, from multicultural and minoritarian knowledges and practices, from what Walter Mignolo, riffing on Mumbimbe and Gloria Anzaldúa, calls "**border gnosis**," or knowledge from a subaltern perspective, knowledge emerging on the borders of the modern/colonial world system.[47] The "new" in art—as opposed to a stagist "modern"—emerges from the transcultural encounters of a Picasso with African sculpture; from the comings and goings between Europe and Latin America of an Alejo Carpentier; or from the encounter of a Mário de Andrade with surrealism, on the one hand, and Amazonian legend and *candomblé*, on the other. "Newness enters the world," as Salman Rushdie puts it, through "hybridity, impurity, inter-mingling, the transformation that comes of new and unexpected combinations of human beings, ideas, politics, movies, songs [from] ... Mélange, hotchpotch, a bit of this and a bit of that."[48] Cultural creativity has often been linked to sites of massive migration and multi-faceted cultural encounters. The idea of an exhausted avant-garde derives from the myopia and amnesia of Westocentric epistemologies and monocultural aesthetics. Within a **polyphonic aesthetics** of mix-and-match, a recombinant art will always be both old and new. Artistic innovation occurs on the transnational and transgenerational borders of cultures and communities and discourses, as artists have deployed magic and trance to go beyond the stale, flat, and unprofitable platitudes of conventional narrative.

We would call, finally, for a **multi-genre radicalism**. The day is long gone when leftist theoreticians could posit a single correct model of cinema that would infallibly lead to revolution. The overall drift of this book, reflected in the wide diversity of terms and strategies explored, has been to argue for a multi-generic, poly-perspectival approach which recognizes that radical art theory/practice needs to develop a constellation of artistic "moods" and genres to fit extremely diverse constituencies and situations. A sense of social affect allows us to understand the differentiated ways in which social subjects feel, experience, and live the social distribution of the sensate life. In aesthetic terms, we might speak of a **radical rasa aesthetics**—a reformulated and radicalized version of the theories enunciated in the ancient Sanskrit texts—now retrofitted for contemporary subversive purposes. The *rasa* correlated the deities with specific moods (love, laughter, fury, terror, wonder) and colors. In an amplified secular version, we might think of radical art as orchestrating positive moods and currents—love, laughter, compassion, wonder—along with the negative moods of anger, disgust, envy, irritation—transfiguring them into kinetic collectivity against injustice, while also recognizing and naming as-yet-unnamed social desires.[49]

A multi-generic strategy would orchestrate genres and formats according to circumstances and audience, thus valuing satire for its political bite, tragedy for its human wisdom, agitprop for its immediate efficacity, melodrama for its emotional impact, reflexivity for its cognitive purchase, realistic drama for its persuasive power, stand-up comedy for its corrosive irreverence, avant-garde provocation for its gay relativity, and experimental films for their capacity to deregulate the senses. We have tried to be attuned to the strains of hegemony and resistance, ideology and utopia, critique and celebration, the hermeneutics of suspicion and the principle of hope, in which critical utopias assume and transform the everyday negativities of social existence into an affective community. A subversive media aesthetics needs both what Ernst Bloch called "cold currents" (the disenchanted analysis of concentrated economic power and its perverse effects) and "warm currents" (the intoxicating thrill of utopian hopes for egalitarian conviviality).[50] This book has been an attempt to radicalize the aesthetic emotion in hopes of achieving that only apparently oxymoronic goal—a **majoritarian avant-garde**.

# Notes

1   See, for example, Philip Rosen, *Change Mummified: Cinema, Historicity, Theory* (Minneapolis: University of Minnesota Press, 2001), pp. 301–349; and D. N. Rodowick, *The Virtual Life of Film* (Cambridge, MA: Harvard University Press, 2007).

2   Alexander R. Galloway, *The Interface Effect* (London: Polity Books, 2012), p. vii.

3   Yiman Wang, "'I Am One of Them' and 'They Are My Actors': Performing, Witnessing, and DV Image-Making in Plebian China," in Chris Berry, Lisa Rofel, and Lu Xinyu (eds.), *The New Chinese Documentary Film Movement: For the Public Record* (Hong Kong: Hong Kong University Press, 2010), p. 234.

4   Ritzer, G. and Jurgenson, N., "Production, Consumption, Prosumption," *Journal of Consumer Culture*, 10(1): 13–36.

5   Dan Harries, "Watching the Internet," in Dan Harries (ed.), *The New Media Book* (London: BFI, 2002), pp. 171–183.

6   See Matthias Krings and Onookome Okome (eds.), *Global Nollywood: The Transnational Dimensions of an African Video Film Industry* (Bloomington: Indiana University Press, 2013).

7   See Alessandro Jedlowski, "From Nollywood to Nollyworld," in *Global Nollywood: The Transnational Dimensions of an African Video Film Industry* (Bloomington: Indiana University Press, 2013).

8   See John L. Comaroff and Jean Comaroff, "Criminal Justice, Cultural Justice: The Limits of Liberalism and the Pragmatics of Difference in the new South Africa," *American Ethnologist*, 31.2 (2004).

9    Diawara, p. 113.

10   Diawara, p. 185.

11   Luke Robinson, *Independent Chinese Documentary: From the Studio to the Street* (Houndmills: Palgrave Macmillan, 2013), p. 29.

12   Zhang Zhen, "Transfiguring the Postsocialist City: Experimental Image-Making in Contemporary China," in Yomi Braester and James Tweedie (eds.), *Cinema at the City's Edge: Film and Urban Networks in East Asia* (Hong Kong: Hong Kong University Press, 2010), p. 106.

13   For more discussion of these transient new media forms, see Voci, "Quasi-Documentary, Cellflix and Web Spoofs: Chinese Movies' Other Visual Pleasures," *Senses of Cinema* 41, October–December 2006, http://www.sensesofcinema. com/2006/41/other-chinese-movies-pleasures (December 15, 2010).

14   Jean Rouch, "The Camera and Man," *Studies in the Anthropology of Visual Communication*, 1.1 (1974): 37–44.

15   Julie Perini, "Relational Filmmaking: A Manifesto," *INCITE: Journal of Experimental Media*, 2 (Spring-Fall 2010), http://www.incite-online.net/ perini2.html

16   In a related move, Ariella Azoulay maps out a notion of the civil contract of photography. Writing about the documentation of the Palestinian occupation by photo-journalists, Azoulay rethinks the relationship of photographer and subject not simply as a tool for enacting a unidirectional power relationship but as an index of a "complex fabric of relations," of gazes, actions, and contexts. See Ariella Azoulay, *The Civil Contract of Photography* (New York: Zone Books, 2008), p. 18.

17   Meg McLagan, "Principles, Publicity, and Politics: Notes on Human Rights Media," *American Anthropologist*, 105(3): 609.

18   Leshu Torchin, *Creating the Witness: Documenting Genocide on Film, Video, and the Internet* (Minneapolis: University of Minnesota Press, 2012), p. 12.

19   Rosen 319ff.

20   Lev Manovich, "Models of Authorship in New Media," www.manovich.net, 2002 <http://www.manovich.net/DOCS/models_of_authorship.doc>

21   Nicolas Bourriaud, *Postproduction: Culture as Screenplay: How Art Reprograms the World* (New York: Lukas & Sternberg, 2002), p. 7.

22   For a discussion of these digital tropes, see Lev Manovich. *The Language of New Media* (Cambridge, MA: MIT Press, 2002), p. 152 and p. 322, respectively.

23   See Vivian Sobchack, "'At the Still Point of the Turning World': Meta-Morphing and Meta-Stasis," in Sobchack (ed.), *Meta-Morphing: Visual Transformation and the Culture of Quick-Change* (Minneapolis: University of Minnesota Press), 2000.

24   Jesse P. Finnegan, "Site Specifics: Chris Marker and Second Life," *Film Comment* (November/December 2010) http://www.filmcomment.com/ article/site-specifics-chris-marker-and-second-life

25   Julian Dibbell, "A Rape in Cyberspace." *The Village Voice*, December 23, 1993, http://www.juliandibbell.com/texts/bungle_vv.html (Accessed 15 October 2012.)

26  Lev Manovich, *The Language of New Media* (Cambridge, MA: MIT Press, 2002), p. 70ff.

27  McKenzie Wark, *Telesthesia: Communication, Culture and Class* (London: Polity, 2012).

28  Henry Jenkins, "Transmedia Storytelling: Moving characters from books to films to video games can make them stronger and more compelling," *Technology Review* (January 15, 2003) http://www.technologyreview.com/news/401760/transmedia-storytelling

29  Dale Hudson and Patricia R. Zimmermann, "Cinephilia, Technophilia, and Collaborative Remix Zones," *Screen* 50.1 "Screen Theorizing Today: A Celebration of Screen's Fiftieth Anniversary" (Spring 2009), pp. 135–136.

30  Barbara Klinger, *Beyond the Multiplex: Cinema, New Technologies and the Home* (Berkeley: University of California Press, 2006).

31  Dale Hudson and Patricia R. Zimmermann, "Cinephilia, Technophilia, and Collaborative Remix Zones," *Screen* 50.1 "Screen Theorizing Today: A Celebration of Screen's Fiftieth Anniversary" (Spring 2009), p. 142.

32  Dale Hudson and Patricia R. Zimmermann, "Cinephilia, Technophilia, and Collaborative Remix Zones," *Screen* 50.1 "Screen Theorizing Today: A Celebration of Screen's Fiftieth Anniversary" (Spring 2009), p. 143.

33  See Anna Siomopoulos and Patrician Rodden Zimmermann, "Silent Film Exhibition and Performative Historiography," *The Moving Image: the Journal of the Association of Moving Image Archivists*, 6(2) (2006): 109–111.

34  Nicholas Rombes, *Cinema in the Digital Age* (New York: Columbia University Press, 2009), p. 27.

35  See McKenzie Wark, *A Hacker Manifesto* (Cambridge, MA: Harvard University Press, 2004), and Gabriella Coleman, "Hacker Politics and Publics," *Public Culture*, 23(3) 65 (Fall 2011): 511–516.

36  Critical Art Ensemble, *Digital Resistance: Explorations in Tactical Media* (Brooklyn, NY: Autonomedia, 2009).

37  See also David Garcia and Geert Lovinck, "The ABCs of Tactical Media" <http://www.nettime.org/Lists-Archives/nettime-l-9705/msg00096.html>; and Rita Raley, *Tactical Media* (Minneapolis: University of Minnesota, 2009).

38  Marianne van den Boomen, Sybille Lammes, Ann-Sophie Lehmann, Joost Raessens, and Mirko Tobias Schäfer, "Introduction: From the Virtual to Matters of Fact and Concern," in *Digital Material: Tracing New Media in Everyday Life and Technology* (Amsterdam: Amsterdam University Press, 2009), p. 10. See also Ed Halter, "The Matter of Electronics," *Vague Terrain* (February 2010) <http://vagueterrain.net/content/2010/02/matter-electronics>

39  For a guide to the people and practices of artisanal moving-image production, see Gregory Zinman's website <http://handmadecinema.com>

40  See Evan Meaney, "On Glitching," *Incite: Journal of Experimental Media*, 2 (Spring–Fall 2010) <http://www.incite-online.net/meaney2a.html> and Hugh S. Manon and Daniel Temkin, "Notes on Glitch," *World Picture*, 6 (Winter 2011), <http://www.worldpicturejournal.com/WP_6/Manon.html>

41 Lisa Klarr "Locating the Material in Digital Materialism," *HASTAC: Humanities, Arts, Science, and Technology Alliance and Collaboratory* (May 2010), <http://www.hastac.org/blogs/lisa-klarr/locating-material-digital-materialism>

42 Paola Voci, *China on Video: Smaller-Screen Realities* (Abingdon: Routledge, 2010), p. 1.

43 Sean Cubitt, Nikos Papastergiadis, and Scott McQuire, "Transient Media: Paper prepared for the *Ubiquitous Media* conference, University of Tokyo, July 2007." Author's website, 2007, <http://homepage.mac.com/waikato screen/talks/TransientMedia3.pdf> (December 15, 2010).

44 David Hogarth, *Realer than Reel: Global Directions in Documentary* (Austin: University of Texas Press, 2006), pp. 128–129.

45 Alexander Kluge, "On New German Cinema, Art, Enlightenment, and the Public Sphere," An Interview with Alexander Kluge, *October*, 46 (Autumn 1988): 58.

46 Paul Feyerabend, *Against Method: Outline of an Anarchistic Theory of Knowledge* (London: Verso, 1988).

47 See Walter Mignolo, *Local Histories/Global Designs* (Princeton: Princeton University Press, 2000).

48 See Salman Rushdie, "In Good Faith: A Pen against the Sword," *Newsweek* (February 12, 1990): 52. Interestingly, Europe itself has begun to recognize the artistic value of these hybrid cultures. It is no accident, in this sense, that Nobel Prizes in literature are now going to postcolonial and minority writers, or that the most recent Cannes Film Festival accorded special honors to the Egyptian film director Youssef Chahine and the Iranian film director/screenwriter/photographer/producer Abbas Kiarostami.

49 Raymond Williams, "Structures of Feeling," in *Marxism and Literature* (Oxford: Oxford University Press, 1977), p. 128, 132.

50 Ernst Bloch, *The Principle of Hope*, 3 Vols (Oxford: Blackwell, 1986).

# Index

*Keywords in Subversive Film/Media Aesthetics*, First Edition. Robert Stam with Richard Porton and Leo Goldsmith.
© 2015 John Wiley & Sons, Inc. Published 2015 by John Wiley & Sons, Inc.

*In the preceding index of terms, the names in parenthesis usually indicate the person who generated or popularized a concept, but at times the names refer to the author of the films or to the films themselves used as examples of a concept. We have tried, whenever possible, to indicate the first user of the term or concept, while also stressing that each concept is embedded in a larger transpersonal history. Where no author is referenced, the reader can assume that the coinage is our own, but with no pretense to originality. If we have failed to give credit to anyone, we will try to correct the oversight in subsequent editions.